DATA MINING WITH R

LEARNING WITH CASE STUDIES

SECOND EDITION

Chapman & Hall/CRC
Data Mining and Knowledge Discovery Series

SERIES EDITOR
Vipin Kumar
University of Minnesota
Department of Computer Science and Engineering
Minneapolis, Minnesota, U.S.A.

AIMS AND SCOPE

This series aims to capture new developments and applications in data mining and knowledge discovery, while summarizing the computational tools and techniques useful in data analysis. This series encourages the integration of mathematical, statistical, and computational methods and techniques through the publication of a broad range of textbooks, reference works, and handbooks. The inclusion of concrete examples and applications is highly encouraged. The scope of the series includes, but is not limited to, titles in the areas of data mining and knowledge discovery methods and applications, modeling, algorithms, theory and foundations, data and knowledge visualization, data mining systems and tools, and privacy and security issues.

PUBLISHED TITLES

ACCELERATING DISCOVERY : MINING UNSTRUCTURED INFORMATION FOR HYPOTHESIS GENERATION
Scott Spangler

ADVANCES IN MACHINE LEARNING AND DATA MINING FOR ASTRONOMY
Michael J. Way, Jeffrey D. Scargle, Kamal M. Ali, and Ashok N. Srivastava

BIOLOGICAL DATA MINING
Jake Y. Chen and Stefano Lonardi

COMPUTATIONAL BUSINESS ANALYTICS
Subrata Das

COMPUTATIONAL INTELLIGENT DATA ANALYSIS FOR SUSTAINABLE DEVELOPMENT
Ting Yu, Nitesh V. Chawla, and Simeon Simoff

COMPUTATIONAL METHODS OF FEATURE SELECTION
Huan Liu and Hiroshi Motoda

CONSTRAINED CLUSTERING: ADVANCES IN ALGORITHMS, THEORY, AND APPLICATIONS
Sugato Basu, Ian Davidson, and Kiri L. Wagstaff

CONTRAST DATA MINING: CONCEPTS, ALGORITHMS, AND APPLICATIONS
Guozhu Dong and James Bailey

DATA CLASSIFICATION: ALGORITHMS AND APPLICATIONS
Charu C. Aggarawal

MINING SOFTWARE SPECIFICATIONS: METHODOLOGIES AND APPLICATIONS
David Lo, Siau-Cheng Khoo, Jiawei Han, and Chao Liu

MULTIMEDIA DATA MINING: A SYSTEMATIC INTRODUCTION TO
CONCEPTS AND THEORY
Zhongfei Zhang and Ruofei Zhang

MUSIC DATA MINING
Tao Li, Mitsunori Ogihara, and George Tzanetakis

NEXT GENERATION OF DATA MINING
Hillol Kargupta, Jiawei Han, Philip S. Yu, Rajeev Motwani, and Vipin Kumar

RAPIDMINER: DATA MINING USE CASES AND BUSINESS ANALYTICS
APPLICATIONS
Markus Hofmann and Ralf Klinkenberg

RELATIONAL DATA CLUSTERING: MODELS, ALGORITHMS,
AND APPLICATIONS
Bo Long, Zhongfei Zhang, and Philip S. Yu

SERVICE-ORIENTED DISTRIBUTED KNOWLEDGE DISCOVERY
Domenico Talia and Paolo Trunfio

SPECTRAL FEATURE SELECTION FOR DATA MINING
Zheng Alan Zhao and Huan Liu

STATISTICAL DATA MINING USING SAS APPLICATIONS, SECOND EDITION
George Fernandez

SUPPORT VECTOR MACHINES: OPTIMIZATION BASED THEORY,
ALGORITHMS, AND EXTENSIONS
Naiyang Deng, Yingjie Tian, and Chunhua Zhang

TEMPORAL DATA MINING
Theophano Mitsa

TEXT MINING: CLASSIFICATION, CLUSTERING, AND APPLICATIONS
Ashok N. Srivastava and Mehran Sahami

TEXT MINING AND VISUALIZATION: CASE STUDIES USING OPEN-SOURCE
TOOLS
Markus Hofmann and Andrew Chisholm

THE TOP TEN ALGORITHMS IN DATA MINING
Xindong Wu and Vipin Kumar

UNDERSTANDING COMPLEX DATASETS: DATA MINING WITH MATRIX
DECOMPOSITIONS
David Skillicorn

DATA MINING WITH R

LEARNING WITH CASE STUDIES

SECOND EDITION

Luís Torgo

University of Porto, Portugal

CRC Press
Taylor & Francis Group
Boca Raton   London   New York

CRC Press is an imprint of the
Taylor & Francis Group, an **informa** business

A CHAPMAN & HALL BOOK

CRC Press
Taylor & Francis Group
6000 Broken Sound Parkway NW, Suite 300
Boca Raton, FL 33487-2742

First issued in paperback 2020

© 2017 by Taylor & Francis Group, LLC
CRC Press is an imprint of Taylor & Francis Group, an Informa business

No claim to original U.S. Government works

ISBN 13: 978-0-367-57398-0 (pbk)
ISBN 13: 978-1-4822-3489-3 (hbk)

Visit the Taylor & Francis Web site at
http://www.taylorandfrancis.com

and the CRC Press Web site at
http://www.crcpress.com

Contents

Preface

The main goal of this book is to introduce the reader to the use of R as a tool for data mining. R is a freely downloadable[1] language and environment for statistical computing and graphics. Its capabilities and the large set of available add-on packages make this tool an excellent alternative to many existing (and expensive!) data mining tools.

The main goal of this book is not to describe all facets of data mining processes. Many books exist that cover this scientific area. Instead we propose to introduce the reader to the power of R and data mining by means of several case studies. Obviously, these case studies do not represent all possible data mining problems that one can face in the real world. Moreover, the solutions we describe cannot be taken as complete solutions. Our goal is more to introduce the reader to the world of data mining using R through practical examples. As such, our analysis of the case studies has the goal of showing examples of knowledge extraction using R, instead of presenting complete reports of data mining case studies. They should be taken as examples of possible paths in any data mining project and can be used as the basis for developing solutions for the reader's own projects. Still, we have tried to cover a diverse set of problems posing different challenges in terms of size, type of data, goals of analysis, and the tools necessary to carry out this analysis. This hands-on approach has its costs, however. In effect, to allow for every reader to carry out our described steps on his/her computer as a form of learning with concrete case studies, we had to make some compromises. Namely, we cannot address extremely large problems as this would require computer resources that are not available to everybody. Still, we think we have covered problems that can be considered large and we have shown how to handle the problems posed by different types of data dimensionality.

This second edition strongly revises the R code of the case studies, making it more up-to-date with recent packages that have emerged in R. Moreover, we have decided to split the book into two parts: (i) a first part with introductory material, and (ii) the second part with the case studies. The first part includes a completely new chapter that provides an introduction to data mining, to complement the already existing introduction to R. The idea is to provide the reader with a kind of bird's eye view of the data mining field, describing more in depth the main topics of this research area. This information should complement the lighter descriptions that are given during the case studies analysis. Moreover, it should allow the reader to better contextualize the solutions of the case studies within the bigger picture of data mining tasks and methodologies. Finally, we hope this new chapter can serve as a kind of backup reference for the reader if more details on the methods used in the case studies are required.

We do not assume any prior knowledge about R. Readers who are new to R and data mining should be able to follow the case studies. We have tried to make the different case studies self-contained in such a way that the reader can start anywhere in the document. Still, some basic R functionalities are introduced in the first, simpler case studies, and are not repeated, which means that if you are new to R, then you should at least start with the first case studies to get acquainted with R. Moreover, as we have mentioned, the first part

---

[1]Download it from `http://www.R-project.org`.

of the book includes a chapter with a very short introduction to R, which should facilitate the understanding of the solutions in the following chapters. We also do not assume any familiarity with data mining or statistical techniques. Brief introductions to different data mining techniques are provided as necessary in the case studies. Still, the new chapter in the first part with the introduction to data mining includes further information on the methods we apply in the case studies as well as other methodologies commonly used in data mining. Moreover, at the end of some sections we provide "further readings" pointers that may help find more information if required. In summary, our target readers are more users of data analysis tools than researchers or developers. Still, we hope the latter also find reading this book useful as a form of entering the "world" of R and data mining.

The book is accompanied by a set of freely available R source files that can be obtained at the book's Web site.[2] These files include all the code used in the case studies. They facilitate the "do-it-yourself" approach followed in this book. We strongly recommend that readers install R and try the code as they read the book. All data used in the case studies is available at the book's Web site as well. Moreover, we have created an R package called DMwR2 that contains several functions used in the book as well as the datasets already in R format. You should install and load this package to follow the code in the book (details on how to do this are given in the first chapter).

---

[2]http://ltorgo.github.io/DMwR2

Acknowledgments

I would like to thank my family for all the support they give me. Without them I would have found it difficult to embrace this project. Their presence, love, and caring provided the necessary comfort to overcome the ups and downs of writing a book. The same kind of comfort was given by my dear friends who were always ready for an extra beer when necessary. Thank you all, and now I hope I will have more time to share with you.

I am also grateful for all the support of my research colleagues and to LIAAD/INESC Tec LA as a whole. Thanks also to the University of Porto for supporting my research, and also to my colleagues at the Department of Computer Science of the Faculty of Sciences of the same University for providing such an enjoyable working environment. Part of the writing of this book was financially supported by a sabbatical grant (SFRH/BSAB/113896/2015) of FCT.

Finally, thanks to all students and colleagues who helped improving the first edition with their feedback, as well as in proofreading drafts of the current edition. In particular, I would like to thank to my students of Data Mining at the Masters on Computer Science of the Faculty of Sciences of the University of Porto, and also my students of the Data Mining with R subject at the Masters of Science on Business Analytics of Stern Business School of NYU — their involvement and feedback on my teaching material is strongly reflected on this new edition of the book.

Luis Torgo
Porto, Portugal

List of Figures

List of Tables

Chapter 1

Introduction

R[1] is a programming language and an environment for statistical computing (R Core Team, 2015b). It is similar to the S language developed at AT&T Bell Laboratories by Rick Becker, John Chambers and Allan Wilks. There are versions of R for the Unix, Windows and MacOS families of operating systems. Moreover, R runs on different computer architectures like Intel, PowerPC, Alpha systems and Sparc systems. R was initially developed by Ihaka and Gentleman (1996), both from the University of Auckland, New Zealand. The current development of R is carried out by a core team of a dozen people from different institutions around the world and it is supported by the R Foundation. R development takes advantage of a growing community that cooperates in its development due to its open source philosophy. In effect, the source code of every R component is freely available for inspection and/or adaptation. This fact allows you to check and test the reliability of anything you use in R and this ability may be crucial in many critical application domains. There are many critics of the open source model. Most of them mention the lack of support as one of the main drawbacks of open source software. It is certainly not the case with R! There are many excellent documents, books and sites that provide free information on R. Moreover, the excellent R-help mailing list is a source of invaluable advice and information. There are also searchable mailing list archives that you can (and should!) use before posting a question. More information on these mailing lists can be obtained at the R Web site in the section "Mailing Lists".

Data mining has to do with the discovery of useful, valid, unexpected, and understandable knowledge from data. These general objectives are obviously shared by other disciplines like statistics, machine learning, or pattern recognition. One of the most important distinguishing issues in data mining is size. With the widespread use of computer technology and information systems, the amount of data available for exploration has increased exponentially. This poses difficult challenges for the standard data analysis disciplines: One has to consider issues like computational efficiency, limited memory resources, interfaces to databases, etc. Other key distinguishing features are the diversity of data sources that one frequently encounters in data mining projects, as well as the diversity of data types (text, sound, video, etc.). All these issues turn data mining into a highly interdisciplinary subject involving not only typical data analysts but also people working with databases, data visualization on high dimensions, etc.

R has limitations with handling enormous datasets because all computation is carried out in the main memory of the computer. This does not mean that you will not be able to handle these problems. Taking advantage of the highly flexible database interfaces available in R, you will be able to perform data mining on large problems. Moreover, the awareness of the R community of this constant increase in dataset sizes has lead to the development of many new R packages designed to work with large data or to provide interfaces to other infrastructures better suited to heavy computation tasks. More information on this relevant work can be found on the High-Performance and Parallel Computing in R task view[2].

---

[1]http://www.r-project.org
[2]http://cran.at.r-project.org/web/views/HighPerformanceComputing.html

1

In summary, we hope that at the end of reading this book you are convinced that you can do data mining on large problems without having to spend any money at all! That is only possible due to the generous and invaluable contribution of lots of people who build such wonderful tools as R.

1.1 How to Read This Book

The main spirit behind the book is

Learn by doing it!

The first part of the book provides you with some basic information on both R and Data Mining. The second part of the book is organized as a set of case studies. The "solutions" to these case studies are obtained using R. All the necessary steps to reach the solutions are described. Using the book Web site[3] and the book-associated R package (DMwR2), you can get all of the code included in the document, as well as all data of the case studies. This should facilitate trying them out by yourself. Ideally, you should read this document beside your computer and try every step as it is presented to you in the book. R code and its respective output is shown in the book using the following font:

```
> citation()
```

```
To cite R in publications use:

  R Core Team (2016). R: A language and environment for
  statistical computing. R Foundation for Statistical Computing,
  Vienna, Austria. URL https://www.R-project.org/.

A BibTeX entry for LaTeX users is

  @Manual{,
    title = {R: A Language and Environment for Statistical Computing},
    author = {{R Core Team}},
    organization = {R Foundation for Statistical Computing},
    address = {Vienna, Austria},
    year = {2016},
    url = {https://www.R-project.org/},
  }

We have invested a lot of time and effort in creating R, please
cite it when using it for data analysis. See also
'citation("pkgname")' for citing R packages.
```

R commands are entered at R command prompt, ">" in an interactive fashion. Whenever you see this prompt you can interpret it as R waiting for you to enter a command. You type in the commands at the prompt and then press the ENTER key to ask R to execute them. This may or may not produce some form of output (the result of the command) and then a new prompt appears. At the prompt you may use the arrow keys to browse and edit

---

[3]http://ltorgo.github.io/DMwR2

previously entered commands. This is handy when you want to type commands similar to what you have done before as you avoid typing them again.

Still, you can take advantage of the code provided at the book Web site to copy and paste between your browser or editor and the R console, thus avoiding having to type all the commands described in the book. This will surely facilitate your learning experience and improve your understanding of its potential.

1.2 Reproducibility

One of the main goals of this book is to provide you with illustrative examples of how to address several data mining tasks using the tools made available by R. For this to be possible we have worked hard to make sure all cases we describe are reproducible by our readers on their own computers. This means that if you follow all steps we describe in the book you should get the same results we describe.

There are two essencial components of this reproducibility goal: (i) the used R code; and (ii) the data of the case studies. Accompanying this book we provide two other means of facilitating your access to the code and data: (i) the book Web page; and (ii) the book R package. Together with the descriptions included in this book, the Web page and the package should allow you to easily replicate what we describe and also re-use and/or adapt it to your own application domains.

The book Web page[4] provides access to all code used in the book in a copy/paste-friendly manner, so that you can easily copy it from your browser into your R session. The code is organized by chapters and sections to facilitate the task of finding it.

The Web page also contains other useful information like the list of packages we use, or the data sets, as well as other files containing some of the objects created in the book, particularly when these can take considerable time to compute on more average desktop computers.

R is a very dynamic "ecosystem". This means that when you read this book most probably some of the packages we use (or even R itself) already have new versions out. Although this will most probably not create any problem, in the sense that the code we show will still work with these new versions, we can not be sure of this. If something stops working due to these new versions we will try to quickly post solutions in the "Errata" section of the book Web page. The book and the R code in it was created and tested in the following R version:

```
> R.version
```

```
                 -
platform      x86_64-apple-darwin13.4.0
arch          x86_64
os            darwin13.4.0
system        x86_64, darwin13.4.0
status
major         3
minor         3.1
year          2016
month         06
day           21
```

---

[4]http://ltorgo.github.io/DMwR2

```
svn rev        70800
language       R
version.string R version 3.3.1 (2016-06-21)
nickname       Bug in Your Hair
```

At the book Web page you will also find the information on the versions of all used packages in our R system when the code was executed.

The book R package is another key element for allowing reproducibility. This package contains several of the functions we describe and/or use in the book, as well as the datasets of the case studies (which as we have mentioned above are also available in the book Web page). This package is available and installable from the usual sources, i.e. the R central repository (CRAN). It is possible that the package evolves to new versions if any bug is found in the code we provide. These corrections will tend to follow a slow pace as recommended by CRAN policies. In this context, for more up-to-date versions of the package, which may include not yet so well tested solutions (so use it at your own risk), you may wish to download and install the development version of the package from its Web page: `https://github.com/ltorgo/DMwR2`

Part I

A Short Introduction to R and Data Mining

Chapter 2

Introduction to R

This chapter provides a very short introduction to the main features of the R language. We do not assume any familiarity with computer programming. Readers should be able to easily follow the examples presented in this chapter. Still, if you feel some lack of motivation to continue reading this introductory material, do not worry. You may proceed to the case studies and then return to this introduction as you get more motivated by the concrete applications.

The material in this chapter should serve as a quick tutorial for those that are not familiar with the basics of the R language. Some other more specific aspects of R will also appear in the next chapter when we introduce the reader to some concepts of Data Mining. Finally, further learning will also take place when presenting the case studies in the second part of the book. Still, some basic knowledge of R is necessary to start addressing these case studies and this chapter should provide that in case you do not have it.

2.1 Starting with R

R is a functional language for statistical computation and graphics. It can be seen as a dialect of the S language (developed at AT&T) for which John Chambers was awarded the 1998 Association for Computing Machinery (ACM) Software award that mentioned that this language "forever altered how people analyze, visualize and manipulate data".

R can be quite useful just by using it in an interactive fashion at its command line. Still, more advanced uses of the system will lead the user to develop his own functions to systematize repetitive tasks, or even to add or change some functionalities of the existing add-on packages, taking advantage of being open source.

The easiest way to install R in your system is to obtain a binary distribution from the R Web site[1] where you can follow the link that takes you to the CRAN (Comprehensive R Archive Network) site to obtain, among other things, the binary distribution for your particular operating system/architecture. If you prefer to build R directly from the sources, you can get instructions on how to do it from the CRAN but most of the times that is not necessary at all.

After downloading the binary distribution for your operating system you just need to follow the instructions that come with it. In the case of the Windows version, you simply execute the downloaded file (`R-3.3.1-win.exe`)[2] and select the options you want in the following menus. In some operating systems you may need to contact your system administrator to fulfill the installation task due to lack of permissions to install software.

To run R in Windows you simply double-click the appropriate icon on your desktop,

---

[1]http://www.R-project.org.

[2]The actual name of the file changes with newer versions. This is the name for version 3.3.1

while in Unix versions you should type R at the operating system prompt. Both will bring up the R console with its prompt ">".

If you want to quit R you can issue the command q() at the prompt. You will be asked if you want to save the current workspace. You should answer yes only if you want to resume your current analysis at the point you are leaving it, later on.

A frequently used alternative way to interact with R is through RStudio[3]. This free software can be downloaded and installed for the most common setups (e.g. Linux, Windows or Mac OS X). It is an integrated development environment that includes on the same graphical user interface several important elements of R, like its console where you can interact with R, a script editor where you can write more complex programs/solutions to your problems, an interface to browse the help pages of R, and many other useful facilities. I strongly recommend its usage, particularly if you are starting with R.[4]

Although the set of tools that comes with R is by itself quite powerful, it is natural that you will end up wanting to install some of the large (and growing) set of add-on packages available for R at CRAN. In the Windows version this is easily done through the "**Packages**" menu. After connecting your computer to the Internet you should select the "Install package from CRAN..." option from this menu. This option will present a list of the packages available at CRAN. You select the one(s) you want, and R will download the package(s) and self-install it(them) on your system. In Unix versions, things may be slightly different depending on the graphical capabilities of your R installation. Still, even without selection from menus, the operation is simple.[5] Suppose you want to download the package that provides functions to connect to MySQL databases. This package name is **RMySQL**.[6] You just need to type the following command at R prompt:

```
> install.packages("RMySQL")
```

The install.packages() function has many parameters, among which there is the repos argument that allows you to indicate the nearest CRAN mirror.[7] Still, the first time you run the function in an R session, it will prompt you for the repository you wish to use.

One thing that you surely should do is to install the package associated with this book, named **DMwR2**. This package will give you access to several functions used throughout the book as well as the datasets. You install the package as any other package available on CRAN, i.e by issuing the following command at your R prompt (or using the respective menu if using RStudio),

```
> install.packages("DMwR2")
```

Once this procedure is finished you may use the book package when necessary by loading it as any other package,

```
> library(DMwR2)
```

The function installed.packages() allows you to know the packages currently installed in your computer,

---

[3]https://www.rstudio.com/

[4]Other alternatives include for instance the excellent Emacs package called ESS (http://ess.r-project.org/), in case you prefer Emacs as your editor.

[5]Please note that the following code also works in other versions, although you may find the use of the menus more practical.

[6]You can get an idea of the functionalities of each of the R packages in the R FAQ (frequently asked questions) at CRAN.

[7]The list of available mirrors can be found at http://cran.r-project.org/mirrors.html.

```
> installed.packages()
```

This produces a long output with each line containing a package, its version information, the packages it depends on, and so on. A more user-friendly, although less complete, list of the installed packages can be obtained by issuing

```
> library()
```

The following command can be very useful as it allows you to check whether there are newer versions of your installed packages at CRAN:

```
> old.packages()
```

Moreover, you can use the following command to update all your installed packages:

```
> update.packages()
```

R has an integrated help system that you can use to know more about the system and its functionalities. Moreover, you can find extra documentation at the R site. R comes with a set of HTML files that can be read using a Web browser[8]. On Windows and Mac OS X versions of R, these pages are accessible through the HELP menu. Alternatively, you can issue `help.start()` at the prompt to launch a browser showing the HTML help pages. Another form of getting help is to use the `help()` function. For instance, if you want some help on the `plot()` function, you can enter the command "`help(plot)`" (or alternatively, `?plot`). A quite powerful alternative, provided you are connected to the Internet, is to use the `RSiteSearch()` function that searches for key words or phrases in the mailing list archives, R manuals, and help pages; for example,

```
> RSiteSearch('neural networks')
```

Finally, there are several places on the Web that provide help on several facets of R, such as the sites `http://www.rseek.org/` or `http://www.rdocumentation.org/`. For more direct questions related to R, stack overflow is a "must"[9].

2.2 Basic Interaction with the R Console

The R console is the place where you carry out most of the interaction with R. This allows for easy interactive exploration of ideas that may solve your data analysis problems. Frequently, after this exploration phase one tends to dump the sequence of R commands that lead to the solution we have found into an R script file. These script files can then be reused, for instance by asking R to execute all commands contained in the script file in sequence.

The interaction with the R console consists of typing some instruction followed by the ENTER key, and receiving back the result of this command. The simplest example of this usage would be to ask R to carry out some calculation:

---

[8]Obviously if you are using RStudio it is even easier to browse the help pages.
[9]`http://stackoverflow.com/questions/tagged/r`

```
> 4 + 3 / 5^2
```

```
[1] 4.12
```

The rather cryptic "[1]" in front of the output can be read as "this output line is showing values starting from the first element of the object". This is particularly useful for results containing many values, as these may be spread over several lines of output. For now we can simply ignore the "[1]" as we will return to this issue later.

More interesting usages of R typically involve some of its many functions, as shown in the following simple examples:

```
> rnorm(4, mean = 10, sd = 2)
```

```
[1] 10.257398 10.552028  9.677471  4.615118
```

```
> mean(sample(1:10, 5))
```

```
[1] 6
```

The first of these instructions randomly generates 4 numbers from a normal distribution with mean 10 and standard deviation 2, while the second calculates the mean of 5 random numbers generated from the interval of integers from 1 to 10. This last instruction is also an example of something we see frequently in R- function composition. This mathematical concept involves applying a function to the result of another function, in this case calculating the mean of the result of the call to the function `sample()`.

Another frequent task we will carry out at the R prompt is to generate some statistical graph of a dataset. For instance, in Figure 2.1 we see a scatter plot containing 5 points whose coordinates were randomly generated in the interval 1 to 10. The code to obtain such a graph is the following:[10]

```
> plot(x=sample(1:10,5),y=sample(1:10,5),
+       main="Five random points",xlab="X values",ylab="Y values")
```

These are just a few short examples of the typical interaction with R. In the next sections we will learn about the main concepts behind the R language that will allow us to carry out useful data analysis tasks with this tool.

2.3   R Objects and Variables

Everything in R is stored as an object. An object is most of the time associated with a variable name that allows us to refer to its content. We can think of a variable as referring to some storage location in the computer memory that holds some content (an object) that can range from a simple number to a complex model.

R objects may store diverse types of information. The simplest content is some value of

---

[10]The "+" sign you see is the continuation prompt. It appears any time you type ENTER before you finish some statement as a way of R reminding you that there is something missing till it can execute your order. You should remember that these prompt characters are not to be entered by you! They are automatically printed by R (as with the normal prompt ">").

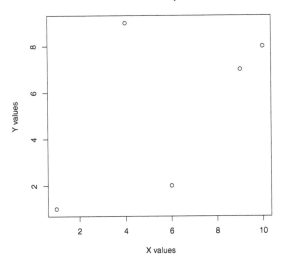

FIGURE 2.1: A simple scatter plot.

one of R basic data types : *numeric*, *character*, or *logical* values[11]. Character values in R are strings of characters[12] enclosed by either single or double quotes (e.g. `"hello"` or `'today'`), while the logical values are either TRUE or FALSE.[13] Please be aware that R is case-sensitive so true and false must be in capital letters!

Other more complex data types may also be stored in objects. We will see examples of this in the following sections.

Content (i.e. objects) may be stored in a variable using the assignment operator. This operator is denoted by an angle bracket followed by a minus sign (`<-`):[14]

```
> vat <- 0.2
```

The effect of the previous instruction is thus to store the number 0.2 on a variable named **vat**. By simply entering the name of a variable at the R prompt one can see its contents:[15]

```
> vat
```

```
[1] 0.2
```

Below you will find other examples of assignment statements. These examples should make it clear that this is a destructive operation, as any variable can only have a single content at any time *t*. This means that by assigning some new content to an existing variable, you in effect lose its previous content:

---

[11]Things are in effect slightly more complex, as R is also able to distinguish between floating point and integer numbers. Still, this is seldom required, unless you are heavily concerned with memory usage and CPU speed. Moreover, R also has complex numbers as another base data type but again this is not frequently used.

[12]This means the character type is in effect a set of characters, which are usually known as strings in some programming languages, and not a single character as you might expect.

[13]You may actually also use T or F.

[14]You may also use the = sign but I would not recommend it as it may be confused with testing for equality.

[15]Or an error message if we type the name incorrectly, a rather frequent error!

```
> y <- 39
> y

[1] 39

> y <- 43
> y

[1] 43
```

You can also assign numerical expressions to a variable. In this case the variable will store the result of the evaluation of the expression, not the expression:

```
> z <- 5
> w <- z^2
> w

[1] 25

> i <- (z * 2 + 45)/2
> i

[1] 27.5
```

This means that we can think of the assignment operation as "evaluate whatever is given on the right side of the operator, and assign (store) the result (an object of some type) of this evaluation in the variable whose name is given on the left side".

Every object you create will stay in the computer memory until you delete it (or you exit R). You may list the objects currently in the memory by issuing the `ls()` or `objects()` command at the prompt. If you do not need an object, you may free some memory space by removing it using the function `rm()`:

```
> ls()

[1] "i"    "vat" "w"    "y"    "z"

> rm(vat,y,z,w,i)
```

Variable names may consist of any upper- and lower-case letters, the digits 0 to 9 (except in the beginning of the name), and also the period, ".", which behaves like a letter. Once again we remind that names in R are *case sensitive*, meaning that `Color` and `color` are two distinct variables with potentially very different content. This is in effect a frequent cause of frustration for beginners who keep getting "object not found" errors. If you face this type of error, start by checking the correctness of the name of the object causing the error.

2.4   R Functions

R functions are a special type of R object designed to carry out some operation. R functions, like mathematical functions, are applied to some set of arguments and produce a result. In R, both the arguments that we provide when we call the function and the result of the function execution are R objects whose type will depend on the function. R functions range from simple objects implementing some standard calculation, e.g. calculating the square root of a number, to more complex functions that can obtain some model of a dataset, e.g. a neural network. R already comes with an overwhelming set of functions available for us to use, but as we will see, the user can also create new functions.

In terms of notation, a function has a name and can have zero or more parameters. When we call (execute) the function we use its name followed by the arguments between parentheses separated by commas[16],

```
> max(4, 5, 6, 12, -4)
```

```
[1] 12
```

In the above example we are calling a function named `max()` that as the name suggests returns the maximum value of the arguments supplied by the user when calling the function.

In R we frequently tend to use function composition that, as mentioned before, consists of applying functions to the result of other functions, as shown in this example where we obtain the maximum of a random sample of 30 integers in the interval 1 to 100[17]:

```
> max(sample(1:100, 30))
```

```
[1] 99
```

R allows the user to create new functions. This is a useful feature, particularly when you want to automate certain tasks that you have to repeat over and over. Instead of typing the instructions that perform this task every time you want to execute it, you encapsulate them in a new function and then simply use it whenever necessary.

R functions are objects that can be stored in a variable. The contents of these objects are the statements that, when executed, carry out the task for which the function was designed. These variables where we store the content of a function will act as the function name. Thus to create a new function we use the assignment operator to store the contents of the function in a variable (whose name will be the name of the function).

Let us start with a simple example. Suppose you often want to calculate the standard error of a mean associated with a set of values. By definition, the standard error of a sample mean is given by

$$\text{standard error} = \sqrt{\frac{s^2}{n}}$$

where s^2 is the sample variance and n the sample size.

Given a set of numbers, we want a function to calculate the respective standard error of the mean of these numbers. Let us decide to call this function `se`. Before proceeding to create the function we should check whether there is already a function with this name in R. If that is the case, then it would be better to use another name, not to "hide" the other R function from the user.[18] We can check the existence of some object with a certain name using the function `exists()`,

---

[16]Note that even if the function takes no arguments we need to call it with the parentheses, e.g. `f()`.

[17]Due to the random nature of the `sample()` function you may get a different maximum if you run this code.

[18]You do not have to worry about overriding the definition of the R function. It will continue to exist, although your new function with the same name will be on top of the search path of R, thus "hiding" the other standard function.

```
> exists("se")
```

```
[1] FALSE
```

The fact that R answered FALSE means that there is no object with the name **se** and thus we are safe to create a function with that name. The following is a possible way to create our function:

```
> se <- function(x) {
+     v <- var(x)
+     n <- length(x)
+     return(sqrt(v/n))
+ }
```

Thus, to create a function object, you assign to its name something with the general form

```
function(<set of parameters>) { <set of R instructions> }
```

A set of R instructions (a block) is delimited by curly braces and it is formed by each instruction on its own line. This means that in our example we have decided that to calculate the standard error of the sample mean of a set of numbers it would be sufficient to execute the above 3 statements. The first of these calls the function **var()** with the content of the variable **x**. This variable is a parameter of the function. Parameters are special variables that will hold the values supplied in the arguments of the function when the user calls it. This means that whenever some user calls our **se** function he will have to supply a set of values in the first (and only) argument of this function. These values will be assigned by R to the parameter (variable) **x**. The function **var()** is an R function that returns the variance of a set of values, that we decided to store in the variable **v**. The second statement uses function **length()** to obtain the number of values in **x**, that we store in another variable named **n**. Having these two quantities we are ready to calculate the standard error, by simply calculating the square root (function **sqrt()**) of the quotient of **v** by **n**. The result of this calculation is then returned back to the user by using the function **return()**.

After creating this function, we could use it as follows:

```
> mySample <- rnorm(100, mean=20, sd=4)
> se(mySample)
```

```
[1] 0.3550299
```

In the above code we have used the function **rnorm()** to obtain a random sample of 100 numbers from a normal distribution with mean 20 and standard deviation 4. We have then called our function with this set of numbers. Please note that due to the random nature of the function **rnorm()** you may get a different result.

Sometimes we want to create functions that may have some parameters that have default values. For instance, we could create a function to convert a value in meters to other units of length. This function could take as a first argument the value in meters and as a second argument the target unit. However, we could allow the user to omit this second argument by setting a default value when we create the function. The following is an illustration of this:

```
> convMeters <- function(val, to="inch") {
+     mult <- switch(to,inch=39.3701,foot=3.28084,yard=1.09361,mile=0.000621371,NA)
+     if (is.na(mult)) stop("Unknown target unit of length.")
+     else return(val*mult)
+ }
> convMeters(23,"foot")

[1] 75.45932

> convMeters(40,"inch")

[1] 1574.804

> convMeters(40)

[1] 1574.804

> convMeters(2.4,"km")

Error in convMeters(2.4, "km"): Unknown target unit of length.
```

The above function is able to convert meters to inches, feet, yards, and miles. As seen in the example calls, the user may omit the second argument as this has a default value ("inch"). This default value was established at the function creation by telling R not only the name of the parameter (to), but also a value that the parameter should take in case the user does not supply another value. Note that this value will always be overridden by any value the user supplies when calling the function.

The code of the function also illustrates a few other functions available in R. Function switch() for instance, allows us to compare the contents of a variable (to in the above code), against a set of options. For each option we can supply the value that will be the result of the function switch(). In the above example, if the variable to has the value "inch" the value assigned to the variable mult will be 39.3701. The function also allows to supply a return value in case the variable does not match any of the alternatives. In this case we are returning the special value NA. The goal here is to foresee situations where the user supplies a target unit that is unknown to this function. The following statement is another conditional statement. The if statement allows us to have conditional execution of other statements. In this case if the value assigned to variable mult was NA (which is checked by a call to the function is.na()), then we want to stop the execution of the function with some sort of error message (using function stop()) because the user has supplied an unknown target unit. Otherwise we simply carry out the conversion calculation and return it as the result of the function execution.

The way we call functions (either existing or the ones we create) can also have some variations, namely in terms of the way we supply the values for the parameters of the functions. The most frequent setup is when we simply supply a value for each parameter, e.g.:

```
> convMeters(56.2,"yard")

[1] 61.46088
```

Calling the function this way we are supplying the values for the parameters "by position", i.e. the value in the first argument (56.2) is assigned by R to the first parameter of the function (val), and the value in the second argument ("yard") is assigned to the second parameter (`to`). We may also supply the parameter values "by name". We could get the same exact result with the following call:

```
> convMeters(to="yard",val=56.2)

[1] 61.46088
```

In effect, we can even mix both forms of calling a function,

```
> convMeters(56.2,to="yard")

[1] 61.46088
```

Calling by name is particularly useful with functions with a lot of parameters, most of which with default values. Say we have a function named `f` with 20 parameters, all but the two first having default values. Suppose we want to call the function but we want to supply a value different from the default for the tenth parameter named `tol`. With the possibility of calling by name we could do something like:

```
> f(10,43.2,tol=0.25)
```

This avoids having to supply all the values till the tenth argument in order to be able to use a value different from the default for this parameter.

2.5 Vectors

The most basic data object in R is a vector. Even when you assign a single number to a variable (like in x <- 45.3), you are creating a vector containing a single element. A vector is an object that can store a set of values of the same base data type. Thus you may have for instance vectors of strings, logical values, or numbers. The length of a vector object is the number of elements in it, and can be obtained with the function `length()`.

Most of the time you will be using vectors with length larger than 1. You can create a vector in R, using the `c()` function, which combines its arguments to form a vector:

```
> v <- c(4, 7, 23.5, 76.2, 80)
> v

[1]  4.0  7.0 23.5 76.2 80.0

> length(v)

[1] 5

> mode(v)

[1] "numeric"
```

The `mode()` function returns the base data type of the values stored in an object. All elements of a vector must belong to the same base data type. If that is not true, R will force it by type coercion. The following is an example of this:

```
> v <- c(4, 7, 23.5, 76.2, 80, "rrt")
> v

[1] "4"     "7"     "23.5" "76.2" "80"     "rrt"

> mode(v)

[1] "character"
```

All elements of the vector have been converted to the character type, i.e. strings.

All vectors may contain a special value called NA. This represents a missing value:

```
> u <- c(4, 6, NA, 2)
> u

[1]   4   6  NA   2

> k <- c(TRUE, FALSE, FALSE, NA, TRUE)
> k

[1]  TRUE FALSE FALSE    NA  TRUE
```

You can access a particular element of a vector through an index between square brackets:

```
> u[2]

[1] 6
```

The example above gives you the second element of the vector **u**. In Section 2.9 we will explore more powerful indexing schemes.

You can also change the value of one particular vector element by using the same indexing strategies:

```
> k[4] <- TRUE
> k

[1]  TRUE FALSE FALSE  TRUE  TRUE
```

R allows you to create empty vectors like this:

```
> x <- vector()
```

The length of a vector can be changed by simply adding more elements to it using a previously nonexistent index. For instance, after creating the empty vector x, you could type

```
> x[3] <- 45
> x

[1] NA NA 45
```

Notice how the first two elements have a missing value, NA. This sort of flexibility comes with a cost. Contrary to other programming languages, in R you will not get an error if you use a position of a vector that does not exist:

```
> length(x)

[1] 3

> x[10]

[1] NA

> x[5] <- 4
> x

[1] NA NA 45 NA  4
```

To shrink the size of a vector, you can take advantage of the fact that the assignment operation is destructive, as we have mentioned before. For instance,

```
> v <- c(45, 243, 78, 343, 445, 44, 56, 77)
> v

[1]  45 243  78 343 445  44  56  77

> v <- c(v[5], v[7])
> v

[1] 445  56
```

Through the use of more powerful indexing schemes to be explored in Section 2.9, you will be able delete particular elements of a vector in an easier way.

2.6 Vectorization

One of the most powerful aspects of the R language is the vectorization of several of its available functions. These functions can be applied directly to a vector of values producing an equal-sized vector of results. For instance,

```
> v <- c(4, 7, 23.5, 76.2, 80)
> sqrt(v)

[1] 2.000000 2.645751 4.847680 8.729261 8.944272
```

The function **sqrt**() calculates the square root of its argument. In this case we have used a vector of numbers as its argument. Vectorization makes the function produce a vector of the same length, with each element resulting from applying the function to the respective element of the original vector.

You can also use this feature of R to carry out vector arithmetic:

```
> v1 <- c(4, 6, 87)
> v2 <- c(34, 32.4, 12)
> v1 + v2

[1] 38.0 38.4 99.0
```

```
> mode(v)
```

What if the vectors do not have the same length? R will use a *recycling rule* by repeating the shorter vector until it reaches the size of the larger vector. For example,

```
> v1 <- c(4, 6, 8, 24)
> v2 <- c(10, 2)
> v1 + v2

[1] 14  8 18 26
```

It is just as if the vector `c(10,2)` was `c(10,2,10,2)`. If the lengths are not multiples, then a warning is issued, but the recycling still takes place (it is a warning, not an error):

```
> v1 <- c(4, 6, 8, 24)
> v2 <- c(10, 2, 4)
> v1 + v2

Warning in v1 + v2: longer object length is not a multiple of shorter object length

[1] 14  8 12 34
```

As mentioned before, single numbers are represented in R as vectors of length 1. Together with the recycling rule this is very handy for operations like the one shown below:

```
> v1 <- c(4, 6, 8, 24)
> 2 * v1

[1]  8 12 16 48
```

Notice how the number 2 (actually the vector `c(2)`!) was recycled, resulting in multiplying all elements of `v1` by 2. As we will see, this recycling rule is also applied with other objects, such as arrays and matrices.

2.7   Factors

Factors provide an easy and compact form of handling categorical (nominal) data. Factors have *levels* that are the possible values they can take. Factors are particularly useful in datasets where you have nominal variables with a fixed number of possible values. Several graphical and summarization functions that we will explore in the following chapters take advantage of this type of information. Factors allow you to use and show the values of your nominal variables as they are, which is clearly more interpretable for the user, while internally R stores these values as numeric codes that are considerably more memory efficient (but this is transparent to the user).

Let us see how to create factors in R. Suppose you have a vector with the sex of ten individuals:

```
> g <- c("f", "m", "m", "m", "f", "m", "f", "m", "f", "f")
> g

[1] "f" "m" "m" "m" "f" "m" "f" "m" "f" "f"
```

You can transform this vector into a factor by:

```
> g <- factor(g)
> g
```

```
[1] f m m m f m f m f f
Levels: f m
```

Notice that you do not have a character vector anymore. Actually, as mentioned above, factors are represented internally as numeric vectors.[19] In this example, we have two levels, 'f' and 'm', which are represented internally as 1 and 2, respectively. Still, you do not need to bother about this as you can use the "original" character values, and R will also use them when showing you the factors. So the coding translation, motivated by efficiency reasons, is transparent to you, as you can confirm in the following example:

```
> g[3]
```

```
[1] m
Levels: f m
```

```
> g[3] == "m"
```

```
[1] TRUE
```

In the above example we asked R to compare the third element of vector g with the character value "m", and the answer TRUE, which means that R internally translated this character value into the respective code of the factor g. Note that if you tried to do g[3] == m you would get an error... why?

Suppose you have five extra individuals whose sex information you want to store in another factor object. Suppose that they are all males. If you still want the factor object to have the same two levels as object g, you must use the following:

```
> other.g <- factor(c("m", "m", "m", "m", "m"), levels = c("f","m"))
> other.g
```

```
[1] m m m m m
Levels: f m
```

Without the levels argument the factor other.g would have a single level ("m").

One of the many things you can do with factors is to count the occurrence of each possible value. Try this:

```
> table(g)
```

```
g
f m
5 5
```

```
> table(other.g)
```

```
other.g
f m
0 5
```

The table() function can also be used to obtain cross-tabulation of several factors.

---

[19]You can confirm it by typing mode(g).

Suppose that we have in another vector the age category of the ten individuals stored in vector **g**. You could cross-tabulate these two factors as follows:

```
> a <- factor(c('adult','adult','juvenile','juvenile','adult',
+                'adult','adult','juvenile','adult','juvenile'))
> table(a, g)

          g
a          f m
  adult    4 2
  juvenile 1 3
```

Sometimes we wish to calculate the marginal and relative frequencies for this type of contingency table. The following gives you the totals for both the sex and the age factors of this dataset:

```
> t <- table(a, g)
> margin.table(t, 1)

a
   adult juvenile
       6        4

> margin.table(t, 2)

g
f m
5 5
```

The "1" and "2" in the function calls represent the first and second dimensions of the table, that is, the rows and columns of **t**.

For relative frequencies with respect to each margin and overall, we do

```
> prop.table(t, 1)

          g
a                  f         m
  adult    0.6666667 0.3333333
  juvenile 0.2500000 0.7500000

> prop.table(t, 2)

          g
a           f   m
  adult    0.8 0.4
  juvenile 0.2 0.6

> prop.table(t)

          g
a           f   m
  adult    0.4 0.2
  juvenile 0.1 0.3
```

Notice that if we wanted percentages instead, we could simply multiply these function calls by 100 making use of the concept of vectorization we have mentioned before.

2.8   Generating Sequences

R has several facilities to generate different types of sequences. For instance, if you want to create a vector containing the integers between 1 and 100, you can simply type

```
> x <- 1:100
```

which creates a vector called **x** containing 100 elements—the integers from 1 to 100.

You should be careful with the precedence of the operator ":". The following examples illustrate this danger:

```
> 10:15 - 1
```

```
[1]  9 10 11 12 13 14
```

```
> 10:(15 - 1)
```

```
[1] 10 11 12 13 14
```

Please make sure you understand what happened in the first command (remember the recycling rule!).

You may also generate decreasing sequences such as the following:

```
> 5:0
```

```
[1] 5 4 3 2 1 0
```

To generate sequences of real numbers, you can use the function **seq()**,

```
> seq(-4, 1, 0.5)
```

```
[1] -4.0 -3.5 -3.0 -2.5 -2.0 -1.5 -1.0 -0.5  0.0  0.5  1.0
```

This instruction generates a sequence of real numbers between -4 and 1 in increments of 0.5. Here are a few other examples of the use of the function **seq()**:[20]

```
> seq(from = 1, to = 5, length = 4)
```

```
[1] 1.000000 2.333333 3.666667 5.000000
```

```
> seq(from = 1, to = 5, length = 2)
```

```
[1] 1 5
```

```
> seq(length = 10, from = -2, by = 0.2)
```

```
[1] -2.0 -1.8 -1.6 -1.4 -1.2 -1.0 -0.8 -0.6 -0.4 -0.2
```

Another very useful function to generate sequences with a certain pattern is the function **rep()**:

---

[20]You may want to have a look at the help page of the function (typing, for instance, '?seq'), to better understand its arguments and variants.

```
> rep(5, 10)
```

```
[1] 5 5 5 5 5 5 5 5 5 5
```

```
> rep("hi", 3)
```

```
[1] "hi" "hi" "hi"
```

```
> rep(1:2, 3)
```

```
[1] 1 2 1 2 1 2
```

```
> rep(1:2, each = 3)
```

```
[1] 1 1 1 2 2 2
```

The function `gl()` can be used to generate sequences involving factors. The syntax of this function is `gl(k,n)`, where `k` is the number of levels of the factor, and `n` is the number of repetitions of each level. Here are two examples,

```
> gl(3, 5)
```

```
[1] 1 1 1 1 1 2 2 2 2 2 3 3 3 3 3
Levels: 1 2 3
```

```
> gl(2, 5, labels = c("female", "male"))
```

```
[1] female female female female female male   male   male   male   male
Levels: female male
```

Finally, R has several functions that can be used to generate random sequences according to different probability density functions. The functions have the generic structure `rfunc(n, par1, par2, ...)`, where *func* is the name of the probability distribution, `n` is the number of data to generate, and `par1, par2, ...` are the values of some parameters of the density function that may be required. For instance, if you want ten randomly generated numbers from a normal distribution with zero mean and unit standard deviation, type

```
> rnorm(10)
```

```
[1] -0.38016381  0.84988686  1.78151879 -0.43124411  0.54127286
[6] -0.36367234  0.18326414 -0.13043720  0.30978034 -0.05407895
```

while if you prefer a mean of 10 and a standard deviation of 3, you should use

```
> rnorm(4, mean = 10, sd = 3)
```

```
[1] 14.231845 12.781868 17.509875  8.088479
```

To get five numbers drawn randomly from a Student t distribution with 10 degrees of freedom, type

```
> rt(5, df = 10)
```

```
[1]  1.6069443  1.6778517 -1.2440164  1.4702562  0.7808423
```

R has many more probability functions, as well as other functions for obtaining the probability densities, the cumulative probability densities, and the quantiles of these distributions.

2.9 Sub-Setting

We have already seen examples of how to get one element of a vector by indicating its position inside square brackets. R also allows you to use vectors within the brackets. There are several types of index vectors. Logical index vectors extract the elements corresponding to true values. Let us see a concrete example:

```
> x <- c(0, -3, 4, -1, 45, 90, -5)
> x > 0

[1] FALSE FALSE  TRUE FALSE  TRUE  TRUE FALSE
```

The second instruction of the code shown above is a logical condition. As x is a vector, the comparison is carried out for all elements of the vector (remember the famous recycling rule!), thus producing a vector with as many logical values as there are elements in x. If we use this vector of logical values to index x, we get as a result the positions of x that correspond to the true values:

```
> x[x > 0]

[1]  4 45 90
```

This reads as follows: Give me the positions of x for which the following logical expression is true. Notice that this is another example of the notion of function composition, which we will use rather frequently. Taking advantage of the logical operators available in R, you can use more complex logical index vectors, as for instance,

```
> x[x <= -2 | x > 5]

[1] -3 45 90 -5

> x[x > 40 & x < 100]

[1] 45 90
```

As you may have guessed, the "|" operator performs logical disjunction, while the "&" operator is used for logical conjunction.[21] This means that the first instruction shows us the elements of x that are either less than or equal to −2, or greater than 5. The second example presents the elements of x that are both greater than 40 and less than 100.

R also allows you to use a vector of integers to extract several elements from a vector. The numbers in the vector of indexes indicate the positions in the original vector to be extracted:

```
> x[c(4, 6)]

[1] -1 90

> x[1:3]
```

---

[21]There are also other operators, && and ||, to perform these operations. These alternatives evaluate expressions from left to right, examining only the first element of the vectors, while the single character versions work element-wise.

```
[1]  0 -3  4
```

```
> y <- c(1, 4)
> x[y]
```

```
[1]  0 -1
```

Alternatively, you can use a vector with negative indexes to indicate which elements are to be excluded from the selection:

```
> x[-1]
```

```
[1] -3  4 -1 45 90 -5
```

```
> x[-c(4, 6)]
```

```
[1]  0 -3  4 45 -5
```

```
> x[-(1:3)]
```

```
[1] -1 45 90 -5
```

Note the need for parentheses in the last example due to the precedence of the ":" operator.

Indexes can also be formed by a vector of strings, taking advantage of the fact that R allows you to name the elements of a vector, through the function **names()**. Named elements are sometimes preferable because their positions are easier to memorize. For instance, imagine you have a vector of measurements of a chemical parameter obtained at five different locations. You could create a named vector as follows:

```
> pH <- c(4.5, 7, 7.3, 8.2, 6.3)
> names(pH) <- c("area1", "area2", "mud", "dam", "middle")
> pH
```

```
 area1  area2    mud    dam middle
   4.5    7.0    7.3    8.2    6.3
```

In effect, if you already know the names of the positions in the vector at the time of its creation, it is easier to proceed this way:

```
> pH <- c(area1 = 4.5, area2 = 7, mud = 7.3, dam = 8.2, middle = 6.3)
```

The vector **pH** can now be indexed using the names shown above:

```
> pH["mud"]
```

```
mud
7.3
```

```
> pH[c("area1", "dam")]
```

```
area1    dam
  4.5    8.2
```

Finally, indexes may be empty, meaning that all elements are selected. An empty index represents the absence of a restriction on the selection process. For instance, if you want to fill in a vector with zeros, you could simply do "x[] <- 0". Please notice that this is different from doing "x <- 0". This latter case would assign to x a vector with one single element (zero), while the former (assuming that x exists before, of course!) will fill in all current elements of x with zeros. Try both!

2.10   Matrices and Arrays

Data elements can be stored in an object with more than one dimension. This may be useful in several situations. Arrays store data elements in several dimensions. Matrices are a special case of arrays with two single dimensions. Arrays and matrices in R are nothing more than vectors with a particular attribute that is the *dimension*. Let us see an example. Suppose you have the vector of numbers c(45,23,66,77,33,44,56,12,78,23). The following would "organize" these ten numbers as a matrix:

```
> m <- c(45, 23, 66, 77, 33, 44, 56, 12, 78, 23)
> m

 [1] 45 23 66 77 33 44 56 12 78 23

> dim(m) <- c(2, 5)
> m

     [,1] [,2] [,3] [,4] [,5]
[1,]   45   66   33   56   78
[2,]   23   77   44   12   23
```

Notice how the numbers were "spread" through a matrix with two rows and five columns (the dimension we have assigned to m using the dim() function). Actually, you could simply create the matrix using the simpler instruction:

```
> m <- matrix(c(45, 23, 66, 77, 33, 44, 56, 12, 78, 23), 2, 5)
```

You may have noticed that the vector of numbers was spread in the matrix by columns; that is, first fill in the first column, then the second, and so on. You can fill the matrix by rows using the following parameter of the function matrix():

```
> m <- matrix(c(45, 23, 66, 77, 33, 44, 56, 12, 78, 23), 2, 5, byrow = TRUE)
```

As the visual display of matrices suggests, you can access the elements of a matrix through a similar indexing scheme as in vectors, but this time with two indexes (the dimensions of a matrix):

```
> m[2, 3]

[1] 12
```

You can take advantage of the sub-setting schemes described in Section 2.9 to extract elements of a matrix, as the following examples show:

```
> m[-2, 1]
```

```
[1] 45
```

```
> m[1, -c(3, 5)]
```

```
[1] 45 23 77
```

Moreover, if you omit any dimension, you obtain full columns or rows of the matrix:

```
> m[1, ]
```

```
[1] 45 23 66 77 33
```

```
> m[, 4]
```

```
[1] 77 78
```

Notice that, as a result of sub-setting, you may end up with a vector, as in the two above examples. If you still want the result to be a matrix, even though it is a matrix formed by a single line or column, you can use the following instead:

```
> m[1, , drop = FALSE]
```

```
     [,1] [,2] [,3] [,4] [,5]
[1,]   45   23   66   77   33
```

```
> m[, 4, drop = FALSE]
```

```
     [,1]
[1,]   77
[2,]   78
```

Functions `cbind()` and `rbind()` may be used to join together two or more vectors or matrices, by columns or by rows, respectively. The following examples should illustrate this:

```
> m1 <- matrix(c(45, 23, 66, 77, 33, 44, 56, 12, 78, 23), 2, 5)
> cbind(c(4, 76), m1[, 4])
```

```
     [,1] [,2]
[1,]    4   56
[2,]   76   12
```

```
> m2 <- matrix(rep(10, 20), 4, 5)
> m2
```

```
     [,1] [,2] [,3] [,4] [,5]
[1,]   10   10   10   10   10
[2,]   10   10   10   10   10
[3,]   10   10   10   10   10
[4,]   10   10   10   10   10
```

```
> m3 <- rbind(m1[1, ], m2[3, ])
> m3
```

```
     [,1] [,2] [,3] [,4] [,5]
[1,]   45   66   33   56   78
[2,]   10   10   10   10   10
```

You can also give names to the columns and rows of matrices, using the functions `colnames()` and `rownames()`, respectively. This facilitates memorizing the data positions.

```
> results <- matrix(c(10, 30, 40, 50, 43, 56, 21, 30), 2, 4, byrow = TRUE)
> colnames(results) <- c("1qrt", "2qrt", "3qrt", "4qrt")
> rownames(results) <- c("store1", "store2")
> results

       1qrt 2qrt 3qrt 4qrt
store1   10   30   40   50
store2   43   56   21   30

> results["store1", ]

1qrt 2qrt 3qrt 4qrt
  10   30   40   50

> results["store2", c("1qrt", "4qrt")]

1qrt 4qrt
  43   30
```

Arrays are extensions of matrices to more than two dimensions. This means that they have more than two indexes. Apart from this they are similar to matrices and can be used in the same way. Similar to the `matrix()` function, there is an `array()` function to facilitate the creation of arrays. The following is an example of its use:

```
> a <- array(1:24, dim = c(4, 3, 2))
> a

, , 1

     [,1] [,2] [,3]
[1,]    1    5    9
[2,]    2    6   10
[3,]    3    7   11
[4,]    4    8   12

, , 2

     [,1] [,2] [,3]
[1,]   13   17   21
[2,]   14   18   22
[3,]   15   19   23
[4,]   16   20   24
```

The above instruction has created an array with 3 dimensions, the first with 4 possible "positions", the second with 3 and the third 2. The 24 integers were "spread" in this data structure.

You can use the same indexing schemes to access elements of an array. Make sure you understand the following examples.

```
> a[1, 3, 2]

[1] 21
```

```
> a[1, , 2]

[1] 13 17 21

> a[4, 3, ]

[1] 12 24

> a[c(2, 3), , -2]

     [,1] [,2] [,3]
[1,]    2    6   10
[2,]    3    7   11
```

The recycling and arithmetic rules also apply to matrices and arrays, although they are tricky to understand at times. Below are a few examples:

```
> m <- matrix(c(45, 23, 66, 77, 33, 44, 56, 12, 78, 23), 2, 5)
> m

     [,1] [,2] [,3] [,4] [,5]
[1,]   45   66   33   56   78
[2,]   23   77   44   12   23

> m * 3

     [,1] [,2] [,3] [,4] [,5]
[1,]  135  198   99  168  234
[2,]   69  231  132   36   69

> m1 <- matrix(c(45, 23, 66, 77, 33, 44), 2, 3)
> m1

     [,1] [,2] [,3]
[1,]   45   66   33
[2,]   23   77   44

> m2 <- matrix(c(12, 65, 32, 7, 4, 78), 2, 3)
> m2

     [,1] [,2] [,3]
[1,]   12   32    4
[2,]   65    7   78

> m1 + m2

     [,1] [,2] [,3]
[1,]   57   98   37
[2,]   88   84  122
```

R also includes operators and functions for standard matrix algebra that have different rules. You may obtain more information on this by looking at Section 5 of the document "An Introduction to R" that comes with R.

2.11 Lists

R lists consist of an ordered collection of other objects known as their *components*. Unlike the elements of vectors, list components do not need to be of the same type, mode, or length. The components of a list are always numbered and may also have a name attached to them. Let us start by seeing a simple example of how to create a list:

```
> my.lst <- list(stud.id=34453,
+                stud.name="John",
+                stud.marks=c(14.3,12,15,19))
```

The object **my.lst** is formed by three components. One is a number and has the name **stud.id**, the second is a character string having the name **stud.name**, and the third is a vector of numbers with name **stud.marks**.

To show the contents of a list you simply type its name as any other object:

```
> my.lst

$stud.id
[1] 34453

$stud.name
[1] "John"

$stud.marks
[1] 14.3 12.0 15.0 19.0
```

You can extract individual elements of lists using the following indexing schema:

```
> my.lst[[1]]

[1] 34453

> my.lst[[3]]

[1] 14.3 12.0 15.0 19.0
```

You may have noticed that we have used double square brackets. If we had used **my.lst[1]** instead, we would obtain a different result:

```
> my.lst[1]

$stud.id
[1] 34453
```

This latter notation extracts a sub-list formed by the first component of **my.lst**. On the contrary, **my.lst[[1]]** extracts the value of the first component (in this case, a number), which is not a list anymore, as you can confirm by the following:

```
> mode(my.lst[1])

[1] "list"

> mode(my.lst[[1]])

[1] "numeric"
```

In the case of lists with named components (as the previous example), we can use an alternative way of extracting the value of a component of a list:

```
> my.lst$stud.id
```

```
[1] 34453
```

The names of the components of a list are, in effect, an attribute of the list, and can be manipulated as we did with the names of elements of vectors:

```
> names(my.lst)
```

```
[1] "stud.id"    "stud.name"  "stud.marks"
```

```
> names(my.lst) <- c("id", "name", "marks")
> my.lst
```

```
$id
[1] 34453
```

```
$name
[1] "John"
```

```
$marks
[1] 14.3 12.0 15.0 19.0
```

Lists can be extended by adding further components to them:

```
> my.lst$parents.names <- c("Ana", "Mike")
> my.lst
```

```
$id
[1] 34453
```

```
$name
[1] "John"
```

```
$marks
[1] 14.3 12.0 15.0 19.0
```

```
$parents.names
[1] "Ana"  "Mike"
```

You can check the number of components of a list using the function **length()**:

```
> length(my.lst)
```

```
[1] 4
```

You can remove components of a list as follows:

```
> my.lst <- my.lst[-5]
```

You can concatenate lists using the **c()** function:

```
> other <- list(age = 19, sex = "male")
> lst <- c(my.lst, other)
> lst

$id
[1] 34453

$name
[1] "John"

$marks
[1] 14.3 12.0 15.0 19.0

$parents.names
[1] "Ana"  "Mike"

$age
[1] 19

$sex
[1] "male"
```

Finally, you can unflatten all data in a list using the function `unlist()`. This will create a vector with as many elements as there are data objects in a list. This will coerce different data types to a common data type,[22] which means that most of the time you will end up with everything being character strings. Moreover, each element of this vector will have a name generated from the name of the list component that originated it:

```
> unlist(my.lst)
```

id	name	marks1	marks2	marks3
"34453"	"John"	"14.3"	"12"	"15"
marks4	parents.names1	parents.names2		
"19"	"Ana"	"Mike"		

2.12 Data Frames

Data frames are the recommended data structure for storing data tables in R. They are similar to matrices in structure as they are also bi-dimensional. However, contrary to matrices, data frames may include data of a different type in each column. In this sense they are more similar to lists, and in effect, for R, data frames are a special class of lists.

We can think of each row of a data frame as an observation (or case), being described by a set of variables (the named columns of the data frame).

You can create a data frame as follows:

```
> my.dataset <- data.frame(site=c('A','B','A','A','B'),
+                          season=c('Winter','Summer','Summer','Spring','Fall'),
```

---

[22]Because vector elements must have the same type (*c.f.* Section 2.5).

```
+                            pH = c(7.4,6.3,8.6,7.2,8.9))
> my.dataset

  site season  pH
1    A Winter 7.4
2    B Summer 6.3
3    A Summer 8.6
4    A Spring 7.2
5    B   Fall 8.9
```

Elements of data frames can be accessed like a matrix:

```
> my.dataset[3, 2]

[1] Summer
Levels: Fall Spring Summer Winter
```

Note that the "season" column has been coerced into a factor because all its elements are character strings. Similarly, the "site" column is also a factor. This is the default behavior of the **data.frame()** function.[23]

You can use the indexing schemes described in Section 2.9 with data frames. Moreover, you can use the column names for accessing the content of full columns of a data frame using the two following alternatives:

```
> my.dataset$pH

[1] 7.4 6.3 8.6 7.2 8.9

> my.dataset[["site"]]

[1] A B A A B
Levels: A B
```

You can perform some simple querying of the data in the data frame, taking advantage of the sub-setting possibilities of R, as shown on these examples:

```
> my.dataset[my.dataset$pH > 7, ]

  site season  pH
1    A Winter 7.4
3    A Summer 8.6
4    A Spring 7.2
5    B   Fall 8.9

> my.dataset[my.dataset$site == "A", "pH"]

[1] 7.4 8.6 7.2

> my.dataset[my.dataset$season == "Summer", c("site", "pH")]

  site  pH
2    B 6.3
3    A 8.6
```

---

[23]Check the help information on the **data.frame()** function to see examples of how you can use the I() function, or the **stringsAsFactors** parameter to avoid this coercion.

In the above examples you could eventually feel tempted to refer to the columns directly, but this would generate an error as R would interpret the column names as names of variables and such variables do not exist:

```
> my.dataset[pH > 7, ]

Error in '[.data.frame'(my.dataset, pH > 7, ): object 'pH' not found
```

To make this possible you would need to resort to the function **attach()**. Let us see some examples of this:

```
> attach(my.dataset)
> my.dataset[site=='B', ]

  site season  pH
2    B Summer 6.3
5    B   Fall 8.9

> season

[1] Winter Summer Summer Spring Fall
Levels: Fall Spring Summer Winter
```

The inverse of the function **attach()** is the function **detach()** that disables these facilities:

```
> detach(my.dataset)
> season

Error in eval(expr, envir, enclos): object 'season' not found
```

Please note that the use of this simplification through the function **attach()** is not recommended if your data frame will change, as this may have unexpected results. A safer approach, when you are simply querying the data frame, is to use the function **subset()**:

```
> subset(my.dataset, pH > 8)

  site season  pH
3    A Summer 8.6
5    B   Fall 8.9

> subset(my.dataset, season == "Summer", season:pH)

  season  pH
2 Summer 6.3
3 Summer 8.6
```

Notice however, that contrary to the other examples seen above, you may not use this sub-setting strategy to change values in the data. So, for instance, if you want to sum 1 to the pH values of all summer rows, you can only do it this way:

```
> my.dataset[my.dataset$season == 'Summer','pH'] <-
+      my.dataset[my.dataset$season == 'Summer','pH'] + 1
```

You can add new columns to a data frame in the same way you did with lists:

```
> my.dataset$NO3 <- c(234.5, 256.6, 654.1, 356.7, 776.4)
> my.dataset

  site season  pH   NO3
1    A Winter 7.4 234.5
2    B Summer 7.3 256.6
3    A Summer 9.6 654.1
4    A Spring 7.2 356.7
5    B   Fall 8.9 776.4
```

The only restriction to this addition is that new columns must have the same number of rows as the existing data frame; otherwise R will complain. You can check the number of rows or columns of a data frame with these functions:

```
> nrow(my.dataset)
```

```
[1] 5
```

```
> ncol(my.dataset)
```

```
[1] 4
```

```
> dim(my.dataset)
```

```
[1] 5 4
```

Usually you will be reading your datasets into a data frame either from some file or from a database. You will seldom type the data using the `data.frame()` function as above, particularly in a typical data mining scenario. In the next chapters we will see how to import several types of data into data frames, namely in Section 3.2.2 (page 46) of the next chapter. In any case, you may want to browse the "R Data Import/Export" manual that comes with R to check all the different possibilities that R has.

R has a simple spreadsheet-like interface that can be used to enter small data frames. You can edit an existent data frame by typing

```
> my.dataset <- edit(my.dataset)
```

or you may create a new data frame with,

```
> new.data <- edit(data.frame())
```

You can use the **names()** function to check and/or change the name of the columns of a data frame:

```
> names(my.dataset)
```

```
[1] "site"   "season" "pH"     "NO3"
```

```
> names(my.dataset) <- c("area", "season", "pH", "NO3")
> my.dataset

  area season  pH   NO3
1    A Winter 7.4 234.5
2    B Summer 7.3 256.6
3    A Summer 9.6 654.1
4    A Spring 7.2 356.7
5    B   Fall 8.9 776.4
```

As the names attribute is a vector, if you just want to change the name of one particular column, you can type

```
> names(my.dataset)[4] <- "PO4"
> my.dataset

  area season  pH   PO4
1    A Winter 7.4 234.5
2    B Summer 7.3 256.6
3    A Summer 9.6 654.1
4    A Spring 7.2 356.7
5    B   Fall 8.9 776.4
```

2.13   Useful Extensions to Data Frames

In the previous section we have presented data frames as the main form of storing datasets in R. The packages **tibble** (Wickham et al., 2016) and **dplyr** (Wickham and Francois, 2015a) provide some useful extensions to data frames that are very convenient for many data manipulation tasks.

The package **tibble** defines *tibbles* that can be regarded as "special" data frames. *Tibbles* change some of the behavior of "standard" data frames. The more important differences between a *tibble* and a data frame are: (i) *tibbles* never change character columns into factors as data frames do by default; (ii) *tibbles* are more relaxed in terms of naming of the columns; and (iii) the printing methods of *tibbles* are more convenient particularly with large datasets. *Tibbles* can be created with the function `tibble()`

```
> dat <- tibble(TempCels = sample(-10:40, size=100, replace=TRUE),
+               TempFahr = TempCels*9/5 + 32,
+               Location = rep(letters[1:2], each=50))
> dat

# A tibble: 100 × 3
   TempCels TempFahr Location
      <int>    <dbl>    <chr>
1        -4     24.8        a
2        21     69.8        a
3        12     53.6        a
4         4     39.2        a
5        38    100.4        a
6        31     87.8        a
7        -9     15.8        a
8        -8     17.6        a
9        24     75.2        a
10        9     48.2        a
# ... with 90 more rows
```

This function works in a similar way as the standard `data.frame()` function but, as you can observe, each column is calculated sequentially allowing you to use the values of previous columns, and character vectors are not converted into factors.

Any standard data frame can be converted into a *tibble*. For illustration purposes we will use the (in)famous *Iris* dataset. This dataset is available directly in R and contains 150 rows with information (5 attributes) on variants of Iris plants.

```
> data(iris)
> dim(iris)

[1] 150   5

> class(iris)

[1] "data.frame"
```

The first statement loads the *Iris* dataset into a standard local R data frame with 150 rows and 5 columns. Even-though this is a rather small dataset, if you accidentally type `iris` at the R command line and press the ENTER key you will get your screen filled with data which would not happen with *tibbles*. To convert this data frame into a *tibble* we can proceed as follows

```
> library(tibble)
> ir <- as_tibble(iris)
> class(ir)

[1] "tbl_df"     "tbl"          "data.frame"

> ir

# A tibble: 150 × 5
   Sepal.Length Sepal.Width Petal.Length Petal.Width Species
          <dbl>       <dbl>        <dbl>       <dbl> <fctr>
1           5.1         3.5          1.4         0.2 setosa
2           4.9         3.0          1.4         0.2 setosa
3           4.7         3.2          1.3         0.2 setosa
4           4.6         3.1          1.5         0.2 setosa
5           5.0         3.6          1.4         0.2 setosa
6           5.4         3.9          1.7         0.4 setosa
7           4.6         3.4          1.4         0.3 setosa
8           5.0         3.4          1.5         0.2 setosa
9           4.4         2.9          1.4         0.2 setosa
10          4.9         3.1          1.5         0.1 setosa
# ... with 140 more rows
```

Using function **as_tibble()** we create the object **ir** that contains the original dataset converted into a *tibble*. It is important to be aware that we did not create a new copy of the data frame! As you see the new object is still of class **data.frame** but it also belongs to two new classes: **tbl_df** and **tbl**. The first is the class of a *tibble* (**tbl_df**), while the second is a further generalization that allows us to look at a dataset independently of the data source used to store it. As you can observe the printing method of *tibbles* is more interesting than that of standard data frames as it provides more information and avoids over cluttering your screen. Please note that if you wish you can still get all output as in standard data frames. One possible way of achieving this is through the method **print()** of objects of the class **tbl_df** that has extra parameters that allow you to control how many rows to show as well as the width of the output. For instance, the following would show the full *Iris* dataset[24],

---

[24]Check the help page of `print.tbl_df()` for further details and examples.

```
> print(ir, n=Inf, width=Inf)
```

On top of printing another crucial difference between standard data frames and *tibbles* is subsetting. In standard data frames subsetting may sometimes lead to some puzzling results, particularly for newcomers to the R language. Check the following example

```
> iris[1:15, "Petal.Length"]

 [1] 1.4 1.4 1.3 1.5 1.4 1.7 1.4 1.5 1.4 1.5 1.5 1.6 1.4 1.1 1.2

> class(iris[1:15, "Petal.Length"])

[1] "numeric"
```

Asking for the first 15 values of `Petal.Length` resulted in a vector! We subsetted a data frame and we obtained as result a different data structure. This is surprising for many people, although you can avoid it by using the construct `iris[1:15, "Petal.Length",drop=FALSE]`. With *tibbles* this never happens. Subsetting a *tibble* always results in a *tibble*,

```
> ir[1:15, "Petal.Length"]

# A tibble: 15 × 1
   Petal.Length
          <dbl>
1           1.4
2           1.4
3           1.3
4           1.5
5           1.4
6           1.7
7           1.4
8           1.5
9           1.4
10          1.5
11          1.5
12          1.6
13          1.4
14          1.1
15          1.2
```

The only way you get a similar result with *tibbles* is by being specific on extracting a single column and then selecting the first 15 values of this set of values

```
> ir$Petal.Length[1:15]

 [1] 1.4 1.4 1.3 1.5 1.4 1.7 1.4 1.5 1.4 1.5 1.5 1.6 1.4 1.1 1.2

> ir[["Petal.Length"]][1:15]

 [1] 1.4 1.4 1.3 1.5 1.4 1.7 1.4 1.5 1.4 1.5 1.5 1.6 1.4 1.1 1.2
```

Please be aware that this difference between *tibbles* and data frames may invalidate the use of some packages with *tibbles*. This will be the case if the functions of these packages somehow assume the above mentioned simplification after subsetting a single column of a data frame. If you provide them with a *tibble* instead of a data frame they will not get the expected result and may return some error. If that is the case then you need to call these functions with a standard data frame and not a *tibble*.

The package **dplyr** defines the class **tbl** that can be regarded as a wrapper of the actual data source. These objects encapsulate the data source and provide a set of uniform data manipulation verbs irrespectively of these sources. The package currently covers several data sources like standard data frames (in the form of *tibbles*), several database management systems, and several other sources. The main advantages of this package are: (i) the encapsulation of the data source; (ii) providing a set of uniform data manipulation functions; and (iii) the computational efficiency of the provided functions. In summary, using **dplyr** you can create **tbl** objects connected with some data source, and once you do this you can mostly ignore this source as all data manipulation statements the package provides work the same way independently of the source.

The package **dplyr** has many functions that allow easy manipulation of these **tbl** objects. We will explore most of these facilities later in the book. For now let us just see some examples involving querying the data. This package provides two main functions for this task. Function `select()` can be used to select a subset of columns of the dataset, whilst function `filter()` is used to select a subset of the rows. Suppose you wish to inspect the petal lengths and widths of the plants of the species Setosa. You could achieve that as follows:

```
> select(filter(ir,Species=="setosa"),Petal.Width,Petal.Length)

# A tibble: 50 × 2
   Petal.Width Petal.Length
         <dbl>        <dbl>
1          0.2          1.4
2          0.2          1.4
3          0.2          1.3
4          0.2          1.5
5          0.2          1.4
6          0.4          1.7
7          0.3          1.4
8          0.2          1.5
9          0.2          1.4
10         0.1          1.5
# ... with 40 more rows
```

A few things are worth noting on the above statement. First of all you may refer to the column names directly (like you could in the function `subset()` mentioned in Section 2.12). Then you do not need to worry about the output that is automatically truncated to the first few rows. Obviously, you may still inspect all output if you wish. You may for instance call the function `View()` with the above statement as argument, and you will get a graphical spreadsheet-like window where you can explore the full output of the statement. The above statement uses the traditional function composition by applying the select function to the output of the filter function. Function composition is a very nice concept but it often gets too difficult to understand the code if a lot of composition is taking place. Unfortunately, this is frequently necessary when querying datasets. The package **dplyr** provides the pipe operator to make our life easier in those cases. The above statement could have been written as follows using this operator:

```
> filter(ir,Species == "setosa") %>% select(Petal.Width,Petal.Length)

# A tibble: 50 × 2
   Petal.Width Petal.Length
         <dbl>        <dbl>
1          0.2          1.4
2          0.2          1.4
3          0.2          1.3
4          0.2          1.5
5          0.2          1.4
6          0.4          1.7
7          0.3          1.4
8          0.2          1.5
9          0.2          1.4
10         0.1          1.5
# ... with 40 more rows
```

The pipe operator is in effect a simple re-writing operator and this can be applied to any R function, not only in this context. The idea is that the left-hand side of the operator is passed as the first argument of the function on the right side of the operator. So x %>% f(y) is translated into f(x,y). Independently of these technicalities, the fact is that for dataset querying these statements using the pipe operator are often significantly easier to "read" than with the standard function composition strategies. For instance, the above code can be read as: "filter the dataset ir by the setosa species and then show the respective petal width and length". This reading is more natural and more related with the way our brain thinks about these querying tasks.

Later in the book we will explore many more facets of this wonderful **dplyr** package. For now it is sufficient to be aware of this alternative way of handling and querying datasets in R.

2.14   Objects, Classes, and Methods

One of the design goals of R is to facilitate the manipulation of data so that we can easily perform the data analysis tasks we have. In R, data are stored as objects. As mentioned before, everything in R is an object, from simple numbers to functions or more elaborate data structures. Every R object belongs to a *class*. Classes define the abstract characteristics of the objects that belong to them. Namely, they specify the attributes or properties of these objects and also their behaviors (or methods). For instance, the **matrix** class has specific properties like the dimension of the matrices and it also has specific behavior for some types of operations. In effect, when we ask R the content of a matrix, R will show it with a specific format on the screen. This happens because there is a specific **print** method associated with all objects of the class **matrix**. In summary, the class of an object determines (1) the methods that are used by some general functions when applied to these objects, and also (2) the representation of the objects of that class. This representation consists of the information that is stored by the objects of this class.

R has many predefined classes of objects, together with associated methods. On top of this we can also extend this list by creating new classes of objects or new methods. These new methods can be both for these new classes or for existing classes. New classes are normally created after existing classes, usually by adding some new pieces of information to their representation.

The representation of a class consists of a set of *slots*. Each slot has a name and an associated class that determines the information that it stores. The operator "@" can be used to access the information stored in a slot of an object. This means that x@y is the value of the slot y of the object x. This obviously assumes that the class of objects to which x belongs has a slot of information named y.

Another important notion related to classes is the notion of inheritance between classes. This notion establishes relationships between the classes that allow us to indicate that a certain new class extends an existing one by adding some extra information. This extension also implies that the new class inherits all the methods of the previous class, which facilitates the creation of new classes, as we do not start from scratch. In this context, we only need to worry about implementing the methods for the operations where the new class of objects differs from the existing one that it extends.

Finally, another very important notion is that of polymorphism. This notion establishes that some functions can be applied to different classes of objects, producing the results that are adequate for the respective class. In R, this is strongly related to the notion of generic functions. Generic functions implement a certain, very general, high-level operation. For instance, as we have already seen, the function plot() can be used to obtain a graphical representation of an object. This is its general goal. However, this graphical representation may actually be different depending on the type of object. It is different to plot a set of numbers, than to plot a linear regression model, for instance. Polymorphism is the key to implementing this without disturbing the user. The user only needs to know that there is a function that provides a graphical representation of objects. R and its inner mechanisms handle the job of *dispatching* these general tasks to the class-specific functions that provide the graphical representation for each class of objects. All this method-dispatching occurs in the background without the user needing to know the "dirty" details of it. What happens, in effect, is that as R knows that plot() is a generic function, it will search for a plot method (that in effect is just another function) that is specific for the class of objects that were included in the plot() function call. If such a method exists, it will use it; otherwise it will resort to some default plotting method. When the user decides to create a new class of objects he needs to decide if he wants to have specific methods for his new class of objects. So if he wants to be able to plot objects of the new class, then he needs to provide a specific plot method for this new class of objects that "tells" R how to plot these objects.

These are the basic details on classes and methods in R. In effect, R even has several general frameworks for handling classes and object oriented programming in general. The creation of new classes and respective methods is outside the scope of this book. More details can be obtained in many existing books on programming with R, such as, the books *Software for Data Analysis* by Chambers (2008) or *Advanced R* by Whickam (2014).

2.15 Managing Your Sessions

When you are using R for more complex tasks, the command line typing style of interaction becomes a bit limited. In these situations it is more practical to write all your code in a text file and then ask R to execute it. To produce such a file, you can use your favorite text editor (like Notepad, Emacs, etc.) or, in case you are using RStudio, you can use the script editor available in the File menu.[25] After creating and saving the file, you can issue the following command at R prompt to execute all commands in the file:

```
> source('mycode.R')
```

This assumes that you have a text file called "mycode.R" in the current working directory of R. In Windows versions the easiest way to change this directory is through the option "Change directory" of the "File" menu. In Mac OS X versions there is an equivalent option under menu "Misc". In RStudio you may use the option "Set working directory" of the "Session" menu. In Unix versions (actually, on all versions) you may use the functions getwd() and setwd() to check and change the current working directory, respectively.

When you are using the R prompt in an interactive fashion you may wish to save some of the objects you create for later use (such as some function you have typed in). The following example saves the objects named f and my.dataset in a file named "mysession.RData":

```
> save(f,my.dataset,file='mysession.RData')
```

Later, for instance in a new R session, you can load these objects by issuing

```
> load('mysession.RData')
```

You can also save all objects currently in R workspace,[26] by issuing

```
> save.image()
```

This command will save the workspace in a file named ".RData" in the current working directory. This file is automatically loaded when you run R again from this directory. This kind of effect can also be achieved by answering Yes when quitting R.

Further readings on R

The online manual *An Introduction to R* that comes with every distribution of R is an excellent source of information on the R language. The "Contributed" subsection of the "Documentation" section at the R Web site, includes several free books on different facets of R. For more advanced aspects of the R language we recommend Chambers (2008) and Whickam (2014) (which is also freely available at http://adv-r.had.co.nz/).

---

[25]Windows and Mac OS X versions of R also include a dedicated script editor.
[26]These can be listed issuing ls(), as mentioned before.

Chapter 3

Introduction to Data Mining

The approach followed in this book is to learn Data Mining through solving a set of case studies. This means that concepts of this discipline are introduced as they are needed. Although we are strongly supportive of this approach as a way of easily motivating people to understand the concepts, we agree that there are also some drawbacks. The most important is probably the fact that you do not get a global perspective of the organization and relationship between different data mining topics, i.e. you do not get a global overview of the discipline. This is the main goal of this chapter. We introduce the reader to the main topics and concepts of Data Mining and provide a short introduction to their main questions and how they are related to each other. This should give the reader a global perspective of this research field as well as allowing her/him to better place the approaches that will be followed in the case studies, in the context of this larger picture of Data Mining.

Data Mining is a vast discipline, so this chapter will necessarily provide a short introduction to this area. We have tried to explain the key concepts within the different steps of a typical Data Mining workflow. For each of these steps we describe some of the main existing techniques and provide simple illustrations of how these are implemented in R. Further details and broader descriptions of this field will have to be found elsewhere as this is not the main goal of the current book. Good examples of manuscripts with an extensive coverage of current Data Mining topics include the books by Aggarwal (2015) and Han et al. (2012). For a more "statistically" oriented perspective the books by Hastie et al. (2009) and James et al. (2013) are good references. Finally, a Machine Learning perpective can be obtained in the books by Flach (2012) and Kononenko and Kukar (2007).

A second goal of this chapter is to provide links between the main topics and tasks of Data Mining and some key R packages that may help with these tasks. We will provide short illustrations of some of these packages but more detailed usage will be left to the second part of the book where we use them in concrete applications.

3.1 A Bird's Eye View on Data Mining

Data is present in most of our activities. With the widespread usage of computational devices, storing these data is more and more frequent. This obviously leads to a huge amount of available data on a large set of human activities. There are several factors that have, and still are, contributing a lot for this dawn of the age of data[1]. Among them we can highlight: (i) the widespread availability of all sorts of cheap sensors that can collect a diverse set of data values; (ii) the ever increasing power of all sorts of computation devices; (iii) the fact that we have networking available almost everywhere; and also (iv) the recent trend on the Internet of Things (IoT) where we have many physical objects inter connected and

---

[1]This is a shameless copy of the title of an interesting talk I listened to by Bernhard Pfahringer - thank you Bernhard!

able to collect and share data. These and several other aspects of our current societies lead to an overwhelming collection of data and also to pressure on making use of these data to optimize our activities. In this context, it should not come as a surprise that data mining analysts[2] are one of the hottest professions these days and it does not look like this is going to change in the near future, on the contrary.

Data Mining is a relatively recent research field. So much that the name is still evolving, as we frequently witness the dawn of new terms, like for instance the recent Data Science. Its main goals are the analysis of data in the search for useful knowledge. The field has been receiving lots of attention from many actors of the society as a consequence of the amount of data we are collecting in most of our activities. This data potentially hides useful information on these activities and uncovering this knowledge may prove to be a key advantage for many organizations. Analyzing data is not a novel task, so it does not come as a surprise to find out that Data Mining shares many goals and methods with other fields like Statistics, Machine Learning, Pattern Recognition and other areas. At the end of the day all these fields strive to analyze data, and that is also the main goal of Data Mining.

When people talk about Data Mining they are frequently referring to the overall process of starting with data and some analysis goals, and trying to obtain unknown, useful and frequently actionable knowledge from the process. This workflow is often cyclic and interactive as the feedback we obtain from end-users or from our own evaluation procedures leads to revising some of the steps taken before. We can summarize the different steps in this data analysis workflow through some main blocks, as shown in Figure 3.1.

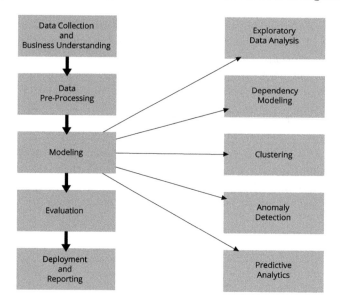

FIGURE 3.1: The Typical Data Mining Workflow.

On the left side of Figure 3.1 we have the main building blocks of the Data Mining workflow. On the right side we have some high level Data Mining Tasks that we frequently use when addressing some particular application. The rest of this chapter will be organized in several sections that will provide details on these main building blocks as well as presenting some R packages and concepts that help in implementing the steps of this workflow.

---

[2]Or if you want to be more trendy, data scientists.

3.2 Data Collection and Business Understanding

The first step in any Data Mining project has to do with collecting the data that will be used in the project as well as meeting with domain experts to better grasp what should be the main goals of the analysis.

Data collection is an important step as it may heavily condition the sort of analysis we can carry out. Still, this is frequently an uncontrollable step for the data analyst. In effect, the analyst can seldom provide advice and/or control what is measured and stored in a given application domain — this is frequently given as a fact. Unfortunately, this also means that one frequently faces several hard problems with the available data. Issues like measurement errors, sampling errors, not measuring necessary variables, among several others, are problems that data analysts need to be able to handle. Suggesting changes to the data collection process is possible, but it usually takes too much time to implement and even more to collect a reasonable sample of data after the changes are implemented. This means that most of the time the task of the analyst at this stage consists essentially of implementing the interface between the analysis tools (R in our case) and the computational infrastructure storing the data, i.e. getting the data into R.

Business understanding is a key task for a successful data mining project. In its essence it involves understanding the goals of the end-user in terms of what he wants to obtain from data mining. This is not an easy task and it is strongly domain-dependent. The difficulty of this task is frequently proportional to the gap between the "culture" of the data analyst and that of the end-user. Normally, there is a serious language problem that stems from these different contexts, and this makes simple communication of goals and of available tools/solutions very hard between the two parts. End-users frequently assign different meanings to words that the analysts take for granted and they often lack the ability to describe in a precise and concrete form what are their goals and their preference biases. Persistence, patience, frequent communication and writing things down, are all important tools at this very relevant step. Still, most probably there will be communication problems, misunderstandings and revisions, and all these are causes for the fact that the data mining workflow is so often a cyclic process. To avoid loss of valuable working hours it is of key importance to frequently involve the end-user in the analysis of the outcome of the data mining steps, as the feedback we get from this interaction may be very important for a successful project. Nevertheless, this is clearly a process that is more dependent on human qualities than on computational tools or data mining knowledge and thus neither R, nor other tools can help much in here.

3.2.1 Data and Datasets

Some of the issues that most distinguish Data Mining from other related fields that also deal with analyzing data are the facts that in Data Mining one tends to deal with a diverse set of data sources (e.g. sensors, Internet, etc.) and also many different types of data (e.g. text, sound, images, etc.). Still, the fact is that most existing modeling techniques are a bit more restrictive on the type of data they can handle. This means that a lot of time is spent on pre-processing these data into some data structure that is manageable by these standard data analysis techniques — and this typically means a standard two-dimensional data table[3].

---

[3]Though relational data mining is a very active field of research that provides models able to handle multiple tables, the fact is that these are still not very common tools.

In this context, let us focus on some properties of these standard data tables, leaving the pre-processing of non-standard data types for later sections. A data table (or dataset) is a two-dimensional data structure where each row represents an entity (e.g. product, person, etc.) and the columns represent the properties (e.g. name, age, temperature, etc.) we have measured for the entities. The terms *entity* and *property* have many synonyms. The entities are frequently referred to as *objects, tuples, records, examples* or *feature-vectors*, while the properties are often called *features, attributes, variables, dimensions* or *fields*.

In terms of the rows of a dataset we can have two main types of setups: (i) each row is independent from the others; or (ii) there is some dependency among the rows. Examples of possible dependencies include some form of time order (e.g. the rows represent the measurements of a set of variables in successive time steps), or some spatial order (e.g. each row has an associated location and this may entail some form of neighborhood relationship among rows).

Regarding the columns of a dataset we can talk about the type of data values they store. The most frequent distinction is between quantitative and categorical variables. A finer taxonomy of the data types can cast these into:

- **interval** - quantitative variables like for instance dates.

- **ratio** - quantitative variables like for instance height of a person or price of a product.

- **nominal** - these are categorical variables whose values are some sort of labels without any ordering among them (e.g. colors).

- **ordinal** - again categorical variables but this time with some implicit ordering among their finite set of values (e.g. small, medium and large).

In spite of these categories, in practice people do tend to distinguish only between quantitative (also referred to as continuous) and categorical (also referred to as discrete) variables.

Columns of a dataset may also be independent from each other or they may be somehow correlated, i.e. the values of one variable may have some form of dependency on the values of other variable(s).

In R data tables typically are stored in a data frame with columns that will store quantitative variables as numeric data types and categorical variables as factors or character strings.

3.2.2   Importing Data into R

One of the first problems you will face for carrying out data analysis in R is the question of loading these data into R. Answering this question depends on the data source from which you need to import your data.

There are many computational infrastructures used to store data. Some common setups include:

- Text files
- Databases
- Spreadsheets
- Other software-specific formats

In this section we will explore some of these common data sources and see how to import data from these sources into an R data frame.

3.2.2.1 Text Files

Text files are frequently used to store and share data. Datasets stored in text files usually follow some fixed format where typically each text line represents a row of the dataset, with the column values separated by some special character. Frequent choices as separator character include spaces, tabs, or commas, among others. When values are separated by commas we have what is usually known as a CSV file. Many software tools include an option to save data as a CSV file, so this is frequently an option when every other way of getting your data into R fails.

Base R has several functions that are able to read different types of text files. Although these functions are perfectly suitable for most setups, we will be mainly using the functions provided by package **readr** (Wickham and Francois, 2015b), instead. The functions provided by this package are more robust in some setups, are much faster, and have the added advantage of returning a **tbl** data frame object (c.f. Section 2.13).

Let us start by learning how to read the content of CSV files in R. Suppose we have a file named **x.csv** with the following content:

```
ID, Name, Age
23424, Ana, 45
11234, Charles, 23
77654, Susanne, 76
```

The following code will read its content into an R data frame table:

```
> library(readr)
> dat <- read_csv("x.csv")

Parsed with column specification:
cols(
ID = col_integer(),
Name = col_character(),
Age = col_integer()
)

> dat

# A tibble: 3 × 3
     ID    Name   Age
  <int>   <chr> <int>
1 23424     Ana    45
2 11234 Charles    23
3 77654 Susanne    76

> class(dat)

[1] "tbl_df"      "tbl"           "data.frame"
```

Function `read_csv()` takes the name of the CSV file as the first argument and may include a series of other arguments that allow to fine tune the reading process. The result of the function is a data frame table object from package **dplyr**.

Some countries use the comma character as decimal separator in real numbers. In these countries the CSV format uses the semi-colon as the values separator character. Function `read_csv2()` works exactly as the above function, but assumes the semi-colon as the values separator instead of the comma, which is used as decimal separator.

Some files simply use spaces as separators between the values. Suppose we have a file named `z.txt` with the following content:

```
ID Name Age Phone
23424 Ana 40 ???
11234 Charles 12 34567678
77654 Susanne 45 23435567
```

The content of this file could be read as follows:

```
> d <- read_delim("z.txt", delim=" ", na="???")

Parsed with column specification:
cols(
ID = col_integer(),
Name = col_character(),
Age = col_integer(),
Phone = col_integer()
)

> d

# A tibble: 3 × 4
      ID    Name   Age     Phone
   <int>   <chr> <int>     <int>
1 23424     Ana    40        NA
2 11234 Charles    12  34567678
3 77654 Susanne    45  23435567
```

You may have noticed that the file included a strange value ("???") in the first record. We are assuming that we were informed by the owner of the file that such values were used to represent missing data. Missing data in R are represented by the special value NA. All these functions from the package **readr** that read data from text files have a parameter (**na**) that accepts as values a vector of strings that are to be interpreted as missing values in the files.

There are several other similar functions to read text files. Most of them are simply special cases of the function `read_delim()` with some specific values of its parameters to match some concrete text format. In effect, function `read_delim()` includes many parameters that allow fine tuning the reading process to your specific files. You may wish to browse the help page and the vignettes of package **readr** to check these parameters. Some of the more frequently used are:

- `delim` - allowing you to indicate the character used as separator of the column values.

- `col_names` - a Boolean indicating whether the first line contains the column names.

- `na` - provides a vector of strings that are to be taken as missing values.

The result of all these functions is a **dplyr** data frame table.

A word of warning on reading text files. A frequent source of frustrating errors is character encoding. Different countries or event different operating systems may be using different character encodings and reading files created on these other environments may lead to some strange results. The above functions also include facilities to handle such situations through parameter `locale` that you may wish to explore in the respective help pages.

The functions of package **readr** are considerably faster than the equivalent functions of base R. Still, for extremely large files you may consider the alternative provided by function `fread()` from package **data.table** (Dowle et al., 2015), or function `read.csv.raw()` from package **iotools** (Urbanek and Arnold, 2015).

3.2.2.2 Databases

Databases are a frequently used infra-structure to store data in organizations. R has many packages that provide an interface with the most common relational database systems (e.g. Oracle, MySQL, PostgreSQL, etc.). Package **DBI** (R Special Interest Group on Databases, 2014) introduces another layer of abstraction by providing a series of functions that are independent of the back-end database management system that is being used. Figure 3.2 provides an illustration of the way this works. On one end you have your own R scripts from which you want to access some data that is stored in some database management system (the other end). Package **DBI** allows you to write your code with almost 100% independence of which database management system is on the other end. You basically select in the beginning which system you are using and then the code querying the database remains unchanged irrespective of the database system on the other end.

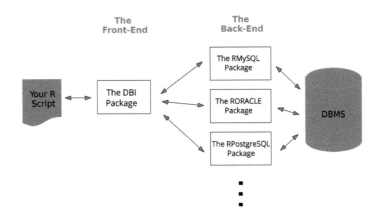

FIGURE 3.2: The front end interface provided by package DBI.

The following example code illustrates this concept with MySQL as the back-end database management system:

```
> library(DBI)
> ## The DBMS-specific code starts here
> library(RMySQL)
> drv <- dbDriver("MySQL")  # Loading the MySQL driver
> con <- dbConnect(drv,dbname="transDB",  # connecting to the DBMS
+                 username="myuser",password="mypasswd",
+                 host="localhost")
> ## The DBMS-specific code ends here
>
> ## getting the results of an SQL query as a data frame
> data <- dbGetQuery(con,"SELECT * FROM clients")
>
```

```
> ## closing up stuff
> dbDisconnect(con)
> dbUnloadDriver(drv)
```

After loading the package **DBI** the above code includes three instructions that are the only part that is specific to the connection to MySQL. All the remaining code would stay untouched if we were to change the back-end database management system from MySQL to any of the other supported systems. Functions `dbDisconnect()` and `dbUnloadDriver()` finish the connection to the database management system that was started with the calls to `dbDriver()` and `dbConnect()`.

The main function of package **DBI** is `dbGetQuery()` that allows you to enter an SQL query that will be sent to the database with the result being returned as an R data frame. This simple process allow us to easily retrieve data stored in one or more database tables into an R data frame.

Sometimes the result of a database query may be too large to be handled at the same time inside R. Package **DBI** also allows you to retrieve the results of a query in chunks. Here is an illustration of this,

```
> library(DBI)
> library(RMySQL)
> drv <- dbDriver("MySQL")   # Loading the MySQL driver
> con <- dbConnect(drv,dbname="transDB",   # connecting to the DBMS
+                     username="myuser",password="mypasswd",
+                     host="localhost")
>
> res  <- dbSendQuery(con,"SELECT * FROM transactions")
> while (!dbHasCompleted(res)) {
+     # get the next 50 records on a data frame
+     someData <- fetch(res, n = 50)
+     # call some function that handles the current chunk
+     myProcessingFunction(someData)
+ }
> dbClearResult(res) # clear the results set
>
> dbDisconnect(con)   # closing up stuff
> dbUnloadDriver(drv)
```

Notice that this time we are using function `dbSendQuery()`. This function retrieves an object (called a result set) from which we can then iteratively obtain successive chunks of results using the function `fetch()` that allows you to specify how many records you want to retrieve (as a data frame) from the result set. Function `dbHasCompleted()`, when applied to a result set, allows you to check if there are still some records remaining for retrieval. The `while()` loop instruction allows you to repeat a block of instructions while the Boolean condition you supply is true. In this case we can read the above loop as follows: while there are still some records to retrieve, get 50 more records and process them.

Further information on this powerful **DBI** package can be obtained in the documentation that is available in its help pages.

Package **dplyr** (Wickham and Francois, 2015a) can also be used for interfacing R with databases. This alternative has the advantage of making your code even less dependent on the database requirements. In effect, one of the key issues of the data manipulation facilities provided by **dplyr** is exactly to make your code independent from the data source, be it a local data frame or a database. In this context, using **dplyr** may actually be a better alternative if you do not want to delve into the SQL language at all, or if your are already used to the data manipulation strategies provided by **dplyr**.

Let us see an example with a database containing a (large) table with values of several sensors along time. The only time you need to "worry" about databases is when you establish the connection to the database management system. Using **dplyr** this connection consists of a single statement,

```
> library(RMySQL)
> library(dplyr)
> dbConn <- src_mysql("sonae",
+                  host="localhost",user="prodUser",password="myPassword")
```

The above statement establishes a connection with the MySQL database management system on your own computer. Equivalent functions are provided for other database management systems. Once this connection is successfully established we can create **dplyr tbl** objects using the tables of the "sonae" database as data sources,

```
> sensors <- tbl(dbConn,"sensor_values")
```

The object **sensors** can be used in the same way as any other **dplyr tbl** object. This means that we can query it in the same exact way as if the data source was a local data frame. For instance, the following example checks when a certain sensor has shown a value higher than 100,

```
> sensors %>%
+     filter(sid==274,value > 100) %>%
+     select(time,value)

Source:   query [?? x 2]
Database: mysql 5.7.14 [prodUser@localhost:/sonae]

                 time   value
                <chr>   <dbl>
1  2009-04-01 06:31:56  100.60
2  2009-04-01 06:32:04  103.11
3  2009-04-01 06:38:21  104.05
4  2009-04-01 06:38:29  103.87
5  2009-04-01 06:44:46  101.29
6  2009-04-01 06:44:54  100.16
7  2009-04-01 08:00:01  100.25
8  2009-04-01 08:55:52  101.64
9  2009-04-01 09:00:14  100.44
10 2009-04-01 09:11:50  102.33
# ... with more rows
```

Note that given that **dplyr** has several functions for querying datasets that result from joining several data sources, you are not restricted to using a single table of your database. In effect, you can easily query datasets that result from joining several tables of your database using the several join functions of **dplyr**, and all that without needing to know anything about SQL, i.e. you may focus on learning a single data manipulation language, in this case the set of functions provided by package **dplyr**.

3.2.2.3 Spreadsheets

Spreadsheets are another frequently used platform for holding datasets. There are several ways of importing data from spreadsheets, in particular from the common Excel spreadsheets. We are going to illustrate a few of the simplest.

Most spreadsheets (all?) should easily allow to export some data table into a CSV text file, or even other text formats. This means that we could first export the data from the spreadsheet into a text file and then use one of the procedures described in Section 3.2.2.1 to load data from these files into a data frame. Although this is a simple process it is still a bit indirect.

When the data tables are small there is a very simple form of getting the data from the spreadsheet into an R data frame. Open your spreadsheet and select the data range you want to import. Copy this range into the clipboard (for instance on Excel in Windows by doing `Ctrl+C`). Now go to R and type the following:

```
> d <- read.table("clipboard", header=TRUE)
```

Function `read.table()` is one of the base R functions for reading text files. The first argument of theses functions is the name of the file from which you want to import data. However, these functions allow you to specify as the filename a special string — "clipboard". With this "filename" these functions will read the data from the contents of the clipboard into a data frame. In the above example we are assuming that we have selected and copied a range that included the column names in the first row and thus the `header=TRUE` argument. Sometimes we may need a few more tweaks of the parameters of the `read.table()` function, but it should be straightforward most of the times. Please note that you can not use this special filename with the functions from package **readr** that we have explored before.

For larger data tables stored in Excel the usage of the clipboard may not be so convenient. For such situations the package **readxl** (Wickham, 2015a) contains a function named `read_excel()` that is very handy. The following is an example of its usage:

```
> library(readxl)
> fc <- "c:\\Documents and Settings\\xpto\\My Documents\\calc.xls"
> dat <- read_excel(fc,sheet=1)
```

This reads the contents of the first sheet of the Excel spreadsheet named "calc.xls" into a data frame named `dat`. Please note the way paths should be indicated in R[4].

3.2.2.4 Other Formats

R includes many other packages and functions that may help you in getting your data into an R data frame. The manual "R Data Import/Export" that comes with any R installation is a good starting point if you are searching for some specific format. Formats used in other statistical and data mining software packages can be read using the functions provided by package **foreign** (R Core Team, 2015a). As usual, searching the Web is most probably the fastest way of getting an answer on how to read some strange data format using R.

---

[4]You may also use the slash ("/") instead of the double backslashes.

3.3 Data Pre-Processing

Data pre-processing is one of the most time-consuming steps in a typical data mining project. It has to do with the steps that are typically required to transform the data you have read into R in a way that allows you to apply further analysis tools. This may involve cleaning up the data (sometimes also known as data munging or data wrangling), transforming the data (e.g. changes of the scale of variables), or even creating new variables that may bring useful information for your analysis steps. In this section we will give you some examples of some typical data pre-processing steps and how to carry them out in R. Further examples will appear in the concrete case studies to be addressed later in the book.

3.3.1 Data Cleaning

Data is frequently not made available in a state that is susceptible to be used for modeling. In this section we will mention some common problems, and some possible solutions available in R to address them.

3.3.1.1 Tidy Data

Wickham (2014) presented the notion of tidy data as a general objective we should pursue to make our posterior analysis in R easier. The key properties of tidy data are that: (i) each value belongs to a variable and an observation; (ii) each variable contains all values of a certain property measured across all observations; and (iii) each observation contains all values of the variables measured for the respective case. These properties lead to a kind of rectangular data table made up of rows (representing the observations) and columns (representing the variables).

Sometimes data is not provided in such a tidy format, which is required by most modeling tools available in R. Package **tidyr** (Wickham, 2015c) can be used to clean up the data and make it more standard.

TABLE 3.1: The grades of some students.

	Math	English
Anna	86	90
John	43	75
Catherine	80	82

Table 3.1 contains the grades of three students in two subjects. These data do not follow the guidelines mentioned above. The variables involved in this problem that describe each student performance are "StudentName", "Subject", and "Grade", so a tidy version of these data should look like what is shown in Table 3.2.

The first version of the data (Table 3.1) is sometimes said to be in a *wide* format, while the version in Table 3.2 is said to be in a *long* format. Package **tidyr** has two functions

TABLE 3.2: The grades of some students in a tidy format.

StudentName	Subject	Grade
Anna	Math	86
Anna	English	90
John	Math	43
John	English	75
Catherine	Math	80
Catherine	English	82

that can be used to easily convert between the two formats. Let us see how. Suppose file "stud.txt" is a text file containing the original data:

```
Math English
Anna 86 90
John 43 75
Catherine 80 82
```

The contents of this file could be read as follows:

```
> library(readr)
> std <- read_delim("stud.txt", delim=" ",
+                   skip=1, col_names=c("StudentName","Math","English"))

Parsed with column specification:
cols(
StudentName = col_character(),
Math = col_integer(),
English = col_integer()
)

> std

# A tibble: 3 × 3
  StudentName  Math English
        <chr> <int>   <int>
1        Anna    86      90
2        John    43      75
3   Catherine    80      82
```

Because the first line of the file contained one less value we had to use the parameter **skip** to make **read_delim()** ignore it, and thus we needed to supply the column names "by hand".

Now we can proceed to move from this wide format into a long (tidy) format using the function **gather()** of the package **tidyr**,

```
> library(tidyr)
> stdL <- gather(std, Subject, Grade, Math:English)
> stdL

# A tibble: 6 × 3
  StudentName Subject Grade
        <chr>   <chr> <int>
1        Anna    Math    86
2        John    Math    43
```

```
3    Catherine    Math    80
4        Anna English    90
5        John English    75
6    Catherine English    82
```

The `stdL` object is in a standard tidy format. Function `gather()` receives the data in wide format as first argument. We then provide the name for the new variable whose values are currently being shown as column names (in our case we selected the name "Subject"). The next argument is the name of the column that will contain the values, and the final argument is the range of columns of the current format that are to be used as source data for these values (notice that we can supply a range of columns using the ":" operator).

Package **tidyr** also provides function `spread()` that reverts the operation putting the data back to the wide format,

```
> spread(stdL, Subject, Grade)

# A tibble: 3 × 3
  StudentName English  Math
*       <chr>   <int> <int>
1        Anna      90    86
2   Catherine      82    80
3        John      75    43
```

Suppose that the text file also included an extra column of data where the degree and the enrollment year were supplied. Sometimes data files include several values encoded as a single one and we want to disaggregate these values into separate variables. Function `separate()` from package **tidyr** becomes handy in these situations,

```
> std2 <- read_delim("stud2.txt", delim=" ",
+                    skip=1, col_names=c("StudentName","Math","English","Degree_Year"))

Parsed with column specification:
cols(
StudentName = col_character(),
Math = col_integer(),
English = col_integer(),
Degree_Year = col_character()
)

> std2

# A tibble: 3 × 4
  StudentName  Math English Degree_Year
        <chr> <int>   <int>       <chr>
1        Anna    86      90    Bio_2014
2        John    43      75   Math_2013
3   Catherine    80      82    Bio_2012

> std2L <- gather(std2, Subject, Grade, Math:English)
> std2L <- separate(std2L, Degree_Year, c("Degree","Year"))
> std2L

# A tibble: 6 × 5
  StudentName Degree  Year Subject Grade
*       <chr>  <chr> <chr>   <chr> <int>
```

```
1        Anna    Bio  2014    Math   86
2        John   Math  2013    Math   43
3   Catherine    Bio  2012    Math   80
4        Anna    Bio  2014 English   90
5        John   Math  2013 English   75
6   Catherine    Bio  2012 English   82
```

Function `separate()` includes a parameter (`sep`) that sets the separator that is used to divide the values to extract. It has reasonable defaults both for character columns (as in the above example) and numeric columns. Still, you may use it to fine tune the function to your own needs. The function also assumes you want to remove the original column but that can also be changed. The help page of the function may be checked for further details on other parameters of this useful clean-up function. The package **tidyr** also includes the function `unite()` that reverses the actions carried out by the function `separate()`, i.e. merge several columns into a single one.

3.3.1.2 Handling Dates

Dates are values that are becoming more and more common in datasets. With the existence of a wide range of formats for storing a date, converting between these formats or extracting information from the provided values turns out to be a frequent task we need to carry out during data pre-processing.

R has many packages and classes devoted to store and process date and time information. On the web page[5] of the Time Series Analysis task view available on the R central repository (CRAN), you may find a section devoted to describing the many packages that handle dates and times.

Package **lubridate** (Grolemund and Wickham, 2011) is particularly handy in terms of parsing different date and time formats, as well as extracting different components of these dates. This package includes a series of functions that can be used to parse strings that contain dates and times into proper **POSIXct** objects that are one of the most flexible classes R provides to store dates and times. These functions have names composed by the letters "y", "m", "d", "h", "m" and "s" arranged in a way to match the format of the string you are trying to parse. Here are a few examples:

```
> library(lubridate)
> ymd("20151021")

[1] "2015-10-21"

> ymd("2015/11/30")

[1] "2015-11-30"

> myd("11.2012.3")

[1] "2012-11-03"

> dmy_hms("2/12/2013 14:05:01")

[1] "2013-12-02 14:05:01 UTC"

> mdy("120112")

[1] "2012-12-01"
```

---

[5]https://cran.r-project.org/web/views/TimeSeries.html

These functions can also be applied to vectors returning a vector of results. Moreover, they are very robust even to vectors containing dates in different formats,

```
> dates <- c(20120521, "2010-12-12", "2007/01/5", "2015-2-04",
+            "Measured on 2014-12-6", "2013-7+ 25")
> dates <- ymd(dates)
> dates

[1] "2012-05-21" "2010-12-12" "2007-01-05" "2015-02-04" "2014-12-06"
[6] "2013-07-25"
```

Frequently we also want to extract some of the temporal information on the dates and/or times we have received. For instance, we could be interested in having an extra column with the weekday corresponding to some dates. Package **lubridate** also includes an extensive set of functions to help you with these operations. For instance, with the previous vector with dates we could build the following data frame that includes some extra columns with information extracted from these dates,

```
> data.frame(Dates=dates,WeekDay=wday(dates),nWeekDay=wday(dates,label=TRUE),
+            Year=year(dates),Month=month(dates,label=TRUE))

    Dates WeekDay nWeekDay Year Month
1 2012-05-21       2      Mon 2012   May
2 2010-12-12       1      Sun 2010   Dec
3 2007-01-05       6      Fri 2007   Jan
4 2015-02-04       4      Wed 2015   Feb
5 2014-12-06       7      Sat 2014   Dec
6 2013-07-25       5    Thurs 2013   Jul
```

There are several other similar functions for extracting other components of dates and times. You may wish to check the vignette accompanying the package to see further examples.

Time zones are another critical aspect of dates and times. These may be measured in places under different time zones and we may wish to either keep that information or eventually convert between time zones. Once again **lubridate** can help you with that. Suppose some measurement took place in Berlin, Germany, at some date. If we want to store the time zone information with the date we should parse it as follows:

```
> date <- ymd_hms("20150823 18:00:05",tz="Europe/Berlin")
> date

[1] "2015-08-23 18:00:05 CEST"
```

Converting this to the New Zealand time zone would give,

```
> with_tz(date,tz="Pacific/Auckland")

[1] "2015-08-24 04:00:05 NZST"
```

You may also force the time zone associated with some date/time,

```
> force_tz(date,tz="Pacific/Auckland")

[1] "2015-08-23 18:00:05 NZST"
```

You may check the available names of the time zones with function `OlsonNames()`.

The package **lubridate** also includes several other functions that help with handling time intervals or carrying out arithmetic operations with dates/times. Information on these features can be obtained in the respective package vignette.

3.3.1.3   String Processing

String processing is a tool frequently required when cleaning up data or extracting information from raw data. Base R contains several functions for string processing but their names and interface are frequently not too coherent. Package **stringr** (Wickham, 2015b) was designed to solve these issues and provide a set of simple functions that address the most common needs of users. Our description will be based on the functionality provided by this package. Still, for more complex string processing needs you should also explore package **stringi**[6] (Gagolewski and Tartanus, 2015).

We will now present a simple example that illustrates a few of the functions of package **stringr** as well as some common string processing operations. Our example consists of reading a dataset from the UCI dataset repository (Lichman, 2013). The most common format of the datasets in this repository consists of having the information spread over two files, one with extension ".data" and the other with the extension ".names". The first contains the data in a CSV format without column headers. The second usually contains some textual information on the dataset authors and donors (that we will discard for the purposes of reading the data into R) and also information on the column names and types of data. If the dataset contains many columns it would be tedious to manually assign the names to the data frame based on the information in this file. We will use string processing to filter and process the information in this ".names" file to do this automatically.

```
> library(dplyr)
> library(stringr)
> library(readr)
> uci.repo <- "https://archive.ics.uci.edu/ml/machine-learning-databases/"
> dataset <- "audiology/audiology.standardized"
> dataF <- str_c(uci.repo,dataset,".data")
> namesF <- str_c(uci.repo,dataset,".names")
> ## Reading the data file
> data <- read_csv(url(dataF), col_names=FALSE, na="?")
> data
```

```
# A tibble: 200 × 71
      X1       X2    X3       X4      X5     X6    X7    X8    X9   X10
   <chr>    <chr> <chr>    <chr>   <chr>  <chr> <chr> <chr> <chr> <chr>
1      f     mild     f   normal  normal   <NA>     t  <NA>     f     f
2      f moderate     f   normal  normal   <NA>     t  <NA>     f     f
3      t     mild     t     <NA>  absent  mild     t  <NA>     f     f
4      t     mild     t     <NA>  absent  mild     f  <NA>     f     f
5      t     mild     f   normal  normal  mild     t  <NA>     f     f
6      t     mild     f   normal  normal  mild     t  <NA>     f     f
7      f     mild     f   normal  normal  mild     t  <NA>     f     f
8      f     mild     f   normal  normal  mild     t  <NA>     f     f
9      f   severe     f     <NA>    <NA>   <NA>     t  <NA>     f     f
10     t     mild     f elevated  absent  mild     t  <NA>     f     f
# ... with 190 more rows, and 61 more variables: X11 <chr>, X12 <chr>,
```

---

[6]Package **stringr** is actually a wrapper for some of the functions provided by **stringi**, the advantage of the former being its increased simplicity.

```
#   X13 <chr>, X14 <chr>, X15 <chr>, X16 <chr>, X17 <chr>, X18 <chr>,
#   X19 <chr>, X20 <chr>, X21 <chr>, X22 <chr>, X23 <chr>, X24 <chr>,
#   X25 <chr>, X26 <chr>, X27 <chr>, X28 <chr>, X29 <chr>, X30 <chr>,
#   X31 <chr>, X32 <chr>, X33 <chr>, X34 <chr>, X35 <chr>, X36 <chr>,
#   X37 <chr>, X38 <chr>, X39 <chr>, X40 <chr>, X41 <chr>, X42 <chr>,
#   X43 <chr>, X44 <chr>, X45 <chr>, X46 <chr>, X47 <chr>, X48 <chr>,
#   X49 <chr>, X50 <chr>, X51 <chr>, X52 <chr>, X53 <chr>, X54 <chr>,
#   X55 <chr>, X56 <chr>, X57 <chr>, X58 <chr>, X59 <chr>, X60 <chr>,
#   X61 <chr>, X62 <chr>, X63 <chr>, X64 <chr>, X65 <chr>, X66 <chr>,
#   X67 <chr>, X68 <chr>, X69 <chr>, X70 <chr>, X71 <chr>

> dim(data)

[1] 200  71

> ## Now reading the names file
> text <- read_lines(url(namesF))
> text[1:3]

[1] "WARNING: This database should be credited to the original owner whenever"
[2] "         used for any publication whatsoever."
[3] ""

> length(text)

[1] 178

> text[67:70]

[1] "   age_gt_60:\t\t      f, t."
[2] "   air():\t\t      mild,moderate,severe,normal,profound."
[3] "   airBoneGap:\t\t     f, t."
[4] "   ar_c():\t\t      normal,elevated,absent."
```

Function `str_c()` is equivalent to the function **paste0()** of base R that concatenates strings. Function `read_lines()` can be used to read a text file producing a vector of strings with as many elements as there are text lines in the file. Checking these lines we can confirm that the information we are searching for (the names of the columns) starts at line 67 and it goes till line 135. This information is stored in the format "**name : type**", so we need to extract the part before the ":" to get the column names. Function `str_split_fixed()` can be used with this purpose as we can see below,

```
> nms <- str_split_fixed(text[67:135],":",n=2)[,1] # get the names
> nms[1:3]

[1] "   age_gt_60"  "   air()"       "   airBoneGap"

> nms <- str_trim(nms) # trim white space
> nms[1:3]

[1] "age_gt_60"  "air()"       "airBoneGap"

> nms <- str_replace_all(nms,"\\(|\\)","") # delete invalid chars.
> nms[1:3]

[1] "age_gt_60"  "air"         "airBoneGap"
```

```
> colnames(data)[1:69] <- nms
> data[1:3,1:10]
```

```
# A tibble: 3 × 10
  age_gt_60       air airBoneGap   ar_c    ar_u  bone boneAbnormal  bser
      <chr>     <chr>      <chr>  <chr>   <chr> <chr>        <chr> <chr>
1         f      mild              f normal normal  <NA>            t  <NA>
2         f  moderate              f normal normal  <NA>            t  <NA>
3         t      mild              t   <NA> absent  mild            t  <NA>
# ... with 2 more variables: history_buzzing <chr>,
#   history_dizziness <chr>
```

After extracting the names we still had some clean-up to do. Namely, we have used function `str_trim()` to trim out the spaces around the names, and also function `str_replace_all()` to replace all occurrences of some strange characters by the empty string. Because some of these characters have special meaning in the context of regular expressions, we had to "escape" some of them to "remove" this special meaning. This is achieved by preceding these characters by double backslashes. Regular expressions are a key element in many string-related R functions, and actually for many other programming languages. They can be used to specify patterns to match to real strings. In the above example we want to say that any "(" or ")" characters should be replaced by the empty string, i.e. eliminated. Explaining the large number of details involved in regular expressions is clearly out of the scope of this book. Several tutorials can be easily found around the Web. Functions `str_view()` and `str_view_all()` may also be interesting to explore as they provide an HTML rendering (appearing in your browser) of the matches of a regular expression against a set of strings (check the help page of these functions for examples).

Package **stringr** contains several other functions for string processing. They typically follow the same type of interface with strings to be processed in the first argument and some pattern in the second. Further details and examples of several other functions can be found in the respective package vignette.

3.3.1.4 Dealing with Unknown Values

Unknown values occur very frequently in many real world applications. They can be caused by measurement errors, typing errors, equipment failures, etc. The first thing we must do is to read them properly into R. By properly we mean to use the special value R has (value NA) to denote these values. We have already seen in Section 3.2.2.1 that the functions we have used to read data stored in text files allow you to indicate, through parameter `na`, the characters that are to be interpreted as missing values. Still, it may happen that you are forced to use other reading methods and that you end up with a data frame where missing values are not coded as NA's, and you need to make this change in the data frame. Suppose you have a data frame where a column contains a few values that should be interpreted as missing values,

```
> dat

      X   Y
1 green  56
2  blue   ?
3 green 100
4   red -10

> class(dat$Y)
```

```
[1] "factor"
```

As you see, probably caused by some wrong reading procedure, the column Y is currently a factor (i.e. a nominal variable), because of the presence of the "?" that was not interpreted as a missing value indicator. How can we solve this problem a posteriori? An easy way is to resort to the facilities of the **readr** package once again,

```
> library(readr)
> dat$Y <- parse_integer(dat$Y, na="?")
> dat

      X   Y
1 green  56
2  blue  NA
3 green 100
4   red -10

> class(dat$Y)
```

```
[1] "integer"
```

Function `parse_integer()` can be used to parse a vector of values into integers. This function allows you to specify values that should be interpreted as unknown values through the parameter **na**. As you can observe, we now have our column with the correct values and data type.

Once we have all missing values properly coded using the R special NA value, we may still need to carry out some further pre-processing. This will depend on the posterior analysis steps we will carry out with the data. In effect, some tools can not handle datasets with unknown values. In these situations we need to do something about this before we proceed. Still, we will see examples of data mining tools that can easily handle datasets with unknown values by having their treatment embedded in the tool. For the other situations there are several ways of trying to overcome missing values, some of the most frequently used being:

- remove any row containing an unknown value

- fill-in (impute) the unknowns using some common value (typically using statistics of centrality)

- fill-in the unknowns using the most similar rows

- using more sophisticated forms of filling-in the unknowns

These alternatives range from computationally cheap (removing the rows) to more demanding alternatives that may involve using predictive models to estimate the missing values. Which alternative is the best is clearly domain dependent and also a function of the size of the problem. For instance, if we have a very large dataset and a few rows with unknown values, then removing them will probably have a small impact on the quality of your analysis.

R has several packages that provide tools to handle unknown values. Examples include functions on our **DMwR2** package, to more specific packages like **imputeR** (Feng et al., 2014). In Chapter 4 we will see concrete examples of these techniques applied to a dataset with unknown values.

3.3.2   Transforming Variables

Sometimes the original data needs to go through some extra modification steps to make it more useful for our analysis. The procedures described in this section fall in this category that does not have to do with cleaning up as in previous sections, but more with somehow enriching the data to make our analysis more effective. In this section we describe some examples of this type of step, and further illustrations will appear throughout the case studies described in the second part of the book.

3.3.2.1   Handling Different Scales of Variables

Numeric variables sometimes have rather different scales. This can create problems for some data analysis tools. In effect, anything that involves calculating and comparing differences among values in different rows of the dataset will make the differences of variables with a larger range of values stand out, when compared to differences involving variables with a smaller scale. This may make the former differences artificially prevail and decrease the impact of the variables with smaller scale, thus strongly biasing our analysis as a result of these different scales. To avoid these effects we frequently apply some transformation to the original values of these numeric variables. Let us see some examples.

Standardization is a frequently used technique that creates a new transformed variable with mean zero and unit standard deviation. It consists of applying the following formula to the original values:

$$Y = \frac{X - \bar{x}}{s_X} \tag{3.1}$$

where $\bar{x}$ is the sample mean of the original variable X, while s_X is its sample standard deviation.

Other scaling statistics can be used, for instance using the median instead of the mean and the inter-quartile range instead of the standard deviation to ensure more robustness to the presence of outlying values that may distort the more standard statistics. Some people also refer to the previous technique as *normalization*, although this name is more frequently assigned to a transformation method that creates a new variable in the range $[0, 1]$, as follows:

$$Y = \frac{X - \min_X}{\max_X - \min_X} \tag{3.2}$$

Taking the log of the original values is also frequently used as a means to "squash" the scale of the variables. However, this can only be applied to variables with positive values, as the log is not defined for zero and negative values.

The function `scale()` can be used to apply many of these standardization techniques. For instance, if we wish to apply the normal standardization (Equation 3.1) to a set of columns of a dataset we can use it as follows,

```
> library(dplyr)
> data(iris)
> iris.stand <- cbind(scale(select(iris,-Species)),select(iris,Species))
> summary(iris.stand)
```

Sepal.Length	Sepal.Width	Petal.Length	Petal.Width
Min. :-1.86378	Min. :-2.4258	Min. :-1.5623	Min. :-1.4422
1st Qu.:-0.89767	1st Qu.:-0.5904	1st Qu.:-1.2225	1st Qu.:-1.1799
Median :-0.05233	Median :-0.1315	Median : 0.3354	Median : 0.1321
Mean : 0.00000	Mean : 0.0000	Mean : 0.0000	Mean : 0.0000

```
3rd Qu.: 0.67225    3rd Qu.: 0.5567    3rd Qu.: 0.7602    3rd Qu.: 0.7880
Max.    : 2.48370    Max.    : 3.0805    Max.    : 1.7799    Max.    : 1.7064
        Species
setosa    :50
versicolor:50
virginica :50
```

Function `scale()` works as follows. You provide it a numeric matrix (or a data frame with numeric only columns) and it will (by default) apply to each of the columns the standardization process described in Equation 3.1. Note that we can use the function `select()` from the package **dplyr** to more easily select columns of the data frame `iris`, even-though this is a standard data frame and not a *tibble*[7]. The function `scale()` can also be used in other ways if the user wants to have control of the constant to be used for centering the columns ($\bar{x}$ by default), and scaling them (s_X by default). These constants can be supplied through parameters `center` and `scale`, respectively. They both accept vectors with as many values as there are numeric columns to standardize. The following illustrates this usage to implement the normalization of Equation 3.2,

```
> mxs <- apply(select(iris,-Species), 2, max, na.rm=TRUE)
> mns <- apply(select(iris,-Species), 2, min, na.rm=TRUE)
> iris.norm <- cbind(scale(select(iris,-Species), center=mns, scale=mxs-mns),
+                    select(iris,Species))
> summary(iris.norm)
```

```
  Sepal.Length       Sepal.Width        Petal.Length       Petal.Width
Min.    :0.0000    Min.    :0.0000    Min.    :0.0000    Min.    :0.00000
1st Qu.:0.2222    1st Qu.:0.3333    1st Qu.:0.1017    1st Qu.:0.08333
Median :0.4167    Median :0.4167    Median :0.5678    Median :0.50000
Mean    :0.4287    Mean    :0.4406    Mean    :0.4675    Mean    :0.45806
3rd Qu.:0.5833    3rd Qu.:0.5417    3rd Qu.:0.6949    3rd Qu.:0.70833
Max.    :1.0000    Max.    :1.0000    Max.    :1.0000    Max.    :1.00000
        Species
setosa    :50
versicolor:50
virginica :50
```

We have used the function `apply()` to easily obtain the maximums and minimums of the numeric columns. We then used `scale()` by supplying the centering and scaling values according to what is specified by Equation 3.2, leading to columns that range between $[0, 1]$ as confirmed by the call to `summary()`.

3.3.2.2 Discretizing Variables

Another frequently used data pre-processing technique is the discretization of numeric variables by transforming them into factors with meaningful bins. This can be motivated by

---

[7]A small word of caution here — any row names that eventually existed in the original data frame are silently dropped when applying these **dplyr** functions to standard data frames.

the analysis objectives or even for reducing the computational complexity of some modeling tools that have this factor dependent on the number of different values of the variables. Whatever the motivation this involves changing a numeric variable into an ordinal variable, though frequently it ends up being treated as a nominal variable because some tools do not distinguish between these two different types of variables.

Most of the time discretization is carried out based on some domain knowledge that provides the bins on the range of the original variable that make sense for the end users. For instance, if we have a numeric column with the age of some clients, it may make sense for some applications to discretize these ages into "young", "adults", or "seniors", with the limits of these bins being determined by the background knowledge of the application (i.e. the end users). If no such domain knowledge exists one can use other criteria to determine the break points of the continuous variables domains. Two frequent choices are: (i) equal width that consists of splitting the range of the variable into k equal size bins; and (ii) equal frequency that makes sure every bin contains the same number of values appearing in the original dataset.

Whatever method we select we can easily implement it through the functions `cut2()` of package **Hmisc** (Harrell Jr. et al., 2015) and `cut()` from base R. The former is a slight variation of the latter that is more convenient on some situations. Let us see an example of discretization in R using the Boston Housing dataset available in package **MASS** (Venables and Ripley, 2002).

```
> library(Hmisc) # for cut2()
> data(Boston, package="MASS") # loading the data
> summary(Boston$age) # the numeric variable we are going to discretize

   Min. 1st Qu.  Median    Mean 3rd Qu.    Max.
   2.90   45.02   77.50   68.57   94.07  100.00
```

If you want to apply equal width discretization to this variable then it is simpler to use the `cut()` function by specifying the number of bins you want,

```
> Boston$newAge <- cut(Boston$age,5)
> table(Boston$newAge)


 (2.8,22.3] (22.3,41.7] (41.7,61.2] (61.2,80.6]  (80.6,100]
         45          71          70          81         239

> Boston$newAge <- cut(Boston$age,5, # alternative using our own labels for the bins
+                 labels=c("verynew","new","normal","old","veryold"))
> table(Boston$newAge)


verynew     new  normal     old veryold
     45      71      70      81     239
```

If we want to apply equal frequency to this variable then the function `cut2()` is more convenient,

```
> Boston$newAge <- cut2(Boston$age, g=5)
> table(Boston$newAge)


[ 2.9, 38.1) [38.1, 66.1) [66.1, 86.1) [86.1, 95.7) [95.7,100.0]
         102          101          101          101          101
```

One drawback of the `cut2()` function is that is does not allow you to specify the labels of the bins which you need to do separately,

```
> Boston$newAge <- factor(cut2(Boston$age, g=5),
+                          labels=c("verynew","new","normal","old","veryold"))
> table(Boston$newAge)


 verynew    new normal    old veryold
     102    101    101    101     101
```

Other more sophisticated discretization methods exist. For instance, there are methods that try to optimize the selection of the break points of the bins according to the resulting performance of some modeling tool. This is frequently applied when your goal is to use your data as training set for a classification task (c.f. Section 3.4.5). These methods are usually known as supervised discretization methods. Further information can be obtained for instance in Dougherty et al. (1995).

3.3.3 Creating Variables

Sometimes we need to create new variables from the available data in order to be able to properly address our data mining goals. This necessity may be caused by several factors. For instance, we may create a new variable whose values are calculated as a function of other measured variables because we think the result of this relationship is useful for mining the data. More frequently, the need for creating new variables arises from limitations of the data mining tools we have available in terms of being able to handle the original data format. Most data mining tools assume a data table where each row is described by a set of variables. Moreover, many of these tools assume that each row is independent from each other, and there are even tools that assume independence among the columns (or at least suffer when that is not the case). Finally, another motivation for feature construction may be the fact that the level of detail at which the data is measured is too high (leading for instance to a too large dataset to be manageable), and we prefer to create and use some form of aggregated summaries of these original values.

3.3.3.1 Handling Case Dependencies

Data observations (rows of a dataset) may not be completely independent. Some frequent dependencies among observations are time and/or space. The fact that some sort of dependency exists between cases has a big impact on the data mining process. In effect, data mining has to do with finding useful patterns in the data. If some sort of dependencies exist among the observations this will change the way we look at the data and also what we find useful on these data.

Aggarwal (2015) proposes to consider two types of information on datasets with dependencies: (i) contextual; and (ii) behavioral. The former describes the information of the context where the data was measured. For instance, for time dependent data this would typically be the time stamps, while for geo-referenced datasets with space dependencies this could be the latitude and longitude. Behavioral information consists of the measurements (variable values) that are collected for each context. For instance, for each time tag we could record the values of several variables that would be the behavioral information associated with a certain time context.

When handling this type of case dependencies there are essentially two main approaches: (i) either one is constrained on using data analysis tools that are able to cope and model the type of dependencies that exist in our dataset; or (ii) we carry out some sort of data transformation that somehow fits the independence assumptions of the "standard" models and moreover, is able to provide information to these models on the dependencies so that they are used when mining the data. The latter of these options is less limited in terms of the tools we are able to use. Still, it is more demanding from the analyst perspective in the sense that it requires extra data pre-processing steps. In the next paragraphs we will see some examples of this second alternative for different types of case dependencies.

Time dependencies

Time dependencies occur when observations are tagged by time stamps and thus there is an implicit ordering among them. For instance, suppose air temperature is being measured at each time stamp. Naturally, one expects that there is some form of correlation between the values of temperature at time t and $t+1$, unless the actual time difference between these time stamps is too large. The possibility of existence of this correlation has consequences on the type of analysis we can carry out with these data. These data are usually known as time series (uni-variate or multi-variate depending on the dimension of the behavioral information being measured at each time stamp). Time series analysis is a vast area of research with many specific tools being developed for this type of dataset. These specific tools directly cope with several types of time dependencies, like trends or seasonal effects. R has many packages providing implementations of these standard time series analysis tools. The TimeSeries CRAN task view[8] is a good starting point for knowing what is available in R.

R has several facilities for dealing with data with time dependencies. As we have seen there are many forms of processing dates and times. Moreover, there are also specific data structures for storing time series data. For instance, package **xts** (Ryan and Ulrich, 2014) defines the class of **xts** objects that can be used to store uni- and multi-variate time series data. This data structure allows creating objects where the contextual information (time stamps) is clearly separated from the behavioral data, as well as providing useful tools for making temporal queries (i.e. queries involving the contextual information) to the datasets. Let us see some examples.

```
> library(lubridate)
> library(xts)
> sp500 <- xts(c(1102.94,1104.49,1115.71,1118.31),
+             ymd(c("2010-02-25","2010-02-26","2010-03-01","2010-03-02"),
+                 tz=Sys.getenv("TZ"))
+                )
> sp500

                [,1]
2010-02-25 1102.94
2010-02-26 1104.49
2010-03-01 1115.71
2010-03-02 1118.31
```

The above example uses function **xts()** from the package with the same name to create a univariate time series object with the prices of S&P 500 at some concrete dates. The function accepts the measurements (the behavioral information) in the first argument, and the time stamps (the context) in the second. We have used the function **ymd()** from package **lubridate** to create and parse the time stamps from a vector of character representations of these dates. In the call to **ymd()**, and just for illustration purposes, we have indicated that

---

[8]https://cran.r-project.org/web/views/TimeSeries.html

the time stamps should be taken as dates using the current time zone of the computer where the code is executed. To obtain this local time zone we have used the function `Sys.getenv()` to query the corresponding environment variable in the operating system of our computer. Note that the returned object is printed with the time stamps as row names, and with the measurements as columns (in this case a single one). If you supply a matrix with k columns in the first argument of the function `xts()`, it will assume that you are creating a multivariate time series formed by k measurements at each time stamp. Obviously, such matrix should have as many rows as there are time stamps supplied in the second argument of the function `xts()`.

Using these `xts` objects has several advantages. For instance, there are plotting methods that take care of selecting the adequate labels for representing times in the X-axis (try doing `plot(sp500)`). More importantly, there are several facilities to make temporal queries on these time series objects[9]. Here are a few examples:

```
> sp500["2010-03-02"]

             [,1]
2010-03-02 1118.31

> sp500["2010-03"]

             [,1]
2010-03-01 1115.71
2010-03-02 1118.31

> sp500["2010-03-01/"]

             [,1]
2010-03-01 1115.71
2010-03-02 1118.31

> sp500["2010-02-26/2010-03-01"]

             [,1]
2010-02-26 1104.49
2010-03-01 1115.71
```

Temporal queries consist of strings following the ISO:8601 time format. As you see from the above examples you may include things like time intervals and so on.

There are many different types of time dependencies. One frequently occurring dependency is trend effects. These consist of series of values that exhibit some consistent tendency (e.g. upwards) along time. This type of dependency may create difficulties in some data analysis tasks. Imagine we are trying to forecast the future values of some time series with a strong upwards tendency based on some historical observation of its values. Due to the tendency, the future values (that we need to forecast) will most probably be significantly larger than the ones observed in the historical record. Without knowledge about this tendency, or without modeling it, the forecasting models will have strong difficulties in correctly predicting the future values because nothing similar was observed in the past. Motivated by these issues sometimes analysts prefer to transform the original time series variables to try to remove these trend effects. One relatively easy way of proceeding consists of working with the series of relative variations instead of the original values. This consists of creating a new variable using the following formula,

---

[9]Note that you may still use the normal indexing schemes on these objects, e.g. `sp[2,1]` .

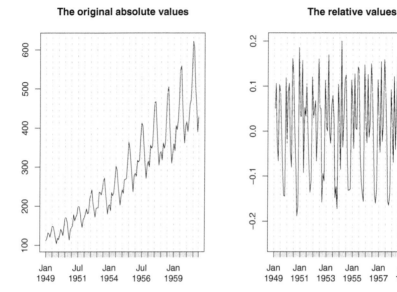

FIGURE 3.3: An example of using relative variations.

$$Y_t = \frac{X_t - X_{t-1}}{X_{t-1}} \tag{3.3}$$

where X_t is the value of the original time series at time stamp t[10].

This type of transformation can be easily obtained in R as shown in the following example, whose results you may check in Figure 3.3. This figure clearly shows that the initial trend was "removed" by this simple pre-processing step.

```
> library(xts)
> data(AirPassengers)
> ap <- as.xts(AirPassengers)
> apRel <- diff(ap)/ap[-length(ap)]
```

Using such a process we would then proceed with trying to obtain a model that forecasts the next variation (i.e. the next value of variable Y) instead of the next value of the original series (X). Obviously, if at time t we observe the value of X_t, and our model forecasts a certain value for Y_{t+1}, it is straightforward to obtain the predicted value of X_{t+1} using the relationship between the original values and the variations established by Equation 3.3. There is however, a caveat. In spite of eliminating the trend effects, we do not eliminate the case dependencies. In effect, if there is some sort of time dependency between the successive values of X, then such a dependency will also exist among the values of Y, i.e. the variation between the original values at time t (captured by Y_t), will naturally depend on the variation at time $t - 1$. This means that once again we can not assume that the values of Y are independent. What can we do about this if we want to use some modeling tools that assume the observations are independent? There are several possible paths with time series data. One is based on the idea of time delay embedding (Takens,

---

[10]Note that there are potential division-by-zero problems with this transformation.

1981). Time delay embedding consists of describing the state of the dynamic system that generates the observed time series values by a set of k recently observed values. The value k is the dimension of the embedding, and needs to be determined. Function `embed()` can be used to generate an embedding from a time series. It receives a time series and an embed dimension k and generates a data matrix where row i contains the values of the series at time $i, i-1, \cdots, i-k+1$, e.g.

```
> head(ap)
```

```
          [,1]
Jan 1949  112
Fev 1949  118
Mar 1949  132
Abr 1949  129
Mai 1949  121
Jun 1949  135
```

```
> head(embed(ap,4))
```

```
     [,1] [,2] [,3] [,4]
[1,]  129  132  118  112
[2,]  121  129  132  118
[3,]  135  121  129  132
[4,]  148  135  121  129
[5,]  148  148  135  121
[6,]  136  148  148  135
```

The following simple function[11] could be used to generate a data frame from a given `xts` object with a uni-variate time series,

```
> createEmbedDS <- function(s, emb=4) {
+       d <- dim(s)
+       if (!is.null(d) && d[2] > 1) stop("Only applicable to uni-variate time series")
+       if (emb < 2 || emb > length(s)) stop("Invalid embed size")
+       e <- embed(s,emb)
+       colnames(e) <- c("T",paste("T",1:(emb-1),sep="_"))
+       if (is.xts(s)) return(xts(e,index(s)[emb:length(s)])) else return(e)
+ }
> dataSet <- createEmbedDS(ap,emb=5)
> head(dataSet)
```

```
           T T_1 T_2 T_3 T_4
Mai 1949 121 129 132 118 112
Jun 1949 135 121 129 132 118
Jul 1949 148 135 121 129 132
Ago 1949 148 148 135 121 129
Set 1949 136 148 148 135 121
Out 1949 119 136 148 148 135
```

Assuming that the time dependency among the series observations is not larger than the embed size, using such simple transformation would ensure we can safely use any "standard" modeling tool. In effect, although there is still some form of dependency between the rows of `dataSet`, we can "safely" ignore it. The reason is that the information on the time

---

[11]You do not need to type it as it is available in the book package.

dependency between the k recent values of the original time series was "moved" to different features of the data set we have created. This means that the time dependencies among the k past values can be modeled as relationships between the variables of the new dataset, and for this we can use "standard" modeling tools. Still, we should not ignore the time ordering that continues to exist between the rows of `dataSet`. This is particularly important when carrying out experiments involving the estimation of the predictive performance of models. We will address this critical issue later in the book in a case study that uses time series data.

Other alternative transformations are possible for time series data. Discrete wavelet transform (DWT) and discrete Fourier transform (DFT) are two of the most frequently used. Symbolic representations where we move from the original numeric values of a time series into a sequence of symbols are also popular ways of representing a series.

The idea of wavelet transformations is to decompose a time series into a set of coefficient-weighted wavelet basis vectors, with each of the coefficients presenting the rough variation of the series between two halves of some time range of the series (Aggarwal, 2015). The calculation of these coefficients is typically followed by a feature selection process where only larger coefficients are retained. Haar wavelet transforms are one of the most commonly used. If n is the length of the time series the Haar coefficients are defined for the orders 1 to $log_2(n)$, assuming the length n is a power of 2. For each order k, 2^{k-1} coefficients are obtained that represent information on a time segment of the series of size $n/2^{k-1}$. The coefficient i of order k is the average difference between the average values of the series for two consecutive time segments. Imagine the time series is formed by the values $10, 9, 11, 13$. The first set of coefficients are given by $(10 - 9)/2, (11 - 13)/2$, i.e. they are $0.5, -1$. The second set works at a lower granularity, namely at the averages of the original values, i.e. it works with the series $(10 + 9)/2 = 9.5, (11 + 13)/2 = 12$. The coefficient is thus $(9.5 - 12)/2 = -1.25$. Finally, the last average is $(9.5 + 12)/2 = 10.75$, which is the overall average of the original time series. With this last average value (10.75) and the 3 coefficients $(0.5, -1, -1.25)$, it is possible to reconstruct the original series. Obviously, these are 4 numbers, which is the size of the original series, thus this seems a waste of time. However, the idea is that some of these coefficients can be thrown away without too much loss of information.

Independently of the process followed to deal with temporal dependencies, the general approach involves passing the information on temporal correlation between the rows into new features (columns) so that it can be used in the construction of models. This happens both with simple approaches like time-delay embedding, but also with more sophisticated approaches like wavelets.

Spatial dependencies

Datasets with spatial dependencies involve observations that are collected at different nearby locations. This neighborhood relationship between observations may entail some form of dependency between the measured behavioral attribute values. In effect, according to the first law of Geography (Tobler, 1970), everything is related with everything else but near things are more related than distant things. In this context, as with temporal data, one should take these potential effects into account when analyzing this type of data. With the advent of GPS-enabled devices, this sort of data is becoming more and more prevalent and thus tools for handling and analyzing it are essential.

The contextual information on spatial datasets may take several forms but the usual is some form of geo-reference, e.g. latitude and longitude. Once again R includes many packages devoted to this type of dataset[12]. Spatial coordinates are just numbers and thus we could simply include this contextual information as extra columns of the dataset. Still, more sophisticated data structures provide other facilities, like easier plotting and querying. Package **sp** (Pebesma and Bivand, 2005) contains a series of classes of objects for handling these data. Several other packages build upon the classes defined in this package. These classes include structures to store data about geographical locations (spatial points), but also for trajectories and other types of geo-referenced datasets. We will see a concrete illustration of its usage with a dataset on forest fires in Portugal. The dataset is available in a CSV file[13],

```
> library(readr)
> ff <- read_csv("forestFires.txt")
> ff
```

```
# A tibble: 25,000 × 14
     FID_    CID ano1991 ano1992 ano1993 ano1994 ano1995 ano1996 ano1997
   <chr>  <int>   <int>   <int>   <int>   <int>   <int>   <int>   <int>
1    <NA>      1       0       0       0       0       0       0       0
2    <NA>      2       0       0       0       0       0       0       0
3    <NA>      3       0       0       0       0       0       0       0
4    <NA>      4       0       0       0       0       0       0       0
5    <NA>      5       0       0       0       0       0       0       0
6    <NA>      6       0       0       0       0       0       0       0
7    <NA>      7       0       0       0       0       0       0       0
8    <NA>      8       0       0       0       0       0       0       0
9    <NA>      9       0       0       0       0       0       0       0
10   <NA>     10       0       0       0       0       0       0       0
# ... with 24,990 more rows, and 5 more variables: ano1998 <int>,
#   ano1999 <int>, ano2000 <int>, x <dbl>, y <dbl>
```

The dataset contains information on different locations (i.e. each row refers to a location). The two first columns are essentially irrelevant for the analysis. They are followed by 10 columns (named "ano....") that contain information on whether the location had or did not have (a binary 0/1 variable) a fire in a certain year ("ano" means year in Portuguese). The last two columns, named "x" and "y", are the longitude and latitude, respectively. For now, let us focus our study on a concrete year, which turns this into a spatial dataset (otherwise it would be a spatio-temporal dataset). Looking only at a single year (say 2000) what we have is information on a series of spatial locations. We can store this on a **SpatialPointsDataFrame** object as follows:

```
> library(sp)
> library(dplyr)
> spatialCoords <- select(ff,long=x,lat=y) # the contextual data
> firesData <- select(ff,ano2000) # the behavioral data
> coordRefSys <- CRS("+proj=longlat +ellps=WGS84")
> fires2000 <- SpatialPointsDataFrame(spatialCoords,
+                                     firesData,
+                                     proj4string=coordRefSys)
> fires2000[1:3,]
```

```
          coordinates ano2000
```

---

[12]Extensive information may be obtained at the Spatial Task View of CRAN (`https://cran.r-project.org/web/views/Spatial.html`) or in the book by Roger S. Bivand (2013).

[13]You can download the CSV file from the book Web page.

```
1 (-7.31924, 38.5406)        0
2 (-7.63557, 40.5022)        0
3 (-7.90273, 40.3418)        0
```

The object `fires2000` is an object of class **SpatialPointsDataFrame**. As we see from the output of the last statement it has special printing methods that show the geographical coordinates associated with each behavioral attribute value. To create such object we need to provide a matrix or data frame with two columns containing the longitude and latitude of each location, the behavioral data measured at each location and also information on the coordinate reference system to use.

Package **sp** contains several utility functions that can provide useful information on our data. Below are a few examples:

```
> bbox(fires2000)

        min      max
long -9.49174 -6.20743
lat  36.98050 42.14360


> coordinates(fires2000)[1:3,]

         long      lat
[1,] -7.31924 38.5406
[2,] -7.63557 40.5022
[3,] -7.90273 40.3418


> summary(fires2000)

Object of class SpatialPointsDataFrame
Coordinates:
        min      max
long -9.49174 -6.20743
lat  36.98050 42.14360
Is projected: FALSE
proj4string : [+proj=longlat +ellps=WGS84]
Number of points: 25000
Data attributes:
    ano2000
 Min.    :0.00000
 1st Qu.:0.00000
 Median :0.00000
 Mean    :0.01612
 3rd Qu.:0.00000
 Max.    :1.00000
```

Function `bbox()` returns the coordinates of the bounding box where all locations are included. The function `coordinates()` can be used to access the matrix with the coordinates of all locations (i.e. the matrix with the contextual information). Function `summary()` can also be applied to **SpatialPointsDataFrame** objects, producing an adequate summary of the dataset.

R also provides many possibilities in terms of spatial data visualization. Here we describe a small illustration using package **ggmap** (Kahle and Wickham, 2013). This package includes, among other things, an interface to several map providers (e.g. Google Maps) and it is based on the excellent infra-structure provided by package **ggplot2** (Wickham, 2009),

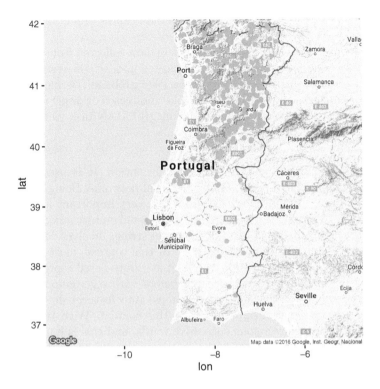

FIGURE 3.4: Forest fires in Portugal during 2000.

that we will be using extensively for data visualization. The following is a simple illustration for visualizing the forest fires in the year 2000 with the result shown on Figure 3.4:

```
> library(ggmap)
> library(tibble)
> mapPT <- get_map("Portugal",zoom=7)
> d4plot <- as_tibble(cbind(coordinates(fires2000),burnt=fires2000$ano2000))
> ggmap(mapPT) +
+     geom_point(data=filter(d4plot, burnt==1),aes(x=long,y=lat),col="orange")
```

Function **get_map()** was used to obtain a map (by default from Google Maps) of the region where we want to plot our data. Then we have created a data frame with the data required to build the plot, which includes the coordinates and the binary variable that indicates whether each location has or has not burned in 2000. Finally, we generate the map calling function **ggmap()** that draws the downloaded map and then super-imposing the points on the locations where there were fires.

Other dependencies

R has several packages that can help with other types of dependencies. For instance, a frequent format of data dependency is spatio-temporal correlation. This refers to data observations that include both time and space contexts. Package **spacetime** (Pebesma, 2012) includes facilities for handling this type of dataset. The classes provided by this package can handle many different setups in terms of spatio-temporal dependencies and are based upon the classes provided by packages **sp** and **xts** that we have covered before. More information on facilities for analyzing this type of data can be found in the SpatioTemporal CRAN task view[14].

Another frequent type of dependency appears in data collected from networks. Networks are frequently represented as graphs (sets of connected nodes). These structures are covered by several packages in R, like for instance the package **gRbase** (Dethlefsen and Højsgaard, 2005) that can handle frequent data structures like undirected or direct acyclic graphs. More information on this type of data is available in the gR CRAN task view[15].

3.3.3.2   Handling Text Datasets

Text is a very frequent form of conveying information. It is used in many different communication channels like reports, emails, or social networks. Being able to analyze this type of data and extract useful knowledge from it is very important for many application domains. There is a large volume of research being invested on text mining. A text document is a string of characters. Analyzing text documents as strings involves deep knowledge about linguistic rules and semantics of the languages. In this context, most approaches tend to transform text documents into the more common attribute-based representation. In a way this exercise is similar to what we have seen before with e.g. temporal data, where we tried to move contextual information (time stamps) into features describing the cases to allow capturing relevant relationships involving this context. With textual data there is also some obvious dependency among successive words, and this is important for properly analyzing the documents. Which attributes/properties should be used to represent a text document? There are several answers to this question, with different degrees of complexity. One of the simplest, and most frequently used approach, is known as the *bag of words* representation. In this approach a text document is transformed into a vector of features where each feature is associated with one word of the language in which the document is written. Some approaches use simple binary features stating whether the word is or is not present in the document. Other approaches are counts of the number of occurrences of the words or other more sophisticated values like TF-IDF, that integrates term frequency with inverse document frequency that tries to measure the amount of information brought by each term. The idea of TF-IDF is to cope with terms (words) that are very frequent but do not bring much information (say the word "the" in English). Once we have a feature vector representation of a set of documents, we have in effect a standard dataset, where each row is a document and each column a feature. Still, because of the large number of words available in any language, this is typically a dataset with a "difficult dimensionality" because it will have many more columns than rows, something that creates problems to several data analysis methods. Please note that bag of words representations completely ignore the order of words in a text. More sophisticated representations try to incorporate some information on this ordering by using *n-grams* instead. N-grams are successive sets of n words that occur in a text. Again we can count their occurrences or use more sophisticated scores.

R has many packages devoted to the analysis of text data. Extensive information on these facilities can be obtained in the Natural Language Processing CRAN task view[16]. Many of these packages are in effect interfaces to existing external linguistic resources (e.g. WordNet or OpenNLP). A good starting point is the **tm** (Feinerer and Hornik, 2015) package that provides a general text mining framework within R. This package includes several functions for reading text documents from many different sources and formats, functions for carrying out the most frequent pre-processing steps of these documents, and also other functions for

---

[14]https://cran.r-project.org/web/views/SpatioTemporal.html
[15]https://cran.r-project.org/web/views/gR.html
[16]https://cran.r-project.org/web/views/NaturalLanguageProcessing.html

analyzing the documents. Moreover, it provides specific classes of objects for adequately storing this type of data. Let us see a concrete example of how to use this package.

Suppose you were given a set of text files, each with a text document that you wish to analyze. Assume these files were stored in a sub-folder of the current folder, named **Documents**. The following code would read these files into R,

```
> library(tm)
> docs <- Corpus(DirSource("Documents"))
> docs

<<VCorpus>>
Metadata:  corpus specific: 0, document level (indexed): 0
Content:   documents: 300
```

The function **Corpus()** can be used to create objects of class **Corpus** that contain a text-based dataset. In this case we can observe that it is formed by 300 documents that were read using the **DirSource()** function. This function assumes the provided path leads to a folder containing plain text files that are to be read into R. Package **tm** provides many other possibilities for reading different types of text documents and using different sources. Check the package documentation for further details and examples.

Each individual document can be inspected as follows:

```
> docs[[2]]

<<PlainTextDocument>>
Metadata:  7
Content:   chars: 1543

> content(docs[[2]])[1:3]

[1] "Africa Fashion Week London kicks off"
[2] "Article By: Simamkele Matuntuta Fri, 07 Aug 2015 12:05 PM"
[3] "Your Email Photo Credit: Africa Fashion Week London"
```

Individual documents are treated as elements of a list as you can observe from the above code. The content (text) of each document can be inspected (and changed) with the function **content()** that returns a vector of strings, each being a text line of the document. This means the above code shows the first three lines of the second document. Documents and corpus can also have meta information (e.g. document heading, document language) associated with them.

As we have mentioned before, instead of analyzing the strings forming the documents directly, it is common to carry out a series of transformations to these documents in order to represent them as feature vectors. Package **tm** includes several functions that help in this task, as shown below:

```
> docs <- docs %>%
+        tm_map(removePunctuation) %>%
+        tm_map(content_transformer(tolower)) %>%
+        tm_map(removeNumbers) %>%
+        tm_map(removeWords, stopwords("en")) %>%
+        tm_map(stripWhitespace) %>%
+        tm_map(stemDocument)
> content(docs[[2]])[1:3]
```

```
[1] "africa fashion week london kick"
[2] "articl simamkel matuntuta fri aug pm"
[3] " email photo credit africa fashion week london"
```

The above code includes some typical pre-processing steps that are applied to the corpus using the function `tm_map()`. These include self-explanatory things like removing punctuation, numbers, transforming everything to lowercase, or stripping white space. Also common is to eliminate from further analysis the stop words (e.g. "the", "a", etc.) of the language of the documents that bring no information. Finally, to make all linguistic variations of some words the same term, we carry out word stemming in the documents. The last statement shows again the same three sentences of the second document after all these steps.

Finally, we can transform the pre-processed documents into a dataset by using some feature vectors to describe them. The example below uses TF-IDF to represent each document:

```
> data <- DocumentTermMatrix(docs, control=list(weighting=weightTfIdf))
> data

<<DocumentTermMatrix (documents: 300, terms: 13276)>>
Non-/sparse entries: 67308/3915492
Sparsity           : 98%
Maximal term length: 43
Weighting          : term frequency - inverse document frequency (normalized) (tf-idf)

> inspect(data[1:2,1:5])

<<DocumentTermMatrix (documents: 2, terms: 5)>>
Non-/sparse entries: 0/10
Sparsity           : 100%
Maximal term length: 7
Weighting          : term frequency - inverse document frequency (normalized) (tf-idf)

          Terms
Docs       aadid aapl abalon abandon abat
  1.text       0    0      0       0    0
  10.text      0    0      0       0    0
```

Function `DocumentTermMatrix()` can be used to create these feature representations. It accepts several arguments that allow for instance to select the way each feature is calculated (in this case using TF-IDF). The result is an object of class **DocumentTermMatrix** that is typically a very sparse matrix, given that most documents contain only a small fraction of all words. Function `inspect()` can be used to see some entries of this large data matrix.

Package **tm** also contains several functions that allow some form of exploration of these document term matrices. For instance, we can use function `findFreqTerms()` to filter out the terms that have a feature value above a certain threshold,

```
> findFreqTerms(data,0.9)

 [1] "can"      "cent"     "compani"  "corbyn"   "famili"   "food"
 [7] "govern"   "like"     "million"  "music"    "new"      "offic"
[13] "olymp"    "peopl"    "per"      "polic"    "race"     "report"
[19] "research" "said"     "say"      "show"     "team"     "use"
[25] "water"    "will"     "work"     "world"    "year"
```

We can also find terms that are correlated with each other,

```
> findAssocs(data,"race",0.5)

$race
finish    sail
  0.53    0.53
```

Function `findAssocs()` allows you to specify a term and correlation threshold, and returns the terms in the document collection that have a correlation with the supplied term higher than the threshold.

Finally, we can use function `removeSparseTerms()` to filter out terms in the document term matrix that have most of their values zero, i.e. sparse terms that occur in very few of the documents. For instance, if we want to filter all terms for which 70% of the entries are zero, we would proceed as follows,

```
> newData <- removeSparseTerms(data,0.7)
> newData

<<DocumentTermMatrix (documents: 300, terms: 49)>>
Non-/sparse entries: 6280/8420
Sparsity           : 57%
Maximal term length: 6
Weighting          : term frequency - inverse document frequency (normalized) (tf-idf)
```

As you see we have moved from an original matrix with 13276 terms (i.e. columns) to a matrix with only 49! For further modelling steps it would be interesting to have this dataset representing the 300 text documents in a more "standard" data structure, i.e. a data frame type object. This could be easily obtained as follows:

```
> library(tibble)
> as_tibble(as.matrix(newData))

# A tibble: 300 × 49
         also         back         call          can         come          day
        <dbl>        <dbl>        <dbl>        <dbl>        <dbl>        <dbl>
1   0.002696966 0.002393000 0.002767608 0.005681151 0.002644988 0.000000000
2   0.000000000 0.000000000 0.000000000 0.012779535 0.000000000 0.000000000
3   0.003398828 0.000000000 0.003487853 0.002386540 0.000000000 0.005922018
4   0.000000000 0.000000000 0.000000000 0.000000000 0.000000000 0.000000000
5   0.000000000 0.000000000 0.000000000 0.005268159 0.000000000 0.000000000
6   0.002988376 0.010606261 0.006133301 0.008393339 0.000000000 0.000000000
7   0.005282822 0.000000000 0.000000000 0.003709416 0.000000000 0.000000000
8   0.000000000 0.000000000 0.005588645 0.000000000 0.000000000 0.000000000
9   0.003896446 0.006914579 0.000000000 0.005471900 0.003821350 0.003394527
10  0.000000000 0.004286092 0.000000000 0.000000000 0.014212281 0.004208283
# ... with 290 more rows, and 43 more variables: dont <dbl>, even <dbl>,
#   first <dbl>, get <dbl>, includ <dbl>, just <dbl>, know <dbl>,
#   last <dbl>, like <dbl>, look <dbl>, made <dbl>, make <dbl>,
#   mani <dbl>, may <dbl>, month <dbl>, much <dbl>, need <dbl>, new <dbl>,
#   now <dbl>, one <dbl>, part <dbl>, peopl <dbl>, report <dbl>,
#   right <dbl>, said <dbl>, say <dbl>, see <dbl>, show <dbl>, sinc <dbl>,
#   take <dbl>, think <dbl>, time <dbl>, told <dbl>, two <dbl>, use <dbl>,
#   want <dbl>, way <dbl>, week <dbl>, well <dbl>, will <dbl>, work <dbl>,
#   world <dbl>, year <dbl>
```

3.3.4   Dimensionality Reduction

The amount and diversity of data sources often leads to datasets whose dimensionality raises serious challenges to most analysis tools, even if extreme computation power is available. This dimensionality problem can take several forms. The data can be too large to handle by the available hardware, but it can also have a dimensionality that goes against the assumptions of some modeling tools. That is the case of datasets where there are many more variables (columns) than observations (rows), as it is often the case in text mining, for instance. While these datasets may fit perfectly well in our available hardware, they still can be problematic for some tools due to this imbalance between the number of columns and rows.

3.3.4.1   Sampling Rows

A large number of rows is one of the most frequently encountered facets of large dimensionality. As datasets grow in size it becomes difficult to fit all data in memory. R uses a computation model that requires data to fit in the central memory of computers. Although memory is becoming cheaper and larger, datasets grow at an even faster rate. Solutions have been appearing trying to overcome this limitation of R for big data. More information on some of these solutions can be found in the Hig Performance Computing task view[17].

Another possible path to handle this type of datasets is not to use all available rows. This typically involves sampling the rows of the data table. Random sampling of a subset of the rows can be easily achieved in R. Below you may find a simple example, where a small dataset is used for illustration purposes,

```
> data(iris)
> prop2sample <- 0.5
> rowIDs <- sample(1:nrow(iris), as.integer(prop2sample*nrow(iris)))
> iris.sample <- iris[rowIDs,]
```

This simple example illustrates the use of the **sample()** function to draw random numbers from a certain range. When both the range and the required size are integers (as in the example above) we can use **sample.int()** instead.

In case you prefer sampling with replacement, you may use the **replace** argument,

```
> data(iris)
> prop2sample <- 0.5
> rowIDs <- sample(1:nrow(iris), as.integer(prop2sample*nrow(iris)), replace=TRUE)
> iris.sample <- iris[rowIDs,]
```

In spite of the virtues of the above approach, the fact is that it requires that the full dataset fits in memory. If that is a problem because the dataset is to big to be loaded into R, then this method is useless. In those situations we need a method that does not involve reading the full dataset into memory. We are going to consider two possible situations: (i) the full dataset is stored in a text file; and (ii) the dataset is in a relational database.

Let us assume our extremely large dataset is stored in a CSV file. We will illustrate how we could obtain a random sample of the lines in this text file. Even simple operations (e.g knowing the number of lines of the file) on very large files can be taxing in terms of computation time. This means that this apparent straightforward task of picking some random lines from a text file is not as simple as one may think. It is indeed a source of big debates as you may easily confirm by a Web search. We are going to provide a

---

[17]https://cran.r-project.org/web/views/HighPerformanceComputing.html

solution that has its drawbacks. Solving these problems would either compromise seriously the performance of the solution or involve much more complex computations. You may find alternative approaches/solutions around the Web[18].

Our solution has the following limitations: (i) it is based on command-line tools of unix-based operating systems; (ii) it is not guaranteed to obtain the exact number of observations we want. The first of these limitations is justified by the efficiency of the tools we use. Overcoming this limitation would involve either implementing a similar solution in some efficient programming language (e.g. C), or compromising the applicability to very large files by using a solution within R. The second limitation is again justified by efficiency reasons. The strategy we use essentially goes through each line of the original large file and draws a random number between 0 and 1. If the number is below a certain percentage the line is selected for the final sample, otherwise we move to the next line. For instance, suppose we want a 10% sample. On each line we check if the random number is below 0.1 — if yes we pick the line otherwise we step to the next. The problem with this approach is that as drawing a random number is a probabilistic task, we may end-up with less than 10% of the lines because there is no guarantee that there will be 10% numbers below 0.1. We limit a bit this drawback by using a threshold larger than 0.1, and then in the end just pick the first 10% of the lines that were selected, but still there is no guarantee that this will always work as expected. The function we show below will issue a warning on those occasions.

```
> nrLinesFile <- function(f) {
+     if (.Platform$OS.type == "unix")
+         as.integer(strsplit(trimws(system(paste("wc -l",f),intern=TRUE)),
+                             " ")[[1]][1])
+     else
+         stop("This function requires unix-based systems")
+ }
>
> sampleCSV <- function(file, percORn, nrLines, header=TRUE, mxPerc=0.5) {
+     if (.Platform$OS.type != "unix")
+         stop("This function requires unix-based systems")
+     require(readr, quietly=TRUE)

+     if (missing(nrLines)) nrLines <- nrLinesFile(file)

+     if (percORn < 1)
+         if (percORn > mxPerc)
+             stop("This function is not adequate for that big samples.")
+         else percORn <- as.integer(percORn*nrLines)
+     perc <- min(2*percORn/nrLines, mxPerc)

+     system(paste0("perl -ne 'print if (rand() < ",perc,")' ",file,
+                   " > ",file,".tmp.csv"))
+     dt <- read_csv(paste0(file,".tmp.csv"),col_names=header, n_max=percORn)
+     file.remove(paste0(file,".tmp.csv"))
+     if (nrow(dt) != percORn)
+         warning(paste("Expecting",percORn,"rows, but got",nrow(dt)))
+     dt
+ }
```

We split the solution in two functions, one that determines the number of lines of a text file and the other that obtains the random sample. The first uses the unix command **wc** that

---

[18]e.g. http://stackoverflow.com/questions/22261082

can be used to compute this number of lines in a very efficient manner. The second function does the heavy part (randomly selecting the rows) using the Perl scripting language. The selected rows are then read into a data frame using the function **read_csv()** from package **readr**.

If the user knows beforehand the number of lines in the original large file it can provide this information through the parameter **nrLines**, thus saving some computation. Otherwise the function will calculate this number. The user may specify the size of the random sample either as a percentage (in the interval $[0, 1]$) or as the desired number of lines. We should note that the function will not work with percentages higher than 0.5. The reason has to do with using a percentage higher than what the user specifies to try to overcome the limitation of the probabilistic nature of drawing random numbers. Still, we should refer that this is not a very serious limitation. In effect, as we are talking about a function to be applied over extremely large files, having a 50% sample may even be too much to fit in memory, so typically we will use much lower percentages.

We now present an example by drawing a 1% random sample from a file with roughly 135 million rows (the file size is $\approx$ 5Gb),

```
> t <- Sys.time()
> d <- sampleCSV("allsensors.csv", 0.01, header=FALSE)

Parsed with column specification:
cols(
X1 = col_datetime(format = ""),
X2 = col_double(),
X3 = col_integer()
)

> Sys.time()-t

Time difference of 34.91942 secs

> nrow(d)

[1] 1349305
```

We use the function **Sys.time()** to access the system clock and time the sampling operation. As you can observe, even using the fast utility programs we get a computation time around 30 seconds (this will obviously vary with the hardware you have available).

In the second setup we are going to address the case when our large dataset is stored in a relational database. We are going to provide a simple illustration using a MySQL database. The solution we are going to describe should work well with other databases. Obtaining a random sample from a database table is again surprisingly not straightforward. If you search around the Web you will see that there are long debates and a huge number of (often complex) solutions proposed. The solution we are going to describe has its drawbacks and it is not the most efficient of the solutions. Still, it has the advantage of being relatively simple so if very fast performance for obtaining the sample is not a critical issue this should be more than enough. For more efficient (but considerably more complex) solutions we recommend you search the Web for other solutions[19].

Our source database contains roughly 135 million rows. Let us assume we want a sample of 10,000 rows from this large table to carry out some analysis in R. We first establish the connection to the database,

---

[19]Two possible starting points are http://jan.kneschke.de/projects/mysql/order-by-rand/ and http://mysql.rjweb.org/doc.php/random

```
> library(DBI)
> library(RMySQL)
> drv <- dbDriver("MySQL")   # Loading the MySQL driver
> con <- dbConnect(drv,dbname="transDB",
+                    username="myuser",password="mypassword",
+                    host="localhost")
```

The following function obtains the random sample from a table of a given database connection,

```
> sampleDBMS <- function(dbConn, tbl, percORn, mxPerc=0.5) {
+     nrRecords <- unlist(dbGetQuery(dbConn, paste("select count(*) from",tbl)))

+     if (percORn < 1)
+         if (percORn > mxPerc)
+             stop("This function is not adequate for that big samples.")
+         else percORn <- as.integer(percORn*nrRecords)
+     perc <- min(2*percORn/nrRecords, mxPerc)

+     dt <- dbGetQuery(dbConn,paste("select * from (select * from",tbl,
+                                   "where rand() <= ",perc,") as t limit ",percORn))
+     if (nrow(dt) != percORn)
+         warning(paste("Expecting",percORn,"rows, but got",nrow(dt)))
+     dt
+ }
```

The solution is similar in strategy to the previous one for datasets stored in a CSV file. We again use a random number generator to decide which rows to pick. This time we use the **rand()** SQL function to draw these random numbers.

We can use the above function to obtain our random sample with 10,000 rows, storing it in a data frame,

```
> t1 <- Sys.time()
> d <- sampleDBMS(con,"sensor_values",10000)
> Sys.time()-t1

Time difference of 5.192664 secs

> nrow(d)

[1] 10000
```

We have again used the function **Sys.time()** to time the execution of our code that obtains the random sample. As you see, it is reasonably fast, though we are talking of a table with 135 million rows.

As with the function for CSV files, this function can also be used by specifying a percentage of the rows of the original database table. Note that the function is also limited to small values of this percentage.

Finally, we can close the connection to the DBMS,

```
> dbDisconnect(con)

[1] TRUE

> dbUnloadDriver(drv)

[1] TRUE
```

3.3.4.2 Variable Selection

The selection of a subset of variables (also known as feature selection) is a very frequent task we carry out in data analysis. This may have several motivations, like for instance trying to remove irrelevant variables or variables that are highly correlated with others. Applying these methods for these reasons is usually motivated by the use some modeling tools that do not handle these "problems" very well, or make some strong assumptions on the variables describing the cases that are violated by the original dataset. Another motivation for feature selection is simply reducing the dimensionality of the dataset. A frequent setting that creates problems to most tools are datasets where the number of variables is considerably larger than the number of cases. We have seen such example in Section 3.3.3.2 when exploring document-based data.

There are many methods we can use to select features. These are frequently cast into (i) filter methods, and (ii) wrapper methods. Filter methods involve looking at variables individually and asserting their value using some metric, which is then used to rank them and remove the less relevant ones (in terms of the selected metric). Wrapper methods work by taking into consideration the objectives of the analysis we plan to carry out with the dataset. This means that they try to search for the subset of variables that are more adequate in terms of the criteria used to evaluate the results of the posterior modeling stages. In this context, the models we plan to apply after the variable selection are brought back to the feature selection step so that we can select the subset of variables that best optimize their performance. These methods typically involve an iterative search procedure where at each step a candidate set of features is used to obtain a model, which is evaluated and the results of this evaluation are used to decide if the features are good enough or if we need to try other set. Because of this iterative search process, wrapper methods are typically more demanding in computation terms. In summary, while filter methods are one-shot approaches, wrapper techniques involve an iterative search process.

Another way of grouping existing feature selection methods is into (i) unsupervised and (ii) supervised methods. Unsupervised methods look at each feature individually and calculate its relevance using only the values of the variable. Supervised methods explore the existence of a "special" variable in the dataset, the so-called target variable. As we will see, this forms the basis of predictive analytics that we will address in Section 3.4.5. These supervised methods evaluate each feature by looking at its relationship with the target variable. This may be as simple as calculating the correlation of each feature with the target, but it may also involve other metrics. Wrapper methods are most of the time supervised methods because they typically use some predictive model to assert the value of a set of candidate features.

Examples of simple unsupervised filter methods include for instance, checking for constant variables (i.e. variables that have a constant value on all observations), or for ID-like variables (i.e. variables that are different on all observations, like for instance the product ID on a dataset of products). In the case study of Chapter 7 we will see another example of this type of simple filter where we will eliminate features that have very low variability as measured by some statistic of spread. These unsupervised filering methods typically search for irrelevant and/or noisy features that we can safely discard from our analysis.

Supervised filtering methods try to obtain some statistic that relates the values of a variable to those of a target variable (a variable whose values are supposed to depend on the values of the other variables). A simple example is to calculate the correlation between the two variables, given by

$$\rho_{\hat{y},y} = \frac{\sum_{i=1}^{N_{test}} (\hat{y}_i - \bar{\hat{y}})(y_i - \bar{y})}{\sqrt{\sum_{i=1}^{N_{test}} (\hat{y}_i - \bar{\hat{y}})^2 \sum_{i=1}^{N_{test}} (y_i - \bar{y})^2}} \tag{3.4}$$

Other examples include information theoretic metrics. These metrics are based on the concept of entropy which is the expected information contained in a message. In the context of supervised classification tasks (i.e. with a nominal target variable) we can talk about the class entropy,

$$H(Y) = - \sum_{c_i \in \mathcal{Y}} P(Y = c_i) \cdot \log P(Y = c_i) \tag{3.5}$$

where $\mathcal{Y}$ is the domain of the target, i.e. the set of classes of the problem; and $P(Y = c_i)$ is the probability of class c_i.

We can also talk about the conditioned class entropy given the value of a certain predictor variable,

$$H(Y|X) = - \sum_{v_i \in \mathcal{X}} P(X = v_i) \sum_{c_k \in \mathcal{Y}} \frac{P(Y = c_k \vee X = v_i)}{P(X = v_i)} \log \frac{P(Y = c_k \vee X = v_i)}{P(X = v_i)} \tag{3.6}$$

Based on these notions we can defined the Information Gain of a variable (which is also referred to as mutual information) as the difference between the class entropy and the conditioned class entropy,

$$IG(X) = H(Y) - H(Y|X) \tag{3.7}$$

A variant of this metric is the Gain Ratio which is the information gain normalized by the variable entropy, i.e.

$$GR(X) = \frac{IG(X)}{H(X)} \tag{3.8}$$

where $H(X) = - \sum_{v_i \in \mathcal{X}} P(X = v_i) \cdot \log P(X = v_i)$.

All these quantities are easy to estimate using frequencies calculated from the available training data. For continuous variables it is harder to calculate, as the summations turn into integrals.

These and other metrics have been implemented in packages **FSelector** (Romanski and Kotthoff, 2014) and **CORElearn** (Robnik-Sikonja and Savicky, 2015). Below we show a few examples using the latter,

```
> library(CORElearn)
> data(iris)
> attrEval(Species ~ ., iris, estimator="GainRatio")

Sepal.Length  Sepal.Width Petal.Length  Petal.Width
   0.5919339    0.3512938    1.0000000    1.0000000

> attrEval(Species ~ ., iris, estimator="InfGain")

Sepal.Length  Sepal.Width Petal.Length  Petal.Width
   0.5572327    0.2831260    0.9182958    0.9182958

> attrEval(Species ~ ., iris, estimator="Gini")

Sepal.Length  Sepal.Width Petal.Length  Petal.Width
   0.2277603    0.1269234    0.3333333    0.3333333

> attrEval(Species ~ ., iris, estimator="MDL")

Sepal.Length  Sepal.Width Petal.Length  Petal.Width
   0.5112764    0.2465980    0.8311280    0.8311280
```

The above examples consider the task of forecasting the species of *Iris* plants using four biometric properties of the plants. We show four examples of supervised metrics for problems with a nominal target variable: the Gain Ratio, the Information Gain, the Gini index, and the MDL score. All of them somehow agree that the predictors related with the petals are the more relevant, followed by the sepal length.

Package **CORElearn** contains many more metrics that you can apply to this type of problem, as shown by the following list of available metrics for supervised classification tasks (check the package help pages for full descriptions),

```
> infoCore(what="attrEval")
```

```
 [1] "ReliefFequalK"     "ReliefFexpRank"    "ReliefFbestK"
 [4] "Relief"            "InfGain"           "GainRatio"
 [7] "MDL"               "Gini"              "MyopicReliefF"
[10] "Accuracy"          "ReliefFmerit"      "ReliefFdistance"
[13] "ReliefFsqrDistance" "DKM"               "ReliefFexpC"
[16] "ReliefFavgC"       "ReliefFpe"         "ReliefFpa"
[19] "ReliefFsmp"        "GainRatioCost"     "DKMcost"
[22] "ReliefKukar"       "MDLsmp"            "ImpurityEuclid"
[25] "ImpurityHellinger" "UniformDKM"        "UniformGini"
[28] "UniformInf"        "UniformAccuracy"   "EqualDKM"
[31] "EqualGini"         "EqualInf"          "EqualHellinger"
[34] "DistHellinger"     "DistAUC"           "DistAngle"
[37] "DistEuclid"
```

For supervised problems with numeric target (known as regression problems) we also have several alternative metrics for feature importance. Here are a few examples again using the package **CORElearn**,

```
> data(algae, package ="DMwR2")
> attrEval(a1 ~ ., algae[,1:12], estimator="MSEofMean")
```

```
    season       size      speed       mxPH       mnO2         Cl        NO3
-453.2142  -395.9696  -413.5873  -413.3519  -395.2823  -252.7300  -380.6412
      NH4       oPO4        PO4       Chla
-291.0525  -283.3738  -272.9903  -303.5737
```

```
> attrEval(a1 ~ ., algae[,1:12], estimator="RReliefFexpRank")
```

```
       season          size         speed          mxPH          mnO2
-0.031203465  -0.028139035  -0.035271926   0.080825823  -0.072103230
           Cl           NO3           NH4          oPO4           PO4
-0.152077352  -0.011462467  -0.009879109  -0.134034483  -0.076488066
         Chla
-0.142442935
```

```
> infoCore(what="attrEvalReg")
```

```
[1] "RReliefFequalK"    "RReliefFexpRank"   "RReliefFbestK"
[4] "RReliefFwithMSE"   "MSEofMean"         "MSEofModel"
[7] "MAEofModel"        "RReliefFdistance"  "RReliefFsqrDistance"
```

The second metric in the above examples is a variant of the adaptation of the Relief metric (Kira and Rendell., 1992) to regression tasks (Robnik-Sikonja and Kononenko, 2003). Relief is a powerful feature evaluation metric because it does not evaluate each variable independently of the others, which is interesting when we suspect there is strong correlation between the variables of our dataset.

We should remark that, in the context of supervised methods, there are tools that include the feature selection process "inside" the modeling stage or associated with it. Examples include tree-based models that carry out some feature selection as part of the modeling stage, or even tools that can be used to estimate the relevance of each feature for their modeling approach (we will see examples of this with random forests later in the book).

Another strongly related topic that sometimes is also used as a means for reducing the dimensionality of the problem by using less variables, is the transformation of the feature space by axis rotation. Each case in a dataset is described by a set of p variables. In this context, we can look at each case as a point in a p-dimensional hyper-space. Axis rotation methods try to change the axes used to describe each case. Typically, one of the objectives is to find a smaller set of axes that still captures most of the variability in the original dataset, but using fewer variables to describe each case. These "new" constructed variables are normally functions of the original variables. An example of such techniques is the Principle Components Analysis (PCA). In short, this method searches for a set of "new" variables, each being a linear combination of the original variables. The idea is that a smaller set of these new variables could be able to "explain" most of the variability of the original data, and if that is the case we can carry out our analysis using only this subset. Let us see an example of this in R using the *Iris* dataset,

```
> data(iris)
> pca.data <- iris[,-5] # each case is described by the first 4 variables
> pca <- princomp(pca.data)
> loadings(pca)
```

```
Loadings:
             Comp.1 Comp.2 Comp.3 Comp.4
Sepal.Length  0.361 -0.657 -0.582  0.315
Sepal.Width         -0.730  0.598 -0.320
Petal.Length  0.857  0.173        -0.480
Petal.Width   0.358         0.546  0.754

             Comp.1 Comp.2 Comp.3 Comp.4
SS loadings    1.00   1.00   1.00   1.00
Proportion Var 0.25   0.25   0.25   0.25
Cumulative Var 0.25   0.50   0.75   1.00
```

The function `princomp()` can be used to obtain the PCAs of a certain dataset. The associated function `loadings()` was used to check what were the found (rotated) axes, as well as the proportion of the original variance that is captured by each of them. From the analysis of the output of this function one can conclude that, in this example, if we used only the first three components (each component is a "new" feature) to describe the data, then we would only be capturing 75% of the original variance of the cases. This is a bit on the short side, but if we decide to go with four components then we have no dimensionality reduction at all, so we may as well stay with the original data! The first part of the output produced by `loadings()` shows us that each of the new variables is a linear combination of the original features. For instance, in the above example we see that the 1st component is calculated as $0.361 \times Sepal.Length + 0.857 \times Petal.Length + 0.358 \times Petal.Width$. We do not need to do these calculations by hand. We can obtain the values of the new features for all cases as follows (we only show them for the first 5 cases):

```
> pca$scores[1:5,]
```

```
           Comp.1      Comp.2       Comp.3      Comp.4
[1,] -2.684126  -0.3193972  -0.02791483  0.002262437
[2,] -2.714142   0.1770012  -0.21046427  0.099026550
[3,] -2.888991   0.1449494   0.01790026  0.019968390
[4,] -2.745343   0.3182990   0.03155937 -0.075575817
[5,] -2.728717  -0.3267545   0.09007924 -0.061258593
```

Suppose we are happy with the proportion of variance explained by a small subset of the components (say the first 2). We could carry out the posterior modeling stages on this new (and reduced) feature space. For instance, instead of using the original *Iris* dataset we could use the scores of the first two components,

```
> dim(iris)
```

```
[1] 150   5
```

```
> reduced.iris <- data.frame(pca$scores[,1:2],Species=iris$Species)
> dim(reduced.iris)
```

```
[1] 150   3
```

```
> head(reduced.iris)
```

```
     Comp.1      Comp.2  Species
1 -2.684126  -0.3193972   setosa
2 -2.714142   0.1770012   setosa
3 -2.888991   0.1449494   setosa
4 -2.745343   0.3182990   setosa
5 -2.728717  -0.3267545   setosa
6 -2.280860  -0.7413304   setosa
```

There are other methods that work in a similar way as the PCA (e.g. Independent Component Analysis or Singular Value Decomposition). Still, most of these methods have a few drawbacks. They typically require the original features to be numeric[20], and the resulting dataset is clearly less comprehensible for the end-user as the new features are combinations of the original variables.

Further readings on variable importance

Several books include chapters/sections on the important issue of variable/feature importance metrics. A good example with an extensive survey is Chapter 6 in Kononenko and Kukar (2007). Several survey articles also exist like for instance the work by Guyon and Elisseeff (2003). Regarding methods involving axis rotation and other types of transformations of the original variables prior to the selection stage, a good overview can be found in Section 2.4.3 of the book by Aggarwal (2015).

---

[20]If that is not the case we can use the so-called *dummy* variables, but for nominal variables with lots of values this becomes impractical.

3.4 Modeling

Before we start to provide details and examples of concrete models of a dataset it may be interesting to clarify what we mean by a model. This word is obviously used in many different contexts but in our case we are talking about some scientific activity based on observations of a phenomena in the form of a dataset. It is interesting to look at a reference definition of a scientific model. According to Wikipedia[21],

> "Scientific modelling is a scientific activity, the aim of which is to make a particular part or feature of the world easier to **understand, define, quantify, visualize, or simulate** by referencing it to existing and usually commonly accepted knowledge. It requires **selecting and identifying relevant aspects of a situation in the real world** and then using different types of models for different aims, such as conceptual models to better understand, operational models to operationalize, mathematical models to quantify, and graphical models to visualize the subject."

We have highlighted in bold several aspects of this definition that are particularly relevant for the type of modeling one carries out in data mining. In the following sections we will see some examples of data mining techniques that address some of these aspects. We will group our description of these techniques into 5 main groups of tasks as already hinted at in Figure 3.1 (page 44): (i) exploratory data analysis; (ii) dependency modeling; (iii) clustering; (iv) anomaly detection; and (v) predictive analytics.

Data mining can be seen as a search for interesting, unexpected, and useful relationships in a dataset. These findings may be interesting mainly because either they are unusual patterns or because they are very common in the sense of being considered key characteristics of the phenomena. Most data mining techniques we will explore can be regarded as either: (i) searching for relationships among the features (columns) describing the cases in a dataset (e.g. anytime some patient shows some set of symptoms, described by some feature values, the diagnostic of a medical doctor is a certain disease); or (ii) searching for relationships among the observations (rows) of the dataset (e.g. a certain subset of products (rows) show a very similar sales pattern across a set of stores; or a certain transaction (a row) is very different from all other transactions). In the following sections we will see instances of data mining techniques that address these tasks in different ways with the goal of helping to answer some questions the user may have concerning the available dataset.

3.4.1 Exploratory Data Analysis

Exploratory data analysis includes a series of techniques that have as the main goal to provide useful summaries of a dataset that highlight some characteristics of the data that the users may find useful. We will consider essentially two main types of summaries: (i) textual summaries; and (ii) visual summaries.

3.4.1.1 Data Summarization

Most datasets have a dimensionality that makes it very difficult for a standard user to inspect the full data and find interesting properties of these data. As the size of the datasets keeps increasing this task gets even harder. Data summaries try to provide overviews of key properties of the data. More specifically, they try to describe important properties of the

---

[21]https://en.wikipedia.org/wiki/Scientific_modelling

distribution of the values across the observations in a dataset. Examples of these properties include answers to questions like:

- What is the "most common value" of a variable?

- Do the values of a variable "vary" a lot?

- Are there "strange" / unexpected values in the dataset?

  - e.g. outliers or unknown values

In the next paragraphs we will describe a few ways of answering these questions with illustrations using R code.

Finding the "most common value" of a variable given a sample of its values is the goal of statistics of centrality/location. In the case of numeric variables two common examples are the sample mean and median. The sample mean of a variable X is an estimate of the (full) distribution/population mean (μ_x) and is given by,

$$\bar{x} = \frac{1}{n} \sum_{i=1}^{n} x_i \tag{3.9}$$

The sample median, $\tilde{x}$, involves ordering the observed values of the variable and picking the value in the middle as the median (in case of an even number of values we take the average of the two values in the middle). Computationally, the median is considerably more expensive to compute than the mean due to the sorting operation, though this would only be noticeable on very large samples. However, this statistic has the advantage of not being sensitive to outlying values, which is not the case of the mean, and thus it is said to be a more "robust" statistic of centrality.

The mode is another statistic of central tendency. It is the most frequent value in the sample. It is often used with nominal variables given that for numeric variables the values may not appear repeated too often. The main drawback of this statistic is which value to select when more than one have the same observed frequency of occurrence in a given dataset.

R has specific functions for obtaining both the mean and the median, as shown in the next short examples,

```
> data(algae,package="DMwR2")
> mean(algae$a1)

[1] 16.9235

> mean(algae$NO3)

[1] NA

> mean(algae$NO3, na.rm=TRUE)

[1] 3.282389

> median(algae$a3)

[1] 1.55

> median(algae$mxPH, na.rm=TRUE)

[1] 8.06
```

The **mean()** and **median()** functions have a parameter (**na.rm**) that can be used to ignore the unknown values of a variable when calculating the statistic and thus avoid having an NA as result. Both these functions can also be used with the **summarise()** function of package **dplyr**,

```
> library(dplyr)
> alg <- tbl_df(algae)
> summarise(alg, avgNO3=mean(NO3,na.rm=TRUE), medA1=median(a1))

# A tibble: 1 × 2
    avgNO3 medA1
     <dbl> <dbl>
1 3.282389  6.95

> select(alg, mxPH:Cl) %>%
+     summarise_each(funs(mean(.,na.rm=TRUE),median(.,na.rm=TRUE)))

# A tibble: 1 × 6
   mxPH_mean mnO2_mean  Cl_mean mxPH_median mnO2_median Cl_median
       <dbl>     <dbl>    <dbl>       <dbl>       <dbl>     <dbl>
1  8.011734  9.117778 43.63628        8.06         9.8     32.73
```

The **summarise()** function can be used to apply any function that produces a scalar value to any column of a data frame table.

The second example above shows how to apply a set of functions to all columns of a data frame table using function **summarise_each()** together with function **funs()**.

Sometimes we are interested in obtaining summaries for sub-groups of our datasets. Often these sub-groups can be defined using the values of some nominal variable (e.g. obtaining the mean age per sex of our clients). These conditional summaries are easy to obtain using package **dplyr**[22]. The following is an example of this type of summaries,

```
> group_by(alg, season, size) %>%
+     summarize(nObs=n(), mA7=median(a7)) %>%
+         ungroup() %>% arrange(desc(mA7))

# A tibble: 12 × 4
    season   size  nObs   mA7
   <fctr> <fctr> <int> <dbl>
1   spring  large    12  1.95
2   summer  small    14  1.45
3   winter medium    26  1.40
4   autumn medium    16  1.05
5   spring medium    21  1.00
6   summer medium    21  1.00
7   autumn  large    11  0.00
8   autumn  small    13  0.00
9   spring  small    20  0.00
10  summer  large    10  0.00
11  winter  large    12  0.00
12  winter  small    24  0.00
```

The function **group_by()** can be used to form sub-groups of a dataset using all combinations of the values of one or more nominal variables (in this case we are using **season**

---

[22]Please not that base R also allows this type of summaries. e.g. check functions by() and aggregate().

and `size`). Subsequent calls to the `summarise()` function will be applied not to all dataset but to each of these sub-groups, thus returning one result for each sub-group. This is particularly interesting if you want to study potential differences among the sub-groups. As we will see, we can carry out similar sub-group comparisons with visual summaries.

Please note the above use of function `ungroup()` to remove the grouping information before ordering the results of the summary. Without this, the ordering provided by the `arrange()` function would take place within each group, which does not make sense in this case.

To obtain the mode of a variable we can create a function[23] for that given that base R does not have it,

```
> Mode <- function(x, na.rm = FALSE) {
+    if(na.rm) x <- x[!is.na(x)]
+    ux <- unique(x)
+    return(ux[which.max(tabulate(match(x, ux)))])
+ }
> Mode(algae$mxPH, na.rm=TRUE)

[1] 8

> Mode(algae$season)

[1] winter
Levels: autumn spring summer winter
```

Function `centralValue()` in our book package can be used to obtain the more adequate statistic of centrality of a given sample of values. It will return the median in the case of numeric variables and the mode for nominal variables,

```
> library(DMwR2)
> centralValue(algae$a1)

[1] 6.95

> centralValue(algae$speed)

[1] "high"
```

In terms of the "variability" of the values of a variable we can use statistics of spread to obtain that information. The most common for numeric variables are the standard deviation or the variance. These statistics depend on the value of the mean and thus share the problems in terms of sensitivity ot outliers (and also skewed distributions). The sample variance of a continuous variable is an estimate of the population variance (σ_x^2) and is given by,

$$s_x^2 = \frac{1}{n-1} \sum_{i=1}^{n} (x_i - \bar{x})^2 \tag{3.10}$$

where $\bar{x}$ is the sample mean.

The sample standard deviation is the square root of the sample variance.

A more robust statistic of spread is the inter-quartile range. This is given by the difference between the 3rd and 1st quartiles. The x-quantile is the value below which there are $x\%$ of the observed values. This means that the inter-quartile range (IQR) is the interval that

---

[23]This function was taken from `http://stackoverflow.com/questions/2547402`

contains 50% of the most central values of a continuous variable. A large value of the IQR means that these central values are spread over a large range, where a small value represents a very packed set of values.

The range is another measure of variability, though less used as it is even more susceptible to outliers than the standard deviation or the variance. It is defined as the difference between the maximum and minimum values of the variable.

Below you may find a few examples of how to obtain these statistics in R,

```
> var(algae$a1)

[1] 455.7532

> sd(algae$Cl, na.rm=TRUE)

[1] 46.83131

> IQR(algae$mxPH, na.rm=TRUE)

[1] 0.7

> quantile(algae$a3)

   0%    25%    50%    75%   100%
0.000  0.000  1.550  4.925 42.800

> quantile(algae$a3, probs=c(0.2,0.8))

20% 80%
0.00 7.06

> range(algae$a1)

[1]  0.0 89.8

> max(algae$a5)-min(algae$a5)

[1] 44.4
```

As you see the function **quantile()** can be used to obtain any of the quantiles of a continuous variable.

The functions that return scalar values can also be used with the **summarise()** function of **dplyr**,

```
> select(alg,a1:a7) %>% summarise_each(funs(var))

# A tibble: 1 × 7
      a1       a2       a3       a4       a5       a6       a7
   <dbl>    <dbl>    <dbl>    <dbl>    <dbl>    <dbl>    <dbl>
1 455.7532 121.6212 48.28217 19.51346 56.1211 135.9722 26.61078
```

This constraint of requiring summarization functions to return a scalar is one of the reasons we may sometimes prefer to use functions from base R over those provided by **dplyr**. In the context of the *Iris* dataset, suppose you want to obtain the quantiles of the variable **Sepal.Length** by **Species**. You could feel tempted to use the grouping facilities of **dplyr** as follows, but this would generate an error,

```
> data(iris)
> group_by(iris,Species) %>% summarise(qs=quantile(Sepal.Length))

Error in eval(expr, envir, enclos): expecting a single value
```

The error is caused by the fact that the **quantile()** function returns a vector of values. In these contexts, it would be easier to use the **aggregate()** function from base R,

```
> aggregate(iris$Sepal.Length, list(Species=iris$Species), quantile)

     Species  x.0% x.25% x.50% x.75% x.100%
1     setosa 4.300 4.800 5.000 5.200  5.800
2 versicolor 4.900 5.600 5.900 6.300  7.000
3  virginica 4.900 6.225 6.500 6.900  7.900
```

The second argument of the **aggregate()** function is a list that can include as many factors as you want to form the sub-groups of the data. For each sub-group the function supplied in the third argument is applied to the values of the variables specified in the first. The **aggregate()** function can also be used with a formula-like interface that may actually be simpler for this particular example,

```
> aggregate(Sepal.Length ~ Species, data=iris, quantile)

     Species Sepal.Length.0% Sepal.Length.25% Sepal.Length.50%
1     setosa           4.300            4.800            5.000
2 versicolor           4.900            5.600            5.900
3  virginica           4.900            6.225            6.500
  Sepal.Length.75% Sepal.Length.100%
1            5.200             5.800
2            6.300             7.000
3            6.900             7.900
```

Regarding the issue of "strange" values in our dataset we will consider two types of situations: (i) unknown values; and (ii) outliers. As we have mentioned in Section 3.3.1.4 (page 60), R contains several packages that implement different methods for dealing with unknown values (NA in R). We will use several of these facilities in the practical case study presented in Chapter 4. Here we will simply illustrate different forms of detecting that some dataset contains these values. If we want to check how many unknown values exist in a dataset we can proceed as follows,

```
> data(algae, package="DMwR2")
> nasRow <- apply(algae,1,function(r) sum(is.na(r)))
> cat("The Algae dataset contains ",sum(nasRow)," NA values.\n")

The Algae dataset contains  33  NA values.

> cat("There are ",sum(!complete.cases(algae)),
+       " rows that have at least one NA value.\n")

There are  16  rows that have at least one NA value.
```

The function **is.na()** can be used to check if a value is NA. If applied to a vector

we get a vector of Booleans, which we can sum to know how many are TRUE[24]. Function
`complete.cases()` returns a vector of Boolean values, one for each row of a dataset. Each
value is TRUE if the respective row does not contain any NA, and FALSE otherwise.

In terms of outliers, we first need to settle on what we consider an outlier. According
to Hawkins (1980), an outlier is "an observation which deviates so much from other observations as to arouse suspicions that it was generated by a different mechanism". We can distinguish between univariate outliers where we are talking about finding unusual values in a
sample of observations of a single variable, and multivariate outliers where each observation
is in effect a vector of values of a set of variables. For univariate outlier detection a frequently
used method is the boxplot rule. This rules states that a value in a sample of a continuous
variable is considered an outlier if it is outside of the interval $[Q_1 - 1.5 \times IQR, Q_3 + 1.5 \times IQR]$,
where $Q_1 (Q_3)$ is the first (third) quartile, and $IQR = Q_3 - Q_1$ the interquartile range. This
rule can be easily implemented as follows,

```
> bpRule <- function(x, const=1.5, positions=FALSE) {
+       x <- x[!is.na(x)]
+       qs <- quantile(x,probs = c(0.25,0.75))
+       iqr <- qs[2]-qs[1]
+       if (!positions) x[x < qs[1]-const*iqr | x > qs[2]+const*iqr]
+       else which(x < qs[1]-const*iqr | x > qs[2]+const*iqr)
+ }
> bpRule(algae$a1)

 [1] 69.9 74.2 66.0 75.8 89.8 81.9 82.7 66.9 64.2 64.9 64.3 86.6

> bpRule(algae$NO3)

[1] 10.416  9.248  9.773  9.715 45.650

> bpRule(algae$NO3, positions=TRUE)

[1]   5   6 139 144 152
```

Although very simple to implement and understand, this rule also has some drawbacks,
like for instance its inadequacy when the distribution of the values is multi-modal.

Further methods both for univariate as well as multivariate outlier detection will be
described in Section 3.4.4 that deals with anomaly detection tasks.

R has several functions that try to provide useful summaries of the full datasets. The
simplest of these consists of applying the function **summary()** to any data frame. The result
is a summary of basic descriptive statistics of the dataset,

```
> data(iris)
> summary(iris)

  Sepal.Length    Sepal.Width     Petal.Length    Petal.Width
 Min.   :4.300   Min.   :2.000   Min.   :1.000   Min.   :0.100
 1st Qu.:5.100   1st Qu.:2.800   1st Qu.:1.600   1st Qu.:0.300
 Median :5.800   Median :3.000   Median :4.350   Median :1.300
 Mean   :5.843   Mean   :3.057   Mean   :3.758   Mean   :1.199
 3rd Qu.:6.400   3rd Qu.:3.300   3rd Qu.:5.100   3rd Qu.:1.800
 Max.   :7.900   Max.   :4.400   Max.   :6.900   Max.   :2.500
```

---

[24]As you may have guessed TRUE corresponds to a 1, while FALSE is a 0.

```
        Species
setosa    :50
versicolor:50
virginica :50
```

For numeric variables this returns some of the metrics we have discussed before, while for nominal variables the summary consists of showing the number of occurrences of each value (if there are too many, only the most frequent are shown).

Another global summary of a dataset can be obtained using the function `describe()` from package **Hmisc** (Harrell Jr. et al., 2015),

```
> library(Hmisc)
> describe(iris)

iris

 5  Variables        150  Observations
---------------------------------------------------------------------------
Sepal.Length
        n missing  unique    Info    Mean     .05     .10     .25     .50
      150       0      35       1   5.843   4.600   4.800   5.100   5.800
      .75     .90     .95
    6.400   6.900   7.255

lowest : 4.3 4.4 4.5 4.6 4.7, highest: 7.3 7.4 7.6 7.7 7.9
---------------------------------------------------------------------------
Sepal.Width
        n missing  unique    Info    Mean     .05     .10     .25     .50
      150       0      23    0.99   3.057   2.345   2.500   2.800   3.000
      .75     .90     .95
    3.300   3.610   3.800

lowest : 2.0 2.2 2.3 2.4 2.5, highest: 3.9 4.0 4.1 4.2 4.4
---------------------------------------------------------------------------
Petal.Length
        n missing  unique    Info    Mean     .05     .10     .25     .50
      150       0      43       1   3.758    1.30    1.40    1.60    4.35
      .75     .90     .95
     5.10    5.80    6.10

lowest : 1.0 1.1 1.2 1.3 1.4, highest: 6.3 6.4 6.6 6.7 6.9
---------------------------------------------------------------------------
Petal.Width
        n missing  unique    Info    Mean     .05     .10     .25     .50
      150       0      22    0.99   1.199     0.2     0.2     0.3     1.3
      .75     .90     .95
      1.8     2.2     2.3

lowest : 0.1 0.2 0.3 0.4 0.5, highest: 2.1 2.2 2.3 2.4 2.5
---------------------------------------------------------------------------
Species
        n missing  unique
```

```
      150          0        3
```

```
setosa (50, 33%), versicolor (50, 33%)
virginica (50, 33%)
------------------------------------------------------------------------
```

Sometimes we want this sort of summary involving several variables applied over sub-groups of data. As we have seen, using the **group_by()** function of **dplyr** limits us to summarization functions that return scalars. If we want to use a function that does not return a scalar we can either use the function **aggregate()** as we have seen before, or the function **by()** that is more interesting if the summary is not easily transformable to a matrix-like structure. Here is an example,

```
> by(algae[,2:5], algae$season, summary)
```

```
algae$season: autumn
     size          speed          mxPH              mn02
 large :11    high  :15    Min.   :5.700    Min.   : 6.50
 medium:16    low   : 8    1st Qu.:7.588    1st Qu.:10.22
 small :13    medium:17    Median :8.060    Median :10.90
                           Mean   :7.952    Mean   :10.60
                           3rd Qu.:8.400    3rd Qu.:11.43
                           Max.   :8.870    Max.   :12.90
---------------------------------------------------------------
algae$season: spring
     size          speed          mxPH              mn02
 large :12    high  :21    Min.   :5.600    Min.   : 1.800
 medium:21    low   : 8    1st Qu.:7.790    1st Qu.: 6.000
 small :20    medium:24    Median :8.070    Median : 8.900
                           Mean   :8.024    Mean   : 8.010
                           3rd Qu.:8.400    3rd Qu.: 9.875
                           Max.   :9.500    Max.   :12.500
                                            NA's   :1
---------------------------------------------------------------
algae$season: summer
     size          speed          mxPH              mn02
 large :10    high  :20    Min.   :6.400    Min.   : 4.400
 medium:21    low   : 7    1st Qu.:7.600    1st Qu.: 8.125
 small :14    medium:18    Median :8.000    Median :10.100
                           Mean   :7.905    Mean   : 9.415
                           3rd Qu.:8.200    3rd Qu.:10.875
                           Max.   :8.800    Max.   :12.100
                                            NA's   :1
---------------------------------------------------------------
algae$season: winter
     size          speed          mxPH              mn02
 large :12    high  :28    Min.   :6.600    Min.   : 1.500
 medium:26    low   :10    1st Qu.:7.800    1st Qu.: 7.625
 small :24    medium:24    Median :8.100    Median : 9.500
                           Mean   :8.119    Mean   : 8.880
                           3rd Qu.:8.430    3rd Qu.:10.650
                           Max.   :9.700    Max.   :13.400
                           NA's   :1
```

In the above example the function `summary()` was applied to sub-groups of the columns 2 to 5 of the `algae` dataset, formed according to the value of the variable `season`.

3.4.1.2 Data Visualization

Data visualization is an important tool for exploring and understanding our datasets. Humans are outstanding at capturing visual patterns, and data visualization tries to capitalize on these abilities. In this section we will go through some of the more relevant tools for data visualization and at the same time introduce the reader to the capabilities of R in terms of visual representations of a dataset. This is one of the areas where R excels.

We will organize our description by talking about tools for visualizing: (i) a single variable; (ii) two variables; and (iii) multivariate plots.

Before that, let us briefly introduce the reader to R graphics. R has two main graphics systems: (i) the standard graphics and (ii) the grid graphics. The first is implement by the package **graphics**, while the second is provided by functions of the package **grid**, both being part of any base R installation. These two packages create an abstraction layer that is used by several graphics packages that provide higher level plotting functions. In this short description we will focus on two main approaches to statistical plots: (i) the one provided by standard plotting functions that build upon the facilities provide by the **graphics** system; and (ii) the tools available in the **ggplot2** package (Wickham, 2009) that build upon the **grid** graphics system.

R graphics architecture can be seen as a series of layers providing increasingly higher level facilities to the user. At one end we have concrete graphics devices (the most common being the computer screen) where the plots will be shown. On the other end we have the graphics functions we will use to produce concrete statistical plots. An interesting aspect of this layered architecture is that it allows users to almost completely ignore the output devices in the sense that to obtain a plot in the screen or as, say, a PDF file, the process is the same minus one specific instruction where you "tell" R where to "show" the plot. For instance, the following instruction produces on your screen the plot shown in Figure 3.5,

```
> plot(sin(seq(0,10,by=0.1)),type="l")
```

If instead of on the screen, you want this plot in a PDF file, you simply type,

```
> pdf("myplot.pdf")
> plot(sin(seq(0,10,by=0.1)),type="l")
> dev.off()
```

And if you prefer a JPEG file instead, you do,

```
> jpeg("myplot.jpg")
> plot(sin(seq(0,10,by=0.1)),type="l")
> dev.off()
```

As you see, you simply open the target device (that defaults to the screen) and then type the instructions that produce your plot that are the same irrespective of the output device. In the end you close your device using the `dev.off()` function. Check the help pages of these functions for pointers to other available devices as well as many parameters of the functions that allow you to fine tune the output.

Most of the functions in R standard graphics system produce complete plots, like the above example using the `plot()` function. There are also other functions that allow you to add information (e.g. text, legends, arrows, etc.) to these plots.

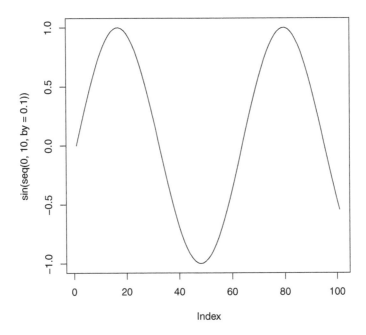

FIGURE 3.5: An example plot.

Package `ggplot2` follows a different approach. This package implements the ideas proposed by Wilkinson (2005) on a grammar of graphics that resulted from a theoretical study on what is a statistical plot. The package builds upon this theory by implementing the concept of a layered grammar of graphics (Wickham, 2009). This grammar defines a statistical graphic as a mapping from data properties into **aesthetic attributes** (color, shape, size, etc.) of **geometric objects** (points, lines, bars, etc.). For instance, within the *Iris* dataset we could decide to map the values of the variable `Petal.Length` into the coordinates of the X axis, the values of `Petal.Width` as the values of coordinates in the Y axis, and the values of the variable `Species` as different colors. With these mappings we could decide to plot each of the 150 plants in the dataset as a point, which would produce a plot like that shown in Figure 3.6.

Let us now explore a few examples of statistical plots. We start our exploration by considering the visualization of the values of a nominal variable. If we want to explore the distribution of these values we can use a *barplot* with this purpose. These graphs will show as many bars as there are different values of the variable, with the height of the bars corresponding to the frequency of the values. Figure 3.7 shows one barplot obtained with the standard graphics of R (left plot), and an equivalent barplot obtained using ggplot (right plot). They were obtained with the following code,

```
> library(ggplot2)
> data(algae, package="DMwR2")
> ## Plot on the left (standard)
> freqOcc <- table(algae$season)
```

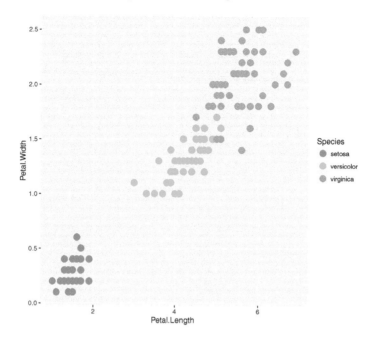

FIGURE 3.6: An example of ggplot mappings with the *Iris* dataset.

```
> barplot(freqOcc,main='Frequency of the Seasons')
> ## Plot on the right (ggplot2)
> ggplot(algae,aes(x=season)) + geom_bar() + ggtitle("Frequency of the Seasons")
```

In standard graphics we start by using the function `table()` to obtain the frequency of each of the values of the nominal variable. Then we use the function `barplot()` to obtain the graph using the parameter `main` to set the plot title.

For the ggplot graphic we build a kind of expression where each "term" defines a layer of the plot. The first layer is the call to the function `ggplot()` that allows you to specify the data source of your graph, and also the aesthetic mappings the plot will use through function `aes()`. In this case it is enough to say that the `season` variable is mapped into the X axis of the graph. Using the `geom_bar()` function we create the graphical objects ("geoms" in ggplot jargon), which in this case are bars. This function takes care of the frequency calculation for us, so we only need to add another layer with the title of the plot using the function `ggtitle()`.

A few notes on barplots (also known as barcharts). When the labels of the values of the nominal variable are too long it may be easier to read the graph if you plot the bars horizontally. To achieve this with the above barplot in **ggplot2** it is enough to do,

```
> ggplot(algae,aes(x=season)) + geom_bar() +
+       ggtitle("Frequency of the Seasons") + coord_flip()
```

The `coord_flip()` function can be used to swap the X and Y coordinates of the plot. Note that you could alternatively rotate the labels in the X axis if you prefer to maintain the bars in the vertical direction.

Another important warning on barplots is the problem that one sometimes faces of having a few of the bar differences being almost undistinguishable (e.g. the frequencies of the 3 values of a nominal variable are 989, 993 and 975). To try to make the differences

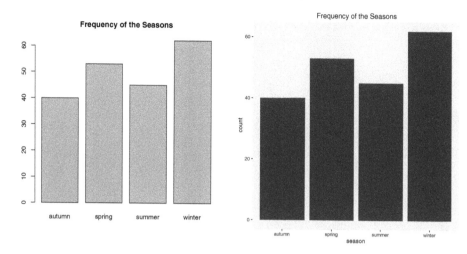

FIGURE 3.7: A barplot using standard graphics (left) and ggplot2 (right).

more visible, you might feel tempted to change the limits of the Y axis, so that it does not start at zero, thus making the differences more noticeable. Do not do this! It is wrong. The differences are not noticeable because that is what they are! Do not use the graphs to "lie" about your data.

Finally, the information provided by barplots could also be shown as a pie chart. Although used very frequently, this is generally a bad idea. The idea of barplots and pie charts is to compare the frequencies of several values. In barplots these frequencies are associated with the height of bars, while in pie charts they are associated with areas of pie slices. Comparing the heights of the bars is much easier for the eyes than comparing areas of slices, particularly if there are many slices/values.

Let us now consider continuous variables. To study the distribution of these variables there are several options. The first we will explore is the histogram that is strongly related to the barplot we have seen above. The idea of the histogram is to divide the range of the numeric variable into bins and then count the frequency of these bins and show this information as heights of bars. The key issue here is how to select the size of the bins. This is a subject of debate and there are several alternative algorithms to determine these bins. This is an important issue as the shape of the distribution as shown by the histogram may change considerably with changes in the bin sizes.

In Figure 3.8 we have two histograms of the variable `Petal.Length` of the *Iris* dataset, one obtained with the base graphics and the other with ggplot. They were obtained with this code,

```
> library(ggplot2)
> data(iris)
> ## Plot on the left (standard)
> hist(iris$Petal.Length,xlab='Petal Length')
> ## Plot on the right (ggplot2)
> ggplot(iris,aes(x=Petal.Length)) + geom_histogram() + xlab("Petal Length")
```

In standard graphics we use the function `hist()` to obtain the histogram of the variable. We have used the parameter `xlab` to set the label for the X axis.

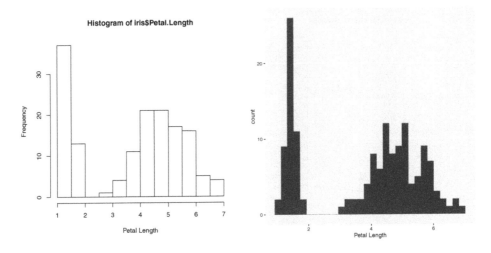

FIGURE 3.8: A histogram using standard graphics (left) and ggplot2 (right).

In ggplot, after setting the aesthetic mappings, we use the `geom_histogram()` function to obtain the plot. We also use the function `xlab()` to set the axis label.

As you can observe, due to the different settings in terms of bin size used by default on both methods for obtaining an histogram, the plots we obtain transmit a slightly different idea on the way the values of this variable are distributed. This highlights the importance of this decision.

A different way of showing information on the distribution of the values of a continuous variable is through the boxplot. This statistical graphic provides several information on some descriptive statistics of the variable. The boxplot tries to convey information on the centrality of variable, its spread, and also the eventual existence of outliers. For this purpose it uses robust statistics, namely the median and inter-quartile range, and also the boxplot rule we have described before, to signal outliers. Below you have the code to generate boxplots in the two graphics systems. The results are shown in Figure 3.9.

```
> library(ggplot2)
> data(iris)
> ## Plot on the left (standard)
> boxplot(iris$Sepal.Width, ylab='Sepal Width')
> ## Plot on the right (ggplot2)
> ggplot(iris, aes(x=factor(0), y=Sepal.Width)) + geom_boxplot() +
+     xlab("") + ylab("Sepal Width") + theme(axis.text.x=element_blank())
```

The function `boxplot()` is used in standard graphics to obtain these plots.

For the ggplot graph, the code is slightly more complex. We use the `geom_boxplot()` function to obtain adequate geom. However, we need a few more tweaks in order to obtain a similar plot. First of all, we need to create a fake variable for the X axis. Then we need to hide its guides in this axis to make the plot look nicer. This is clearly much more cumbersome than with the standard graphics system.

A boxplot shows a rectangle whose horizontal limits represent the first and third quartiles (thus the height of the rectangle is the inter-quartile range). Inside this rectangle an horizontal line shows the median of the sample. From the rectangle two vertical lines exend till the limits above (below) which a value is considered an outlier (the limits established by the boxplot rule). If any such values exist they are shown as separate dots in the graph.

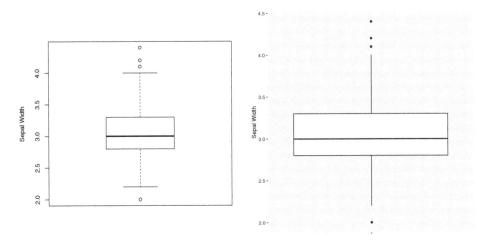

FIGURE 3.9: A boxplot using standard graphics (left) and ggplot2 (right).

Boxplots provide interesting and useful information on the distribution of a continuous variable, and are one of the best options when analyzing these variables.

Frequently, we want to obtain this type of descriptive graphs for sub-groups of our dataset, as we did for textual summaries. Conditioned plots provide this type of analysis. With the exception of the `boxplot()` function, this is not possible with the functions of standard graphics. Within the ggplot "ecosystem" this is usually achieved through the notion of faceting. Facets are variations of the same plot that are obtained with different subsets of a dataset. That is different from showing several plots on the same screen. Conditioned plots are designed with the goal of comparing behaviors across sub-groups and this imposes some design criteria that are not compatible with multiple individual plots shown on the same screen. For instance, the different plots should have the same exact ranges in the axes to facilitate their visual comparison. Moreover, as they are the same plots (just obtained with different data) we can take advantage of this to avoid repeating extra information (e.g. axes labels) and thus optimize the use of the available space.

It is worth mentioning that conditioned graphs are also possible through the use of the excellent **lattice** (Sarkar, 2010) package. This package implements most of the ideas behind Trellis graphics (Cleveland, 1993). We will not cover this package in the book as most facilities are also available within ggplot; still this is an important package for data visualization within R.

The first example we are going to show involves boxplots. Conditioned boxplots allow us to compare the distribution of a continuos variable along subsets defined by the values of another variable (typically nominal to constrain the number of subsets). For instance, the example in Figure 3.10 shows the distribution of the variable `Sepal.Length` for the plants of the different species. The figure was obtained with the following code,

```
> library(ggplot2)
> data(iris)
> ## Plot on the left (standard)
> boxplot(Sepal.Length ~ Species, iris, ylab="Sepal.Length")
> ## Plot on the right (ggplot2)
> ggplot(iris,aes(x=Species,y=Sepal.Length)) + geom_boxplot()
```

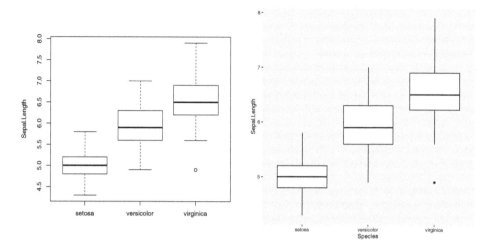

FIGURE 3.10: A conditioned boxplot using standard graphics (left) and ggplot2 (right).

The function `boxplot()` also accepts in the first argument a formula that specifies the variables to use on each axis of the condition boxplot. The second argument in this case is the source data.

For the ggplot graph we use the aesthetic mappings to provide the same type of information and then use again the `geom_boxplot()` function to obtain the plot.

The ggplot graphics system provides more sophisticated conditioning through facets. For instance, suppose we want to check the distribution of algal "a1" for the different types of rivers (in terms of water speed and river size), through a histogram. What we need are as many histograms as there are combinations of river size and speed. Figure 3.11 shows us these graphs. Note that in this case we do not show a solution with base graphics as this is not directly feasible. The plot in Figure 3.11 was obtained as follows,

```
> library(ggplot2)
> data(algae, package="DMwR2")
> ggplot(algae,aes(x=a1)) + geom_histogram() + facet_grid(size ~ speed)
```

The function `facet_grid()` allows us to set up a matrix of plots with each dimension of the matrix getting as many plots as there are values of the respective variable. For each cell of this matrix the graph specified before the facet is shown using only the subset of rows that have the respective values on the variables defining the grid.

Graphs involving two variables allow us to try to understand the relationship between their values across the observations in the dataset. The typical example of such plots is the scatterplot. Scatterplots represent each observation by a point whose coordinates are the values on two variables we want to analyze. In Figure 3.12 we have two scatterplots: one obtained with base graphics and the other with ggplot. The code to obtain them is as follows,

```
> library(ggplot2)
> data(iris)
> ## Plot on the left (standard)
> plot(iris$Sepal.Length,iris$Sepal.Width,
+       main="Relationship between Sepal Length and Width",
```

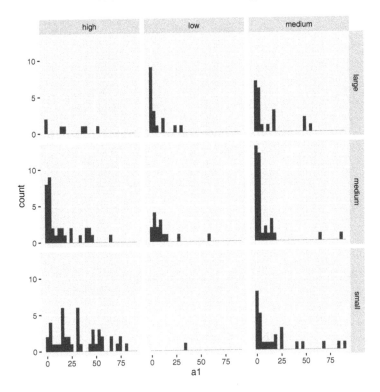

FIGURE 3.11: Conditioned histograms through facets.

```
+        xlab="Sepal Length", ylab="Sepal Width")
> ## Plot on the right (ggplot2)
> ggplot(iris,aes(x=Sepal.Length,y=Sepal.Width)) + geom_point() +
+        xlab("Sepal Length") + ylab("Sepal Width") +
+        ggtitle("Relationship between Sepal Length and Width")
```

The function **plot()** accepts as the first two parameters the vectors of X and Y coordinates of the points. The remaining arguments of the above call have obvious meaning.

For the ggplot graph the only novelty is the usage of the **geom_point()** function to draw points.

Looking at the scatterplots in Figure 3.12 there is no obvious relationship between the two variables we have used. The dots are rather widespread and there is no obvious conclusion of the type "if one variable has a certain pattern (e.g. upward trend) then the other variable shows this other pattern (e.g. decreases)".

As mentioned before, sometimes it is useful to split the analysis by subgroups defined by some nominal variable. With scatterplots there are several ways to achieve this effect. For instance, we could associate the color of the points to the values of a nominal variable, or even the size of these points, or any other aesthetic property (e.g the character used to represent the points). With the ggplot we can also use facets in addition to these aesthetic changes. Let us see some examples. In Figure 3.13 we show two illustrations using base graphics where we split the data by the values of a nominal variable,

```
> data(algae, package="DMwR2")
> ## Plot on the left (standard)
```

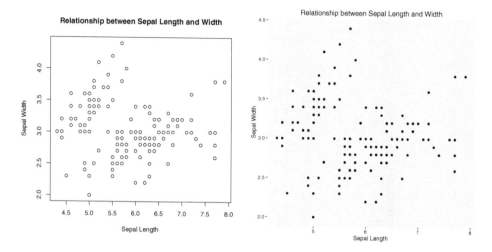

FIGURE 3.12: A scatterplot using standard graphics (left) and ggplot2 (right).

```
> plot(algae$a1, algae$a2, col=algae$season,
+        main="Relationship between A1 and A2 by Season",
+        xlab="A1", ylab="A2")
> legend("topright",legend=levels(algae$season),
+        col=palette()[1:nlevels(algae$season)],pch=1)
> ## Plot on the right (ggplot2)
> plot(algae$a4, algae$a7, pch=as.integer(algae$speed),
+        main="Relationship between A4 and A7 by River Speed",
+        xlab="A4", ylab="A7")
> legend("topright",legend=levels(algae$speed),
+        pch=1:nlevels(algae$season))
```

The function `plot()` accepts several parameters to control several aesthetic properties of the plot. The parameter `col` can be used to specify the color of the points. In the first call we set this to the value of the *season* variable. This may seem strange, as the values of this variable are not colors. In effect, R transforms these values into integers[25], and uses a standard palette to obtain the colors to use in the plot. This standard palette is obtained with the function `palette()` that returns the names of the colors. We have used the function `legend()` to create a legend in the plot to allow the user to interpret the graph. Creating the legend involves setting its position, the labels associated with each color, the colors and the characters used to plot the points. The second call to the `plot()` function is similar but this time we associate the values of the nominal variable to different plotting characters through the parameter `pch`.

This type of comparison becomes clearer with facets, although at the cost of space as we move from one single plot into as many plots as there are values of the nominal variables. For instance the left plot of Figure 3.13 could be obtained as follows using facets in ggplot,

```
> data(algae, package="DMwR2")
> ggplot(algae, aes(x=a1,y=a2,color=season)) + geom_point() + facet_wrap(~ season)
```

The result of this code is shown in Figure 3.14. Note that as each subset is shown in a

---

[25]Actually, any factor is stored internally as a set of integer codes, one associated with each value of the nominal variable.

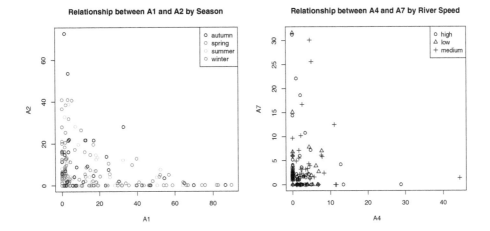

FIGURE 3.13: Two scatterplots with points differentiated by a nominal variable.

different plot we could even avoid the color (and thus the legend). The faceting was obtained with function `facet_wrap()`. This function allows you to indicate a nominal variable whose values will create a set of subplots that will be presented sequentially with reasonable wrapping around the screen space. Note that the specification of the legend is much simpler in ggplot. Although it is possible to tune its settings (like position and so on), the defaults are sufficiently reasonable for most setups. Finally, although we do not show the code for this, we could also obtain the graphs of Figure 3.13 with ggplot using adequate aesthetic mappings[26] and avoiding facets.

Some common pitfalls with scatterplots have to do with the scales used on the axes. If one of the variables has a few extreme values the interpretation of the graph may be difficult due to the fact that the scale of that variable needs to be stretched to cope with these extremes, which squashes all other values, making the analysis of their variability very difficult. In those cases we can either eliminate those outliers from our visualization or we can use logarithmic scales for the axes that suffer those problems. We will see an example of this in Chapter 6.

Another interesting concept related to scatterplots are scatterplot matrices. This involves producing a matrix of scatterplots which allows us to make several pairwise comparions among a set of variables. Obviously, if this set is large the analysis of each individual scatterplot becomes impractical and this is clearly not recommended.

Scatterplot matrices can be obtained with base graphics through function `pairs()`, as shown in Figure 3.15, produced with the following code,

```
> data(algae, package="DMwR2")
> pairs(algae[,12:16])
```

This function has many parameters that provide several extra functionalities, allowing for instance to have differentiated visualizations on the upper and lower parts of the matrix avoiding the repetition of the scatterplots. The same happens with the diagonal of the matrix as well as other elements. Several examples can be found on the help page of this function.

Package **GGally** (Schloerke et al., 2016) provides a series of interesting additions to

---

[26]More specifically, through the "color" and "shape" aesthetic properties.

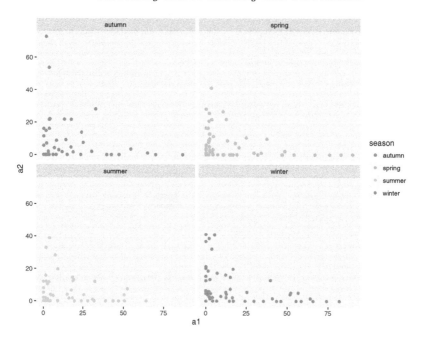

FIGURE 3.14: Faceting a scatterplot in ggplot.

the graphs available in package **ggplot2**. Among these are scatterplot matrices obtained with function **ggpairs()**. Figure 3.16 shows the result of this function produced with the following code,

```
> library(GGally)
> ggpairs(algae,columns=12:16)
```

This function will automatically take advantage of the symmetry of the graphs and use the upper part of the matrix to show the correlation values between each pair of variables. Moreover, in the diagonal we get a continuous approximation of the distribution of the respective variable. Once again, several other variants are possible, and in particular if the columns include nominal variables we get different types of plots on each cell of the matrix, as shown in Figure 3.17 that was obtained as follows,

```
> library(GGally)
> ggpairs(algae,columns=2:5)
```

As you can observe we get different types of statistical plots depending on the types of the variables in the respective matrix cell. Analyze the figure carefully and try to understand each of the graphs (they were already described in this section).

Another statistical graph provided by package **GGally** that also involves the visualization of several variables at the same time, is the parallel coordinate plot. These graphs try to show all observations of a dataset in a single plot, each being represented by a line. This is clearly not feasible for large datasets, but sometimes these graphs are very interesting for detecting strongly deviating cases in a dataset. Figure 3.18 shows an example of this type of graph where we try to compare the frequency values of all 200 observations of the **algae** dataset, with the color of the lines representing the season of the year when the respective water sample was collected. The following code obtained that figure,

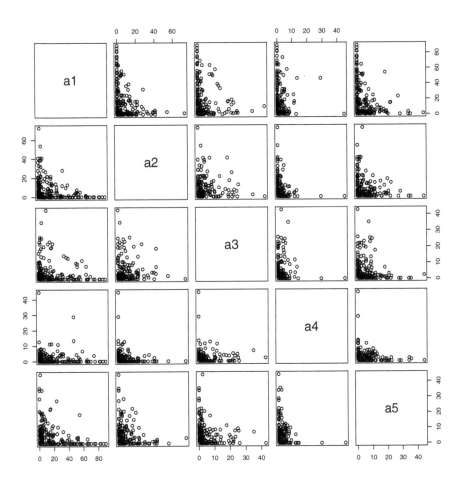

FIGURE 3.15: Scatterplot matrices with function pairs().

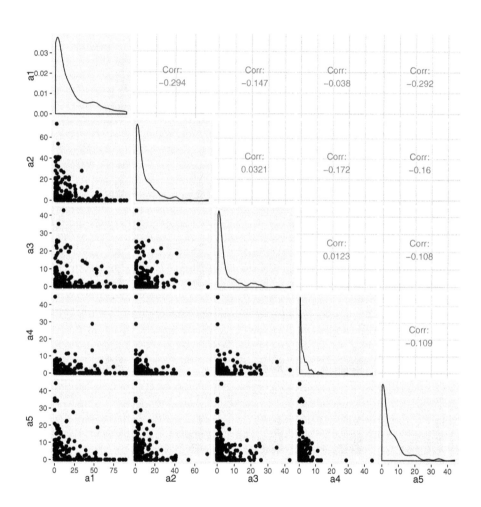

FIGURE 3.16: Scatterplot matrices with function ggpairs().

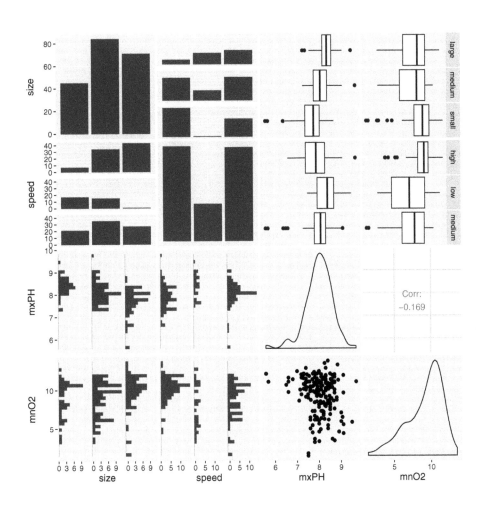

FIGURE 3.17: Scatterplot matrices involving nominal variables.

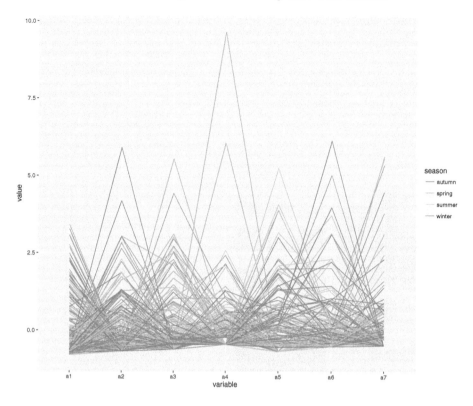

FIGURE 3.18: A parallel coordinates plot.

```
> library(GGally)
> ggparcoord(algae,columns=12:18,groupColumn="season")
```

In parallel coordinate plots the X axis represents the variables being used to characterize each row of the dataset that is represented as a line (with color depending on the season in this example). The Y axes represents the standardized (c.f. Equation 3.1, page 62) value of each variable. As we can see there are a few observations that clearly stand out from the others.

Further readings on data visualization

An excellent document on data visualization is the book by Cleveland (1993). A more formal follow-up of this work is the book *The Elements of Graphing Data* (Cleveland, 1995). A more recent and outstanding contribution is the *Handbook of Data Visualization* edited by Chen et al. (2008). Other nice books include Tufte (2001) and Steele and Iliinsky (2010). More related with R we have Murrell (2006), and Wilkinson (2005) that establish the theoretical grounds for the graphs implemented in package **ggplot2** that are described in Wickham (2009).

3.4.2   Dependency Modeling using Association Rules

Dependency modeling has to do with finding relationships between groups of variables. The most common approach to this task uses association rules that are also frequently associated with market basket analysis, due to the fact that one of the most common applications is exactly the analysis of market baskets of consumers in search for associations between products (i.e. products that are bought together frequently). The formalization of these tasks typically uses a terminology that is also related with market basket analysis. We have a set of transactions $\mathcal{D}$ (our dataset), each described as a set of itens, $i \in \mathcal{I}$ (basically binary variables that represent whether each item is present or not in the transaction). An association rule is defined as an implication $X \rightarrow Y$, where X and Y are sets of items (itemsets), i.e. $X, Y \subseteq \mathcal{I}$, where $X \neq \emptyset$, $Y \neq \emptyset$, and $X \cap Y = \emptyset$. Within an association rule X is usually known as the *antecedent*, while Y is known as the *consequent*.

Finding association rules requires a search process over an extremely large space of possible rules. This search is usually constrained by some minimal requirements on two important properties of a rule: the *support* and the *confidence*. The support of an itemset, $sup(X)$, is defined as the proportion of the transactions in the dataset that include this set of items, i.e. the estimated probability of the itemset, $P(X)$. In this context, the support of an association rule is defined as $sup(X \rightarrow Y) = sup(X \cup Y)$. The confidence of an association rule $X \rightarrow Y$ is defined as the proportion of times that the itemset Y is included in a transaction, when X is also included defined as $conf(X \rightarrow Y) = sup(X \cup Y)/sup(X)$, i.e. the estimated probability of Y given $X - P(Y|X)$. The support of an itemset is estimated by counting the number of times the itemset occurs in the available dataset of transactions.

Algorithms for finding association rules involve an iterative process that starts by: (i) finding all frequent itemsets that have a certain minimal support, *minsup*; and then (ii) generating candidate association rules from these frequent itemsets. For a task with k different items there are $2^k - 1$ distinct subsets, which makes brute force not a feasible approach for even small values of k. Moreover, counting the support of candidate itemsets can also be computationally very demanding depending on the size of the dataset (number of transactions). This means that association rule mining is only possible with clever algorithmic tricks that minimize this search effort.

The Apriori algorithm (Agrawal and Srikant, 1994) is among the most well-known implementations of association rules. The algorithm proceeds in an iterative fashion by producing itemsets of increasing size. Itemsets of size $k + 1$ are efficiently generated from itemsets of size k. The efficiency of this is ensured by imposing a lexicographical ordering among the itemsets of size k and using this ordering to generate the new itemsets with size $k+1$. Apriori uses other tricks to further reduce the computational requirements of this task, some of which take advantage of some well-known properties of itemsets, like for instance, the *downward closure property* that states that every non-empty subset of a frequent itemset (i.e. an itemset with $sup() > minsup$) is also frequent. After all itemsets are generated one needs to obtain their support, which can be very demanding depending on the size of the dataset. Once again Apriori makes use of hash tree data structures to improve the efficiency of the task.

There are many other algorithms for finding frequent itemsets in a dataset. Goethals and Zaki (2004) provide a nice comparison of some of the fastest implementations, among which there were the implementations of Apriori (Agrawal and Srikant, 1994) and Eclat (Zaki et al., 1997) algorithms by Borgelt (2003). Package **arules** (Hahsler et al., 2016) provides an interface to these implementations in R.

The second step of the algorithms for finding association rules consists of building them from the obtained set of frequent itemsets. The generated association rules are constrained by having a minimum support, *minsup*, and a minimum confidence, *minconf*. This consists of a two step process: (i) generate all non-empty subsets of each frequent itemset; and (ii) for each subset s of itemset i generate the association rule $s \rightarrow (i - s)$ if $sup(i)/sup(s) \geq minconf$.

In R the package **arules** can be used to find association rules. We will explore its facilities by applying it to the Boston housing dataset. Succinctly, this dataset has to do with a study carried out in 1978 concerning the median prices of housing in 506 residential areas of Boston, MA, USA. Originally one of the motivations of the study was to check if the pollution levels were having an impact on these prices. The dataset contains a series of descriptive socio-economic variables on each residential area and also the measurements of a pollutant (nitrogen oxides concentration), as well as characteristics of the houses in each area. There is also a "target" variable, the median price of the houses in each region (variable medv), whose values are supposed to somehow depend on the values of the other descriptor variables. The dataset contains both numeric and nominal variables. More details on their meaning can be obtained on the help page associated with the dataset available in package **MASS** (Venables and Ripley, 2002).

In order to be able to use this type of "standard" dataset with the **arules** package functions we need some pre-processing stages in order to transform the dataset into a "transactions" dataset, where each row is described by a series of binary variables (the items). An easy way to achieve this involves first discretizing the numeric variables into factors of ordered bins of the original values (c.f. Section 3.3.2.2, page 63). Once we do this we can associate each bin to a binary variable, such that a variable with k bins will be transformed into k binary variables. In the illustration below we have decided to arbitrarily discretize all numeric variables into 4 equal width bins. Obviously, in a real world scenario this should be done with the help of domain experts so that meaningful bins are used. Note that we will not apply this strategy to the variables chas and rad because although they are provided as integers in the original dataset, they are in effect nominal variables (ordinal in the case of rad). We have also treated the variable black differently. This variable is related to the proportion of black people in the region. However, as you may check using the help page of the dataset, the variable is a (non-linear) function of this proportion. We have "decoded" the values of this function so that the values of the nominal variable translate to the proportion of black people, which makes the rules more comprehensible. The following code prepares the data for usage with the **arules** package,

```
> library(arules)
> library(dplyr)
> data(Boston,package="MASS")
> b <- Boston
> b$chas <- factor(b$chas,labels=c("river","noriver"))
> b$rad <- factor(b$rad)
> b$black <- cut(b$black,breaks=4,labels=c(">31.5%","18.5-31.5%","8-18.5%","<8%"))
> discr <- function(x) cut(x,breaks=4, labels=c("low","medLow","medHigh","high"))
> b <- select(b,-one_of(c("chas","rad","black"))) %>%
+       mutate_each(funs(discr)) %>%
+       bind_cols(select(b,one_of(c("chas","rad","black"))))
> b <- as(b,"transactions")
> b

transactions in sparse format with
 506 transactions (rows) and
 59 items (columns)
```

We have used the facilities of **dplyr** to manipulate the dataset more easily. Try to understand what was done for discretizing the numeric variables into 4 bins. The last step involved transforming the data frame resulting from the discretization into a transactions dataset, which consists of creating the binary variables as mentioned above. The **arules** package allows us to do that easily through the function as() that can be used to convert a data frame into an object of class **transactions**. As you can observe, the resulting transactions dataset contains items (binary variables), instead of the original 14 variables.

The following code allows us to obtain some further information on this dataset, both textually and visually (resulting in Figure 3.19),

```
> summary(b)

transactions as itemMatrix in sparse format with
 506 rows (elements/itemsets/transactions) and
 59 columns (items) and a density of 0.2372881

most frequent items:
   crim=low chas=river  black=<8%     zn=low    dis=low     (Other)
        491        471        452        429        305        4936

element (itemset/transaction) length distribution:
sizes
 14
506

    Min. 1st Qu.  Median   Mean 3rd Qu.    Max.
      14      14      14      14      14      14

includes extended item information - examples:
       labels variables  levels
1    crim=low       crim    low
2 crim=medLow       crim medLow
3 crim=medHigh      crim medHigh

includes extended transaction information - examples:
   transactionID
1              1
2              2
3              3


> itemFrequencyPlot(b, support=0.3,cex.names=0.8)
```

Once we have a transactions dataset we can apply the Apriori algorithm to it. The following code does this, using some minimal support and confidence,

```
> ars <- apriori(b, parameter=list(support=0.025, confidence=0.75))

Apriori

Parameter specification:
 confidence minval smax arem  aval originalSupport support minlen maxlen
       0.75    0.1    1 none FALSE            TRUE   0.025      1     10
 target    ext
  rules FALSE

Algorithmic control:
 filter tree heap memopt load sort verbose
    0.1 TRUE TRUE  FALSE TRUE    2    TRUE

Absolute minimum support count: 12

set item appearances ...[0 item(s)] done [0.00s].
set transactions ...[59 item(s), 506 transaction(s)] done [0.00s].
sorting and recoding items ... [52 item(s)] done [0.00s].
```

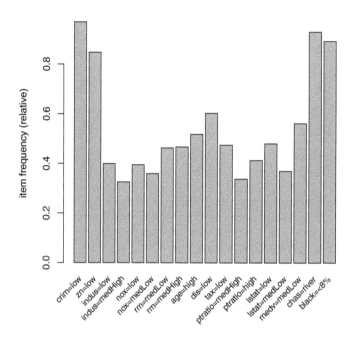

FIGURE 3.19: Some frequent itemsets for the Boston Housing dataset.

```
creating transaction tree ... done [0.00s].
checking subsets of size 1 2 3 4 5 6 7 8 9 10 done [0.07s].
writing ... [408638 rule(s)] done [0.08s].
creating S4 object  ... done [0.32s].

> ars

set of 408638 rules
```

You may wonder why we have used such low values of support. The reason is that we wanted to check if we could find some association rules involving the bins of the target variable (medv) corresponding to the cheapest and most expensive houses, and the latter are very few (see below) so to have chances of finding rules involving these houses we had to lower the minimum support.

```
> table(discr(Boston$medv))


   low  medLow medHigh    high
   116     284      74      32
```

As you see, and as is frequently the case[27], we obtained a large set of rules. Checking all these rules is obviously not feasible. Fortunately, package **arules** contains a series of functions that can help in querying an analyzing these rules. For instance, the following

---

[27]Though our parameter settings have not helped.

code shows us the top 5 rules in terms of confidence that have the regions with houses of highest median price on the right-hand side (rhs) of the rules,

```
> inspect(head(subset(ars, subset=rhs %in% "medv=high"),5,by="confidence"))
```

```
  lhs                   rhs            support confidence   lift
1 {rm=high,
   ptratio=low} => {medv=high} 0.02964427        1 15.8125
2 {rm=high,
   ptratio=low,
   lstat=low}  => {medv=high} 0.02964427        1 15.8125
3 {rm=high,
   ptratio=low,
   black=<8%}  => {medv=high} 0.02964427        1 15.8125
4 {crim=low,
   rm=high,
   ptratio=low} => {medv=high} 0.02964427        1 15.8125
5 {rm=high,
   ptratio=low,
   lstat=low,
   black=<8%}  => {medv=high} 0.02964427        1 15.8125
```

We have used the **subset()** method applied to the set of association rules. The method for this class of objects includes a parameter (**subset**) that allows us to indicate a logical condition for filtering the rules. This logical condition may involve tests on the left- and right-hand sides of the rules (*lhs* and *rhs*), and also on the quality metrics that the package produces to qualify each rule. These are the support and confidence, but also the *lift*. The lift of an association rule is given by $lift(X \to Y) = sup(X \cup Y)/(sup(X)sup(Y))$. The higher the value of the lift the stronger the association. It is based on the fact that if the occurrence of the itemset X is independent from that of itemset Y, then $P(X \cup Y) = P(X)P(Y)$. Otherwise there exists some form of dependency or correlation between X and Y. So the higher the value of $lift(X \to Y)$, the higher the confidence on the existence of this dependency relationship. Note that if the value of the lift is negative, the itemsets are said to be negatively correlated, which means that the occurrence of X is likely to lead to the absence of Y. For instance, if $lift(X \to Y) = 4$ this has the interpretation that the occurrence of X will increase the likelihood of Y by a factor of 4. The function **head()** applied to the result allows us to pick the top x rules according to some of the quality metrics (we are selecting the top 5 in terms of confidence). Finally, the **inspect()** function provides a textual representation of the rules together with their metrics.

The rules all seem to have an intuitive and sociologically expected interpretation (remember this is data from the 1970s). We always see itemsets including houses with a large number of rooms and located in areas with a low pupil-teacher ratio. Other items associated with these extremely expensive houses include a low percentage of lower status population, low crime rate and low percentage of black people. We should remark that all these 5 rules have 100% confidence, meaning that every time the left-hand side happens the right-hand side is true.

We may carry out a similar analysis for rules involving lower median price regions on the right-hand side,

```
> inspect(head(subset(ars, subset=rhs %in% "medv=low"),5,by="confidence"))
```

```
  lhs                   rhs            support confidence   lift
1 {nox=medHigh,
```

```
     lstat=medHigh} => {medv=low} 0.05928854          1 4.362069
2 {nox=medHigh,
   lstat=medHigh,
   rad=24}         => {medv=low} 0.05928854          1 4.362069
3 {nox=medHigh,
   tax=high,
   lstat=medHigh} => {medv=low} 0.05928854          1 4.362069
4 {indus=medHigh,
   nox=medHigh,
   lstat=medHigh} => {medv=low} 0.05928854          1 4.362069
5 {nox=medHigh,
   ptratio=high,
   lstat=medHigh} => {medv=low} 0.05928854          1 4.362069
```

Once again we find expected items in the left-hand side. However, it is interesting to remark, in the context of the original goals of this study, that above average pollution level appears in the rules.

Again, in the context of the goals of the study, we may wish to look at the rules that involve high pollution levels either in the left- or right-hand sides of the rules,

```
> inspect(head(subset(ars, subset=lhs %in% "nox=high" | rhs %in% "nox=high"),
+              5,by="confidence"))
```

```
   lhs              rhs              support    confidence lift
38 {nox=high} => {indus=medHigh} 0.04743083 1          3.066667
40 {nox=high} => {age=high}      0.04743083 1          1.931298
41 {nox=high} => {dis=low}       0.04743083 1          1.659016
42 {nox=high} => {zn=low}        0.04743083 1          1.179487
44 {nox=high} => {crim=low}      0.04743083 1          1.030550
```

Apriori has not found any rule with this high pollution level on the right-hand side. However, when this occurs we observe a series of other interesting items occurring, like industrialization, lower levels of residential areas, or old houses. The association with a low crime rate may seem strange but maybe can be explained by the fact that crime will tend to happen in areas with more wealthy people/houses (still we should note that the lift of this rule is rather low).

Package **arulesViz** (Hahsler and Chelluboina, 2016) provides a series of interesting facilities to visualize the association rules produced by package **arules**. For instance, we can have a visual overview of the main quality metrics of all produced rules as follows,

```
> library(arulesViz)
> plot(ars)
```

The result of this code is shown in Figure 3.20. The `plot` method provided by this package includes many parameters that allow to obtain several interesting variants of this plot. In particular, for interactive exploration of the graph, you can add the argument `interactive=TRUE` to the above call, which allows you to use the mouse to select points (rules) in the plot that you which to see, with the corresponding lhs and rhs of the selected rule appearing in the R terminal — try it.

Another type of exploration that is possible with this package are the so-called matrix representations of the rules. These plots show the rules antecedents in the X axis and the consequents in the Y axis. At each intersection of lhs and rhs we have the corresponding quality measure (e.g. lift). The following example, whose result is shown in Figure 3.21, should illustrate this concept,

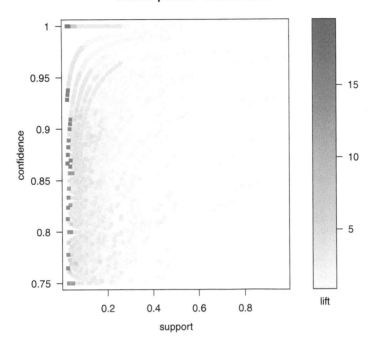

FIGURE 3.20: Support, confidence and lift of the rules.

```
> somerules <- subset(ars,
+               subset=rhs %in% c("medv=high","medv=medHigh") & confidence>0.75)
> plot(somerules, method="matrix", measure="lift")
```

In the figure the lhs and rhs are referred to using numbers to avoid filling too much of the graphs. The association of the numbers with the respective itemsets is shown in the R console when you call the `plot()` function.

Yet another interesting visualization is to look at a small subset of the rules as graphs. For instance, the following code obtains a graph (Figure 3.22) of the rules involving expensive houses on the rhs whose confidence is higher than 95%,

```
> somerules <- subset(ars, subset=rhs %in% "medv=high" & confidence > 0.95)
> plot(somerules, method="graph", control=list(type="itemsets"))
```

Package **arulesViz** includes several other interesting ways of exploring the association rules visually. Check the vignette accompanying the package for more examples.

Further readings on association rules

Chapter 4 of the book by Aggarwal (2015) provides an excellent and extensive overview of the area of association rule mining. The same happens in Chapter 6 of the book by Han et al. (2012). More related with R implementations the vignettes accompanying both the **arules** and the **arulesViz** packages are very good sources of information.

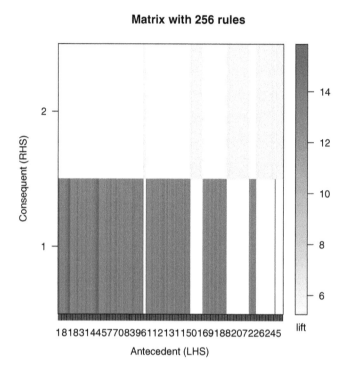

FIGURE 3.21: A matrix representation of the rules show the lift.

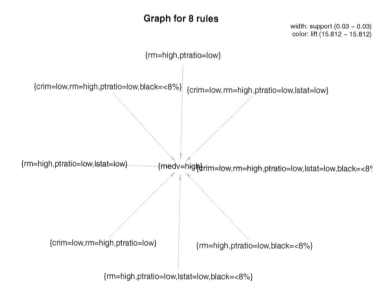

FIGURE 3.22: A graph representation of a subset of rules.

3.4.3 Clustering

Clustering has to do with finding similar sub-groups of the rows in a dataset. In this context, at the basis of clustering is the definition of *row similarity*. Similarity is usually asserted through the definition of some *distance function* between any pair of rows.

The results of a clustering method is usually a *partitioning* of the data observations in a set of groups (the clusters). Cases inside each group are supposed to be very similar to each other and at the same time rather different from cases in other groups. A typical practical application of clustering methods is to perform customer segmentation given a dataset containing information about the customers of some company. Nevertheless, clustering has many other applications across a wide range of domains.

3.4.3.1 Measures of Dissimilarity

Given the goals of clustering it is of utmost importance to be able to correctly assert the (dis)similarity between any pair of cases of a dataset. This issue is in effect relevant to other data mining tasks, as we will see in other sections of this book. The dissimilarity of two cases is usually calculated by a distance function. These functions receive as arguments two cases (two vectors of feature values) and return a distance value — the higher, the more different the cases are supposed to be. Distance functions use the information of the values in the variables describing the cases to come up with this score. In this context, there are other issues that become important to avoid unwanted biases in the distance calculation. These include, among others, issues of the different scales of the variables, the relevance of the variables, the type of the variables, etc.

The definition of the distance function is often a crucial step in the application of data mining models. Incorrect distance functions may easily lead to biased results of the posterior modeling stages with potentially serious consequences to the conclusions drawn from the data mining workflow.

For numeric variables one of the most common choices is the Euclidean distance, defined as,

$$d(\mathbf{x}, \mathbf{y}) = \sqrt{\sum_{i=1}^{d} (x_i - y_i)^2} \tag{3.11}$$

where x_i is the value of case $\mathbf{x}$ on variable i

This function is in effect a special case of the general Minkowski distance function[28],

$$d(\mathbf{x}, \mathbf{y}) = \left(\sum_{i=1}^{d} |x_i - y_i|^p \right)^{1/p} \tag{3.12}$$

If $p = 2$ in the above equation we have the Euclidean distance, while for $p = 1$ we have what is usually known as the Manhattan distance.

In R these, and other distance functions applicable to numeric vectors, are implemented in the function `dist()`, as shown in the following simple examples,

```
> set.seed(1234)
> randDat <- matrix(rnorm(50), nrow=5)
> dist(randDat) # Euclidean distance (default)
```

---

[28] Also known as the L_p norm.

```
            1          2          3          4
2 4.261667
3 4.038030 2.060117
4 3.456732 3.726399 4.037978
5 5.307253 4.415046 4.111230 4.814393

> dist(randDat, method="manhattan")

             1          2          3          4
2 11.382197
3 10.016795   4.536827
4  9.887932   8.845512   8.829131
5 14.683770  10.617871   9.091241 11.362705

> dist(randDat, method="minkowski", p=4)

            1          2          3          4
2 2.899494
3 2.875467 1.653824
4 2.208297 2.814135 3.453336
5 3.488531 3.192217 3.398721 3.643788
```

For nominal variables typically one simply distinguishes whether the values on each feature are equal or not, though some specialized functions exist for binary variables. Function vegdist() from package **vegan** (Oksanen et al., 2016) contains a larger set of distance functions and also allows the specification of further metrics through the use of function designdist().

The more challenging setups occur when we have mixed mode data, i.e. datasets that include both nominal and numeric features. One of the main challenges of this type of data is the question of how to make sure the importance given to the differences in the values of both nominal and numeric variables is equivalent. A possible solution to this problem is the following distance function,

$$d(\mathbf{x}, \mathbf{y}) = \sum_{i=1}^{d} \delta_i(x_i, y_i) \tag{3.13}$$

where,

$$\delta_i(v_1, v_2) = \begin{cases} 1 & \text{if } i \text{ is nominal and } v_1 \neq v_2 \\ 0 & \text{if } i \text{ is nominal and } v_1 = v_2 \\ \frac{|v_1 - v_2|}{range(i)} & \text{if } i \text{ is numeric} \end{cases}$$

This distance function makes sure all differences (either in numeric or nominal variables) have a score in the interval $[0, 1]$. It does this by normalizing the differences in the numeric variables by their range. Still, this is not very satisfactory if any of these variables has outliers. This distance function is implemented in function daisy() of package **cluster** (Maechler et al., 2015). The function also allows the specification of weights to be used in the distance calculation that enables you to assign different importance to the feature differences (the default is to use equal weights).

3.4.3.2   Clustering Methods

The are many clustering methods some of which follow quite different approaches to the general problem of finding groups of the cases in a dataset. Usually, we can classify the different methods into one of the following categories:

- Partitioning methods
- Hierarchical methods
- Density-based methods
- Grid-based methods

Partitioning methods receive as input a dataset and a target number of clusters k. They use the information on the distances between the cases in the dataset to obtain the k "best" groups according to a certain criterion. This is normally an iterative process where at each step some of the cases may be moved between the clusters in order to improve the overall quality of the solution.

Contrary to partitioning methods, hierarchical methods obtain a hierarchy of alternative clustering solutions, known as a dendrogram. These methods can follow a divisive or an agglomerative approach to the task of building the hierarchy. The former starts with a single group containing all the observations and then it iteratively keeps splitting one of the current groups into two separate clusters according to some criterion, until n groups with a single observation are obtained, where n is the number of cases in the dataset. Agglomerative methods, on the other hand, proceed from n groups to a single group. At each iteration the two most similar groups are selected for being merged.

Methods based on the distances between cases have limitations on the "shape" of the clusters they can obtain. Density-based methods try to overcome these limitations through the notion of density. These methods try to find regions of the feature space where cases are packed together with high density, and because of this they are frequently also used as a way of finding outliers as these are by definition rather different from other cases and thus should not belong to these high-density regions of the features space.

Finally, grid-based methods obtain clusters using a division of the feature space into a grid-like structure. Compared to the other approaches this leads to high computational efficiency as the clustering operations are performed within the cells of this grid. This approach to the computational complexity of building clusters is often integrated with hierarchical or density-based methods.

In our necessarily succinct description of clustering methods we will focus on the first three approaches.

Partitioning a dataset into a set of k groups requires the specification of some sort of criteria that allows us to evaluate each candidate solution that is tried in the iterative process by following these methods. Two important criteria that can be used to evaluate a clustering solution are: (i) compactness — how similar are the cases on each cluster; and (ii) separation — how different is a cluster from the others.

Having chosen a certain criterion that assigns a score for each cluster/group of cases, $h(c)$, and given a clustering solution formed by a set of k clusters, $C = c_1, c_2, \cdots, c_k$, we can obtain the overall score of this clustering, $H(C, k)$, in several ways, among which we can include the following common solutions,

- $H(C, k) = \sum_{c \in C} \frac{h(c)}{|C|}$
- $H(C, k) = \min_{c \in C} h(c)$
- $H(C, k) = \max_{c \in C} h(c)$

In terms of evaluating each cluster, for numeric data only, common criteria include,

- The sum of squares to the center of each cluster

$$h(c) = \sum_{x \in c} \sum_{i=1}^{d} (v_{x,i} - \hat{v}_i^c)^2 \tag{3.14}$$

where $\hat{v}_i^c = \frac{1}{|c|} \sum_{j=1}^{|c|} v_{j,i}$

- The L_1 measure with respect to the centroid of the cluster

$$h(c) = \sum_{x \in c} \sum_{i=1}^{d} |v_{x,i} - \tilde{v}_i^c| \tag{3.15}$$

where $\tilde{v}_i^c$ is the median value of variable i in the cluster c

Using an approach similar to that used in Equation 3.13 we can easily come up with similar formulations when using mixed-mode datasets.

One of the simplest and most well-known partitioning methods is the k-means clustering algorithm. This algorithm is very simple and consists, in its simplest form, of,

- Initialize the centers of the k groups to a set of randomly chosen observations

- Repeat

  - Allocate each observation to the group whose center is nearest
  - Re-calculate the center of each group

- Until the groups are stable

A few observations on this simple clustering method. The method is based on distance calculations, and typically Euclidean distance is the used function. This algorithm results in maximizing the inter-cluster dissimilarity, i.e. the cluster separation. However, the word maximizing must be taken with care as there are no guarantees of an optimal clustering solution. Moreover, using different starting points as cluster centers may lead the algorithm to converge to a different solution. Obviously, in the research literature we can find some approaches that try to overcome some of these limitations.

In R the k-means algorithm is implemented in function `kmeans()`. The following is a simple illustrative example of applying this function to the *Iris* dataset ignoring the target variable. As we know that there are 3 species of these plants, assuming we did not know the species information for the 150 plants, we could try to use a clustering algorithm to form 3 groups with these plants, expecting that the algorithm would allocate to each cluster plants of the same species.

```
> set.seed(1234) # setting a seed for the random number generator
> data(iris)
> ir3 <- kmeans(iris[,-5], centers=3, iter.max=200) # not using Species info.
> ir3

K-means clustering with 3 clusters of sizes 50, 62, 38

Cluster means:
  Sepal.Length Sepal.Width Petal.Length Petal.Width
1     5.006000    3.428000     1.462000    0.246000
2     5.901613    2.748387     4.393548    1.433871
3     6.850000    3.073684     5.742105    2.071053

Clustering vector:
  [1] 1 1 1 1 1 1 1 1 1 1 1 1 1 1 1 1 1 1 1 1 1 1 1 1 1 1 1 1 1 1 1 1 1 1 1
 [36] 1 1 1 1 1 1 1 1 1 1 1 1 1 1 1 2 2 3 2 2 2 2 2 2 2 2 2 2 2 2 2 2 2 2 2
 [71] 2 2 2 2 2 2 3 2 2 2 2 2 2 2 2 2 2 2 2 2 2 2 2 2 2 2 2 3 2 3 3 3
[106] 3 2 3 3 3 3 3 3 2 2 3 3 3 3 2 3 2 3 2 3 3 2 2 3 3 3 3 3 2 3 3 3 3 2 3
```

```
[141] 3 3 2 3 3 3 2 3 3 2

Within cluster sum of squares by cluster:
[1] 15.15100 39.82097 23.87947
 (between_SS / total_SS =  88.4 %)

Available components:

[1] "cluster"      "centers"      "totss"        "withinss"
[5] "tot.withinss" "betweenss"    "size"         "iter"
[9] "ifault"
```

The object returned by the function contains a series of useful information, among which is a vector with as many elements as there are cases in the dataset, with the number of the cluster assigned to each case.

One of the key issues with any clustering algorithm is the question of how to decide if an obtained solution is good or not, i.e. *cluster validation*. This question becomes even more relevant when we face a new problem and we have a series of alternative clustering methods that we can apply to the available data. Cluster validation is related to several questions one may ask once we get a solution from a method, like for instance: (i) is the obtained group structure random? or (ii) what is the "right" number of clusters for this dataset?

Validation measures are usually split into internal and external metrics. External measures require the existence of information that was not available when obtaining the clustering solution, that can be used to compare against the structure obtained by the clustering algorithm. For instance, in the above example with the *Iris* dataset, this external information could consist of the class labels of each of the 150 plants. This information was not used in the clustering process and we could use it as a kind of ground truth to validate the results of the *k*-means method. The following code illustrates this idea,

```
> table(ir3$cluster, iris$Species)


    setosa versicolor virginica
  1     50          0         0
  2      0         48        14
  3      0          2        36

> cm <- table(ir3$cluster, iris$Species)
> 1-sum(diag(cm))/sum(cm)

[1] 0.1066667
```

As you can observe, the clustering that was obtained assigns 10.7% of the plants to the wrong cluster, at least according to the class label. While the first cluster is clearly right in that it contains all **setosa** plants, the other two clusters mix the remaining species (particularly cluster 2).

While external validation measures are interesting they are often not applicable in practice. In effect, having access to this sort of class label is not very frequent in real problems, because having them reduces the need for the clustering step in the first place.

Internal validation metrics only use information available during the clustering process. They essentially evaluate the cluster quality from the point of view of issues like cluster compactness or cluster separation, among others. A typical example of such a metric is the Silhouette coefficient (Rousseeuw, 1987). This metric is calculated as follows. For each

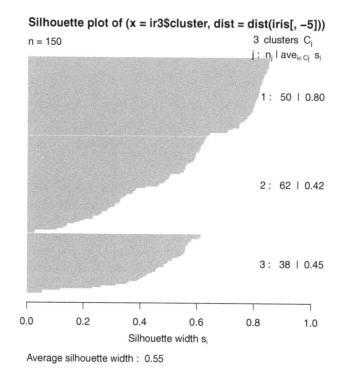

FIGURE 3.23: A silhouette plot.

observation i we start by obtaining the average distance to all objects in the same group as i and call this average a_i. For each observation we also calculate the average distance to the cases belonging to the other groups to which this observation does not belong, calling this value b_i. Finally, the *silhouette coefficient* of any observation, s_i, is equal to

$$s_i = \frac{b_i - a_i}{\max(a_i, b_i)} \tag{3.16}$$

The coefficient takes values between -1 and 1. Ideally all objects should have positive values (meaning $a_i < b_i$), and the a_i's should be near zero. This metric is implemented in R through function `silhouette()` available in package **cluster** (Maechler et al., 2015). The following is an illustration of its usage on the results obtained above with the k-means algorithm,

```
> library(cluster)
> s <- silhouette(ir3$cluster, dist(iris[,-5]))
```

Note that the function requires the distance matrix of the dataset used in the clustering process. The result of this function can be given to the `plot()` function producing the output shown in Figure 3.23,

```
> plot(s)
```

As you may observe in the figure, the overall average silhouette coefficient of all 150 cases is 0.55, which is a reasonable value (the nearer 1 the better). We can also observe that the best cluster is number 1, with an average silhouette of 0.8, while the other two clusters have lower scores. This clearly confirms what we have observed when using the true class labels for an external evaluation of the results.

The silhouette coefficient can be used to compare different clustering solutions or even to select the "ideal" number of clusters for a given method. The following code illustrates this idea with the k-means method applied to the *Iris* dataset. We check for the best number of groups in the interval $[2, 6]$,

```
> set.seed(1234)
> d <- dist(iris[,-5])
> avgS <- c()
> for(k in 2:6) {
+     cl <- kmeans(iris[,-5],centers=k,iter.max=200)
+     s <- silhouette(cl$cluster,d)
+     avgS <- c(avgS,mean(s[,3]))
+ }
> data.frame(nClus=2:6,Silh=avgS)

  nClus      Silh
1     2 0.6810462
2     3 0.5528190
3     4 0.4152074
4     5 0.4609502
5     6 0.3712570
```

As we can observe, the maximum average silhouette is obtained with 2 groups.

There are many other internal and external validation measures of the clustering results. A good survey of this important topic can be found in Chapter 23 of the book by Aggarwal and Reddy (2014). Package **clv** (Nieweglowski, 2013) contains an extensive list of both internal and external measures that you may wish to try.

Another widely used partitioning algorithm is the k-medoids method. This is a slight variation of the ideas used in the k-means method, but revolving around the medoids as cluster centers instead of means, which leads to better robustness against outliers. Moreover, instead of squared distances the implementations of this algorithm typically use sums of dissimilarities as search criterion. The method is implemented in the function **pam()** of the **cluster** package. The following is a similar application to the *Iris* dataset,

```
> library(cluster)
> set.seed(1234)
> pc <- pam(iris[,-5],k=3)
> (cm <- table(pc$clustering, iris$Species))

    setosa versicolor virginica
  1     50          0         0
  2      0         48        14
  3      0          2        36

> 100*(1-sum(diag(cm))/sum(cm))

[1] 10.66667

> pc$silinfo$avg.width

[1] 0.552819
```

As you can observe, the **pam()** function already provides the average silhouette coefficient so in this case we do not need to use the function to calculate it (though we could do it anyway). In this particular example the results obtained with the k-medoids algorithm were the same as with the k-means.

A short remark on the computational cost of these methods. For large datasets these methods can be computationally too demanding. Package **cluster** contains a more efficient implementation of **pam()** in the function **clara()**. This is achieved through a sampling mechanism that leads to the application of **pam()** to smaller samples, with the results being aggregated in the end (check the complete details in the help page of **clara()**).

Finally, a note on the issue of determining the number of clusters for these methods. We have seen a simple way of searching for this "ideal" number using a simple **for()** loop. We could apply the same strategy to the **pam()** function. However, in package **fpc** (Hennig, 2015) we have function **pamk()** that does that with more flexibility in terms of options. This function allows us to supply a range of possible number of clusters and then we can use different criteria (including the silhouette coefficient) to search for the best solution, using either **pam()** or **clara()**. Here is a simple example of its usage,

```
> library(fpc)
> data(iris)
> sol <- pamk(iris[,-5], krange=2:10, criterion="asw", usepam=TRUE)
> sol

$pamobject
Medoids:
        ID Sepal.Length Sepal.Width Petal.Length Petal.Width
[1,]   8          5.0         3.4          1.5         0.2
[2,] 127          6.2         2.8          4.8         1.8
Clustering vector:
  [1] 1 1 1 1 1 1 1 1 1 1 1 1 1 1 1 1 1 1 1 1 1 1 1 1 1 1 1 1 1 1 1 1 1 1 1
 [36] 1 1 1 1 1 1 1 1 1 1 1 1 1 1 1 2 2 2 2 2 2 2 2 2 2 2 2 2 2 2 2 2 2 2 2
 [71] 2 2 2 2 2 2 2 2 2 2 2 2 2 2 2 2 2 2 2 2 2 2 2 2 2 1 2 2 2 2 2 2 2 2 2
[106] 2 2 2 2 2 2 2 2 2 2 2 2 2 2 2 2 2 2 2 2 2 2 2 2 2 2 2 2 2 2 2 2 2 2 2
[141] 2 2 2 2 2 2 2 2 2
Objective function:
    build      swap
0.9901187 0.8622026


Available components:
 [1] "medoids"   "id.med"    "clustering" "objective"  "isolation"
 [6] "clusinfo"  "silinfo"   "diss"       "call"       "data"

$nc
[1] 2


$crit
 [1] 0.0000000 0.6857882 0.5528190 0.4896972 0.4867481 0.4703951 0.3390116
 [8] 0.3318516 0.2918520 0.2918482
```

The output of the function is a list with 3 components: **pamobject** with the object resulting from running **pam()** (or **clara()**) with the "optimal" number of clusters; **nc** with this number of clusters; and **crit** with the scores of the internal validation metric used for the different values of the number of clusters. In the above example we have tried from 2 to 10 and selected the best using the average silhouette width ("asw").

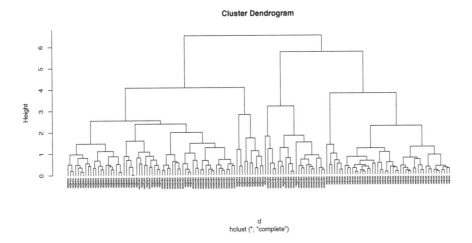

FIGURE 3.24: The dendrogram for *Iris*.

We will now shift our attention to **hierarchical clustering** methods. As mentioned before, their goal is to obtain a hierarchy of possible solutions ranging from one single group to n groups, where n is the number of observations in the dataset.

Agglomerative hierarchical clustering methods start with as many groups as there are cases in the dataset. At each iteration the pair of groups that is most similar is merged into a single group. Several criteria exist to select this pair of groups. The *single linkage* criterion measures the difference between two groups by the smallest distance between any two observations in each group. The *complete linkage* method measures this difference using the largest distance, instead. On the other hand, the *average linkage* uses the average distance between any two observations of the two groups. Several other criteria exist, but the general idea is similar: select the pair of groups that are more likely to be similar to each other and merge them into a single group at the next level of the hierarchy.

This type of clustering is implemented in function `hclust()`. This function takes in the first argument the distance matrix of the dataset, while the second argument specifies the criterion used to select the two groups for merging at each step. The following is an example of its application,

```
> d <- dist(scale(iris[,-5]))
> h <- hclust(d)
```

The first statement obtains the distance matrix of the cases. We have standardized the data before to avoid different scale effects. The second statement obtains the clustering. In this call we have not specified the merging method, thus accepting its default value that is *complete linkage*. The resulting hierarchy, usually known as a dendrogram, can be shown by applying the function `plot()` to the object resulting from the call to `hclust()`,

```
> plot(h,hang=-0.1,labels=iris[["Species"]],cex=0.5)
```

The result of this code is shown in Figure 3.24. We have used a negative value for the `hang` parameter so that the labels are all at the bottom, and then used the `labels` parameter to show the actual species of the plants instead of the respective row numbers (the default).

A dendrogram corresponds to a set of possible clustering solutions. Cutting this hierarchy at different heights corresponds to selecting a particular number of clusters (i.e. a solution), depending on how many vertical lines of the dendrogram are crossed by the cut.

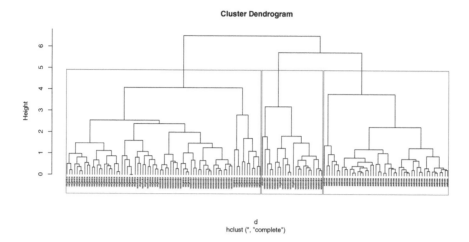

FIGURE 3.25: The dendrogram cut at three clusters.

For instance, suppose we want three clusters, we would proceed as follows,

```
> clus3 <- cutree(h, 3)
> (cm <- table(clus3, iris$Species))


clus3 setosa versicolor virginica
    1     49          0         0
    2      1         21         2
    3      0         29        48

> 100*(1-sum(diag(cm))/sum(cm))

[1] 21.33333
```

The function `cutree()` can be used to perform the cutting by specifying the desired number of groups. The result of this function is a vector with the number of the cluster to which each observation was assigned, according to the dendrogram cut. In the above example we observe that this particular solution is considerably worse than the previous ones we have tried, at least from the perspective of the external validation provided by the class labels.

This cutting of the dendrogram can also be represented graphically thanks to the function `rect.hclust()`. Figure 3.25 shows this effect, and was obtained with the following code,

```
> plot(h,hang=-0.1,labels=iris[["Species"]],cex=0.5)
> rect.hclust(h,k=3)
```

The function `rect.hclust()` was used to draw in the dendrogram the actual cutting corresponding to three clusters.

Once again, and given the variants we may consider for applying this clustering algorithm, we may question which is the best for a given problem. In the example we are going to show we assume the lack of external information and resort to the silhouette coefficient to compare a few of these variants,

```
> set.seed(1234)
> d <- dist(scale(iris[,-5]))
> methds <- c('complete','single','average')
> avgS <- matrix(NA,ncol=3,nrow=5,
+               dimnames=list(2:6,methds))
> for(k in 2:6)
+   for(m in seq_along(methds)) {
+     h <- hclust(d,meth=methds[m])
+     c <- cutree(h,k)
+     s <- silhouette(c,d)
+     avgS[k-1,m] <- mean(s[,3])
+   }
> avgS
```

```
   complete    single   average
2 0.4408121 0.5817500 0.5817500
3 0.4496185 0.5046456 0.4802669
4 0.4106071 0.4067465 0.4067465
5 0.3520630 0.3424089 0.3746013
6 0.3106991 0.2018867 0.3248248
```

According to this simple example it seems the best scores are obtained with the single and average linkage methods. Please note that this experiment is far from exhaustive, being simply another illustration of the use of the silhouette coefficient for selecting a clustering solution when no external information is available.

Divisive hierarchical methods proceed in a top down fashion to build the dendrogram. They are less common than agglomerative methods. In package **cluster** we may find an example of these methods — the DIANA algorithm. This algorithm selects the cluster to be split in two during the iterative process of building the dendrogram by looking at the cluster diameter. This diameter is estimated as the largest dissimilarity between any two observations of the cluster. Once this group is identified, the observation in that group with the largest average dissimilarity to the other members of the group is selected. Then all observations are allocated to either the cluster of this selected observation or to the "old" group (represented by its center), depending on which one is nearest. Function `diana()` from package **cluster** implements this algorithm. Here is another simple illustration of its usage,

```
> di <- diana(iris[,-5], metric='euclidean', stand=TRUE)
> di3 <- cutree(di, 3)
> (cm <- table(di3, iris$Species))
```

```
di3 setosa versicolor virginica
  1     50          0         0
  2      0         11        33
  3      0         39        17
```

```
> 100*(1-sum(diag(cm))/sum(cm))
```

```
[1] 48
```

The function can internally calculate the distance between the observations, which in the above example was done through Euclidian distance after standardization of the variables. Alternatively, it is also possible to supply a dissimilarity matrix in the first argument. The results seem rather bad in terms of the external validation. However, looking closer we can observe a problem with the procedure we have been using. In effect, we have been assuming that the order of the clusters corresponds to the order of values in the target variable. In this case, looking at the numbers in the confusion matrix it is obvious that cluster 2 should be regarded as the cluster of the `virginica` species, and cluster 3 of the `versicolor` species. This means we should swap rows 2 and 3 before calculating the error,

```
> cm <- cm[c(1,3,2),]
> 100*(1-sum(diag(cm))/sum(cm))
```

```
[1] 18.66667
```

As expected, this leads to a considerably lower error.

We will now mention a **density-based clustering** method. These methods search for regions of the input space where cases are packed tightly. An instance of this idea is the DBSCAN algorithm (Ester et al., 1996). The key idea of this method is to estimate the density of a single observation as the number of observations that are within a certain radius of the observation, the radius being a key parameter of the method known as the reachability distance. Based on this idea the method defines three classes of observations in the provided dataset: (i) *core points* are cases that have a number of observations within its radius above a certain threshold; (ii) *border points* that have a number of observations within their radius that does not reach that threshold but are within the radius of a core point; and (iii) *noise points* that do not have enough observations within their radius nor are sufficiently close to any core point. Based on the classification of all cases into one of these three classes, the algorithm starts by removing the noise points into a separate cluster that contains cases that are too different up to a point of not making sense to use them in the cluster formation. These cases can actually be regarded as outliers from the perspective of this method. Then all core points that are within a certain distance of each other are put together in the same cluster, leading to a set of clusters containing at this stage core points that are nearer to each other. Finally, all border points are allocated to the cluster to which they are nearer. This means that, contrary to the methods we have seen before, this algorithm does not require the user to specify the number of clusters. In effect, it is a result of the method to determine the "correct" number of groups according to the parameter settings selected by the user.

Function `dbscan()` from package **fpc** (Hennig, 2015) contains an implementation of this density-based clustering algorithm. The function contains two main parameters (`eps` and `MinPts`) that control the reachability distance and the minimum number of observations within this distance for a case to be considered a core point, respectively. The following is a simple illustration of the application of this method to the *Iris* dataset,

```
> library(fpc)
> d <- scale(iris[,-5])
> db <- dbscan(d, eps=0.9, MinPts=5)
> db
```

```
dbscan Pts=150 MinPts=5 eps=0.9
          0  1  2
border  4  1  4
seed    0 48 93
total   4 49 97
```

```
> table(db$cluster,iris$Species)
```

	setosa	versicolor	virginica
0	1	0	3
1	49	0	0
2	0	50	47

Cluster 0 contains the set of observations that the algorithm has decided to tag as too different from the remaining cases. With the parameter settings used the algorithm has clustered the remaining cases in two groups. Looking at the confusion matrix it seems cluster 1 contains the **setosas**, with the exception of one that was put in the group of outliers. Cluster 2 contains the plants of the other two species. This seems to be a bad result, but in effect, as we have seen previously when analyzing the silhouette coefficients for different clustering settings, creating two groups often appeared as the best option. Moreover, it is well known that in this dataset the **versicolor** and **virginica** species are very hard to differentiate.

Further readings on clustering

The book by Aggarwal and Reddy (2014) contains an extensive set of interesting articles that address most of the different aspects involved in clustering data. Most reference books on data mining (e.g. Aggarwal (2015) or Han et al. (2012)) will also contain chapters on clustering, that is one of the major tasks in data mining.

3.4.4 Anomaly Detection

Anomaly detection has to do with finding observations that are too different from the remaining cases. This task is obviously related with that of clustering. In clustering we aim at putting together similar cases, while here we want to identify the more deviating observations. This means that these anomalies should be hard to cluster together with other cases, as they are too different. Still, we should note that what we have just described are the most common types of anomalies (or outliers), known as *point outliers*. There are other types of deviations whose identification requires different analysis. That is the case of *contextual outliers* whose identification requires looking at the context in which they appear, given that in isolation they look "normal". For instance, a certain value of some medical indicator of a patient may be normal from the perspective of all patients, but may also be anomalous given some context of the particular patient (e.g. having some type of disease). This is related with case dependencies that we have mentioned in Section 3.3.3.1 (page 65). In effect, in these applications cases are described by both contextual properties that provide information on the specific context of the observation under analysis, and behavioral features that describe the case in itself. In the case of contextual outlier detection we use the contextual properties to decide whether the behavioral feature values are or are not anomalous. Finally, another type of anomalies is known as *collective outliers*. These are cases that individually can not be considered anomalous but when taken together as a whole they are indeed anomalous. Take for instance the scenario of computer network security. Some types of events (e.g. denial of service) when occurring in isolation may be seen as normal. However, when we observe these events happening in succession, this may provide clear indications that something strange is occurring (e.g. an attack). Our brief description of the main approaches to outlier detection will be focussed on point outliers.

Outlier detection raises several challenges to analysis methods, mainly due to the intrinsic nature of these events. In effect, by definition anomalies are infrequent and thus being able to identify them means to work with higher uncertainty given the lack of statistical support of any conclusions from these small number of samples. Moreover, being able to differentiate anomalies from noisy observations or simple typing (or other types of) errors is not easy. Other types of challenges include the fact that characterizing what is "normal" behavior may also not be an easy task as the frontier between normal and deviating cases may be imprecise. Moreover, anomalies are frequently associated with malicious activities, which means that the authors of these activities will typically make a big effort to try to disguise their activities as normal. Finally, in many applications the notion of outlier evolves with time (or may even be different depending on the location).

In terms of types of outlier detection methods we can distinguish the following three main approaches:

- Supervised methods
  When we have access to a historical record of observations that have been audited by some domain expert that has tagged them as being normal or anomalous.

- Non-supervised methods
  When there is no previous information on the available data concerning the cases being or not being outliers.

- Semi-supervised methods
  When some of the available cases are tagged while others are not (the latter being frequently the majority).

In spite of the clear differences among these approaches, as we will see in Chapter 6, it is sometimes possible to apply all of them to the same problem.

Even in terms of output of outlier detection methods we can also distinguish between methods that simply tag cases as being or not being anomalous, from methods that output a kind of probability of being an outlier. The latter are more flexible, particularly in applications where the outcome of the method is used to guide some sort of auditing activities, as they allow for different types of inspection resource management strategies. For instance, a company may have limited auditing resources and if a method outputs as potential outliers more cases than it is possible to inspect with the available resources, we are left with no guidance on which cases should be audited. When probabilities (or scores) are available we can use them to create a kind of inspection ranking that is more flexible for managing limited resources.

3.4.4.1 Univariate Outlier Detection Methods

The simplest outlier detection methods only look at a single variable. In Section 3.4.1.1 (page 87) we have already mentioned one frequently used uni-variate outlier detection method — the *boxplot rule*. This rule can be applied to a sample of a numeric variable and tags any value outside the interval $[Q_1 - 1.5 \times IQR, Q_3 + 1.5 \times IQR]$, where $Q_1(Q_3)$ is the first (third) quartile and $IQR = Q_3 - Q_1$ the interquartile range, as an outlier. In that section we have created an R function (`bpRule()`) that can be used to find these outlying values.

A related method is the so-called *Grubb's test* that starts by calculating the following z score for each observation x,

$$z = \frac{|x - \bar{x}|}{s_x} \tag{3.17}$$

where $\bar{x}$ is the sample mean of the variable X and s_x the respective sample standard deviation. Using this score a case is declared an outlier if the following holds,

$$z \geq \frac{N-1}{\sqrt{N}} \sqrt{\frac{t^2_{\alpha/(2N),N-2}}{N-2+t^2_{\alpha/(2N),N-2}}} \tag{3.18}$$

where N is the sample size and $t^2_{\alpha/(2N),N-2}$ is the value of the t-distribution at the significance level of $\alpha/(2N)$.

Package **outliers** (Komsta, 2011) contains function `grubbs.test()` that can be used for applying this method. Unfortunately, the function can not be used to obtain all outliers in a sample, at least without writing another function that iteratively calls the package function. Let us write such a function copying the part of the code of the function `grubbs.test()` that is useful for our objective,

```
> grubbs.outliers <- function(x, p.thresh=0.05) {
+     require(outliers, quietly=TRUE)
+     x <- x[!is.na(x)]
+     n <- length(x)
+     zs <- abs(x - mean(x)) / sd(x)
+     outs <- 1 - sapply(zs, function(z) pgrubbs(z, n, type=10))
+     posOuts <- which(outs <= p.thresh)
+     return(list(zs=zs,
+                 pvals=outs,
+                 outliers=x[posOuts],
+                 positions=posOuts))
+ }
> data(algae, package="DMwR2")
> grubbs.outliers(algae$a2)$outliers

[1] 53.6 72.6
```

Package **outliers** contains other tests that can be used for uni-variate outlier detection.

In the case of categorical variables we can only resort to observed frequencies of each value on the available sample. Whether the frequency of some value is too unusual to indicate that it may be an outlying value, depends on the distribution you assume for the values. For instance, if your prior expectations for a variable (say the sex of some sample of clients) is roughly uniform, and you observe that one of the values hardly appears, then you may suspect a problem. Finding the frequencies of the values of some nominal variable is easy in R,

```
> data(algae, package="DMwR2")
> table(algae$season)/length(algae$season)


autumn spring summer winter
 0.200  0.265  0.225  0.310
```

3.4.4.2 Multi-Variate Outlier Detection Methods

For multi-variate outlier detection we can use different types of approaches, as we have mentioned before: unsupervised, supervised, or semi-supervised methods. We start our description with the unsupervised approaches.

We have already seen an example of unsupervised methods that can be used to identify outliers. In effect, in Section 3.4.3.2 we have described the DBSCAN density-based clustering method (Ester et al., 1996) that returns a special cluster containing cases that are too isolated to be part of the "normal" clusters created by this method. According to this algorithm, these are observations that do not have a minimum number of cases (set as a parameter) within a certain distance (another parameter), and moreover, are not part of the neighborhood of any *core* case. These are the outliers according to DBSCAN. The following simple function can be used to identify the outliers in a dataset using DBSCAN,

```
> dbscan.outliers <- function(data, ...) {
+     require(fpc, quietly=TRUE)
+     cl <- dbscan(data, ...)
+     posOuts <- which(cl$cluster == 0)
+     list(positions = posOuts,
+          outliers = data[posOuts,],
+          dbscanResults = cl)
+ }
```

In the illustrations of this section we will use a dataset available in package **mlbench** (Leisch and Dimitriadou, 2010). The dataset is named `Glass` and each observation consists of a sample of glass from a crime scene. For each sample a series of chemical properties is provided and also the type of glass assigned by a human expert. The goal of this problem is to try to forecast the type of glass based on the measured chemical properties. Among the different types of glass some are less frequent. We will slightly change this data to make it more interesting for outlier detection. We will group the rare types into a "rare" class and tag the remaining as "normal" glasses,

```
> library(dplyr)
> library(forcats)
> data(Glass, package="mlbench")
> count(Glass,Type)   # a dplyr alternative to "table(Glass$Type)"

# A tibble: 6 × 2
    Type     n
  <fctr> <int>
1      1    70
2      2    76
3      3    17
4      5    13
5      6     9
6      7    29

> g <- mutate(Glass,
+             Type=fct_collapse(Type,
+                       rare   = as.character(c(3,5,6)),
+                       normal = as.character(c(1,2,7))
+                       )
+             )
> g %>% count(Type) %>% mutate(prop=100*n/nrow(g))

# A tibble: 2 × 3
    Type     n    prop
  <fctr> <int>   <dbl>
1 normal   175 81.7757
2   rare    39 18.2243
```

We have used the function `fct_collapse()` from package **forcats** Wickham (2016) to create the new factor levels that consist in joining the less frequent glass types into a "rare" class and the remaining as "normal". This package contains several other interesting and useful functions to work with factors in R.

Let us now illustrate the use of the function for detecting outliers using DBSCAN on this dataset,

```
> outs <- dbscan.outliers(g[,-10], eps=1, scale=TRUE)
> head(outs$outliers)

      RI    Na   Mg   Al    Si    K    Ca   Ba   Fe
22 1.51966 14.77 3.75 0.29 72.02 0.03  9.00 0.00 0.00
48 1.52667 13.99 3.70 0.71 71.57 0.02  9.82 0.00 0.10
51 1.52320 13.72 3.72 0.51 71.75 0.09 10.06 0.00 0.16
57 1.51215 12.99 3.47 1.12 72.98 0.62  8.35 0.00 0.31
62 1.51977 13.81 3.58 1.32 71.72 0.12  8.67 0.69 0.00
67 1.52152 13.05 3.65 0.87 72.22 0.19  9.85 0.00 0.17

> nrow(outs$outliers)

[1] 66

> slice(g, outs$positions) %>% count(Type)

# A tibble: 2 × 2
    Type      n
  <fctr> <int>
1 normal    42
2   rare    24

> count(g, Type)

# A tibble: 2 × 2
    Type      n
  <fctr> <int>
1 normal   175
2   rare    39
```

The DBSCAN-based outlier detection method has signalled 66 cases as outliers. However, according to the external information provided by the **Type** column, we observe that from these only 24 are real outliers. Moreover, we can also observe that there are 39 outliers in the dataset, so this method is missing some of the outliers.

Note that any extra parameters you give the function on top of the data, will be passed down to the **dbscan()** function. This simple example shows that from the outliers detected by DBSCAN 24 are outliers, from the 39 available in the full dataset.

Another example of an outlier detection method strongly related with clustering is the OR_h method (Torgo, 2007). This method uses the results of a hierarchical agglomerative clustering process to assign an outlyingness score to each case in a dataset. This means that contrary to the DBSCAN method, OR_h will output a score of outlyingness that can be used to produce rankings. The idea of OR_h is simple: cases that are outliers should be harder to merge with other cases because they are too different. In this context, this fact should be evident by looking at their path in the dendrogram. In effect, the merging process used to obtain the dendrogram is guided by some criterion that tries to put together observations that are more similar to each other. The function **hclust()** of the base package **stats** implements several variants of hierarchical agglomerative clustering, as we have seen in Section 3.4.3.2. The object returned by this function includes a data structure (**merge**) that has information on which cases are involved in each merging step. The OR_h method uses the information in this data structure as the basis for the following outlier ranking method. The basic idea is that outliers should offer greater resistance to being merged and thus, when they are finally merged, the size difference between the group in to which they belong and the group to which they are being merged should be very large. This reflects the idea that outliers are rather different from other observations, and thus their inclusion in groups with more "normal" observations should clearly decrease the homogeneity of the resulting group. Occasionally, outliers are merged at initial stages with other observations, but only if these are similar outliers. Otherwise, they will only be merged at later stages of the clustering process and usually with a much larger group of cases. This is the general idea that is captured by the OR_h method. This method calculates the outlier score of each case as follows. For each merging step i involving two groups (g_x^i and g_y^i), we calculate the following value:

$$of_i(x) = \max\left(0, \frac{|g_y^i| - |g_x^i|}{|g_y^i| + |g_x^i|}\right) \tag{3.19}$$

where g_x^i is the group to which x belongs at iteration i of the merging process, and $|g_x^i|$ is the group cardinality.

At each merging step i any case x belongs to some group. This group may: (i) not be involved in the merging taking place at iteration i, and thus the score of the case at this step will be 0; (i) be the larger (in size) of the two groups involved in the merge, and according to the above definition the score at this iteration will also be 0; or (iii) be the smaller group, and then the score will be positive, and the larger the size difference between the two groups, the larger the score the case will get at this step i.

Each observation can be involved in several merges throughout the iterative process of the hierarchical clustering algorithm — sometimes as members of the larger group, other times as members of the smaller group. The final outlier score of each case in the data sample is given by

$$OF_H(x) = \max_i of_i(x) \tag{3.20}$$

The function `outliers.ranking()` of our book package implements this method. The following is an example of using it with the `Glass` dataset,

```
> library(DMwR2)
> library(dplyr)
> og <- outliers.ranking(select(g, -Type))
> slice(g, og$rank.outliers[1:40]) %>% count(Type)

# A tibble: 2 × 2
    Type      n
  <fctr> <int>
1 normal    30
2   rare    10
```

Although you can control the clustering process used by this method through the parameter `clus` of the function, most of the time you can simply use the defaults. The function returns a list with several components one of which is named `rank.outliers` and contains a ranking of the rows of the dataset with higher "probability" of being an outlier. Above we are using it to check the `Type` value of the top 40 outliers according to this method. From these 40 only 10 seem to belong to the rare class, which is not an interesting result.

One of the most well-known unsupervised methods for multi-variate outlier detection is

LOF (Breunig et al., 2000). As with OR_h, the result of this method is an outlier score for each case. The main idea of *LOF* is to try to obtain an outlyingness score for each case by estimating its degree of isolation with respect to its local neighborhood. The method is based on the notion of the local density of the observations. Cases in regions with very low density are considered outliers. The estimates of the density are obtained using the distances between cases. The authors defined a few concepts that drive the algorithm used to calculate the outlyingness score of each point. These are: the (1) concept of *core distance* of a point p, $dist_k(p)$, which is defined as its distance to its kth nearest neighbor; (2) the k-distance neighborhood of p, $N_k(o)$, which is the set of k nearest neighbors of p; (3) the concept of *reachability distance* between the case p_1 and p_2, which is given by the maximum of the core distance of p_1 and the distance between both cases, i.e. $reach.dist_k(p_1, p_2) = \max\{dist_k(p_1), d(p_1, p_2)\}$; and (4) the *local reachability distance* of a point p, which is inversely proportional to the average reachability distance of its k neighbors, i.e.

$$lrd_k(p) = \frac{|N_k(p)|}{\sum_{o \in N_k(p)} reach.dist_k(p, o)} \tag{3.21}$$

The *LOF* score of a case p captures the degree to which we can consider it an outlier and it is calculated as a function of its local reachability distance,

$$LOF_k(p) = \frac{\sum_{o \in N_k(p)} \frac{lrd_k(p)}{lrd_k(o)}}{N_k(p)} \tag{3.22}$$

This factor is the average of the ratio between the local reachability-distance of p and those of its k-nearest neighbors. This ratio can be seen as a kind of normalization that allows for this method to cope with problems where observations belong to clusters with different data density, that are problems for which methods that rely on establishing a global threshold on the distances (e.g. DBSCAN) will not be able to address properly.

This method was implemented in package **dprep** (Acuna et al., 2009) that was redrawn from the CRAN repository. In our book package we include function `lofactor()` based on the code that was available in package **dprep**. This function receives as arguments a dataset and the value of k that specifies the size of the neighborhood used in calculating the *LOF* of the observations. This implementation of the *LOF* method is limited to datasets described by numeric variables. Package **Rlof** (Hu et al., 2015) contains a similar implementation but is optimized for parallel execution and thus should be preferred for large datasets. Below we show a small illustrative example of its usage,

```
> library(DMwR2)
> library(dplyr)
> lof.scores <- lofactor(select(g, -Type),10)
> slice(g, order(lof.scores,decreasing=TRUE)[1:40]) %>% count(Type)

# A tibble: 2 × 2
    Type      n
  <fctr> <int>
1 normal    25
2   rare    15
```

The function `lofactor()` takes as arguments the data and the number of k neighbors used in the formulae we have described above. The results of the function are the *LOF* scores for each of the rows of the dataset. Once again we check the Type value of the top 40 outliers according to *LOF*. We get a slightly better result than with OR_h, but still not very impressive taking into account that we know that there are 39 cases belonging to the "rare" class.

In terms of supervised approaches to multi-variate outlier detection we usually define this task as a binary classification problem. Classification tasks are part of predictive analytics that will be described in detail in Section 3.4.5. For now we can informally describe these tasks as having the objective of forecasting the values of a nominal target variable using the values of other variables. In the case of binary classification this target variable only has two possible values. Within outlier detection, supervised approaches assume the existence of a dataset where all observations were previously audited by some human expert that has tagged the cases as either "normal" or "outliers". The results of this auditing are stored in the target variable, thus having as possible values "normal" or "outlier". With this dataset we can apply any of the algorithms we are going to describe in Section 3.4.5. However, there is a caveat. The distribution of the values of the target variable for these outlier detection tasks is typically very imbalanced. This means that one of the values ("outlier") will usually be much less frequent than the other. This type of datasets creates all sorts of problems for standard classification algorithms (see Branco et al. (2016b) for a survey on these problems and some of the available solutions). Section 3.4.5 will describe in detail different classification methods, while in Chapter 6 we will address a concrete case study where the classification methods will be applied. Moreover, in this chapter we will see one of the possible solutions for overcoming the class imbalance problem that consists of trying to re-sample the available training data in a biased way in order to try to obtain a more balanced distribution to use for obtaining the classification models.

Handling imbalanced classification tasks raises problems at two different levels: (i) the metrics used to evaluate the performance; and (ii) the modeling stages. The former has to do with the fact that standard classification metrics, like the percentage of correct predictions (accuracy), will be misleading if one of the classes is too rare, and moreover, this is the more interesting class for the user. This is the case of our problems where the rare class ("outlier") is the more important. If in our datasets say 95% of the cases are "normal", it is easy to achieve a percentage of accurate predictions of 95% — it is enough to always predict "normal"! However, such a model is useless from the perspective of outlier detection. This means we need to use evaluation metrics that are more adequate for these problems. In Section 3.4.5.1 we will describe several metrics that can be used for this class of problems. The second issue where class imbalance has a strong impact is on the development of the models. Predictive modeling is strongly based on finding regularities in the provided data sample. Outliers are so rare that they are often disregarded due to their low frequency. Given that they are the most relevant cases for the end-user of these applications something needs to be done to avoid this. The more frequent approaches involve either manipulating the data used for obtaining the models, or by somehow changing the learning algorithms. The former may involve strategies like under-sampling the more frequent cases, or over-sampling the outliers, always with the goal of obtaining a more balanced distribution between the two classes. Package **UBL** (Branco et al., 2016a) contains several functions that implement these strategies. The following is an example of trying to obtain a more balanced sample of the `Glass` dataset that we have used before,

```
> library(UBL)
> library(dplyr)
> count(g,Type)

# A tibble: 2 × 2
    Type     n
  <fctr> <int>
```

```
1 normal    175
2   rare     39
```

```
> ## Undersampling the largest class
> newg <- RandUnderClassif(Type ~ ., g)
> count(newg,Type)
```

```
# A tibble: 2 × 2
    Type      n
  <fctr> <int>
1 normal     39
2   rare     39
```

```
> ## Now specifying the degree of undersampling by hand
> newg2 <- RandUnderClassif(Type ~ ., g, list(normal=0.4, rare=1))
> count(newg2,Type)
```

```
# A tibble: 2 × 2
    Type      n
  <fctr> <int>
1 normal     70
2   rare     39
```

```
> ## Oversampling the minority class
> newg3 <- RandOverClassif(Type ~ .,g)
> count(newg3,Type)
```

```
# A tibble: 2 × 2
    Type      n
  <fctr> <int>
1 normal    175
2   rare    175
```

You may check the package vignette accompanying package **UBL** for further alternative methods (and examples) for changing the distribution of the original dataset to make it more in accordance with the goals of the end-user (which in this case is performance on a rare class).

Regarding changes to the learning process there are several alternatives that try to bias the methods for the cases most relevant to the end-user. Examples include the use of cost matrices or the usage of different evaluation metrics to guide the search for patterns that are more biased towards the performance on the "outliers".

Given the imbalanced problem another frequently used alternative for supervised outlier detection is to use the so-called one-class models. Contrary to standard classification methods these algorithms focus on obtaining a description of the "normal" (and more prevailing) class. Given this description any case that does not satisfy it will be tagged as an "outlier". The main advantage of these methods is that they do not suffer from a lack of cases of the rare class. For instance, in package **e1071** (Dimitriadou et al., 2009), that we will use extensively later in the book, there is an implementation of a classification algorithm — the SVM — that can handle one-class problems. Let us see an example of how to use this function for the `Glass` data,

```
> library(e1071)
> trainD <- filter(g, Type == "normal") %>% select(-Type)
> s <- svm(trainD, y=NULL, type="one-classification", nu=0.5)
```

```
> (cm <- table(g$Type, predict(s,select(g, -Type))))
```

```
          FALSE  TRUE
  normal     86    89
  rare       28    11
```

We start by training the one-class SVM on the normal cases only. Then we apply it to the full dataset to check which ones are not tagged as normal (predicted value of **FALSE**). As we can observe, the from the 39 cases that are outliers, this approach predicts 28 as being outliers. Moreover, it predicts as outliers 86 cases that are in effect normal, i.e. a large number of false positives.

Semi-supervised methods are able to handle datasets where some of the available observations were tagged by a human expert, but where the remaining (frequently the largest portion) were not audited. In these contexts, we can either ignore the cases without tag, and apply a supervised classification method to the others, or ignore the labels and apply an unsupervised method to the full data. Both approaches waste some information and this is the motivation for using semi-supervised methods. These methods are not very common (see Chapelle et al. (2006) for a reference on these methods). Still, they usually revolve around: (i) improving supervised methods by trying to take advantage of the non-tagged cases; or (ii) improving the unsupervised methods by imposing constraints based on the information of the available labels. For instance, for the latter we could try to make sure that a clustering algorithm does not create groups that contain both outliers and normal cases. For the former we could try to use the results of a clustering method to assign labels to the cases that are not tagged. For instance, if as the result of clustering the data we find a group that contains a few outliers and also some non tagged observations, then we have some confidence in assigning the outlier tag to these other observations because the clustering method found them to be similar enough to cluster them together with outliers. In Chapter 6 we will see yet another example of a semi-supervised method where we start by building a classifier using only the labeled data and then iteratively use it to predict the labels for the unlabeled cases, assuming this prediction is true for the ones in which the classifier has more confidence, thus extending our training set that is then used to obtain another classifier.

Further readings on anomaly detection

The book by Aggarwal (2013) contains an extensive description of anomaly detection methods for different types of data and applications. It is an excellent reference for the state of the art on this topic within the data mining field. Chandola et al. (2007) and Hodge and Austin (2004) provide shorter surveys of outlier detection. More "classical" references are the books by Hawkins (1980) and Barnett and Lewis (1994). Finally, most data mining reference books (e.g. Aggarwal (2015) or Han et al. (2012)) will contain chapters devoted to anomaly detection.

3.4.5 Predictive Analytics

Predictive analytics has to do with obtaining models using a sample of observations for solving predictive tasks. Predictive tasks involve trying to obtain an approximation of an unknown function f that maps the values of a set of variables (the predictors) into the values of a target variable. For instance, in a medical domain we may have access to a historical record of patient analysis where some medical doctor has assigned a certain diagnosis to each patient based on a set of measurements of symptoms. This means that there is an unknown function that we are trying to approximate based on a historical record of mappings from symptoms into diagnoses.

The main goal of the obtained models is to predict the target variable for new observations of the problem at hand. Still, sometimes we also have the goal of understanding how the predictor variables influence the value of the target variable, i.e. we want to uncover eventually unknown relationships between the predictors and the target.

Obviously, to develop prediction models we must assume that there is some regularity on what we observe (the historical dataset), i.e. that the phenomenon is not completely random. Our goal is then to uncover these regularities based on the dataset provided and according to some preference criteria that allow us to compare possible alternative "explanations" of what we observe. In summary, we want to obtain a model, h, of the unknown function $Y = f(X_1, X_2, \cdots, X_p)$, using a dataset $D = \{\langle x_1^i, \cdots, x_p^i, y^i \rangle\}_{i=1}^N$, where Y is a target variable, the X's are predictor variables and N is the dataset size (number of rows of our data table).

Depending on the type of the target variable Y, we are going to distinguish two types of prediction tasks: (i) *classification tasks* where Y is nominal; and (ii) *regression tasks* where Y is numeric. For instance, re-visiting our *Iris* dataset we can look at it as a classification task where we are trying to find the function that maps the biometric properties of the plants into the species of *Iris*, which is a nominal variable with three possible values. On the other hand, looking at the *Algae* dataset that we have explored before, we can see a regression task when we try to estimate the frequency of say Algal A1 using the 11 descriptors of the water sample.

Both regression and classification tasks share many relevant questions and we are going to see that several available techniques can handle both tasks. However, there are obvious differences between the tasks that are frequently related with the criteria used to evaluate and compare different candidate models.

Independently of facing a regression or a classification task we have to : (i) make some assumptions on the shape of the unknown function $f()$ that we are trying to approximate; and then (ii) try to search for the "optimal" instance of this assumed form taking into account the dataset provided and also some preference criteria that allow us to compare the different candidate instances.

There are many alternatives in terms of assumptions of functional forms, i.e. types of models. These include simple linear models (e.g. linear regression or linear discriminants), logical approaches (e.g. trees or rules), probabilistic approaches (e.g. Naive Bayes), more complex models (e.g. neural networks or support vector machines), or even sets of models (ensembles). These different classes of models typically entail different compromises in terms of: (i) the strictness of the assumed functional form of the unknown function; (ii) the computational complexity of the task of obtaining the best instance of this form; (iii) or the interpretability of the resulting model; among other less relevant characteristics.

Given this wide variety of modeling approaches users typically face the question of which technique to apply given a new prediction task. This is usually known as the *model selection* problem and will be the topic of Section 3.5. Nevertheless, this will always involve the question of the preference criteria, i.e. the metrics that are used to evaluate the different models we may consider for a given task. In the next section we will describe some of the most common metrics.

3.4.5.1 Evaluation Metrics

In classification tasks the target variable is nominal. Given a set of N_{test} test cases we can use an obtained model $h()$ to obtain predictions for these test cases. Assuming we have access to the true value of the target variable of these test cases (sometimes known as the ground truth) we can compare the predictions of the model against these true values. The results of this comparison can be summarized in a matrix, usually known as the *confusion*

TABLE 3.3: An example of a confusion matrix.

		\multicolumn Pred.		
		c_1	c_2	c_3
Obs.	c_1	n_{c_1,c_1}	n_{c_1,c_2}	n_{c_1,c_3}
	c_2	n_{c_2,c_1}	n_{c_2,c_2}	n_{c_2,c_3}
	c_3	n_{c_3,c_1}	n_{c_3,c_2}	n_{c_3,c_3}

TABLE 3.4: An example of a cost/benefit matrix.

		Pred.		
		c_1	c_2	c_3
Obs.	c_1	$B_{1,1}$	$C_{1,2}$	$C_{1,3}$
	c_2	$C_{2,1}$	$B_{2,2}$	$C_{2,3}$
	c_3	$C_{3,1}$	$C_{3,2}$	$B_{3,3}$

matrix. This is a square matrix with dimensions $n_c \times n_c$, where n_c is the number of possible values of the target variable, frequently known as the *number of classes*. Assuming $n_c = 3$, Table 3.3 shows an example of a confusion matrix for a problem where the target variable takes values from the domain $\{c_1, c_2, c_3\}$.

Each cell of a confusion matrix has a number and the sum of all numbers is equal to the number of test cases, N_{test}. For instance, the number n_{c_2,c_3} represents the number of times for the given test cases the model has predicted the class c_3, when the true value was c_2. This means that the ideal model (perfect predictions) will only have numbers greater than zero at the diagonal of this matrix.

Using the numbers of the confusion matrix we can calculate several metrics that are often used to evaluate classification models. The most common is the *Error Rate* (also known as the 0/1 loss), defined as,

$$L_{0/1} = \frac{1}{N_{test}} \sum_{i=1}^{N_{test}} I(\hat{h}(\mathbf{x}_i) \neq y_i) \tag{3.23}$$

where $I()$ is an indicator function such that $I(x) = 0$ if x is false and 1 otherwise; and $\hat{h}(\mathbf{x}_i)$ is the prediction of the model being evaluated for the test case i that has as true class the value y_i.

Please note that the error rate can also be obtained as the proportion of the N_{test} cases that are outside of the diagonal of the confusion matrix.

Some people prefer to use the *Accuracy* that is basically the complement of the error rate, i.e. $Acc = 1 - L_{0/1}$.

There are applications where errors (or accurate predictions) do not have the same value. For instance, in a medical domain having a model forecasting that a patient is OK when it suffers from a serious disease is much more serious than the opposite. In these contexts, one often resorts to the use of cost/benefit matrices. These matrices have the same dimension as confusion matrices but they specify the costs and benefits associated with each pair of predicted/true class values. For instance, the value $B_{1,1}$ in Table 3.4 is the benefit of an accurate prediction of class c_1 ,while the value $C_{1,3}$ is the cost of forecasting c_3 for a true class value of c_1. Typically, benefits are positive, while costs are negative.

In the context of these applications the performance of a model is measured by the total utility of the model predictions for a given test set. If CM is the confusion matrix of the model predictions and CB the cost/benefit matrix of the problem, then the total utility is given by,

TABLE 3.5: A confusion matrix for prediction of a rare positive class.

		Preds.	
		Pos	Neg
Obs.	Pos	True Positives (TP)	False Negatives (FN)
	Neg	False Positives (FP)	True Negatives (TN)

$$totU = \sum_{i=1}^{n_c} \sum_{k=1}^{n_c} CM_{i,k} \times CB_{i,k} \tag{3.24}$$

Another frequent application setup within classification tasks is that of binary classification where one of the classes is not only more relevant for the user but is also less frequent in the available dataset. Example application domains include fraud detection or any type of outlier detection task based on supervised techniques. As we have mentioned in Section 3.4.4 using the standard error rate (or its complement accuracy) will lead to over-optimistic estimates of the capacities of a model. In effect, these metrics will be dominated by the performance of the model on the prevailing class, which is the least important in these applications.

For these applications it is common to call the class of interest (and least frequent) the *positive class*, while the other class is the *negative class*. A confusion matrix for these applications with the nomenclature one usually applies in these contexts is shown in Table 3.5.

In these applications the main goal of the end-user is to maximize the number of *true positives* (TP). From the numbers in the above confusion matrix one usually defines two key metrics for these applications: (i) *precision* that is the proportion of the positive predictions of the model that are correct; and (ii) *recall* that is the proportion of real positive events that are captured by the model. These metrics are calculated as follows,

$$Prec = \frac{TP}{TP + FP} \tag{3.25}$$

$$Rec = \frac{TP}{TP + FN} \tag{3.26}$$

There is typically a trade-off between these two metrics. For instance, it is easy to get 100% recall by having a model that always predicts a positive class. However, this model would score poorly in terms of precision as the positive class is rare.

It is common to aggregate these two metrics into a single score — the F-measure. This metric is a weighted average of precision and recall and it is given by,

$$F_\beta = \frac{(\beta^2 + 1) \cdot Prec \cdot Rec}{\beta^2 \cdot Prec + Rec} \tag{3.27}$$

where β controls the relative importance of $Prec$ and Rec. If $\beta = 1$ then F is the harmonic mean between $Prec$ and Rec; When $\beta \to 0$ the weight of Rec decreases. When $\beta \to \infty$ the weight of $Prec$ decreases.

For regression tasks the target variable is numeric. In this context, the available evaluation metrics revolve around the numeric differences between the true and predicted values. The most frequently used metric is the *mean squared error* (MSE) defined as,

$$MSE = \frac{1}{N_{test}} \sum_{i=1}^{N_{test}} (\hat{y}_i - y_i)^2 \tag{3.28}$$

where $\hat{y}_i$ is the prediction of the model under evaluation for the case i and y_i the respective true target variable value.

Note that the MSE is measured in units that are the square of those of the original variable. Because of this it is sometimes common to use the *root mean squared error* ($RMSE$) instead, which is defined as $RMSE = \sqrt{MSE}$.

Another frequently used metric is the *mean absolute error* (MAE) defined as,

$$MAE = \frac{1}{N_{test}} \sum_{i=1}^{N_{test}} |\hat{y}_i - y_i| \tag{3.29}$$

Note that the MAE is measured in the same units as the original variable.

Relative error metrics are also very common for regression tasks. They are unit-less measures that compare the performance of a model against some baseline. The relative score is expected to be a value between 0 and 1, with values nearer (or even above) 1 representing performances as bad as the baseline model, which is usually chosen as something too naive. The most common baseline model is the constant model consisting of predicting for all test cases the average target variable value calculated with the training data. An example of such a metric is the *normalized mean squared error* ($NMSE$) given by,

$$NMSE = \frac{\sum_{i=1}^{N_{test}} (\hat{y}_i - y_i)^2}{\sum_{i=1}^{N_{test}} (\bar{y} - y_i)^2} \tag{3.30}$$

where $\bar{y}$ is the sample average of the target variable in the training data.

Similarly, we can also calculate the *normalized mean absolute error* ($NMAE$) using,

$$NMAE = \frac{\sum_{i=1}^{N_{test}} |\hat{y}_i - y_i|}{\sum_{i=1}^{N_{test}} |\bar{y} - y_i|} \tag{3.31}$$

Another popular relative metric is the *mean average percentage error* ($MAPE$) given by,

$$MAPE = \frac{1}{N_{test}} \sum_{i=1}^{N_{test}} \frac{|\hat{y}_i - y_i|}{y_i} \tag{3.32}$$

Note, however, that the $MAPE$ has problems when the target variable can be zero.

Finally, the correlation between the predictions and the true values is also used as a metric of success. In this case the nearer the correlation gets to one, the better. This metric is given by,

$$\rho_{\hat{y},y} = \frac{\sum_{i=1}^{N_{test}} (\hat{y}_i - \bar{\hat{y}})(y_i - \bar{y})}{\sqrt{\sum_{i=1}^{N_{test}} (\hat{y}_i - \bar{\hat{y}})^2 \sum_{i=1}^{N_{test}} (y_i - \bar{y})^2}} \tag{3.33}$$

Many R packages provide these and other evaluation metrics for classification and regression tasks. Examples include the function `mmetric()` from package **rminer** (Cortez, 2015) that contains an extensive list of classification and regression metrics, the functions `classificationMetrics()` and `regressionMetrics()` from package **performanceEstimation** (Torgo, 2014a), the function `performance()` from package **ROCR** (Sing et al., 2009), or the function `performance()` from package **mlr** (Bischl et al., 2016), among others.

3.4.5.2 Tree-Based Models

We now start our brief description of some of the most relevant modeling techniques that can be used to solve predictive tasks. The first we are going to present are tree-based models. This is a rather popular approach that is known for producing reasonably interpretable models with acceptable predictive performance, and moreover, is able to address both classification and regression tasks. Other key characteristics of tree-based models are their computational efficiency, the ability to handle datasets with unknown values, the embedded feature selection and also the lack of very strong assumptions on the functional form of the function we are trying to approximate, which makes them a good alternative for a wide range of applications. On the other hand these models are not known for achieving top predictive performance, meaning that if this is the key goal of your application, they are probably not the best choice. Still, trees are at the basis of many ensemble models (c.f. Section 3.4.5.5) that achieve top performance, so it is important to understand how these models work.

A tree-based model is a hierarchy of logical tests on some of the predictor variables. This inverted tree ends at the so-called leaf nodes where we have the predictions of the model. Any path from the top (root) node till a leaf can be seen as a conjunction of logical tests that leads to some conclusion (the prediction at the leaf). Figure 3.26 shows two examples of tree-based models: on the left side a classification tree for the *BreastCancer* dataset available in package **mlbench**, and on the right side a regression tree for the *Boston Housing* dataset available in package **MASS**. Each node of the tree has a logical test (e.g. `Cell.siz < 2.5`) on one of the predictors. The left branch of the node is followed if the condition is true, otherwise we follow the right branch. We keep going down the tree until we reach a leaf node where we have the predictions — class labels in the case of classification trees, and numeric predictions for regression trees. For instance, the leftmost path on the classification tree can be read as: "if cell size is less than 2.5 and bare nuclei is less than 5.5 then we predict that the case is of class benign". We have as many of these "rules" as there are leaves in the tree. To use these models for making predictions we simply "drop" the test case down the tree starting at the root node until a leaf is reached, where we have the prediction for the case. You may have noticed that both trees do not use all predictors of the respective datasets, which means that they automatically carry out feature selection. Moreover, the trees are able to easily handle data with unknown values, as is the case of the *BreastCancer* dataset.

Tree-based models can be seen as providing a partitioning of the predictors space into a set of hyper-rectangles where all test cases are assigned the same prediction. Figure 3.27 shows an example of this for a simple 2-dimensional illustration dataset. As you can observe each path (a conjunction of logical conditions) that leads to a leaf corresponds to a certain rectangle in the predictors space.

Trees are obtained using a very simple algorithm (Algorithm 1) that builds these partitions recursively. This algorithm has three key issues: (i) the termination criterion that decides when we stop growing the tree creating a leaf node; (ii) the value that is selected for these leaves (the representative of the cases in each leaf); and (iii) the procedure used for selecting the best logical test for each non-leaf node. The answer to these questions is different for classification and regression trees. They are both grown using the recursive partitioning algorithm but they differ in the preference criterion guiding the tree building process. Classification trees typically use criteria related to the minimization of the error rate (e.g. the Gini index, the Gain ratio, entropy, etc.). Regression trees typically use the least squares error criterion that minimizes the mean squared error of the tree.

Let us focus on classification trees built with the Gini index. The Gini index of a dataset D where each example belongs to one of C classes is given by,

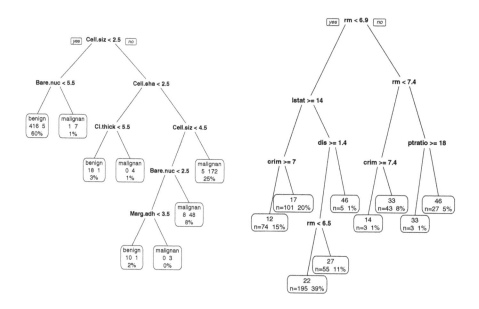

FIGURE 3.26: A classification (left) and a regression (right) tree.

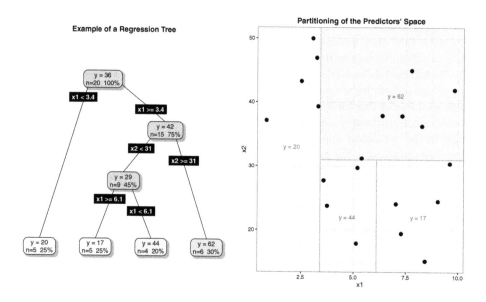

FIGURE 3.27: The partitioning provided by trees.

Algorithm 1 The recursive partitioning algorithm.

1: **function** RECURSIVEPARTITIONING(D)
    Input : D, a sample of cases, $\{\langle x_{i,1}, \cdots, x_{i,p}, y_i \rangle\}_{i=1}^{N_{train}}$
    Output : t, a tree node

2:    **if** <TERMINATION CRITERION> **then**
3:        **Return** a leaf node with the <REPRESENTATIVE> of D
4:    **else**
5:        $t \leftarrow$ new tree node
6:        $t.split \leftarrow$ <FIND THE BEST PREDICTORS TEST>
7:        $t.leftNode \leftarrow$ RecursivePartitioning($\mathbf{x} \in D : \mathbf{x} \rightarrow t.split$)
8:        $t.rightNode \leftarrow$ RecursivePartitioning($\mathbf{x} \in D : \mathbf{x} \not\rightarrow t.split$)
9:        **Return** the node t
10:   **end if**
11: **end function**

$$Gini(D) = 1 - \sum_{i=1}^{C} p_i^2 \tag{3.34}$$

where p_i is the probability of class i usually estimated with the observed frequency of this class on the training data.

If the dataset is split on a logical test s then the resulting Gini index is given by,

$$Gini_s(D) = \frac{|D_s|}{|D|} Gini(D_s) + \frac{|D_{\neg s}|}{|D|} Gini(D_{\neg s}) \tag{3.35}$$

where D_s is the subset of cases of set D that satisfies the test s and $D_{\neg s}$ is the subset of cases in D that do not satisfy this test.

Therefore, the reduction in impurity provided by the test s is,

$$\Delta Gini_s(D) = Gini(D) - Gini_s(D) \tag{3.36}$$

These equations are used to compare and select the best test for a given node of the tree.

The tests that are considered as candidates depend on the type of predictor variable. For numeric predictors, we start by sorting the values in the set of cases of the node, and then consider as candidates all tests of the form $X < k$, where k is a mid-point between the successive sorted values. For instance, if the sorted values of a numeric variable X are $\{4, 6, 10, 12\}$, the tried tests would be $X < 5$, $X < 8$ and $X < 11$. For nominal predictors, in principle all possible combinations of the values in the node should be tried. If there are L different values, this would correspond to 2^L candidate tests. However, Breiman et al. (1984) have proven a theorem that allows reducing the complexity of finding the best test on a nominal variable to a complexity of the order of L. In summary, all these tests are tried and the best according to Equation 3.36 is selected for each test node.

For regression trees, the most frequent method for selecting the best logical test is to use the least squares (LS) criterion. According to the LS criterion the error in a dataset D is given by,

$$Err(D) = \frac{1}{|D|} \sum_{\langle \mathbf{x}_i, y_i \rangle \in D} (y_i - k_D)^2 \tag{3.37}$$

where D is the sample of cases in a node, $|D|$ is the cardinality of this set and k_D is the constant used in the node. It can be easily proven that the constant k_D that minimizes this error is the sample average target variable value of the cases in D. Any logical test s divides the cases in D in two partitions, D_s and $D_{\neg s}$. As with classification trees, the resulting pooled error is given by,

$$Err_s(D) = \frac{|D_s|}{|D|} \times Err(D_s) + \frac{|D_{\neg s}|}{|D|} \times Err(D_{\neg s}) \tag{3.38}$$

where $|D_s|/|D|$ ($|D_{\neg s}|/|D|$) is the proportion of cases going to the left (right) branch of the node.

We can estimate the value of the split s by the respective error reduction,

$$\Delta Err_s(D) = Err(D) - Err_s(D) \tag{3.39}$$

The tests tried for each node of a regression tree are similar to those tried on classification trees, which we have described before.

The second key issue of the recursive partitioning algorithm (Algorithm 1) is the decision on which value to select as the representative of the cases in a leaf node. This decision is related to the criterion used to grow the trees. As we have seen above, for regression trees, the constant that minimizes the LS criterion is the average value of the target variable estimated using the cases in the leaf node. For classification trees the value is the majority class of the cases in the node.

Finally, the last issue is the decision on when to stop the tree growth process. This question is related with a problem known as *overfitting*. A too large tree will most probably capture spurious patterns on the training data that will hardly generalize to new test cases, thus leading to poor predictive performance. On the other hand a very small tree will be too general and will fail to capture more detailed patterns, again leading to poor predictive performance. This results from the models being obtained based on a sample of the unknown full distribution of the problem. This means that all decisions are based on estimates of the true value of each test in the tree. Moreover, given the way the recursive partitioning algorithm works, these decisions are being taken on smaller and smaller samples, and thus are getting potentially less reliable as we go down the tree. In this context, the most frequent method for obtaining reliable tree-based models is to grow an overly large tree and then use some statistical procedure that tries to eliminate branches of the tree that are statistically unreliable, in a procedure usually known as *post-pruning*. This procedure typically involves generating a large sequence of subtrees of the original large tree and then selecting one of them according to some statistical test.

In R there are two main packages for obtaining tree-based models: (i) package **rpart** (Therneau and Atkinson, 2010) and package **party** (Hothorn et al., 2006). Package **rpart** closely follows the ideas in the seminal book *Classification and Regression Trees* by Breiman et al. (1984), while package **party** implements the concept of conditional inference trees (Hothorn et al., 2006). In this book we will use the package **rpart**.

Package **rpart** provides two main functions to assist in obtaining tree-based models: (i) one for growing the trees (named `rpart()`); and (ii) the other for post-pruning them (named `prune.rpart()`). Our book package provides function `rpartXse()` that joins the two steps in a single function call, which is more practical in most cases. This function calls the functions implemented in package **rpart** to obtain trees that are post-pruned using the X-SE rule. Trees in **rpart** are grown till one of three criteria is true: (1) the decrease in the error of the current node goes below a certain threshold; (2) the number of samples in the node is less than another threshold; or (3) the tree depth exceeds another value. These thresholds are controlled by the parameters `cp`, `minsplit`, and `maxdepth`, respectively. Their default values are 0.01, 20, and 30. Function `prune.rpart()` implements a pruning method called *cost complexity* pruning (Breiman et al., 1984). This method uses the values of the parameter `cp` that R calculates for each node of the tree. The pruning method tries to estimate the value of `cp` that ensures the best compromise between predictive accuracy and tree size. Given a tree obtained with the `rpart()` function, R can produce a set of subtrees of this tree and estimate their predictive performance using a procedure based on cross validation estimates (c.f. Section 3.5). For each subtree an error estimate is obtained together with a standard error of this estimate. The X-SE pruning rule determines that the final selected tree is the smallest tree in the sequence whose estimated error is smaller than the lowest error plus the respective standard error. For instance, if the tree in the sequence of subtrees with the lowest error has an estimate of 4.5 ± 0.4 and has 13 nodes, but there is a (smaller) tree in the sequence with 10 nodes and an estimated error of 4.8, this latter tree will be selected if we are using the 1-SE rule because $4.8 < 4.5 + 0.4$ and this rule prefers smaller trees. Function `rpartXse()` allows you to specify the number of standard errors to use in the X-SE pruning rule, i.e the value of X. It then grows a very large tree using very relaxed values of parameters `cp` and `minsplit`, which then is pruned using the procedure described above.

Functions `rpart()` and `rpartXse()` use the standard *formula interface* that most modeling functions in R use. This means specifying the abstract functional form of the model we are trying to obtain in the first argument and the available training data in the second. Say you are trying to obtain a model to forecast variable Y using the values of variables X and Z. The functional form would be specified by the formula Y ~ X + Z. Alternatively, if your dataset only includes these 3 variables you could instead use the simpler form Y ~ ., where the dot means all remaining variables.

The following example obtains two classification trees for the *Iris* dataset,

```
> library(DMwR2)
> set.seed(1234)
> data(iris)
> ct1 <- rpartXse(Species ~ ., iris)
> ct2 <- rpartXse(Species ~ ., iris, se=0)
```

The first tree is obtained with the default parameters of `rpartXse()`, which means using 1-SE post pruning. The second tree is obtained with a less "aggressive" pruning by specifying 0-SE pruning. This corresponds to selecting the lowest estimated error subtree of the original overly large tree. Note the use of the function `set.seed()` as a way of ensuring you get the same trees. Given that there is some random component on the method used to obtain the error estimates of the subtrees, it is possible to obtain a different tree if you run the same code twice.

While we can ask R for the content of the two objects (`ct1` and `ct2`), which will get us a textual representation of the trees, it is more interesting to have a graphical representation. Package **rpart.plot** (Milborrow, 2015) provides powerful graphical visualizations for **rpart** trees. Namely, function `prp()` can be used to plot the trees with many graphical variants, accessible through the large amount of parameters of this function. Figure 3.28 shows the two trees of the above example. The graphs were obtained as follows,

```
> library(rpart.plot)
> prp(ct1, type=0, extra=101)   # left tree
> prp(ct2, type=0, extra=101)   # right tree
```

Regression trees are obtained using the same exact procedure. Function `rpart()` decides

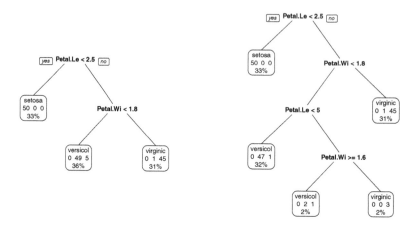

FIGURE 3.28: The two classification trees for Iris.

to obtain either a classification or a regression tree, depending on the type of the target variable you indicate in the formula.

　　Trees obtained with this package can also be used to obtain predictions for a set of test cases. Package **rpart** uses the standard procedure of providing a `predict()` method for the objects produced by function `rpart()`. As with most modeling functions the usage of this `predict()` function requires you to specify the model in the first argument and the test cases (a data frame) in the second. Let us see an example,

```
> set.seed(1234)
> rndSample <- sample(1:nrow(iris),100)
> tr <- iris[rndSample, ]
> ts <- iris[-rndSample, ]
> ct <- rpartXse(Species ~ ., tr, se=0.5)
> ps1 <- predict(ct, ts)
> head(ps1)

   setosa versicolor virginica
1       1          0         0
3       1          0         0
9       1          0         0
11      1          0         0
12      1          0         0
14      1          0         0

> ps2 <- predict(ct, ts, type="class")
> head(ps2)

     1      3      9     11     12     14
setosa setosa setosa setosa setosa setosa
Levels: setosa versicolor virginica

> (cm <- table(ps2, ts$Species))

ps2          setosa versicolor virginica
```

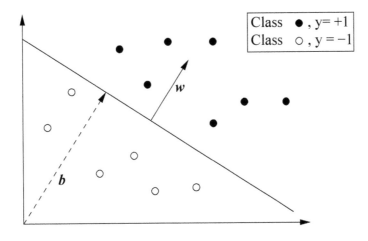

FIGURE 3.29: Two linearly separable classes.

setosa	12	0	0
versicolor	0	21	3
virginica	0	0	14

```
> 100*(1-sum(diag(cm))/sum(cm))   # the error rate

[1] 6
```

If called without any further argument with a classification tree in the first argument, the **predict()** method of these **rpart** objects will output a matrix with the estimated probabilities of each class for each test case. With the extra argument **type="class"** we get a vector with the predicted classes for all test cases (which are the classes with highest probability).

To obtain predictions using regression trees we use the same **predict()** function. However, in this case the argument **type="class"** does not make sense as the predictions are numbers and there are no class probabilities.

Further readings on tree-based models

The book by Breiman et al. (1984) can be seen as the major reference on tree-based models. The book covers most of the aspects related with this type of modeling approach. The book by Quinlan (1993) provides a less formal approach to classification trees, while in Torgo (1999a) you can find extensive coverage on regression trees and several variants of these models.

3.4.5.3 Support Vector Machines

Support vector machines (SVMs) are one of the most successful modeling approaches. To explain their approach it is easier to start with one particularly simple classification problem — binary classification where the two classes can be separated by a linear model as is the case in Figure 3.29.

These simple problems have a very elegant solution in the form of a linear model whose additive form is usually considered very interpretable. In spite of their attractiveness, linearly separable classes do not abound in the real world. In effect, one frequently encounters

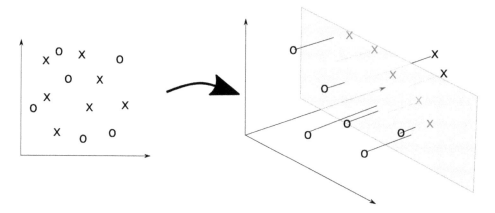

FIGURE 3.30: Mapping into a higher dimensionality.

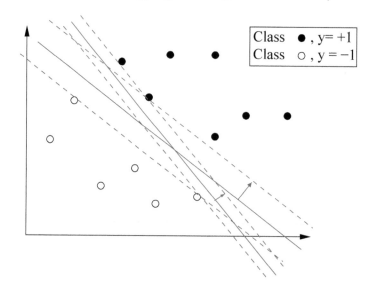

FIGURE 3.31: Maximum margin hyperplane.

non-linear domains where such solutions are not applicable. SVMs try to overcome this problem by using a non-linear mapping of the original data into a very high dimension space where the classes can be separated linearly (by an hyperplane) as illustrated in Figure 3.30.

The question of finding the hyperplane separating the classes is also relevant. There is a potentially infinite number of hyperplanes that are able to separate the cases of the two classes. Which one should we choose? Our goal is to ensure that the selected hyperplane leads to higher classification accuracy. In this context, the best hyperplane is the one that maximizes the separating margin between the points of the two classes, because this decreases the probability of confusion between the classes. The idea is illustrated in Figure 3.31 where we see two hyperplanes (red and blue) that are able to separate the cases of the two classes. However, the blue hyperplane has a larger separating margin between the cases so we prefer it over the red.

To determine the maximum margin hyperplane SVMs use a quadratic optimization process. Going back to Figure 3.29, the equation of the separating hyperplane is,

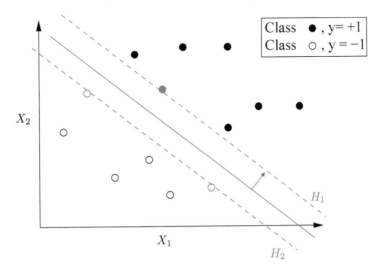

FIGURE 3.32: The maximum margin hyperplane and the support vectors.

$$\mathbf{w} \cdot \mathbf{x} + b = 0 \qquad (3.40)$$

where $\mathbf{w}$ is a vector of coefficients and b is the distance to the origin.

If we assume that the points of one of the classes have $Y = +1$ while the others have $Y = -1$, then we have that the separating hyperplane is such that,

$$\begin{aligned} \mathbf{w} \cdot \mathbf{x}_i + b \geq 0 \qquad & \forall i : y_i = +1 \\ \mathbf{w} \cdot \mathbf{x}_i + b \leq 0 \qquad & \forall i : y_i = -1 \end{aligned} \qquad (3.41)$$

These constraints still do not introduce the notion of margin. Assuming that the separating hyperplane is in the center of the two maximum margin hyperplanes, H_1 and H_2, as shown in Figure 3.32, and assuming that m is the distance from the maximum margin hyperplane to both H_1 and H_2, we can say that the equations defining these two hyperplanes are,

$$\begin{aligned} \mathbf{w} \cdot \mathbf{x}_i + b \; &= +m \\ \mathbf{w} \cdot \mathbf{x}_i + b \; &= -m \end{aligned} \qquad (3.42)$$

The points in these two hyperplanes are known as the *support vectors* (in red in Figure 3.32).

Without loss of generality we can scale the variables so that $m = 1$. Moreover, by definition of H_1 and H_2, we know that there are no cases between the two, which means that,

$$\begin{aligned} \mathbf{w} \cdot \mathbf{x}_i + b \geq +1 \qquad & \forall i : y_i = +1 \\ \mathbf{w} \cdot \mathbf{x}_i + b \leq -1 \qquad & \forall i : y_i = -1 \end{aligned} \qquad (3.43)$$

which can be re-written as,

$$y_i(\mathbf{w} \cdot \mathbf{x}_i + b) \geq +1 \qquad \forall i \tag{3.44}$$

SVMs search to maximize the margin between H_1 and H_2. Using linear algebra we can show that the distance between these two hyperplanes is the normalized difference between their constant terms, where the normalization factor is the L_2-norm, $\|\mathbf{w}\|$, of the coefficients. This means that the distance between H_1 and H_2 is $2/\|\mathbf{w}\|$, which is the margin we want to maximize. This maximization problem is inconvenient because calculating the L_2-norm involves a square root. This can be overcome because maximizing $2/\|\mathbf{w}\|$ is equivalent to minimizing $\frac{1}{2}\|\mathbf{w}\|^2$. Taking into account the constraints of Equation 3.43, this minimization is a convex quadratic programming problem.

This optimization problem can be solved with the help of Lagrange multipliers, through a method known as Lagrangian relaxation. This leads to the *primal* optimization problem defined as,

$$L_P = \frac{\|\mathbf{w}\|^2}{2} - \sum_{i=1}^{N} \lambda_i [y_i(\mathbf{w} \cdot \mathbf{x}_i + b) - 1] \tag{3.45}$$

where $\lambda_1, \cdots, \lambda_N \geq 0$ are the Lagrangian multipliers.

It is possible to derive a simpler *dual* optimization problem that is a lower bound of the solution to the *primal* problem L_P. Under a set of conditions known as the *Karush-Kuhn-Tucker conditions* the solutions to the two problems are equal. SVMs obtain the maximum margin hyperplane by solving this dual optimization problem, that consists of maximizing the following expression,

$$L_D = \sum_{i=1}^{N} \lambda_i - \frac{1}{2} \sum_{i=1}^{N} \sum_{j=1}^{N} \lambda_i \lambda_j y_i y_j (\mathbf{x}_i \cdot \mathbf{x}_j) \tag{3.46}$$

subject to,

$$\sum_{i=1}^{N} \lambda_i y_i = 0$$

$$\lambda_i \geq 0, \qquad 1 \leq i \leq N$$

At this stage it is important to remark that solving the problem of Equation 3.46 only requires knowledge of the class values (y_i's) and of the dot products between the cases in the dataset ($\mathbf{x}_i \cdot \mathbf{x}_j$). This latter issue is particularly relevant when we consider the case of non-linearly separable classes as we will see below.

Till now we have seen that SVMs solve the problem of linearly separable binary classification by finding the maximum margin hyperplane using a quadratic optimization approach that involves solving Equation 3.46. We have also mentioned that when cases are not linearly separable, SVMs move the data into a higher dimension where this is feasible, i.e. where they can apply the same optimization procedure.

When moving the data into a much higher dimension solving Equation 3.46 in this new space would involve dot products of vectors of a much higher size than the original data. This makes the computational complexity of the optimization problem much higher. Enter the so-called *kernel trick*. A kernel function, $K()$ is a function that when evaluated on two vectors of dimension p gives the same result as the dot product of the transformation of these two vectors into a much higher dimension r, i.e. $K(\mathbf{x}, \mathbf{z}) = \phi(\mathbf{x}) \cdot \phi(\mathbf{z})$, where ϕ is a mapping from the original space into a new higher dimension space. Let us see a concrete example. Suppose $\mathbf{x} = \langle x_1, x_2 \rangle$ and $\mathbf{z} = \langle z_1, z_2 \rangle$ are two points in a bi-dimensional space. Take the polynomial kernel of degree 2, defined as $K(\mathbf{x_i}, \mathbf{x_j}) = (\mathbf{x_i} \cdot \mathbf{x_j})^2$. In this context,

$$
\begin{aligned}
(\mathbf{x} \cdot \mathbf{z})^2 &= (\langle x_1, x_2 \rangle \cdot \langle z_1, z_2 \rangle)^2 \\
&= (x_1 z_1 + x_2 z_2)^2 \\
&= x_1^2 z_1^2 + x_2^2 z_2^2 + 2 x_1 x_2 z_1 z_2 \\
&= \langle x_1^2, x_2^2, \sqrt{2} x_1 x_2 \rangle \cdot \langle z_1^2, z_2^2, \sqrt{2} z_1 z_2 \rangle
\end{aligned}
$$

This means that the transformation $\phi(\langle x_1, x_2 \rangle) = \langle x_1^2, x_2^2, \sqrt{2} x_1 x_2 \rangle$ has the property that $K(\mathbf{x}, \mathbf{z}) = \phi(\mathbf{x}) \cdot \phi(\mathbf{z})$. In other words, instead of calculating the dot product of two vectors in a high dimension, $\langle x_1^2, x_2^2, \sqrt{2} x_1 x_2 \rangle \cdot \langle z_1^2, z_2^2, \sqrt{2} z_1 z_2 \rangle$, we can get the same exact result by applying the kernel function to two vectors of smaller dimension! While in this short illustrative example the difference in dimensions is irrelevant, with larger differences this can be crucial when you have to make a large number of dot products. That is the case with SVMs when they need to solve the optimization problem of Equation 3.46, for vectors in a very high dimension, which was necessary to solve the non-linearity in the original low-dimensional space. With this so-called kernel trick we can replace the dot products in this high dimension on Equation 3.46, by cheap kernel calculations in the original low-dimensional space.

Some common kernel functions are:

- Gaussian Kernel

$$K(\mathbf{x_i}, \mathbf{x_j}) = e^{\left(-\frac{\|\mathbf{x_i} - \mathbf{x_j}\|^2}{2\sigma^2} \right)}$$

- Polynomial Kernel with degree d

$$K(\mathbf{x_i}, \mathbf{x_j}) = (\mathbf{x_i} \cdot \mathbf{x_j})^d$$

- Radial Kernel

$$K(\mathbf{x_i}, \mathbf{x_j}) = e^{-\gamma \|\mathbf{x_i} - \mathbf{x_j}\|^2}$$

In summary, SVMs solve binary classification tasks by searching for the maximum margin hyperplane using a quadratic programming formulation. When the classes are not linearly separable this problem needs to be solved in a very high dimensional space. To escape the resulting computational problems due to "moving" into this high-dimension space, SVMs use the kernel trick we described above.

The above procedure works well with two linearly separable classes. Unfortunately, sometimes it is hard to get a perfect linear separation between the classes, even at high dimensions. In this context, SVMs tend to use a slightly more relaxed formulation than the one of Equation 3.46. This is usually known as the *soft margin optimization problem*. Essentially, this resorts to allowing a few cases to be on the "wrong" side of the separating hyperplane. For each of these cases we establish a penalty (frequently a parameter on SVM implementations). In this context, the optimization problem is slightly reformulated to take into account for this penalty for each case on the wrong side of the hyperplane. More specifically, it can be proven that the dual problem of this reformulated optimization task is exactly the same as before (Equation 3.46) with the addition of an extra constraint stating that $\lambda_i \leq C$, where C is the penalty to pay for each case on the wrong side of the hyperplane. This means that the *soft margin* optimization problem consists of finding the solution for Equation 3.46, subject to $\sum_{i=1}^{N} \lambda_i y_i = 0$ and $0 \leq \lambda_i \leq C$.

Till now we have always talked about binary classification tasks. How do SVMs tackle

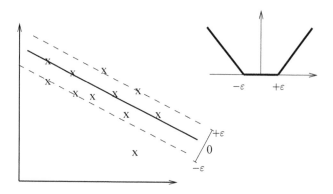

FIGURE 3.33: SVMs for regression.

non-binary classification? These problems are usually handled by solving m binary classification tasks with the previously described optimization method, where m is the number of classes of the problem. In summary, given a problem with m classes, obtain m hyperplanes, each separating the respective class from all others. Given a test case, we assign it to the class whose separating hyperplane is more distant, i.e. we have more confidence that it is on a certain side of the hyperplane.

The idea of SVMs was adapted to regression tasks in Vapnik (1995). The author has proposed ϵ-SV regression as a method that aims at finding an hyperplane whose distance to all training cases is at most ϵ. This means that there is a kind of "envelope" of size ϵ around the hyperplane where all cases are (Figure 3.33).

In the following short description we mostly follow Smola and Schölkopf (1998). ϵ-SV regression uses as an error metric the following,

$$|\xi|_\varepsilon = \begin{cases} 0 & \text{if } |\xi| \leq \varepsilon \\ |\xi| - \varepsilon & \text{otherwise} \end{cases} \tag{3.47}$$

This error metric and the idea of the "envelope" in ϵ-SV regression are synthesized in Figure 3.33.

The theoretical developments that lead to the formalization of the optimization problem for ϵ-SV regression are similar to what we have seen before for classification. For the more general case where we accept some cases outside of the "envelop" (each paying some penalty C) we have the following minimization problem,

$$\text{Minimize}: \quad \tfrac{1}{2}\|\mathbf{w}\|^2 + C\sum_{i=1}^{l}(\xi_i + \xi_i^*) \tag{3.48}$$

$$\text{Subject to}: \quad \begin{cases} y_i - \mathbf{w} \cdot \mathbf{x} - b & \leq \varepsilon + \xi_i \\ \mathbf{w} \cdot \mathbf{x} + b - y_i & \leq \varepsilon + \xi_i^* \\ \xi_i, \xi_i^* & \geq 0 \end{cases}$$

As in classification it is possible to use Lagrangian multipliers to obtain a primal optimization function that also has a dual representation that corresponds to the following optimization problem,

$$\text{Maximize}: \quad \begin{cases} -\tfrac{1}{2}\sum_{i=1}^{N}\sum_{j=1}^{N}(\lambda_i - \lambda_i^*)(\lambda_j - \lambda_j^*)(\mathbf{x}_i \cdot \mathbf{x}_j) \\ -\epsilon\sum_{i=1}^{N}(\lambda_i + \lambda_i^*) + \sum_{i=1}^{N}y_i(\lambda_i - \lambda_i^*) \end{cases} \tag{3.49}$$

$$\text{Subject to :} \qquad \left\{ \begin{array}{ll} \sum_{i=1}^{N}(\lambda_i - \lambda_i^*) & = 0 \\ \lambda_i, \lambda_i^* & \in [0, C] \end{array} \right.$$

Once again, when solving this problem in high dimension spaces we can resort to the kernel trick to avoid the computational burden of the dot products in Equation 3.49.

In R there are two main implementations of SVMs: the one available in package **e1071** (Dimitriadou et al., 2009), and that of package **kernlab** (Karatzoglou et al., 2004). Both follow a similar formula-based interface and are able to handle regression and (multi-class) classification tasks. Package **kernlab** is probably more flexible in terms of the available options. Let us look at a few examples with the simpler **svm()** function from package **e1071**.

```
> library(e1071)
> data(iris)
> set.seed(1234)
> rndSample <- sample(1:nrow(iris), 100)
> tr <- iris[rndSample, ]
> ts <- iris[-rndSample, ]
> s <- svm(Species ~ ., tr)
> ps <- predict(s, ts)
> (cm <- table(ps, ts$Species))
```

```
ps           setosa versicolor virginica
  setosa         12          0         0
  versicolor      0         20         1
  virginica       0          1        16
```

```
> 100*(1-sum(diag(cm))/sum(cm))  # the error rate
```

```
[1] 4
```

Using the default parameter settings as above, the **svm()** function uses a radial kernel with constraints violation cost of 1. For instance, to obtain a solution using a polynomial kernel of degree 3 and with a higher cost of constraints violations, we would do,

```
> s2 <- svm(Species ~ ., tr, cost=10, kernel="polynomial", degree=3)
> ps2 <- predict(s2, ts)
> (cm2 <- table(ps2, ts$Species))
```

```
ps2          setosa versicolor virginica
  setosa         12          0         0
  versicolor      0         20         3
  virginica       0          1        14
```

```
> 100*(1-sum(diag(cm2))/sum(cm2))  # the error rate
```

```
[1] 8
```

Below you will find similar illustrations for handling the regression task of the *Boston Housing* dataset,

```
> data(Boston,package='MASS')
> set.seed(1234)
> sp <- sample(1:nrow(Boston),354)
> tr <- Boston[sp,]
> ts <- Boston[-sp,]
> s1 <- svm(medv ~ ., tr)
> ps1 <- predict(s1, ts)
> mean(abs(ps1-ts$medv))

[1] 2.769211

> s2 <- svm(medv ~ ., tr, kernel="radial", cost=10, epsilon=0.02, gamma=0.01)
> ps2 <- predict(s2, ts)
> mean(abs(ps2-ts$medv))

[1] 2.400234
```

Further readings on support vector machines

A good reference book on SVMs is Cristianini and Shawe-Taylor (2000). A good alternative is also the book by Schölkopf and Smola (2002). The web site http://www.kernel-machines.org contains a large list of up to date references on this active area. For shorter documents Burges (1998) provides a nice tutorial on SVMs. Another good tutorial, this time focused on SVMs for regression, is the report by Smola and Schölkopf (1998).

3.4.5.4   Artificial Neural Networks and Deep Learning

Artificial Neural Networks (ANNs) are non-linear models that can be used to solve both classification and regression tasks. At the origins of these models is a strong biological inspiration. McCulloch and Pitts (1943) have proposed the first artificial model of a neuron. An artificial neural network is composed of a set of units (neurons) that are connected together, with each of these connections having an associated weight. Each of the units has an activation level and carries out a computation that provides means to update this activation level. In simple terms, obtaining an ANN consists of updating the weights of the connections in such a way that leads the model to produce "correct" outputs, i.e. good approximations of the function we are trying to "learn" given a historical record of function mappings (i.e. a training set).

Neurons in ANNs are computation units that receive inputs from other neurons, perform a computation using these inputs, and produce an output value that is fed into other neurons. ANNs also have some special neurons that allow the models to receive input from the outside world and also to output the overall result of their computation. Each connection between nodes has an attached weight that is a metaphor of the strength of synapses in real neural networks. The weights play a key role in the way the values transmitted from one neuron to the others influence the output of these neurons. By changing these weights in an adequate manner we can lead the ANN to produce the correct outputs, i.e. to provide a good approximation of the function we are modeling using some dataset.

Figure 3.34 shows a graphical representation of an artificial neuron. We can describe the computation taking place at these units as consisting of two sequential steps: (i) first we have a linear computation using the input values arriving from other units weighted by the strength of the respective connections; (ii) then a non-linear function (known as the activation function) is applied to the value resulting from the previous computation; (iii) the result of this non-linear function is the output of this neuron that is sent to the neurons to which the unit is connected.

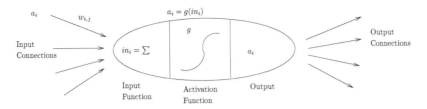

FIGURE 3.34: An artificial neuron.

The linear computation is essentially a weighted sum of the inputs to the neuron,

$$in_i = \sum_{j=1}^{k} w_{j,i} a_j \tag{3.50}$$

where k is the number of input neurons to the neuron i, $w_{x,y}$ is the weight of the connection between neurons x and y, and a_r is the output of neuron r.

The non-linear computation at neuron i is applied to the value in_i. It consists of an activation function that will determine the output of the neuron, a_i. Different activation functions lead to different behaviors of the ANN. Some common activation functions include,

- The Step Function

$$step(x) = \begin{cases} 1 & \text{if } x \geq t \\ 0 & \text{if } x < t \end{cases}$$

- The Sign Function

$$sign(x) = \begin{cases} +1 & \text{if } x \geq 0 \\ -1 & \text{if } x < 0 \end{cases}$$

- The Sigmoid Functions

$$sigmoid(x) = \frac{1}{1 + \exp^{-x}}$$

As we have mentioned before, an ANN is a set of neurons that are connected to each other. Rosenblatt (1958) introduced the *perceptron*, one of the simplest examples of an ANN. This work, later extended by Minsky and Papert (1969), defines a network formed solely by a set of input units (as many as there are predictor variables of the problem) that are directly connected to the output units. This type of network has very limited approximation capabilities (essentially linear tasks) and thus has essentially a historical interest. Multi-layer architectures are much more powerful and are the most frequently used type of networks. There are two main types of multi-layer ANNs: (i) feed-forward (acyclic); and (ii) recurrent (cyclic). The former consist of uni-directional connections between neurons from the input till the output neurons. The latter may include arbitrary connections between nodes. In our short description of this area we will focus on feed-forward multi-layer ANNs, which are the most common models of this type.

On feed-forward ANNs neurons are structured in layers. There is an *input layer* with as many neurons as there are predictor variables in the problem being tackled. At the other end there is the *output layer*. This may consist of a single neuron for regression tasks, or a set of neurons (as many as there are class values) in the case of classification problems. Between these two layers one may have one or more *hidden layers*, though the most common architecture includes a single hidden layer. Figure 3.35 illustrates this most common setup of feed-forward ANNs.

Training a multi-layer feed-forward ANN consists of iteratively presenting each training

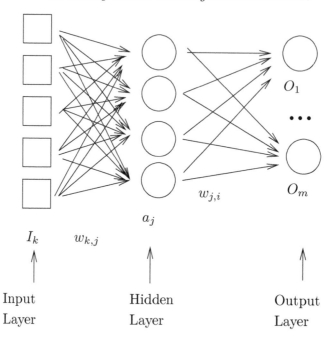

FIGURE 3.35: A feed-forward multi-layer ANN architecture.

case at the input nodes of the network and carrying out the calculations at each node in a forward manner (from the input to the output layers). Once an output is obtained in the output neurons this is compared with the true target variable value of the training case. If there is an error, then this error is used to update the weights of the ANN using a rule that we will discuss below. This iterative process keeps going until the weights of the ANN converge or some other termination criterion is reached.

The process of updating the weights consists of trying to propagate the error at the output neurons back to the neurons in previous layers. This is usually achieved by the application of an algorithm known as *backpropagation*. If O_i is the value at output node i, and T_i is the true target variable value of the training case, we can calculate the error at the output neuron as $Err_i = (T_i - O_i)$. The updating of the weights from the hidden layer units till this output unit is done using,

$$w_{j,i} = w_{j,i} + \eta \cdot a_j \cdot \Delta_i \tag{3.51}$$

where $\Delta_i = g'(in_i) \cdot Err_i$, with $g'(.)$ being the derivative of the activation function $g(.)$ while η is known as the learning rate.

To update the weights of the connections from the input units till the hidden layer units we need a quantity similar to Err_i for each of these units in the hidden layer. This is where the backpropagation idea enters. Each hidden unit j is responsible for a certain fraction of the error Δ_i in the output nodes to which it is connected. Thus each Δ_i value is going to be divided according to the weight of the connection between the respective hidden and output units (i.e. $w_{j,i}$), thus propagating the errors backwards. This corresponds to,

$$\Delta_j = g'(in_j) \cdot \sum_i w_{j,i} \cdot \Delta_i \tag{3.52}$$

where the i's are the output units to which the hidden unit j is connected.

Finally, we can update the weights from the input units to the hidden units using these Δ_j quantities, as follows,

$$w_{k,j} = w_{k,j} + \eta \cdot I_k \cdot \Delta_j \tag{3.53}$$

where k is an input unit and j is a hidden unit.

ANNs are a powerful modeling technique that have been shown to be *universal function approximators*, meaning that with the correct architecture they can approximate any function. Still, this generality comes with two main costs: (i) first we need to know how to correctly define the best network architecture for a given predictive task; and (ii) we must be able to pay the price of a potentially slow and computationally demanding convergence process. Nevertheless, on this latter issue one should add that ANNs architectures are very adequate for parallel computation and there are even specialized computer architectures designed from scratch to learn ANNs in an efficient manner.

In R the most frequently used implementation of feed forward ANNs is that provided by the package **nnet** (Venables and Ripley, 2002) that comes with base R. Other available implementations include the package **RSNNS** (Bergmeir and Benítez, 2012) that provides an interface to the Stuttgart Neural Network Simulator[29], the package **FCNN4R** (Klima, 2016) that provides an interface to the FCNN library[30] that is a fast and highly extensible C++ library for learning ANNs, and also the package **neuralnet** (Fritsch et al., 2012).

The following code illustrates using the function **nnet()** from package **nnet**,

```
> library(nnet)
> data(iris)
> set.seed(1234)
> rndSample <- sample(1:nrow(iris), 100)
> tr <- iris[rndSample, ]
> ts <- iris[-rndSample, ]
> n <- nnet(Species ~ ., tr, size=6 ,trace=FALSE, maxit=1000)
> ps <- predict(n, ts, type="class")
> (cm <- table(ps, ts$Species))
```

ps	setosa	versicolor	virginica
setosa	12	0	0
versicolor	0	20	1
virginica	0	1	16

```
> 100*(1-sum(diag(cm))/sum(cm))  # the error rate
```

```
[1] 4
```

The parameter `size` allows the user to specify how many neurons the hidden layer has (note that this package only allows for a single hidden layer). The parameter `trace` is simply to avoid the output of the convergence process involved in learning the network. Finally, the parameter `maxit` allows you to set a maximum number of iterations of the weight convergence process to limit the computation time. Although not used in the above call, the parameter `decay` can be used to set the learning rate (η in Equation 3.51). By default, the function `nnet()` sets the initial weights of the connections between neurons with random values in the interval $[-0.5 \cdots 0.5]$. This means that two successive runs of the function with exactly the same arguments can actually lead to different solutions. To

---

[29] http://www.ra.cs.uni-tuebingen.de/SNNS/
[30] http://fcnn.sourceforge.net/

ensure you get the same results as we present above, we have added a call to the function `set.seed()` that initializes the random number generator to some seed number.

As you can observe, the predict method of the resulting class of objects also includes the setting `type="class"` like **rpart** ojects, to obtain the actual predicted classes instead of a matrix of class probabilities.

For handling regression tasks the process is similar, but the function **nnet()** requires you to call it with the argument `linout=TRUE`, as seen in the following example,

```
> data(Boston,package='MASS')
> set.seed(1234)
> sp <- sample(1:nrow(Boston),354)
> tr <- Boston[sp,]
> ts <- Boston[-sp,]
> nr <- nnet(medv ~ ., tr, linout=TRUE, trace=FALSE, size=6, decay=0.01, maxit=2000)
> psnr <- predict(nr, ts)
> mean(abs(psnr-ts$medv))
```

```
[1] 3.028373
```

Neural networks are usually considered "black-box" models in the sense that we can not try to understand or show the models. Still, some efforts have been made in terms of trying to get some form of visualization of the outcome of these tools. Package **Neural-NetTools** (Beck, 2015) is an example of a package that provides some interesting tools for exploring these models. Figure 3.36 shows two plots obtained with this package. The left-most graph shows a ranking of the importance given by the network to each of the predictors of the *Boston Housing* dataset, whilst the right-hand graph shows the architecture of the neural network obtained above. The graphs were obtained as follows:

```
> library(ggplot2)
> library(NeuralNetTools)
> ## Feature importance (left graph)
> garson(nr) + theme(axis.text.x = element_text(angle = 45, hjust = 1))
> ## Network diagram (rigth graph)
> plotnet(nr)
```

In the plot of the neural network (right graph) obtained by function **plotnet()**, positive weights of neuron connections are presented in black, while negative weights are in gray. The line thickness is proportional to the relative magnitude of the weights. Function **garson()** obtains and plots (using the **ggplot2** infra-structure) a bar plot with the feature relevance scores of each of the input variables. It is interesting to observe the ranking of the features provided by the **garson()** function. On the top part of the ranking appears the pollution indicator **nox**. This indicator was actually the motivation of the original study with this dataset, i.e. to check if the pollution levels were having some impact on housing prices.

In recent years a new research area, usually known as *deep learning*, has emerged as a consequence of several successful practical applications of this type of technique. As we will see, there are strong relationships with ANNs and there are even critics who say that this is just a rebranding of ANNs that were seeing their popularity decrease.

Deep learning is related to the issue of representation of concepts with the long term objective of having machines that are able to learn concepts, a critical step toward artificial intelligence. The idea is to have a kind of hierarchy of concepts each built upon the previous simpler concepts. Thinking of image recognition, one of the success cases of the deep learning approaches, we can start at the lowest levels with pixels but we can build increasingly more

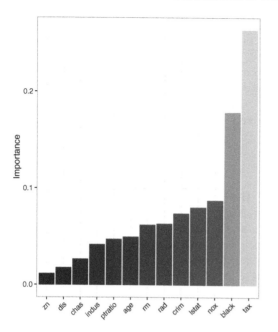

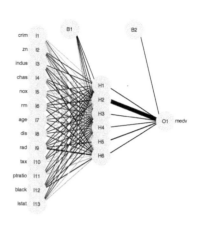

FIGURE 3.36: Visualizing the Boston neural network results.

complex features (e.g. edges) describing an image, with each new concept building up a hierarchy of increasing levels of abstraction. Obtaining this hierarchy of concepts can be seen as a kind of representation learning, i.e. we are trying to infer a new and more useful representation of what we observe by building a hierarchy of abstract concepts that describe these observations. The key to learning these deep representations was a seminal work by Hinton et al. (2006) that presented the idea of using a greedy layerwise unsupervised method to learn a hierarchy of features one level at a time. At each level an unsupervised feature learning method was used to create new features based on those of previous levels. This was achieved by learning weights of a deep (many levels) neural network. The outcome of this feature representation learning stage was a set of layers that were used as a starting point for learning a predictive model, e.g. an ANN.

From a simplistic point a view we can look at standard ANNs as a kind of *shallow* neural network containing just a few layers, while with *deep* learning neural networks we have many more layers (Schmidhuber, 2014). Deep learning neural networks (DLNNs) have been applied to many domains and also to different tasks. Here we will focus on the application to predictive tasks, also known as *supervised learning* tasks. Deep learning experts do not agree at which depth an ANN starts to become deep as opposed to the usual shallow networks we have seen before (Schmidhuber, 2014). Moreover, it is not clear which depth should be chosen for a given problem. As frequently is the case in predictive modeling, one has to try and compare different alternatives to reach a good solution. One potential drawback of DLNNs is that they basically increase the space of possible alternatives a lot, thus increasing the size of the model selection problem.

In R several packages were recently introduced that allow one to obtain DLNNs. Examples include the implementation available in package **h2o** (Aiello et al., 2016), package **mxnet** [31], package **darch** (Drees, 2013), or package **deepnet** (Rong, 2014). In our simple

---

[31]https://github.com/dmlc/mxnet/tree/master/R-package

illustrations we will use the implementation available in the H2O[32] open source machine learning platform. This is a very fast an scalable platform with interfaces to many languages, including R by means of the package **h2o**. This package includes several other predictive modeling techniques that you may also wish to explore, particularly if you are facing very large scale problems. Here we are simply going to provide very basic examples of how to use their deep learning neural network model.

After installing the package the first step is to start an instance of H2O.

```
> library(h2o)
> h2oInstance <- h2o.init(ip="localhost")   # start H2O instance locally
```

Function `h2o.init()` ca be used to start H2O instances. In this simple illustrative example we are running a local instance, but much more complex setups are available (check the documentation of the package for illustrations). We are using all defaults for this H2O instance as this is just an illustration. Once we have the instance up and running we can obtain models in H2O. The following code starts by loading the *Iris* dataset into H2O, creating an **H2OFrame** object, and then learns a deep feed-forward multi-layer ANN using this data.

```
> data(iris)
> set.seed(1234)
> rndSample <- sample(1:nrow(iris), 100)
> trH  <- as.h2o(iris[rndSample, ],"trH")
> tsH <- as.h2o(iris[-rndSample, ],"tsH")
> mdl <- h2o.deeplearning(x=1:4, y=5, training_frame=trH)
> preds <- h2o.predict(mdl,tsH)[,"predict"]
```

Function `as.h2o()` can be used to import a local data frame into the H2O instance. After doing this for the train and test sets we use the function `h2o.deeplearning()` for obtaining the model. This function does not use the standard formula interface. We specify the training data through parameter `training_frame` and then we use the parameters `x` and `y` to indicate the columns with the predictors and the target variables, respectively. Finally, function `h2o.predict()` can be used to obtain the predictions that are provided as a matrix with a column with the predicted class (the one we are selecting), and other columns with the estimated probabilities of each class. With these predicted classes we can calculate the error rate of the model,

```
> (cm <- table(as.vector(preds), as.vector(tsH$Species)))
```

```
           setosa versicolor virginica
setosa         12          0         0
versicolor      0         20         1
virginica       0          1        16
```

```
> 100*(1-sum(diag(cm))/sum(cm))
```

```
[1] 4
```

Note the need to convert both the predicted classes and the true values into vectors as they are both **H2OFrame** objects.

---

[32]http://www.h2o.ai/

The following is a small example of applying a similar strategy for a regression task, using the *Boston Housing* dataset,

```
> library(h2o)
> h2oInstance <- h2o.init(ip="localhost") # start H2O instance locally
> data(Boston,package="MASS")
> rndSample <- sample(1:nrow(Boston), 354)
> trH <- as.h2o(Boston[rndSample, ],"trH")
> tsH <- as.h2o(Boston[-rndSample, ],"tsH")
> mdl <- h2o.deeplearning(x=1:13, y=14, training_frame=trH,
+                          hidden=c(100,100,100, 100), epochs=500)
> preds <- as.vector(h2o.predict(mdl,tsH))
```

In the above example we have used the parameter **hidden** to specify the number of neurons on each hidden layer (four in this example). Moreover, we have also used the parameter **epoch** to specify the number of iterations of the convergence process.

Note that in the case of regression there are no associated probabilities so the result of the **h2o.predict()** function only contains a single column. With these predictions we can calculate the error as usual,

```
> mean(abs(preds-as.vector(tsH$medv)))
```

```
[1] 2.206557
```

Further readings on neural networks and deep learning
The book by Rojas (1996) is a general reference on neural networks. The work of McCulloch and Pitts (1943) presents the first model of an artificial neuron. This work was generalized by Ronsenblatt (1958) and Minsky and Papert (1969). The back-propagation algorithm, the most frequently used weight updating method, although frequently attributed to Rumelhart et al. (1986), was, according to Rojas (1996), invented by Werbos (1974, 1996). Regarding deep learning a good introduction is the article by Bengio (2009). Other good tutorial articles are the works by Bengio et al. (2012) and Schmidhuber (2014). The web page http://deeplearning.net/ is a great source of information on this recent research area including many pointers to documentation and software.

3.4.5.5 Model Ensembles

Ensembles are one of the most successful approaches to predictive analytics. In a nutshell, an ensemble is a set of models that together solve a concrete problem. The individual models are usually called the base learners and each of them is able to solve the predictive task being addressed. The main idea of ensembles is that of being able to capitalize on particularities distinguishing each base learner so that the aggregation of the models is able to perform better than each of them individually. In order to stimulate these gains one of the key aspects is the issue of diversity among ensemble members. The most frequent setting of ensembles is to use the same type of base learners (i.e. using the same modeling approach) that is applied to slightly different variants of the original data. These ensembles are usually knowns as *homogeneous ensembles*. Other types of ensembles use a diverse set of modeling tools leading to *heterogeneous ensembles*.

There are strong theoretical studies that somehow explain why ensembles are so successful (e.g. Dietterich (2000)). Still, intuitively it is easy to understand that for complex problems it is difficult to obtain a single model that is able to "explain" all the observations of the problem. In this context, it seems logical to think that averaging over different perspectives of the observations will usually lead to better performance. In terms of theoretical analysis one of the key explanations revolves around the notion of bias-variance decomposition of the error of a model. This decomposition results from understanding that the errors of predictive models have two main components: (i) the bias component is the part of the error that is due to the poor ability of the model to fit the observed data; while (ii) the variance component has to do with the sensibility of the model to the given training data. Different modeling techniques are more susceptible to one or the other of these causes of prediction errors. For instance, models that make strong assumptions on the functional form of the unknown function we are trying to approximate (e.g. linear models) may have a higher bias component if these assumptions are not completely accurate. On the other hand, models that are very flexible in terms of the functional form tend to suffer more from the problem of overfitting, thus being more sensitive to small variations in the available training sample, that may lead to rather different models. There is a well-known bias-variance tradeoff. In effect, decreasing the bias by adjusting more to the training sample will most probably lead to a higher variance — the overfitting phenomenon — while decreasing the variance by being less sensitive to the given training data will most probably have as a consequence a higher bias. Ensembles are able to reduce both components, which explains their success. By using as base models techniques with a high variance component we obtain models that are able to explain very accurately (often too much due to overfitting) the training sample provided. However, by using slightly different training samples to obtain each individual model, and then averaging over these models, we are able to reduce the variance of the overall set of models in spite of the individual models suffering from this problem.

In our necessarily short overview of this area we will focus on some of the most successful ensemble techniques. One of the first successful examples of an ensemble was *bagging* (Breiman, 1996). This is a very simple idea based on the usage of tree-based models as base learners. Bagging (Bootstrap Aggregating) is a method that obtains a set of k models using different bootstrap samples of the given training data. For each model a sample with replacement of the same size as the available data is obtained. This means that for each model there is a small proportion of the examples that will be different. If the base learner has a high variance (i.e. is very sensitive to variations on the training sample), this will ensure diversity among the k models. In this context, bagging should be applied using base learners with high variance as it is the case of tree-based models, particularly if not post-pruned.

Bagging is implemented in several R packages. An example is the implementation available in the package **adabag** (Alfaro et al., 2013). Below you can find a simple example of applying the function **bagging()** of this package,

```
> library(adabag)
> data(iris)
> set.seed(1234)
> rndSample <- sample(1:nrow(iris), 100)
> tr <- iris[rndSample, ]
> ts <- iris[-rndSample, ]
>  m <- bagging(Species ~ ., tr, mfinal=500)
> ps <- predict(m,ts)
> names(ps)

[1] "formula"   "votes"     "prob"      "class"     "confusion" "error"

> ps$confusion

                Observed Class
Predicted Class setosa versicolor virginica
     setosa         12          0         0
```

```
        versicolor     0       20        1
        virginica      0        1       16
```

```
> ps$error*100 # percentage of errors
```

```
[1] 4
```

The parameter `mfinal` controls the number of trees that is obtained, i.e. the number of base models in the ensemble. The `predict()` method of the obtained models produces a list with several components including the confusion matrix and the corresponding error rate. One drawback of the facilities of this package is that it is only able to handle classification tasks. For regression tasks we can use the implementation of bagging available in the package **ipred** (Peters and Hothorn, 2015). The following is an example of using it with the *Boston* dataset,

```
> library(ipred)
> data(Boston,package='MASS')
> set.seed(1234)
> sp <- sample(1:nrow(Boston),354)
> tr <- Boston[sp,]
> ts <- Boston[-sp,]
> m <- bagging(medv ~ ., tr, nbagg=500)
> ps <- predict(m, ts)
> mean(abs(ps-ts$medv))
```

```
[1] 2.930425
```

The function `bagging()` of package **ipred** uses the parameter `nbagg` to control the number of trees/models. This implementation uses the trees obtained by the function `rpart()` of the package **rpart**. It is possible to control the growth and pruning of these trees through some parameters of this `bagging()` function.

Breiman has evolved the general idea of bagging leading to the well-known and widely successful technique of random forests (Breiman, 2001). The general idea is similar in the sense that random forests are a set of k tree-based models, each obtained using a different bootstrap sample of the original dataset. The main difference to bagging resides in the way the trees are obtained. In order to generate even more variability among the individual models forming the ensemble, random forests grow each tree using a random component in terms of the predictors used. More specifically, as we have seen in Section 3.4.5.2 (page 145), trees are obtained with a recursive partitioning algorithm that includes a step designed to select the best test for each tree node. In "normal" trees this selection involves comparing the possible splits over all predictor variables. In random forests this search for the best split is carried out over a random subset of these variables. Moreover, this random selection is done at each node of the tree. The effect of this is that random forests use trees grown not only with different observations but also using different predictors, thus increasing the diversity of the individual models when compared to bagging. Random forests are currently among the most successful prediction models over a wide range of tasks.

In R there are several implementations of random forests. The main one, based on the original code by Leo Breiman, is available in the package **randomForest** (Liaw and Wiener, 2002). Its usage is fairly standard as the following simple example, using the *Breast Cancer* dataset available in the package **mlbench**, tries to illustrate,

```
> library(randomForest)
> library(DMwR2)
> data(BreastCancer, package="mlbench")
> bc <- cbind(knnImputation(BreastCancer[,-c(1,11)]), # column 1 is an ID
+             Class=BreastCancer$Class)
> set.seed(1234)
> rndSample <- sample(1:nrow(bc), 500)
> tr <- bc[rndSample, ]
> ts <- bc[-rndSample, ]
> m <- randomForest(Class ~ ., tr, ntree=750)
> ps <- predict(m, ts)
> (cm <- table(ps, ts$Class))
```

```
ps          benign malignant
  benign       114         1
  malignant      7        77
```

```
> 100*(1-sum(diag(cm))/sum(cm))  # the error rate
```

```
[1] 4.020101
```

The application of random forests to this particular task required some pre-processing stages. Specifically, we had to use some strategy to handle unknown values that this dataset contains, because this implementation of random forests is not able to use datasets with missing data. We have used the function `knnImputation()` from our book package for this purpose (we have eliminated the first column of the dataset because it was a useless patient ID). Regarding the function `randomForest()` we have used the parameter `ntree` to indicate the number of trees forming the ensemble. The function also includes another important parameter that controls the feature sampling process we have described above. This is the goal of parameter `mtry` that can be set to the number of features to randomly select at each node, when growing the trees.

Both bagging and random forests are examples of what are usually known as ensembles of *independent models*. In this type of ensemble each individual model is obtained independently of the others. This is an interesting property from a computational perspective. In effect, given the number of models typically included in ensembles, the computational cost of applying these approaches to very large datasets can be too high. Having independent base models means that in theory all of them could be obtained at the same time, i.e. these models are highly prone to parallel computation strategies. Packages taking advantage of these strategies for obtaining random forests include for instance, the package **Rborist** (Seligman, 2016) that provides an implementation of these models that can take advantage of multicore architectures and GPUs; the package **randomForestSRC** (Ishwaran and Kogalur, 2016); or the implementation available in the package **h2o** (Aiello et al., 2016) that we have already mentioned when describing deep learning in R.

There is another class of ensembles known as *coordinated models*, where each member of the ensemble is dependent on the others. Boosting algorithms belong to this class of models. Boosting (Schapire, 1990) was originally developed with the goal of answering the question: can a set of weak learners form a single strong learner? In this question a "weak" learner is a model that alone is unable to correctly approximate the unknown predictive function. Boosting algorithms work by iteratively creating a strong learner by adding at each iteration a new weak learner to make the ensemble. Weak learners are added with weights that reflect the learner's accuracy. After each addition the data is re-weighted such that cases that are still poorly predicted by the current set of models, gain more weight. This means that each new weak learner will focus on the errors of the previous ones.

AdaBoost (Adaptive Boosting) (Freund and Shapire, 1996) is one of the most well-known and successful boosting algorithms. It consists of an iterative process where new models are added to form an ensemble. It is adaptive in the sense that at each new iteration of the algorithm, the new models are built to try to overcome the errors made in the previous iterations. At each iteration the weights of the training cases are adjusted so that cases that were wrongly predicted get their weight increased to make new models focus on accurately predicting them. AdaBoost was originally created for classification tasks although variants for regression also exist, as we will see. AdaBoost produces a model that can be seen as an additive model where each term is a base model,

$$H(\mathbf{x}_i) = \sum_k w_k h_k(\mathbf{x}_i) \tag{3.54}$$

where w_k is the weight of the weak model $h_k(\mathbf{x}_i)$.

The AdaBoost algorithm starts by assigning the same weight to all training cases ($d_1(\mathbf{x}_i) = 1/N$, where N is the sample size). At iteration r the algorithm builds the weak model $h_r(\mathbf{x}_i)$ such that this model minimizes the weighted training error. This error is given by $e = \sum_i d_r(\mathbf{x}_i)I(y_i \neq h_r(\mathbf{x}_i))$, where $d_r(\mathbf{x}_i)$ is the weight of case $\langle \mathbf{x}_i, y_i \rangle$ at iteration r. The weight of the weak model $h_r(\mathbf{x}_i)$ is calculated by,

$$w_r = \frac{1}{2} \ln \left(\frac{1-e}{e} \right) \tag{3.55}$$

After obtaining the weak model at iteration r and the respective weight, the next iteration receives the same data sample but with the weights of the cases changed to reflect the failures of the current set of models. More specifically, the case weights for iteration $r + 1$ are updated by,

$$d_{r+1}(\mathbf{x}_i) = d_r(\mathbf{x}_i) \frac{\exp(-w_r I(y_i \neq h_r(\mathbf{x}_i)))}{Z_r} \tag{3.56}$$

where Z_r is a normalization factor chosen to make all d_{r+1} sum up to one.

Once again there are several implementations of boosting in R. The package **adabag** that we have seen before also contains the function `boosting()` that provides an implementation of `AdaBoost.M1` (Freund and Shapire, 1996) and of another boosting algorithm named `SAMME` (Zhu et al., 2009). The following is a simple illustration of its usage,

```
> library(adabag)
> data(iris)
> set.seed(1234)
> rndSample <- sample(1:nrow(iris), 100)
> tr <- iris[rndSample, ]
> ts <- iris[-rndSample, ]
> m1 <- boosting(Species ~ ., tr,   mfinal=500) # AdaBoost.M1
> ps1 <- predict(m1,ts)
> ps1$confusion

               Observed Class
Predicted Class setosa versicolor virginica
      setosa        12          0         0
      versicolor     0         20         1
      virginica      0          1        16
```

```
> ps1$error*100
```

```
[1] 4
```

```
> m2 <- boosting(Species ~ ., tr, coeflearn="Zhu", mfinal=500) # SAMME
> ps2 <- predict(m2,ts)
> ps2$confusion
```

```
                Observed Class
Predicted Class setosa versicolor virginica
       setosa       12          0         0
       versicolor    0         20         1
       virginica     0          1        16
```

```
> ps2$error*100
```

```
[1] 4
```

Gradient boosting (Friedman, 2002, 1999) is a boosting algorithm based on the idea of steepest-descent minimization establishing connections between boosting and optimization. Like other boosting algorithms it builds a model with an additive form as in Equation 3.54. At each iteration of gradient boosting we add a new weak learner that tries to overcome the errors of the current model ensemble. In gradient boosting this new weak learner is obtained by trying to fit the residuals (errors) of the current ensemble. This means that this model is trained with a dataset formed by the cases $\{\langle \mathbf{x}_i, r_i \rangle\}$, where $r_i = -\partial L(y_i, f(\mathbf{x}_i))/\partial f(\mathbf{x}_i)$ and $L(.)$ is a chosen loss function. The gradients for the most common loss functions are easy to obtain. For instance for the squared loss function $\frac{1}{2}[y_i - f(\mathbf{x}_i)]^2$ the value of $-\partial L(y_i, f(\mathbf{x}_i))/\partial f(\mathbf{x}_i)$ is $y_i - f(\mathbf{x}_i)$. Friedman (1999) has proposed the method named *gradient boosting machine* that follows these ideias and can be used to address several types of predictive tasks, including regression and classification.

The gradient boosting machine is implemented in package **gbm** (Ridgeway, 2015). The implementation provided in this package closely follows the original code by Friedman but it adds a few extra features. The following is a short example for the *Boston* dataset,

```
> library(gbm)
> data(Boston,package='MASS')
> set.seed(1234)
> sp <- sample(1:nrow(Boston),354)
> tr <- Boston[sp,]
> ts <- Boston[-sp,]
> m <- gbm(medv ~ ., data=tr, n.trees=5000)
```

```
Distribution not specified, assuming gaussian ...
```

```
> ps <- predict(m, ts, n.trees=5000)
> mean(abs(ps-ts$medv))
```

```
[1] 3.069492
```

Function gbm() can be used to obtain models using the gradient boosting machine. A first small note on the fact that, contrary to most modeling functions in R, this particuar function does not take the training data as the second argument, so we had to specify the parameter by name in the above code. The second parameter is actually **distribution** that allows the user to specify the loss function used in the gradient calculations. The default is to infer it from the type of the target variable, which in the above example leads to a Gaussian distribution that corresponds to the quadratic loss function we have mentioned before. You should check the help page of the `gbm()` function for other alternatives. Parameter `n.trees` allows you to indicate the number of weak learners in the model. The function includes many more parameters that allow fine tuning of the behavior of the model. When using the model for prediction you must specify how many of the trees you wish to use through the parameter `n.trees` of the predict method.

The following example illustrates the application of the function `gbm()` to a classification task, as well as other details of this function.

```
> data(iris)
> set.seed(1234)
> rndSample <- sample(1:nrow(iris), 100)
> tr <- iris[rndSample, ]
> ts <- iris[-rndSample, ]
>
> m <- gbm(Species ~ ., data=tr, n.trees=10000,
+               cv.folds=5, n.cores=4)

Distribution not specified, assuming multinomial ...

> (best <- gbm.perf(m, plot.it=FALSE, method="cv"))

[1] 3035

> ps <- predict(m, ts, n.trees=best, type="response")[,,1]
> ps <- as.factor(colnames(ps)[max.col(ps)])
> (cm <- table(ps, ts$Species))
```

```
ps           setosa versicolor virginica
  setosa         12          0         0
  versicolor      0         20         1
  virginica       0          1        16
```

```
> 100*(1-sum(diag(cm))/sum(cm))   # the error rate

[1] 4
```

With more than two classes, as in the case of *Iris*, the default for the parameter distribution is "bernoulli"[33]. In the above example we have set a large number of trees, and have also used the facilities provided by the package for parallel computation on multicore machines. We have indicated through parameter `n.cores` that we allow the function to use 4 cores of our processor[34]. We have also used parameter `cv.folds` to obtain cross validation estimates of the true prediction error of the model for the different number of trees. This allows us to use the function `gbm.perf()` to obtain the number of trees (from 1 to 10000 we have set in the parameter `n.trees` of `gbm()`) that gives the best predictive performance according to these cross validation estimates[35]. Finally, we use this best number of trees to call the predict method and obtain the final predictions. This required a bit more post-

---

[33]You may check the **gbm** package vignette for the mathematical details of the loss functions corresponding to each distribution.

[34]Please adjust this to your own hardware.

[35]Note the parameter `plot.it` of function `gbm.perf()` that if set to `TRUE` will show a graph with the error for the different alternatives - try it.

processing. With `type="response"` you get the predicted class probabilities for each test case. Unfortunately, if you want to get the label of the most probable class you need to do it yourself. We have obtained this using the function `max.col()` that returns the position of the maximum for each row of a matrix.

We can use the function `summary()` applied to the model to obtain information on the importance of the different features.

```
> summary(m, plotit=FALSE)

                      var    rel.inf
Petal.Length Petal.Length 65.542710
Petal.Width   Petal.Width 28.518834
Sepal.Width   Sepal.Width  4.928013
Sepal.Length Sepal.Length  1.010442
```

Argument `plotit=FALSE` avoids a plot with the same information. Variables are presented by decreasing relevance influence (i.e. feature importance).

Another interesting feature is the marginal plots that allow you to study how the variation on the values of a certain predictor variable will influence the value predicted by the model. The following code shows (c.f. Figure 3.37) the marginal plot between the variable Petal.Length (the third predictor in *Iris*) and the predicted class probabilities,

```
> plot(m, i.var=3, type="response")
> legend("topleft",c("setosa","versicolor","virginica"),
+          col=1:3,lty=1)
```

The graph in Figure 3.37 shows a very marked mapping between the values of `Petal.Length` and the class probabilities estimated by the gradient boosting machine. This somehow explains why the previous call to `summary()` clearly indicated this feature as the most relevant.

Further readings on ensembles

The book by Zhou (2012) is an interesting general reference on the foundations of ensembles. The article by Dietterich (2000) is another interesting reference on this area. Specifically on gradient boosting, the article by Friedman (2002) provides a good summary.

3.5 Evaluation

One of the key issues for a successful data mining project is to be able to correctly evaluate the performance of the proposed models. Reliable estimates of the performance are of utmost importance when it comes to deciding to deploy your models into production. Failing to provide these reliable estimates may eventually lead to disappointing results that may seriously compromise the application of data mining in the organization.

In this section we will focus on the evaluation of one particular type of metric — the predictive performance. Still, some of the things we discuss in this section will be applicable to other types of metrics.

Estimating the predictive performance of a model (or set of models) involves the following main issues:

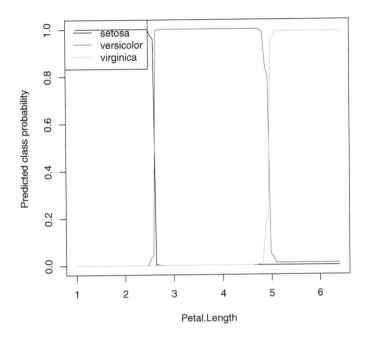

FIGURE 3.37: Marginal plot of Petal.Length.

- A predictive task: trying to approximate an unknown function $Y = f(\mathbf{x})$ that maps the values of a set of predictors into a target variable value (can be a classification or a regression problem, depending on the type of Y)

- A (training) dataset $\{< \mathbf{x}_i, y_i >\}_{i=1}^{N}$: with known values of this mapping

- Performance evaluation criterion(a): metric(s) of predictive performance (e.g. error rate or mean squared error)

In this context, our goal is to decide how to obtain **reliable estimates** of the predictive performance of any solutions we consider to solve the task using the available dataset.

The issue of the reliability of the estimates has to do with the problem of statistical estimation. The key question is whether the values of predictive performance we obtain have a high probability of being observed again, when we apply the same solutions to new samples of the data. Calculating the predictive performance of a model by applying it to the same data used to obtain the model is unreliable. The level of unreliability is proportional to the capacity of the models to overfit the given data. Models that have a higher ability to adjust to the given sample incur the risk of overfitting the sample and thus will obtain a very good score if evaluated on this same data. This however, will hardly occur with a different sample of data.

In this context, a golden rule of predictive performance evaluation is:

Always evaluate the models on unseen data.

This is the best way of obtaining a reliable estimate of the expected prediction error of a model on the unknown data distribution. A simple method of implementing this idea is to split the available data into two random partitions, as we have done in the previous section when presenting different modeling techniques: (i) a training set used to develop the models; and (ii) a test set to calculate their predictive performance. However, we should try to make sure this random splitting is repeated several times to increase the statistical reliability of the estimation process. With several repetitions we get a set of scores that we can then average to obtain a sample mean prediction error that can be seen as an estimate of the true population prediction error. Moreover, we can complement this estimate with the respective standard error.

An experimental methodology should allow us to obtain several prediction error scores that we can use to calculate the sample mean prediction error, $\overline{E} = \frac{1}{k} \sum_{i=1}^{k} E_i$, and also the respective standard error of this estimate, $SE(\overline{E}) = \frac{s_E}{\sqrt{k}}$, where s_E is the sample standard deviation of E measured as $\sqrt{\frac{1}{k-1} \sum_{i=1}^{k} (E_i - \overline{E})^2}$. In the next subsections we will describe a few examples of common experimental methodologies that can be used to obtain reliable estimates of the prediction error of the models.

In R there are several packages that provide facilities to carry out this sort of experiment with the goal of estimating and comparing the predictive performance of different models. Examples include the package **caret** (Kuhn, 2016) or the package **mlr** (Bischl et al., 2016). In our description we will use the package **performanceEstimation** (Torgo, 2014b). This package provides a highly general infrastructure for this type of experiments. The infrastructure is generic in the sense that it can be used to estimate the values of any performance metrics, for any workflow (solution) on different predictive tasks, namely, classification, regression, and time series tasks. The package also includes several standard workflows that allow users to easily set up their experiments limiting the amount of work and information they need to supply.

To use the package **performanceEstimation** the user needs to specify: (i) the predictive task(s) to use in the estimation experiment; (ii) the workflow(s) used to solve the task(s); and (iii) the estimation task, that includes the specification of the evaluation metric(s) and the methodology to use to obtain reliable estimates of this(ese) metric(s).

3.5.1 The Holdout and Random Subsampling

The holdout method consists of randomly dividing the available data sample in two subsets: one used for training the model, and the other for testing/evaluating it. A frequently used proportion is 70% for training and 30% for testing. If we have a small data sample there is the danger of either having too small a test set (unreliable estimates as a consequence), or removing too much data from the training set (worse model than what could be obtained with the available data). In this context, it is not surprising that this method is typically only used for very large data samples, and it is actually the preferred method in these situations. Still, we should remark that this method only leads to one single estimate as there is one single split.

A small variation of this idea, that is usually known as random subsampling, consists of repeating the random split on train and test partitions several times, thus leading to a method that obtains a set of scores, as many as the amount of times we repeat the random split.

The following is a small illustration of using package **performanceEstimation** to estimate the error rate of an SVM on the *Iris* dataset using the holdout method,

```
> library(performanceEstimation)
> library(e1071)
> data(iris)
```

```
> r <- performanceEstimation(PredTask(Species ~ ., iris),
+                            Workflow(learner="svm"),
+                            EstimationTask(metrics="err",method=Holdout(hldSz=0.3))
+                            )
```

```
##### PERFORMANCE ESTIMATION USING  HOLD OUT  #####

** PREDICTIVE TASK :: iris.Species

++ MODEL/WORKFLOW :: svm
Task for estimating  err  using
 1 x 70 % / 30 % Holdout
 Run with seed =  1234
Iteration :  1

> summary(r)


== Summary of a  Hold Out Performance Estimation Experiment ==

Task for estimating  err  using
 1 x 70 % / 30 % Holdout
 Run with seed =  1234

* Predictive Tasks ::  iris.Species
* Workflows  ::  svm

-> Task:  iris.Species
  *Workflow: svm
                err
avg     0.02222222
std             NA
med     0.02222222
iqr     0.00000000
min     0.02222222
max     0.02222222
invalid 0.00000000
```

The example above illustrates several new concepts related to the package **performanceEstimation**. The main function is `performanceEstimation()`, and it takes 3 main arguments specifying: (i) the task(s); (ii) the workflow(s); and (iii) the estimation task. A task is created with `PredTask()` by indicating the formula and the dataset. Using function `Workflow()` you specify the solution to the task(s) that you wish to evaluate. In this simplest form you are using a standard workflow provided by the package **performanceEstimation**. This workflow applies the modeling function whose name you supply through parameter `learner`, to the training set and then uses the `predict()` function to obtain the predictions of the resulting model for the test set. This sort of simple workflow is the most frequent, but as we will see later, further steps can be added to this standard workflow without having to write your own workflow functions, which you can for maximum flexibility. Function `EstimationTask()` allows you to specify the metrics that you wish to estimate and the method used for obtaining the estimates. In the above example we specify the error rate as metric and the holdout with a test size of 30% randomly selected rows, as the estimation methodology.

Function `summary()` can be applied to the object resulting from running the experiments to obtain an overview of the estimation results. In the above example, given that the holdout does not include several repetitions of the train/test split, we only get one score and thus some of the statistics do not make sense.

The following is an example of random subsampling, this time for estimating the mean squared error of a random forest on the *Boston* regression task,

```
> library(performanceEstimation)
> library(randomForest)
> data(Boston, package="MASS")
> r <- performanceEstimation(PredTask(medv ~ ., Boston),
+                            Workflow(learner="randomForest"),
+                            EstimationTask(metrics="mse",
+                                      method=Holdout(nReps=3,hldSz=0.3))
+                            )


##### PERFORMANCE ESTIMATION USING  HOLD OUT  #####

** PREDICTIVE TASK :: Boston.medv

++ MODEL/WORKFLOW :: randomForest
Task for estimating  mse  using
 3 x70 %/ 30 % Holdout
 Run with seed =  1234
Iteration :  1  2  3

> summary(r)


== Summary of a  Hold Out Performance Estimation Experiment ==

Task for estimating  mse  using
 3 x70 %/ 30 % Holdout
 Run with seed =  1234

* Predictive Tasks ::  Boston.medv
* Workflows  ::  randomForest

-> Task:  Boston.medv
  *Workflow: randomForest
             mse
avg      14.012785
std       7.899818
med      11.742487
iqr       7.651238
min       7.496696
max      22.799171
invalid   0.000000
```

The `Holdout()` function has a parameter (`nReps`) that allows you to specify how many random train/test splits you want, which leads to what we know as random subsampling.

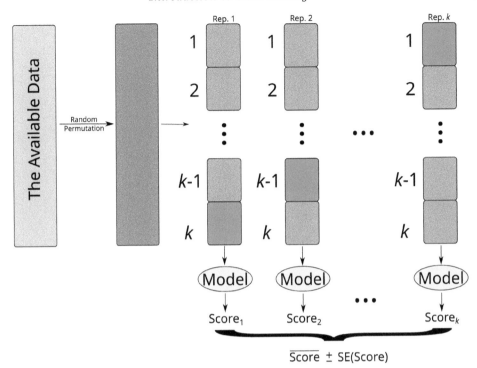

FIGURE 3.38: k-Fold cross validation.

3.5.2 Cross Validation

k-Fold cross validation (CV) is one of the most common methods to estimate the predictive performance of a model. It consists of repeating k times a train/test cycle, but where the test set is carefully chosen instead of randomly selected as in k repetitions of random subsampling. Figure 3.38 provides an illustration of the process. We start by randomly reshuffling the training data to avoid any ordering effects. Then we split the dataset into k equal-sized partitions. These will be the k test sets (in orange in the figure). For each of the test sets the respective training set will be formed by the remaining $k-1$ partitions (dark yellow in the figure). The $k-$fold cross validation estimate will be the average of the k individual scores obtained on each test partition.

$k-$fold CV is frequently the procedure selected for estimating the performance of a model. It is the recommendation for mid-sized datasets (few hundreds to few thousand cases). Sometimes we repeat the process several times and average these repetitions to increase the reliability of the estimates.

Package **performanceEstimation** includes this methodology as one of the possible estimation methods. The following is an example of its usage for estimating the performance of a set of variants of a regression tree in the *Boston* dataset,

```
> library(performanceEstimation)
> library(DMwR2)
> data(Boston, package="MASS")
> r <- performanceEstimation(
+          PredTask(medv ~ ., Boston),
+          workflowVariants(learner="rpartXse",
+                          learner.pars=list(se=c(0,0.25,0.5,1,2))),
+          EstimationTask(metrics=c("mse","mae"),
```

```
+                              method=CV(nReps=3,nFolds=10))
+       )



##### PERFORMANCE ESTIMATION USING  CROSS VALIDATION  #####

** PREDICTIVE TASK :: Boston.medv

++ MODEL/WORKFLOW :: rpartXse.v1
Task for estimating  mse,mae  using
 3 x 10 - Fold Cross Validation
 Run with seed =  1234
Iteration :*****************************


++ MODEL/WORKFLOW :: rpartXse.v2
Task for estimating  mse,mae  using
 3 x 10 - Fold Cross Validation
 Run with seed =  1234
Iteration :*****************************


++ MODEL/WORKFLOW :: rpartXse.v3
Task for estimating  mse,mae  using
 3 x 10 - Fold Cross Validation
 Run with seed =  1234
Iteration :*****************************


++ MODEL/WORKFLOW :: rpartXse.v4
Task for estimating  mse,mae  using
 3 x 10 - Fold Cross Validation
 Run with seed =  1234
Iteration :*****************************


++ MODEL/WORKFLOW :: rpartXse.v5
Task for estimating  mse,mae  using
 3 x 10 - Fold Cross Validation
 Run with seed =  1234
Iteration :*****************************

> rankWorkflows(r, top=3)

$Boston.medv
$Boston.medv$mse
     Workflow Estimate
1 rpartXse.v1 19.33560
2 rpartXse.v4 19.54624
3 rpartXse.v3 19.98751

$Boston.medv$mae
     Workflow Estimate
1 rpartXse.v1 2.937393
```

```
2 rpartXse.v2 3.029241
3 rpartXse.v3 3.077736
```

Trying different parameter variants of a model or a set of models is a frequent task an analyst often needs to carry out. Function `workflowVariants()` is designed to help with this task. It can be used to automatically generate a vector of **Workflow** objects without having to create all of them through the function `Workflow()` and typing all their details. Essentially it works by allowing the user to indicate vectors of values instead of concrete values in some parameters of the **Workflow** constructor. For instance, in the example above, in the parameter of `Workflow()` that allows us to indicate the learning parameters to be used when calling the specified model (the parameter `learner.pars`), we are indicating that the parameter `se` (a parameter of the learner `rpartXse()` that sets the level of pruning), takes a vector of values. These values are interpreted as alternatives and thus the function `workflowVariants()` will generate as many workflows as there are variants. In case you indicate sets of values for more than one parameter, the function will generate as many workflows as there are combinations of the specified values. This is particularly handy when you are searching for the best variant of an algorithm that contains many possible parameters.

In terms of the estimation task, the above code uses 3 repetitions of a 10-fold CV process, to obtain estimates for both mean squared and absolute errors.

Finally, we have used the function `rankWorkflows()` to obtain the top 3 workflows for each of the metrics. You may be curious about the characteristics of the workflow that achieved the best results. Function `getWorkflow()` can be used with this purpose,

```
> getWorkflow("rpartXse.v1", r)
```

```
Workflow Object:
Workflow ID        ::  rpartXse.v1
Workflow Function ::  standardWF
    Parameter values:
 learner.pars  -> se=0
 learner  -> rpartXse
```

As we can observe this is a regression tree with best estimated error, i.e. the 0-SE tree (c.f. Section 3.4.5.2).

We may also explore the results of the estimation experiments visually (c.f. Figure 3.39) as follows,

```
> plot(r)
```

You get a boxplot for each workflow with the distribution of the scores obtained on each repetition (the concrete individual scores are shows as red dots).

3.5.3   Bootstrap Estimates

The bootstrap is another frequently used methodology for obtaining estimates of the predictive performance of a model. The bootstrap is based on the concept of sampling with replacement. This technique can be explained with the simple example of drawing x balls from a closed bag containing x balls. In sampling with replacement, after picking a ball from the bag we put it again inside the bag, which means that the next ball we take may actually be the same. Bootstrap consists of taking k random samples with replacement of size N, where N is the size of the available dataset. This means that the k samples will have

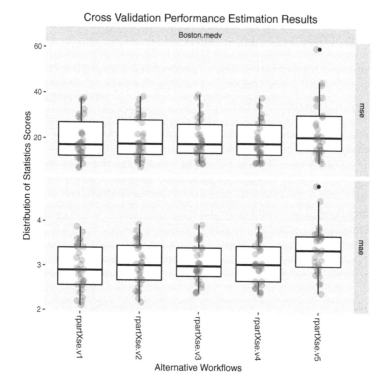

FIGURE 3.39: The results of a 10-fold CV estimation experiment.

the same size as the initial dataset but will contain "repeated" rows of this dataset. It can actually be shown that on average each bootstrap sample will contain 63.2% of the rows in the original dataset. For each bootstrap sample the rows that were not used will form the respective test set. This means that we obtain the model with the bootstrap sample (that will have size N) and obtain the score by applying this model on the test set formed with the rows of the original dataset not present in the training set. ϵ_0 bootstrap estimates are calculated as the average of the k scores obtained by the process we have described. An alternative are the 0.632 bootstrap estimates. These consist of a weighted average between the ϵ_0 estimates and the resubstitution estimate. This latter is obtained by applying the model to the full dataset and then testing it on the same full set. The 0.632 estimate is then obtained as $0.368\epsilon_r + 0.632\epsilon_0$, where ϵ_r is the resubstitution estimate.

Bootstrap estimates are typically obtained using a large number of repetitions of the random sampling (typically 100-200 repetitions). This method is considered one of the best options for small datasets (less than a few hundred cases).

The package **performanceEstimation** contains an implementation of both ϵ_0 and 0.632 bootstrap estimates. The following is an example of its application to the *Iris* dataset (we have hidden the output of the `performanceEstimation()` as there are too many variants and repetitions),

```
> library(performanceEstimation)
> library(DMwR2)
> library(e1071)
> data(iris)
> data(BreastCancer, package="mlbench")
```

```
> bc <- cbind(knnImputation(BreastCancer[,-c(1,11)]),
+             Class=BreastCancer$Class)
> r <- performanceEstimation(
+         c(PredTask(Species ~ ., iris),
+           PredTask(Class ~ ., bc)),
+         workflowVariants(learner="svm",
+                          learner.pars=list(cost=c(1,5,10),
+                                            gamma=c(0.01,0.001))),
+         EstimationTask(metrics="acc",
+                        method=Bootstrap(nReps=200,type=".632"))
+   )
```

In this example we have included two different prediction tasks. Function `performanceEstimation()` allows you to provide a vector of **PredTask** objects in its first argument[36]. As workflows we have indicated six variants of an SVM. Finally, the estimation task consists of using .632 bootstrap (200 repetitions) to estimate the accuracy of these alternative workflows.

We can check the best workflows for each task as follows,

```
> topPerformers(r , maxs=TRUE)

$iris.Species
    Workflow Estimate
acc   svm.v3    0.964

$bc.Class
    Workflow Estimate
acc   svm.v3    0.967
```

Function `topPerformers()` will show the workflow that obtained the best score on each metric, for each predictive task. The notion of "best" depends on the evaluation metric. For accuracy "best" means maximum, while for instance, for error rate "best" would mean minimum. The function assumes minimization by default, but you can use the parameter `maxs` to specify a different criterion for each metric.

3.5.4 Recommended Procedures

In previous sections we have described a few of the existing and most frequently used methods of estimating the predictive performance of a modeling approach. This section provides a few guidelines on this important step of the data mining workflow.

Our recommendations for classification or regression tasks can be summarized as follows:

- Small datasets (less than a few hundred observations) - use 100-200 repetitions of a bootstrap procedure.

- Average-sized datasets (less than a few thousand cases) - use a few repetitions of 10-fold cross validation.

- Large datasets - use Holdout (70%-30% split) or a few repetitions of random subsampling.

---

[36]Please note that they must be the same type of tasks; in this example both are classification tasks.

Although there are other alternative methodologies (and we will see some of them in the case studies to be addressed in Part II of the book), these are reasonable defaults that you can use. Obviously, some of these decisions are dependent on the computing power you have available for carrying out these experiments and also the number of tasks and/or workflows. In this context, it is also important to be aware that several of the R functions include parallel computation options that may allow you to improve the efficiency of your workflows. An example is the `performanceEstimation()` function, which has the possibility of taking advantage of parallel computation backends ranging from the simple local parallelization using the different cores of multicore processors, to more sophisticated settings using computer clusters. Check the help page of this function for further details.

In terms of results analysis sometimes it is important to check the statistical significance of the observed differences between the performance of the alternative workflows you may have considered to solve some task(s). Demsar (2006) provides a well-acknowledged study of this subject. In the following description we mostly follow the recommendations of this study. We are going to distinguish between two basic setups: (i) comparing several workflows on a single predictive task; and (ii) comparing them over multiple tasks. For the former the accepted procedure involves using the Wilcoxon signed rank statistical test to compare the scores of the different workflows. This is a non-parametric statistical hypothesis test that can be used to make paired comparisons of two population mean ranks. It is preferable to the also used *t*-Student paired test on this type of experimental comparisons because most experimental methods break some of the assumptions of this latter test. In this context, we can use the Wilcoxon signed rank test to check the statistical significance of the differences between the performance of any pair of workflows. For the second setup, where we are comparing several workflows over a set of predictive tasks, the recommendations in Demsar (2006) is to proceed in two stages. First we use a Friedman test to check the validity of the null hypothesis that all workflows are equivalent and so their rankings across the tasks are equal. If we can not reject this hypothesis with some selected level of confidence then we stop here, concluding that we can not reject the hypothesis that all workflows perform equally. Otherwise, we can proceed to the second step. If we are interested in all paired comparisons among all pairs of workflows then we should use a Nemenyi post-hoc test to check the null hypothesis that there is no significant difference among the ranks of a certain pair of workflows. If instead we are interested in all paired comparisons against a certain baseline workflow, then we should use the Bonferroni-Dunn post-hoc test to check the null hypothesis that there is no significant difference among the ranks of a certain workflow and the baseline.

The package **performanceEstimation** includes function `pairedComparisons()` that can be used to perform these and other statistical tests based on the outcome of the `performanceEstimation()` function. The package also includes some visual representations of the outcome of these tests, namely through CD diagrams (Demsar, 2006). In several of the case studies we will address in Part II of the book we will illustrate the usage of these facilities.

3.6 Reporting and Deployment

Once we are confident on the quality of our data mining procedures we need to communicate them. This frequently involves: (i) some sort of reporting to other people within some organization; and/or (ii) trying to deploy the outcome of our data mining workflow into production stages. While these steps are sometimes not considered very related to data mining, but more about communication abilities or standard software engineering in the case of deployment, the fact is that these are critical steps for the successful adoption of data mining technologies.

In this context, and given that R includes some packages that were designed to facilitate these important steps, we will provide a short overview of these functionalities.

3.6.1 Reporting Through Dynamic Documents

Reporting can be a key element for a successful data mining project. Being able to correctly and effectively communicate the outcome of your analysis is a crucial step for its acceptance. This communication can occur at different stages of your data mining project and it may involve different types of people. They can be technically-oriented (e.g. other collaborators of the data mining project), or non-technical people (e.g. management). Whatever is the case it is important to have tools that facilitate your task to efficiently report your results.

Classical approaches to reporting involve using software tools that are different from the tools you use for data mining (in our case R). This creates a large potential for inefficiencies and human errors. In effect, these software tools are typically word processing and presentation tools that normally do not have easy ways of communicating with data mining software. This means that a large part of your data mining results will be sent to these reporting tools through manually copy-pasting steps, or manually creating results files that are then inserted in your documents. All this is highly tedious and time-consuming, but also seriously prone to error. Moreover, if any changes are required to your report then you typically need to re-do all (or at least some of) these manual steps. This reporting workflow means that the *analysis* and the *reporting* are separate and someone needs to spend time in making sure they are *in-sync* to avoid reporting inaccuracies. Other drawbacks of this workflow are that it makes sharing your work with other members of the team difficult and it is also hard to re-use your reporting steps for other tasks. Sharing is difficult because the connection between what you report to other members of the team and what you have really implemented to obtain these results, is through a series of manual steps to send your results from the analysis tool into the reporting tool. This means your report does not "contain" your solution and if someone wants to replicate your analysis or pickup from where you are, then you need another effort for communicating the real analysis that lead to the results seen in the report. On the other hand, re-use is hard because a large part of what you see in the report involved manual steps that are not easily automated (e.g. frequent use of graphical user interface operations).

Due to all these "problems" with this classical approach, most modern data mining tools include reporting facilities that try to address these and other issues. R is not an exception. In this section we will describe a particular approach that is available in R that is based on the interesting concept of *dynamic documents*. These documents mix data analysis steps with descriptive text. They are executable by a computer program that produces the final document that you will use to communicate with the end-users. Dynamic documents solve most of the problems we have described before! In effect, by including the analysis steps together with the descriptive text, in a single place, we make sure that what we show to the audience is the real result of some concrete analysis steps with no possibility of reporting errors because there are no manual steps in transforming the analysis into the results — all is done by a computer program. This means that if the analysis contains an error this will show up in the final document, and moreover, whatever appears in this final document is supported by some concrete analysis steps that you can easily share with others for them to replicate your analysis, if necessary.

The idea of dynamic documents is strongly related to the concept of literate programming described by Knuth (1984). The usage of dynamic reports involves the following steps: (i) the analyst writes the dynamic report that includes both the analysis steps and the text to communicate to the audience; (ii) using a specific software tool the dynamic document is parsed separating the analysis parts from the descriptive parts; (iii) the same tool "executes" the analysis steps and grabs the results re-inserting them in the places where the respective analysis steps were, thus producing the final report.

R has several packages that implement this concept. Still, the framework provided by package **knitr** (Xie, 2015)[37] has recently emerged as the most effective. This is a general package that implements the literate programming concept supporting different document formats, including LaTeX, HTML and MARKDOWN, as well as different programming languages to implement the analysis steps. As output format you can have **knitr** produce a wide range of common formats, like PDF, HTML or WORD documents, to name just a few. For instance, this book you are now reading was fully produced using **knitr**, using LaTeX and R as the sources of the original dynamic document.

In our brief description of how to use **knitr** we will focus on a concrete type of dynamic document that uses R markdown as the source document format. Files in R markdown are normal text files that include R code together with text formated in MARKDOWN. This is a very simple markup language that was designed to easily produce Internet content.

You create R markdown files in any standard text editor by writing your text using short annotation tags to format it. Moreover, you can use some special tags to delimit parts that contain R code that carries out some analysis steps you are describing, known as *code chunks*. For instance, writing ****hello**** in your R markdown dynamic document will make the word `hello` appear in bold-face in the final document. There several other annotation tags that allow you to implement the most common formatting procedures (e.g. lists of items, section headings, etc.). The Web page `http://rmarkdown.rstudio.com/` contains extensive information on this document format as well as useful summaries of the main tags[38].

Figure 3.40 shows a simple example of an R markdown dynamic document (left side) and the resulting final document (right side), in this case an HTML document that you can read on any standard Web browser. The dynamic document starts with an optional heading (lines 1 to 6) where some meta information about the document is included. In this case the author name, the title and date of the document, and the type of output for the final document. In case you are using RStudio to produce your R markdown document, which I recommend, all this is automatically filled in by answering a few questions on a dialog box that appears when you select to create a new R markdown report. As you can observe both the author and the title information are adequately inserted in the final document.

Going back to the source document you may observe some "special" parts that are shown in light gray. These are code chunks that are delimited by special tags (e.g. lines 8 and 10 for the first code chunk). Once again if you are using RStudio you will have a button on the text editor that allows you to insert a new code chunk without having to type these delimiters. You may also have noticed that these chunks have some options on the first delimiter. These chunk options control the way they are executed by R. The default (without any option, just the letter "r") tells knitr that the chunk code is to be executed by R[39] and creates two parts in the final document for each code chunk: (i) one with the R code of the chunk properly formatted; and (ii) the other with the result of running the code in the chunk. Chunk options can be used to change this default behavior. For instance, the option `echo=FALSE`

---

[37]`http://yihui.name/knitr/`

[38]`http://www.rstudio.com/wp-content/uploads/2016/03/rmarkdown-cheatsheet-2.0.pdf`

[39]If instead you type "`python`" you can type Python code in your chunk that will be executed by a Python interpreter to produce the final results in the document.

FIGURE 3.40: An example of an R markdown document and the final result.

(e.g. first code chunk) hides the code from the final document, though still executing it and showing its results (if it produces any). On the other hand, if you just want to show a piece of R code without executing it you can use the chunk option `eval=FALSE`. These and many other options that you may browse at `http://yihui.name/knitr/options/`, can be used to control what R does with the chunks in your dynamic document.

On line 12 you have an example of how to create a first-level heading using the character # (further #'s will create other level headings). You may also have noticed that the first paragraph (line 14) includes some special text, called inline code, delimited by '`r ... `'. These are pieces of R code, typically expressions or function calls that you want R to evaluate and return the result that is shown in the document. With inline code you may avoid having to change the document due to some minor changes in your data. For instance, if the *Iris* data frame grows (e.g. someone adds information on a few more plants), you will not have to touch the report, you just need to re-compile it, which in RStudio consists of clicking a button. Moreover, these sort of constructs help in making your reports more general and more re-usable.

Producing the final report from the source R markdown text in RStudio can be achieved by a simple click of the appropriate button in the text editor. In other environments you will have to run the **render()** function on the dynamic report source file, as the following example shows,

```
> library(rmarkdown)
> render("myreport.Rmd")
```

This function also accepts other arguments that can control the output that is generated, which can be used instead of the YALM heading information we have seen in the example shown in Figure 3.40. For instance, the following function call with the same source document would generate a Word docx file named "myreport.docx",

```
> render("myreport.Rmd", output_format="word_document")
```

There are many more features provided by **knitr** dynamic reports that the above example did not tackle. For instance, there are ways of handling bibliographic references, special formatting of tables or the introduction of equations. We strongly advice you to browse through the Web pages of R markdown[40] to check these and other more advanced features. Moreover, you should be aware that it is equally easy to create presentation slides or dashboards using R markdown. The process is very similar with a few specificities of these types of outputs.

A final note on a recent feature of dynamic documents called *interactive documents*. This is an extension of R markdown documents that allows you to include some graphical widgets in these documents that provide the user with ways of interacting with the documents changing the resulting output as a result of this interaction. For instance, you may show a plot in your document and have some drop-down menu or some slider shown beside the plot that allows the user to change the plot dynamically. You should be aware that this is only feasible when the output is an HTML document, although this can be either a report or a presentation. More information about this interesting feature is available at `http://rmarkdown.rstudio.com/authoring_shiny.html` .

3.6.2   Deployment through Web Applications

Deploying the results of your data mining workflow is frequently a task that is highly dependent on the software infrastructure of your organization, particularly if you want to integrate your "tools" with other existing tools. In those cases that is mostly a software engineering task that will require strong communication/collaboration with the software engineering team of the target organization. Nevertheless, in some cases this integration/communication is not required and we can provide our tools to end-users through a simpler process: Web applications.

Web applications are client-server software tools that allow the end-user to run the applications in a standard Web browser without having to install any extra software in their computer. They are becoming highly trendy due to some of their advantages over more standard applications. Among these advantages we can quote: (i) no complex installation and upgrading processes; (ii) "no" requirements from the client side (simply a compatible browser); (iii) cross-platform compatibility; or (iv) extensions to other devices (smartphones, tablets, etc.). Nevertheless, they also have some drawbacks, like: (i) some sacrifice in terms of usability when compared to traditional applications due to the user interface limitations associated with the Web; (ii) potential problems with Internet connectivity; or (iii) concerns with privacy due to the usage of the Web for communicating potentially sensitive information/data.

Shiny[41] is a Web application framework for R. It has a very intuitive and simple workflow that allows developing web applications very easily. It allows you to deploy your data mining results produced with R through a web application. Shiny is developed by RStudio and thus it is not surprising to observe that is very well integrated with recent versions of RStudio integrated development environment.

To create Shiny web applications you need to install the package **shiny** (Chang et al., 2016). The basic building blocks of a Shiny web application are two files named "ui.R" and "server.R". These files should be stored in a separate directory, whose name will be the name of the web application. The file ui.R takes care of the interaction with the user,

---

[40]http://rmarkdown.rstudio.com/
[41]http://shiny.rstudio.com/

i.e. the user interface elements, while file `server.R` implements the server-side logic of your application, i.e. the actual work that produces the results that you want to show in the browser of the user.

Once you have these two files created and stored in a separate directory you may run your application either by pressing the corresponding button in the editor of RStudio if you are using this environment, or by issuing the following commands at R prompt:

```
> library(shiny)
> runApp("myAppFolderName")
```

Let us see a small example of a very simple web application that shows a conditioned boxplot of one of the predictors of the *Iris* dataset. The application allows the user to select the predictor and as a result it shows the distribution of this variable conditioned by `Species`, using boxplots. The following is the code in the `ui.R` file that controls the user interface of this simple application:

```
library(shiny)
data(iris)

shinyUI(fluidPage(
  titlePanel("Exploring the Iris dataset"),
  sidebarLayout(
    sidebarPanel(
      selectInput("var",
                  "Select a Predictor Variable:",
                  choices=colnames(iris)[1:4])
    ),
    mainPanel(
      plotOutput("condBP")
    )
  )
))
```

This script essentially defines the layout of the web application and also creates the user interface elements (in this case a simple drop-down menu and a plot). This layout is defined through function `shinyUI()`. In this case we are selecting a certain type of web page through function `fluidPage()` and then adding several elements to this page. More specifically, a title panel at the top (through function `titlePanel()`) and then a side-bar layout (through function `sidebarLayout()`). This latter part of the interface consists of a sidebar panel (function `sidebarPanel()`) where we will include a drop-down menu using the function `selectInput()`, and then a main panel (function `mainPanel()`) containing the respective conditioned boxplot that will be "created" in the server side script. Note that most user interface elements have names so that we can check or change their content. These elements will be distinguished between input elements, like for instance the drop-down menu widget named "var"; and output elements, like the plot named "condBP" that will be shown in the main panel. As we will see, in the server side we will check the values selected by the user on the input elements and will produce results to be shown through the output elements in the user interface.

The script with the server side logic (`server.R`) for this simple application is the following,

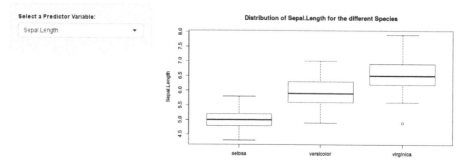

FIGURE 3.41: A simple example of a Shiny web application.

```
library(shiny)
data(iris)

shinyServer(
    function(input, output)
        {
            output$condBP <- renderPlot(
                {
                    form <- as.formula(paste(input$var,"~ Species"))
                    boxplot(form,iris,ylab=input$var,
                        main=paste("Distribution of",input$var,
                            "for the different Species"))
                }
            )
        }
)
```

The server side logic defines a function using **shinyServer()** that receives two lists as arguments: (i) the list named **input** that contains as many named components as there are interface elements in the user interface, allows you to check the user selections on these elements; and (ii) the list named **output** where you can change the content of the output elements that are shown in the user interface. In this case our web application has an input element named **var** containing the selection of the user in the drop-down menu, and it has an output element named **condBP** that is supposed to be a plot that will be shown on the main panel of the application.

If you run this simple application you will get in your browser the interface shown in Figure 3.41.

A key aspect of web applications is the concept of *reactive output*. This has to do with content in web applications that is dependent on user interaction with the application through the widgets. Having reactive output in a page involves two steps: (i) including the object content in the page (in **ui.R**); and (ii) telling Shiny how to get the object content (in **server.R**). If the object value depends on the value of some Shiny widget(s) you have reactive output.

Output functions tell Shiny where to display the content of an R object in the page. These functions have names ending in ...**Output()**. For instance, in the example in Figure 3.41 the plot was placed in the main panel using the function **plotOutput()** in **ui.R**. Before these objects are placed in the page through these functions you need to tell Shiny what their content is in `server.R`. You do this by assigning their content to the respective component in the list `output` (check in the above example to see how the boxplot was created in the script `server.R`). To carry out this assignment you use specific functions for building content. These functions have names starting with `render...()`. For instance, in the above example we have assigned to the component of `output` with the plot (`condBP`) the content produced by function `renderPlot()`. This function transforms an R plot in the respective content that can be placed in the Web page. There are several of these functions for different types of R objects.

The components of the list `input` contain the values of the widgets. The type of value depends on the widget. For instance, a `dateRangeInput()` widget will produce a vector with two values, whilst a `numericInput()` widget will produce a single value. Shiny has many widgets that you can include in your web application for creating your user interface. You may get a list of these widgets together with illustrative code at the web page `http://shiny.rstudio.com/gallery/widget-gallery.html`.

We have described a few of the key elements of Shiny web applications. To build more sophisticated applications you will obviously need more knowledge of Shiny. For more details we strongly recommend that you check the excellent tutorials available at `http://shiny.rstudio.com/tutorial/`.

Part II

Data Mining Case Studies

Chapter 4

Predicting Algae Blooms

This case study will provide concrete illustrations of some basic tasks of data mining: data pre-processing, exploratory data analysis, and predictive model construction. For this initial case study we have selected a small problem by data mining standards. Namely, we are addressing the problem of predicting the frequency occurrence of several harmful algae in water samples. If you are not familiar with the R language and you have not read the short introduction provided in Chapter 2, you may feel the need to review that chapter as you work through this case study.

4.1 Problem Description and Objectives

High concentrations of certain harmful algae in rivers constitute a serious ecological problem with a strong impact not only on river life forms, but also on water quality. Being able to monitor and perform an early forecast of algae blooms is essential to improving the quality of rivers.

With the goal of addressing this prediction problem, several water samples were collected in different European rivers at different times during a period of approximately one year. For each water sample, different chemical properties were measured as well as the frequency of occurrence of seven harmful algae. Some other characteristics of the water collection process were also stored, such as the season of the year, the river size, and the river speed.

One of the main motivations behind this application lies in the fact that chemical monitoring is cheap and easily automated, while the biological analysis of the samples to identify the algae that are present in the water involves microscopic examination, requires trained manpower, and is therefore both expensive and slow. As such, obtaining models that are able to accurately predict the algae frequencies based on chemical properties would facilitate the creation of cheap and automated systems for monitoring harmful algae blooms.

Another objective of this study is to provide a better understanding of the factors influencing the algae frequencies. Namely, we want to understand how these frequencies are related to certain chemical attributes of water samples as well as other characteristics of the samples (like season of the year, type of river, etc.).

4.2 Data Description

The data available for this problem was collected in the context of the ERUDIT[1] research Network and used in the COIL 1999 international data analysis competition. It is available from several sources, such as in the UCI Machine Learning Repository of datasets.[2]

There are two main datasets for this problem. The first consists of data for 200 water samples. To be more precise, each observation in the available datasets is in effect an aggregation of several water samples collected from the same river over a period of 3 months, during the same season of the year.

Each observation contains information on 11 variables. Three of these variables are nominal and describe the season of the year when the water samples to be aggregated were collected, as well as the size and speed of the river in question. The eight remaining variables are values of different chemical parameters measured in the water samples forming the aggregation, namely:

- Maximum pH value

- Minimum value of O_2 (oxygen)

- Mean value of Cl (chloride)

- Mean value of NO_3^- (nitrates)

- Mean value of NH_4^+ (ammonium)

- Mean of PO_4^{3-} (orthophosphate)

- Mean of total PO_4 (phosphate)

- Mean of chlorophyll

Associated with each of these parameters are seven frequency numbers of different harmful algae found in the respective water samples. No information is given regarding the names of the algae that were identified.

The second dataset contains information on 140 extra observations. It uses the same basic structure but it does not include information concerning the seven harmful algae frequencies. These extra observations can be regarded as a kind of test set. The main goal of our study is to predict the frequencies of the seven algae for these 140 water samples. This means that we are facing a predictive data mining task. This is one among the diverse set of problems tackled in data mining as we have seen in Chapter 3. In this type of task our main goal is to obtain a model that allows us to predict the value of a certain target variable given the values of a set of predictor variables. This model may also provide indications on which predictor variables have a larger impact on the target variable; that is, the model may provide a comprehensive description of the factors that influence the target variable.

4.3 Loading the Data into R

We will consider two forms of getting the data into R: (1) one by simply taking advantage of the package accompanying the book that includes data frames with the datasets ready for use; and (2) the other by going to the book Web site, downloading the text files with the data, and then loading them into R. The former is obviously much more practical. We include information on the second alternative for illustrative purposes on how to load data into R from text files.

---

[1]http://www.erudit.de/erudit/.
[2]http://archive.ics.uci.edu/ml/.

If you want to follow the easy path, you simply load the book package,[3] and you immediately have a data frame named **algae** available for use. This data frame contains the first set of 200 observations mentioned above.

```
> library(dplyr)
> data(algae, package="DMwR2")
> algae
```

```
# A tibble: 200 × 18
   season  size   speed  mxPH  mnO2    Cl    NO3     NH4     oPO4      PO4
   <fctr>  <fctr> <fctr> <dbl> <dbl> <dbl>  <dbl>   <dbl>    <dbl>    <dbl>
1  winter  small  medium 8.00   9.8 60.800  6.238 578.000  105.000  170.000
2  spring  small  medium 8.35   8.0 57.750  1.288 370.000  428.750  558.750
3  autumn  small  medium 8.10  11.4 40.020  5.330 346.667  125.667  187.057
4  spring  small  medium 8.07   4.8 77.364  2.302  98.182   61.182  138.700
5  autumn  small  medium 8.06   9.0 55.350 10.416 233.700   58.222   97.580
6  winter  small  high   8.25  13.1 65.750  9.248 430.000   18.250   56.667
7  summer  small  high   8.15  10.3 73.250  1.535 110.000   61.250  111.750
8  autumn  small  high   8.05  10.6 59.067  4.990 205.667   44.667   77.434
9  winter  small  medium 8.70   3.4 21.950  0.886 102.750   36.300   71.000
10 winter  small  high   7.93   9.9  8.000  1.390   5.800   27.250   46.600
# ... with 190 more rows, and 8 more variables: Chla <dbl>, a1 <dbl>,
#   a2 <dbl>, a3 <dbl>, a4 <dbl>, a5 <dbl>, a6 <dbl>, a7 <dbl>
```

Note that if, as in the above code, you load the **dplyr** package before loading the data, then you get a data frame table object instead of a standard data frame, with the added benefits like for instance improved printing of the object contents. We recommend you do this although it is not mandatory for carrying out the rest of the code.

Alternatively, you may use the text files available in the "Data" section of the book Web site. The "Training data" link contains the 200 water samples in a file named "Analysis.txt", while the "Test data" link points to the "Eval.txt" file that contains the 140 test samples. There is an additional link that points to a file ("Sols.txt") that contains the algae frequencies of the 140 test samples. This last file will be used to check the performance of our predictive models and will be taken as unknown information for now. The files have the values for each observation in a different line. Each line of the training and test files contains the values of the variables (according to the description given in Section 4.2) separated by spaces. Unknown values are indicated with the string "XXXXXXX".

The first thing to do is to download the three files from the book Web site and store them in some directory on your hard disk (preferably on the current working directory of your running R session, which you may check issuing the command `getwd()` at the prompt).

After downloading the data files into a local directory, we can start by loading into R the data from the "Analysis.txt" file (the training data, i.e. the data that will be used to obtain the predictive models). To read the data from the file it is sufficient to issue the following command:[4]

```
> algae <- read.table('Analysis.txt',
+          header=FALSE,
+          dec='.',
+          col.names=c('season','size','speed','mxPH','mnO2','Cl',
```

---

[3]Please note that you will have to install the package as it does not come with the standard installation of R. Check Section 2.1 (page 3) to know how to do this.

[4]We assume that the data files are in the current working directory of R. If not, use the command "setwd()" to change this, or use the "Change dir..." option in the "File" menu of Windows versions.

```
+               'NO3','NH4','oPO4','PO4','Chla','a1','a2','a3','a4',
+               'a5','a6','a7'),
+               na.strings=c('XXXXXXX'))
```

Note that we have not used the functions from package **readr** (Wickham and Francois, 2015b) that we introduced in Section 3.2.2.1. The functions of this package are very useful and fast in many contexts but they achieve this by making some compromises in terms of assumptions on the regularity of the text files. This package includes the function `read_table()` that we could try to use to read this text file. However, this function does not allow for lines with arbitrary number of spaces separating each column value in the text file. Sometimes this is not the case and then you need to resort to the standard R function to read datasets from text files, like the above `read.table()` function. They work in a similar way to the functions of the package **readr** but they use different parameter names and are more flexible in some situations at the cost of some lack of efficiency.

The parameter `header=FALSE` indicates that the file to be read does not include a first line with the variables names. Argument `dec='.'` states that the numbers use the '.' character to separate decimal places. These two previous parameter settings could have been omitted as we are using their default values. Parameter `col.names` allows us to provide a vector with the names to give to the variables whose values are being read. Finally, `na.strings` serves to indicate a vector of strings that are to be interpreted as unknown values. These values are represented internally in R by the value NA, as mentioned in Section 2.5.

R has several other functions that can be used to read data contained in text files. You may wish to type "`?read.table`" to obtain further information on this and other related functions. Moreover, R has a manual that you may want to browse named "R Data Import/Export"; it describes the different possibilities R includes for reading data from other applications.

The result of the instruction above is a data frame. You may transform this into a data frame table (*tibble*) as follows:

```
> tibble::as_tibble(algae)
```

Note that we have used the function `as_tibble()` from package **tibble** (Wickham et al., 2016) to obtain the *tibble* object. This function belongs to that package so we could have started by loading the package (using `library(tibble)`) and then using the function as usual. Above we just show an alternative that is practical when you simply want to use one function from a package and will need nothing else from it. In those situations it is frequently more convenient to use the above construct that allows you to use the function provided you refer its "origin" using the construct `packageName::functionName`.

4.4   Data Visualization and Summarization

Given the lack of further information on the problem domain, it is wise to investigate some of the statistical properties of the data, so as to get a better grasp of the problem. Even if that was not the case, it is always a good idea to start our analysis with some kind of exploratory data analysis similar to the one we will show below.

A first idea of the statistical properties of the data can be obtained through a summary of its descriptive statistics:

```
> summary(algae)
```

```
   season        size         speed        mxPH             mnO2
autumn:40    large :45    high  :84    Min.   :5.600    Min.   : 1.500
spring:53    medium:84    low   :33    1st Qu.:7.700    1st Qu.: 7.725
summer:45    small :71    medium:83    Median :8.060    Median : 9.800
winter:62                              Mean   :8.012    Mean   : 9.118
                                       3rd Qu.:8.400    3rd Qu.:10.800
                                       Max.   :9.700    Max.   :13.400
                                       NA's   :1        NA's   :2

      Cl                NO3               NH4              oPO4
Min.   :  0.222   Min.   : 0.050   Min.   :    5.00   Min.   :  1.00
1st Qu.: 10.981   1st Qu.: 1.296   1st Qu.:   38.33   1st Qu.: 15.70
Median : 32.730   Median : 2.675   Median :  103.17   Median : 40.15
Mean   : 43.636   Mean   : 3.282   Mean   :  501.30   Mean   : 73.59
3rd Qu.: 57.824   3rd Qu.: 4.446   3rd Qu.:  226.95   3rd Qu.: 99.33
Max.   :391.500   Max.   :45.650   Max.   :24064.00   Max.   :564.60
NA's   :10        NA's   :2        NA's   :2          NA's   :2

      PO4              Chla               a1               a2
Min.   :  1.00   Min.   :  0.200   Min.   : 0.00    Min.   : 0.000
1st Qu.: 41.38   1st Qu.:  2.000   1st Qu.: 1.50    1st Qu.: 0.000
Median :103.29   Median :  5.475   Median : 6.95    Median : 3.000
Mean   :137.88   Mean   : 13.971   Mean   :16.92    Mean   : 7.458
3rd Qu.:213.75   3rd Qu.: 18.308   3rd Qu.:24.80    3rd Qu.:11.375
Max.   :771.60   Max.   :110.456   Max.   :89.80    Max.   :72.600
NA's   :2        NA's   :12

      a3               a4               a5               a6
Min.   : 0.000   Min.   : 0.000   Min.   : 0.000   Min.   : 0.000
1st Qu.: 0.000   1st Qu.: 0.000   1st Qu.: 0.000   1st Qu.: 0.000
Median : 1.550   Median : 0.000   Median : 1.900   Median : 0.000
Mean   : 4.309   Mean   : 1.992   Mean   : 5.064   Mean   : 5.964
3rd Qu.: 4.925   3rd Qu.: 2.400   3rd Qu.: 7.500   3rd Qu.: 6.925
Max.   :42.800   Max.   :44.600   Max.   :44.400   Max.   :77.600

      a7
Min.   : 0.000
1st Qu.: 0.000
Median : 1.000
Mean   : 2.495
3rd Qu.: 2.400
Max.   :31.600
```

This simple instruction immediately gives us a first overview of the statistical properties of the data.[5] In the case of nominal variables (which are represented by factors in R data frames), it provides frequency counts for each possible value.[6] For instance, we can observe that there are more water samples collected in winter than in the other seasons. For numeric variables, R gives us a series of statistics like their mean, median, quartiles information and extreme values. These statistics provide a first idea of the distribution of the variable values (we return to this issue later on). In the event of a variable having some unknown values, their number is also shown following the string NAs. By observing the difference between

---

[5]As mentioned in Section 3.4.1.1, an interesting alternative with similar objectives is the function `describe()` in package **Hmisc** (Harrell Jr, 2009).

[6]Actually, if there are too many, only the most frequent are shown.

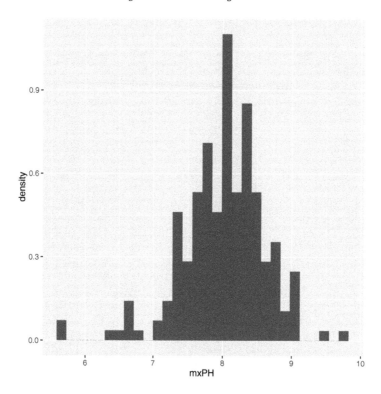

FIGURE 4.1: The histogram of variable *mxPH*.

medians and means, as well as the inter-quartile range (3rd quartile minus the 1st quartile),[7] we can get an idea of the skewness of the distribution and also its spread. Still, most of the time, this information is better captured graphically. Let us see an example:

```
> library(ggplot2)
> ggplot(algae,aes(x=mxPH)) + geom_histogram(aes(y=..density..))
```

This instruction shows us the histogram of the variable *mxPH*. The result appears in Figure 4.1. With `aes(y=..density..)` we get probabilities for each interval of values,[8] while omitting this setting would give us frequency counts.

Figure 4.1 tells us that the values of variable *mxPH* apparently follow a distribution very near the normal distribution, with the values nicely clustered around the mean value. A more precise check of this hypothesis can be obtained using normal Q-Q plots. The function `qqPlot()`, in the **car** (Fox, 2009) package, obtains this type of plot, the result of which is shown in Figure 4.2, together with a slightly more sophisticated version of the histogram. The graphs were obtained with the following code:

---

[7]If we order the values of a variable, the 1st quartile is the value below which there are 25% of the data points, while the 3rd quartile is the value below which there are 75% of the cases, thus implying that between these two values we have 50% of our data. The inter-quartile range is defined as the 3rd quartile minus the 1st quartile, thus being a measure of the spread of the variable around its central value (larger values indicate larger spread).

[8]The areas of the rectangles should sum to one (and not the height of the rectangles as some people might expect).

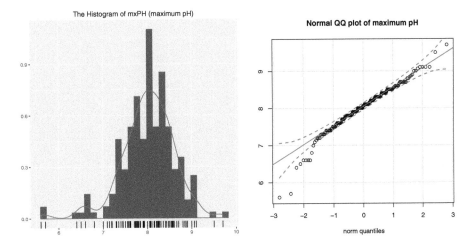

FIGURE 4.2: An "enriched" version of the histogram of variable extitMxPH (left) together with a normal Q-Q plot (right).

```
> ggplot(algae,aes(x=mxPH)) +
+     geom_histogram(aes(y=..density..)) +
+     geom_density(color="red") + geom_rug() +
+     ggtitle("The Histogram of mxPH (maximum pH)") +
+     xlab("") + ylab("")
> library(car)
> qqPlot(algae$mxPH,main='Normal QQ plot of maximum pH',ylab="")
```

The code starts by obtaining the first graph, which is again a histogram of the variable *mxPH*, except that this time we specify an empty X-axis label and we change the title of the graph. Moreover, on top of the histogram we also add other geometric objects (*geoms* in **ggplot2** jargon), namely an object providing a smooth version of the histogram (a kernel density estimate of the distribution of the variable) and also a rug that plots (as vertical dashes) the real values of the variable near the X-axis, thus allowing easy spotting of outliers. For instance, we can observe that there are two values significantly smaller than all others. This kind of data inspection is very important as it may identify possible errors in the data sample, or even help to locate values that are so awkward that they may only be errors, or at least we would be better off by disregarding them in posterior analysis. The second graph shows a Q-Q plot obtained with the `qqPlot()` function, which plots the variable values against the theoretical quantiles of a normal distribution (solid red line). The function also plots an envelope with the 95% confidence interval of the normal distribution (red dashed lines). As we can observe, there are several low values of the variable that clearly break the assumptions of a normal distribution with 95% confidence.

Another example (Figure 4.3) showing this kind of data inspection can be achieved with the following instructions, this time for variable *oPO4*:

```
> ggplot(algae,aes(x=factor(0),y=oPO4)) +
+     geom_boxplot() + geom_rug() +
+     geom_hline(aes(yintercept=mean(algae$oPO4, na.rm = TRUE)),
+              linetype=2,colour="red") +
+     ylab("Orthophosphate (oPO4)") + xlab("") + scale_x_discrete(breaks=NULL)
```

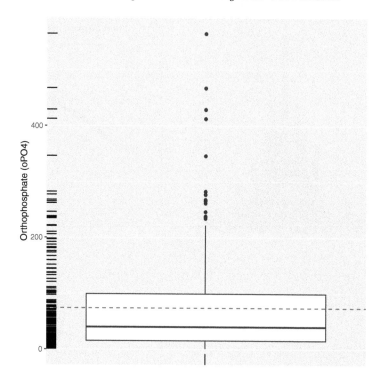

FIGURE 4.3: An "enriched" box plot for *orthophosphate*.

This call to `ggplot()` draws a box plot of variable *oPO4*. As mentioned in Section 3.4.1.2 (page 96), box plots provide a quick summarization of some key properties of a continuous variable distribution. Namely, there is a box whose vertical limits are the 1st and 3rd quartiles of the variable. This box has a horizontal line inside that represents the median value of the variable. Let r be the inter-quartile range. There are two vertical lines starting from the middle of the box. The bottom (upper) line stops at the lower (upper) whisker, calculated as the lowest (highest) value that is within $1.5 \times IQR$ from the 1st (3rd) quartile. The dots below or above these vertical lines represent observations that are extremely low (high) compared to all others, and are usually considered outliers. This means that box plots give us plenty of information regarding not only the central value and spread of the variable, but also eventual outliers.

We also added to the boxplot a rug showing the concrete values of the variable and a horizontal red dashed line[9] at the mean value of the variable, which is obtained using the function `mean()`. By comparing this line with the line inside the box indicating the median, we can conclude that the presence of several outliers has distorted the value of the mean as a statistic of centrality (i.e., indicating the more common value of the variable).

The analysis of Figure 4.3 tells us that the variable *oPO4* has a distribution of the observed values clearly concentrated on low values, thus with a positive skew. In most of the water samples, the value of *oPO4* is low, but there are several observations with high values, and even with extremely high values.

Sometimes when we encounter outliers, we are interested in inspecting the observations that have these "strange" values. We will show two ways of doing this. First, let us do it

---

[9]The argument `linetype=2` is used to obtain a dashed line.

graphically. R base plots allow some form of interaction that facilitates identifying points in a graph that you are interested[10]. For instance, if we plot the values of variable *NH4*, we notice a very large value. We can identify the respective water sample using the following code:

```
> plot(algae$NH4, xlab = "")
> abline(h = mean(algae$NH4, na.rm = T), lty = 1)
> abline(h = mean(algae$NH4, na.rm = T) + sd(algae$NH4, na.rm = T), lty = 2)
> abline(h = median(algae$NH4, na.rm = T), lty = 3)
> identify(algae$NH4)
```

The first instruction plots all values of the variable. The calls to the `abline()` function draw three informative lines, one with the mean value, another with the mean plus one standard deviation, and the other with the median. They are not necessary for this identification task. The last instruction is interactive and allows the user to click on the plotted dots with the left mouse button. For every clicked dot, R will write the respective row number in the **algae** data frame.[11] The user can finish the interaction by clicking the right mouse button.

If we want to inspect the respective observations in the **algae** data frame, then we better proceed in the following way:

```
> plot(algae$NH4, xlab = "")
> clickedRows <- identify(algae$NH4)
> algae[clickedRows, ]
```

As you may have guessed before, the function `identify()`, returns as a result the number of the rows corresponding to the clicked points in the graph and thus we may take advantage of this fact to index the **algae** data frame, thus obtaining the full information on these observations.

We can also perform this inspection without graphics, as shown below:

```
> library(dplyr)
> filter(algae, NH4 > 19000)
```

This instruction illustrates another form of filtering a data frame, using the facilities of the **dplyr** package.

Let us now explore a few examples of another type of data inspection. Suppose we would like to study the distribution of the values of, say, algal *a1*. We could use any of the possibilities discussed before. However, if we wanted to study how this distribution depends on other variables, new tools are required.

As we have seen in Section 3.4.1.2 conditioned plots are graphical representations that depend on a certain factor. Factors are nominal variables with a set of finite values. For instance, we can obtain a set of box plots for the variable *a1*, for each value of the variable *size* (*see* Figure 4.4). Each of the box plots was obtained using the subset of water samples that have a certain value of the variable *size*. These graphs allow us to study how this nominal variable may influence the distribution of the values of *a1*. The following code would obtain such box plots,

---

[10]The **ggplot2** package infra-structure currently does not provide these facilities.

[11]The position where you click relative to the point determines the side where R writes the row number. For instance, if you click on the right of the dot, the row number will be written on the right.

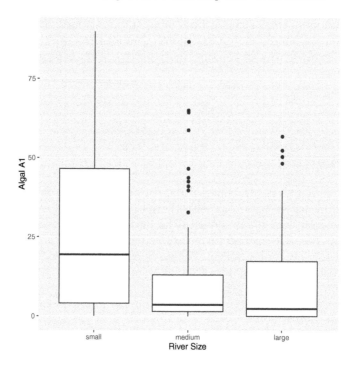

FIGURE 4.4: A conditioned box plot of Algal *a1*.

```
> ggplot(algae,aes(x=size,y=a1)) + geom_boxplot() +
+     xlab("River Size") + ylab("Algal A1")
```

If you run this code you will notice that you get a slightly different graph than that shown in Figure 4.4. The reason is that the ordering of the values of the river size factor variable is not what you expect. You would naturally expect the values to go from small to large and not the opposite. By default the ordering of factor values is done alphabetically by R. Sometimes this is not what we want and in these situations we better "rebuild" the factors telling R what is the ordering of values we want. Actually, this "problem" of unnatural ordering of the factor values occurs in all three nominal variables of this dataset. Let us solve the problem for all of them,

```
> library(forcats)
> algae <- mutate(algae,
+                 size=fct_relevel(size,c("small","medium","large")),
+                 speed=fct_relevel(speed,c("low","medium","high")),
+                 season=fct_relevel(season,c("spring","summer","autumn","winter")))
```

We have used the function **fct_relevel()** from package **forcats** (Wickham, 2016) to set the order of the levels of the nominal variables (factors) the way it makes sense for us. After this code you should be able to obtain the graph shown in Figure 4.4.

Figure 4.4 allows us to observe that higher frequencies of algal *a1* are expected in smaller rivers, which can be valuable knowledge.

An interesting variant of this type of plot that gives us more information on the distribution of the variable being plotted, are violin plots. Let us see an example of its use with the same algal *a1* against the size of rivers:

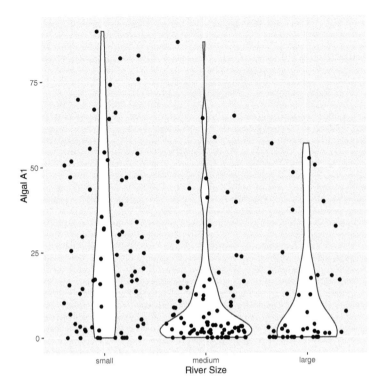

FIGURE 4.5: A conditioned violin plot of Algal *a1*.

```
> ggplot(algae,aes(x=size,y=a1)) +
+     geom_violin() + geom_jitter() + xlab("River Size") + ylab("Algal A1")
```

The result of this call is shown in Figure 4.5. The white areas represent the distribution of *a1* for each of the river sizes. The areas are made to have the same size and thus wider regions represent ranges of values that have larger weight in terms of the distribution of the values. For instance we can observe that for rivers of medium size most values of *a1* are packed near zero, while for smaller rivers the values are more spread across the range (thinner violin). We have also used the function `geom_jitter()` to include the concrete values as dots. Compared to `geom_point()` that we could have used instead, this function randomly jitters the points in the horizontal axis to try to avoid over-plotting of points.

Conditioned plots are not restricted to nominal variables, nor to a single factor. You can carry out the same kind of conditioning study with continuous variables as long as you previously "discretize" them. Let us see an example by observing the behavior of the frequency of algal *a3* conditioned by *season* and *mnO2*, the latter being a continuous variable. Figure 4.6 shows such a graph and the code to obtain it is the following:

```
> data2graph <- filter(algae,!is.na(mnO2)) %>%
+     mutate(minO2=cut(mnO2, quantile(mnO2,c(0,0.25,.5,.75,1)), include.lowest=TRUE))
> ggplot(data2graph,aes(x=a3,y=season, color=season)) + geom_point() +
+     facet_wrap(~ minO2) +
+     guides(color=FALSE)
```

The first instruction builds the data to be used on the graph. We first filter out the rows that have an NA in the continuous variable we want to use in the graph. These values

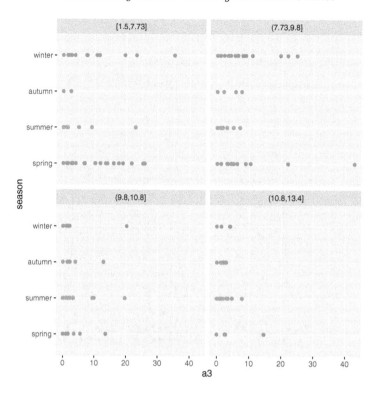

FIGURE 4.6: A conditioned dot plot of Algal *a3* using a continuous variable.

would cause problems in the subsequent instructions and in the graph.[12] We then create a new column in the data frame, named `minO2` that is a discretized version of the orginal continuous variable `mnO2`. The discretization is carried out by function `cut()` that picks a set of numeric values and allows the user to specify either the number of intervals into which to discretize the range of these values, or instead specifying the break points where to split the range into intervals. We have used this second option by means of the outcome of the `quantile()` function to obtain these break points. This function obtains quantiles of any sample of values. A quantile x is a value below which there are $x\%$ of the values in the sample. The way we have specified the quantiles to obtain, makes sure we get four intervals each containing 25% of the original values of the variable `mnO2`. As we have seen in Section 3.3.2.2 (page 63), there are ways of discretizing numeric variables that we could have also used to produce the graph. Finally, the second instruction plots the graph that is a dot plot of `a3` against `season`, conditioned (using faceting of the package **ggplot2**) by the newly created factor, `minO2`.

---

[12]Later, in Section 4.5 we will see a better solution to this.

4.5   Unknown Values

There are several water samples with unknown values in some of the variables. This situation, rather common in real-world problems, may preclude the use of certain techniques that are not able to handle missing values.

Whenever we are handling a dataset with missing values, we can follow several strategies. The most common are:

- Remove the cases with unknowns.

- Fill in the unknown values with the most frequent values.

- Fill in the unknown values by exploring the correlations between variables.

- Fill in the unknown values by exploring the similarity between cases.

- Use tools that are able to handle these values.

The last alternative is the most restrictive, as it limits the set of tools one can use. Still, it may be a good option whenever we are confident in the merit of the strategies used by those data mining tools to handle missing values.

In the following subsections we will show examples of how to implement these strategies in R. If you decide to try the code given in these sections, you should be aware that they are not complementary. This means that as you go into another method of dealing with missing values, you should read in again the original data to have all the unknown cases again, as each section handles them in a different way. The easiest form of doing this is to execute the following code:

```
> library(DMwR2)
> library(dplyr)
> data(algae)
```

Note that the two library loading instructions are not necessary if you have executed them before when following the previous sections. If that is the case simply re-load the data with the third instruction.

4.5.1   Removing the Observations with Unknown Values

The option of removing the cases with unknown values is very easy to implement, and can also be a reasonable choice when the proportion of cases with unknowns is small with respect to the size of the available dataset.

Before eliminating all observations with at least one unknown value in some variable, it is always wise to have a look, or at least count them:

```
> filter(algae, !complete.cases(algae) )
```

```
# A tibble: 16 × 18
    season   size  speed  mxPH  mnO2    Cl   NO3   NH4   oPO4     PO4
    <fctr>  <fctr> <fctr> <dbl> <dbl> <dbl> <dbl> <dbl>  <dbl>   <dbl>
1   autumn  small   high  6.80  11.1 9.000 0.630    20  4.000      NA
2   spring  small   high  8.00    NA 1.450 0.810    10  2.500   3.000
3   winter  small    low    NA  12.6 9.000 0.230    10  5.000   6.000
```

```
 4 winter  small   high 6.60  10.8     NA 3.245   10   1.000   6.500
 5 spring  small medium 5.60  11.8     NA 2.220    5   1.000   1.000
 6 autumn  small medium 5.70  10.8     NA 2.550   10   1.000   4.000
 7 spring  small   high 6.60   9.5     NA 1.320   20   1.000   6.000
 8 summer  small   high 6.60  10.8     NA 2.640   10   2.000  11.000
 9 autumn  small medium 6.60  11.3     NA 4.170   10   1.000   6.000
10 spring  small medium 6.50  10.4     NA 5.970   10   2.000  14.000
11 summer  small medium 6.40    NA     NA   NA    NA      NA  14.000
12 autumn  small   high 7.83  11.7 4.083 1.328   18   3.333   6.667
13 winter medium   high 9.70  10.8 0.222 0.406   10  22.444  10.111
14 spring  large    low 9.00   5.8     NA 0.900  142 102.000 186.000
15 winter  large   high 8.00  10.9 9.055 0.825   40  21.083  56.091
16 winter  large medium 8.00   7.6     NA   NA    NA      NA      NA
# ... with 8 more variables: Chla <dbl>, a1 <dbl>, a2 <dbl>, a3 <dbl>,
#   a4 <dbl>, a5 <dbl>, a6 <dbl>, a7 <dbl>
```

The function `complete.cases()` produces a vector of Boolean values with as many elements as there are rows in the `algae` data frame, where an element is TRUE if the respective row is "clean" of NA values (i.e., is a complete observation). Thus the above instruction shows the water samples with some NA value because the '!' operator performs logical negation, as was mentioned before.

In order to remove these 16 water samples from our data frame, we can simply do

```
> algae <- na.omit(algae)
```

Even if we decide not to use this drastic method of removing all cases with some unknown value, we can remove some observations because the number of unknown values is so high that they are almost useless, and even complex methods of filling in these values will be too unreliable. Note that if you have executed the previous command, you should read in the data again, as this instruction has removed all the unknowns, so the next statements would not make sense! Looking at the cases with unknowns we can see that both the samples 62 and 199 have six of the eleven explanatory variables with unknown values. In such cases, it is wise to simply ignore these observations by removing them:

```
> data(algae, package="DMwR2") # only necessary if you executed the above na.omit()
> algae <- algae[-c(62, 199), ]
```

In problems where the visual inspection of all the cases with unknowns is unfeasible due to their number, we need to be able to find the rows with a large number of NAs. The following code gives you the number of unknown values in each row of the `algae` dataset:

```
> apply(algae, 1, function(x) sum(is.na(x)))
```

The function `apply()` belongs to a set of very powerful functions of R. These functions are sometimes known as meta-functions and allow applying other functions to objects under certain conditions. In the case of the function `apply()`, we can use it to apply any function to one of the dimensions of a multidimensional object. Using the `apply()` function we are executing a function on all rows of the data frame.[13] This function, specified on the third argument of `apply()`, will be called with each row of the data frame. The function we have provided is in this case a temporary function. It is temporary because it only exists within

---

[13]The 1 on the second argument stands for the first dimension of the object in the first argument, i.e., the rows.

the call of the `apply()`. Alternatively, we could have supplied the name of a "normal" function. The temporary function basically calculates the number of NAs on the object x, its argument. It takes advantage of the fact that a TRUE value in R is equivalent to the number 1, and the FALSE to the value 0, which means that when you sum a vector of Boolean values, you obtain the number of TRUEs that exist in the vector.

Based on this code we can create a function that gives us the rows in `algae` that have a certain number of unknowns. Such a function is available in the book package and you can use it as follows:

```
> data(algae, package="DMwR2")
> manyNAs(algae, 0.2)

[1]   62 199
```

The call to `data()` is only necessary if you have previously removed the rows that have lots of unknowns. The `manyNAs()` function gives you the row numbers that, in this case, have more than 20% of the columns with an NA. In the second argument you can alternatively supply the exact number of columns that you want to consider as the limit. So, an alternative to the code given before that does not require you to know the number of the rows with lots of unknowns is

```
> algae <- algae[-manyNAs(algae), ]
```

In this case we have used the default value of the second argument of `manyNAs()`, which is 0.2.

4.5.2   Filling in the Unknowns with the Most Frequent Values

An alternative to eliminating the cases with unknown values is to try to find the most probable value for each of these unknowns, frequently known as missing value imputation. Again, several strategies can be followed, with different trade-offs between the level of approximation and the computational complexity of the method.

The simplest and fastest way of filling in the unknown values is to use some statistic of centrality. These statistics reflect the most frequent value of a variable distribution; thus they are a natural choice for this strategy. Several statistics of centrality exist, like the mean, the median, the mode, etc. The choice of the most adequate value depends on the distribution of the variable. For approximately normal distributions, where all observations are nicely clustered around the mean, this statistic is the best choice. However, for skewed distributions, or for variables with outliers, the mean can be disastrous. Skewed distributions have most values clustered near one of the sides of the range of values of the variable; thus the mean is clearly not representative of the most common value. On the other hand, the presence of outliers (extreme values) may distort the calculation of the mean,[14] thus leading to similar representativeness problems. Therefore, it is not wise to use the mean without a previous inspection of the distribution of the variable using, for instance, some of the graphical tools of R (e.g., Figure 4.2). For skewed distributions or for variables with outliers, the median is a better statistic of centrality.

For instance, the sample `algae[48,]` does not have a value in the variable *mxPH*. As the distribution of this variable is nearly normal (compare with Figure 4.2) we could use its mean value to fill in the "hole". This could be done by

---

[14]The mean of the vector `c(1.2,1.3,0.4,0.6,3,15)` is 3.583.

```
> algae[48, "mxPH"] <- mean(algae$mxPH, na.rm = TRUE)
```

where the function **mean()** gives the mean value of any vector of numbers, and **na.rm=TRUE** disregards any NA values in this vector from the calculation.[15]

Most of the time we will be interested in filling in all unknowns of a column instead of working on a case-by-case basis as above. Let us see an example of this with the variable *Chla*. This variable is unknown on 12 water samples. Moreover, this is a situation where the mean is a very poor representative of the most frequent value of the variable. In effect, the distribution of *Chla* is skewed to lower values, and there are a few extreme values that make the mean value (13.971) highly unrepresentative of the most frequent value. Therefore, we will use the median to fill in all the unknowns in this column,

```
> algae[is.na(algae$Chla), "Chla"] <- median(algae$Chla, na.rm = TRUE)
```

In order to automate this process you may use the function **centralImputation()**, available in the book package. This function fills in all unknowns in a dataset using a statistic of centrality. The function uses by default the median for numeric columns and the most frequent value (the mode) for nominal variables. You may apply it as follows:

```
> data(algae, package="DMwR2")
> algae <- algae[-manyNAs(algae), ]
> algae <- centralImputation(algae)
```

While the presence of unknown values may impair the use of some methods, filling in their values using a strategy as above is usually considered a bad idea. This simple strategy, although extremely fast, and thus appealing for large datasets, may introduce a large bias in the data, which can influence our posterior analysis. However, unbiased methods that find the optimal value to fill in an unknown are extremely complex and may not be adequate for some large data mining problems.

4.5.3   Filling in the Unknown Values by Exploring Correlations

An alternative for getting less biased estimators of the unknown values is to explore the relationships between variables. For instance, using the correlation between the variables values, we could discover that a certain variable is highly correlated with *mxPH*, which would enable us to obtain other, more probable values for the sample number 48, which has an unknown on this variable. This could be preferable to using the mean as we did above.

To obtain the variables correlation we can issue the command,

```
> cor(algae[, 4:18], use = "complete.obs")
```

The function **cor()** produces a matrix with the correlation values between the variables (we have avoided the first 3 variables/columns because they are nominal). The **use="complete.obs"** setting tells R to disregard observations with NA values in this calculation. Values near 1 (−1) indicate a strong positive (negative) linear correlation between the values of the two respective variables. Other R functions could then be used to approximate the functional form of this linear correlation, which in turn would allow us to estimate the values of one variable from the values of the correlated variable.

The result of this **cor()** function is not very legible but we can put it through the function **symnum()** to improve this:

---

[15]Without this 'detail' the result of the call would be NA because of the presence of NA values in this column.

```
> symnum(cor(algae[,4:18],use="complete.obs"))

       mP mO Cl NO NH o P Ch a1 a2 a3 a4 a5 a6 a7
mxPH 1
mnO2    1
Cl         1
NO3           1
NH4         , 1
oPO4    . .      1
PO4     . .    * 1
Chla .            1
a1          .   . . 1
a2      .          .   1
a3                   1
a4      .        .   1
a5                   1
a6        . .         . 1
a7                     1
attr(,"legend")
[1] 0 ' ' 0.3 '.' 0.6 ',' 0.8 '+' 0.9 '*' 0.95 'B' 1
```

This symbolic representation of the correlation values is more legible, particularly for large correlation matrices. Probably even more interesting is to visualize the correlation matrix. Package **corrplot** (Wei, 2013) provides a series of interesting functions with this purpose. Here is an example of its usage with the result shown in Figure 4.7:

```
> library(corrplot)
> cm <- cor(algae[,4:18], use="complete.obs")
> corrplot(cm, type="upper", tl.pos="d")
> corrplot(cm, add=TRUE, type="lower", method="number",
+          diag=FALSE, tl.pos="n", cl.pos="n")
```

The graph is obtained in two steps (two calls to the function `corrplot()`), the first drawing the upper right part of the graph, and the second producing the bottom left part with the correlation values. This function has many more parameter settings that you can use to produce different visual representation of these correlation matrices.

In our data, the correlations are in most cases irrelevant. However, there are two exceptions: between variables *NH4* and *NO3*, and between *PO4* and *oPO4*. These two latter variables are strongly correlated (above 0.9). The correlation between *NH4* and *NO3* is less evident (0.72) and thus it is risky to take advantage of it to fill in the unknowns. Moreover, assuming that you have removed the samples 62 and 199 because they have too many unknowns, there will be no water sample with unknown values on *NH4* and *NO3*. With respect to *PO4* and *oPO4*, the discovery of this correlation[16] allows us to fill in the unknowns on these variables. In order to achieve this we need to find the form of the linear correlation between these variables. This can be done as follows:

```
> data(algae, package="DMwR2")
> algae <- algae[-manyNAs(algae), ]
> lm(PO4 ~ oPO4, data = algae)
```

---

[16] According to domain experts, this was expected because the value of total phosphates (*PO4*) includes the value of orthophosphate (*oPO4*).

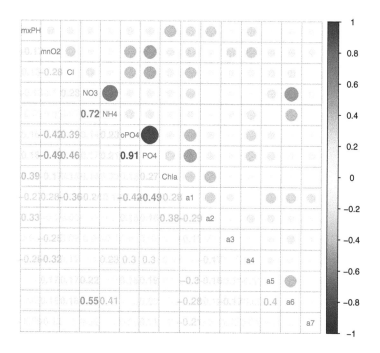

FIGURE 4.7: A visualization of a correlation matrix.

```
Call:
lm(formula = PO4 ~ oPO4, data = algae)

Coefficients:
(Intercept)            oPO4
      42.897           1.293
```

The function `lm()` can be used to obtain linear models of the form $Y = \beta_0 + \beta_1 X_1 + \ldots + \beta_n X_n$. We will describe this function in detail in Section 4.6. The linear model we have obtained tells us that $PO4 = 42.897 + 1.293 \times oPO4$. With this formula we can fill in the unknown values of these variables, provided they are not both unknown.

After removing the sample 62 and 199, we are left with a single observation with an unknown value on the variable *PO4* (sample 28); thus we could simply use the discovered relation to do the following:

```
> algae[28, "PO4"] <- 42.897 + 1.293 * algae[28, "oPO4"]
```

However, for illustration purposes, let us assume that there were several samples with unknown values on the variable *PO4*. How could we use the above linear relationship to fill all the unknowns? The best way would be to create a function that would return the value of *PO4* given the value of *oPO4*, and then apply this function to all unknown values:

```
> data(algae, package="DMwR2")
> algae <- algae[-manyNAs(algae), ]
> fillPO4 <- function(oP) ifelse(is.na(oP),NA,42.897 + 1.293 * oP)
```

```
> algae[is.na(algae$PO4), "PO4"] <- sapply(algae[is.na(algae$PO4), "oPO4"], fillPO4)
```

We first create a function called `fillPO4()` with one argument, which is assumed to be the value of *oPO4*. Given a value of *oPO4*, this function returns the value of *PO4* according to the discovered linear relation (try issuing "`fillPO4(6.5)`"). This function is then applied to all samples with unknown value on the variable *PO4*. This is done using the function `sapply()`, another example of a meta-function. This function has a vector as the first argument and a function as the second. The result is another vector with the same length, with the elements being the result of applying the function in the second argument to each element of the given vector. This means that the result of this call to `sapply()` will be a vector with the values to fill in the unknowns of the variable *PO4*. The last assignment is yet another example of the use of function composition. In effect, in a single instruction we are using the result of the function `is.na()` to index the rows in the data frame, and then to the result of this data selection we are applying the function `fillPO4()` to each of its elements through function `sapply()`.

The study of the linear correlations enabled us to fill in some new unknown values. Still, there are several observations left with unknown values. We can try to explore the correlations between the variables with unknowns and the nominal variables of this problem. We can use conditioned histograms with this objective. For instance, Figure 4.8 shows an example of such a graph. This graph was produced as follows:

```
> library(ggplot2)
> library(forcats)
> algae <- mutate(algae,
+                 size=fct_relevel(size,c("small","medium","large")),
+                 speed=fct_relevel(speed,c("low","medium","high")),
+                 season=fct_relevel(season,c("spring","summer","autumn","winter")))
> ggplot(algae, aes(x=mxPH)) + geom_histogram(binwidth=0.5) + facet_wrap(~ season)
```

This instruction obtains a histogram of the values of *mxPH* for the different values of *season*. Each histogram is built using only the subset of observations with a certain *season* value. We have changed the order of the factors again because you have most probably loaded again the original data in the package that includes the factors with the values ordered alphabetically.

Notice that the histograms in Figure 4.8 are rather similar, thus leading us to conclude that the values of *mxPH* are not seriously influenced by the season of the year when the samples were collected. If we try the same thing using the size of the river, we can observe a tendency for smaller rivers to show lower values of *mxPH*. We can extend our study of these dependencies using several nominal variables. For instance,

```
> ggplot(algae, aes(x=mxPH)) + geom_histogram(binwidth=0.5) +
+     facet_wrap(size ~ speed)
```

shows the variation of *mxPH* for all combinations of size and speed of the rivers. It is curious to note that there is no information regarding small rivers with low speed.[17] The single sample that has these properties is exactly sample 48, the one for which we do not know the value of *mxPH*!

Another alternative used to obtain similar information but now with the concrete values of the variable is

---

[17] Actually, if you have executed the instruction given before to fill in the value of *mxPH* with the mean value of this variable, this is not true any more!

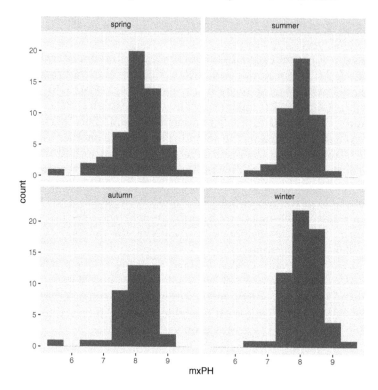

FIGURE 4.8: A histogram of variable *mxPH* conditioned by *season*.

```
> ggplot(algae, aes(x=mxPH, y=size, color=size)) + geom_point() +
+     facet_wrap(~speed) + geom_jitter(height = 0.4)
```

The result of this instruction is shown in Figure 4.9. The `geom_jitter()` function was used to perform a small random permutation of the values in the Y-direction to avoid plotting observations with the same values over each other, thus losing some information on the concentration of observations with some particular value.

This type of analysis could be carried out for the other variables with unknown values. Still, this is a tedious process because there are too many combinations to analyze. Nevertheless, this is a method that can be applied in small datasets with few nominal variables.

4.5.4 Filling in the Unknown Values by Exploring Similarities between Cases

Instead of exploring the correlation between the columns (variables) of a data set, we can try to use the similarities between the rows (observations) to fill in the unknown values. We will illustrate this method to fill in all unknowns with the exception of the two samples with too many NAs. Let us again read in the data to override the code of the previous sections (assuming you have tried it).

```
> data(algae, package="DMwR2")
> algae <- algae[-manyNAs(algae), ]
```

The approach described in this section assumes that if two water samples are similar,

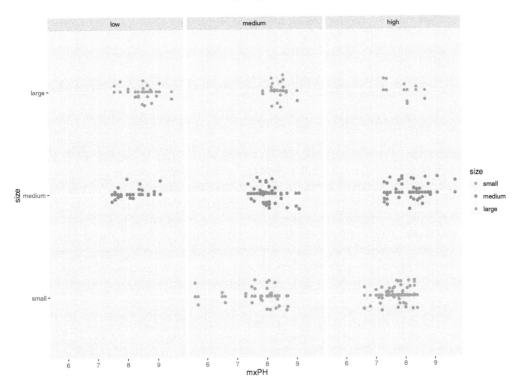

FIGURE 4.9: The values of variable *mxPH* by river size and speed.

and one of them has an unknown value in some variable, there is a high probability that this value is similar to the value of the other sample. In order to use this intuitively appealing method, we need to define the notion of similarity. This notion is usually defined using a metric over the multivariate space of the variables used to describe the observations, as we have seen in Section 3.4.3.1 (page 119).

The method we describe below will use the Euclidean distance (Equation 3.11 on page 119) to find the ten most similar cases of any water sample with some unknown value in a variable, and then use their values to fill in the unknown. We will consider two ways of using their values. The first simply calculates the median of the values of the ten nearest neighbors to fill in the gaps. In case of unknown nominal variables (which do not occur in our `algae` data set), we would use the most frequent value (the mode) among the neighbors. The second method uses a weighted average of the values of the neighbors. The weights decrease as the distance to the case of the neighbors increases. We use a Gaussian kernel function to obtain the weights from the distances. If one of the neighbors is at distance d from the case to fill in, its value will enter the weighted average with a weight given by

$$w(d) = e^{-d} \tag{4.1}$$

This idea is implemented in function `knnImputation()` available in the book package. The function uses a variant of the Euclidean distance to find the k nearest neighbors of any case. This variant allows the application of the function to datasets with both nominal and continuous variables. The used distance function was described in Equation 3.13 on page 120. These distances are calculated after standardizing the numeric values (c.f. Equation 3.1 on page 62).

Let us now see how to use the `knnImputation()` function:

```
> algae <- knnImputation(algae, k = 10)
```

In case you prefer to use the strategy of using the median values for filling in the unknowns, you could use the call

```
> algae <- knnImputation(algae, k = 10, meth = "median")
```

In summary, after these simple instructions we have the data frame free of NA values, and we are better prepared to take full advantage of several R functions.

In terms of deciding which of the methods for filling in unknowns that were described in the previous sections should be used, the answer is domain dependent most of the time. The method of exploring the similarities between cases seems more rational, although it suffers from some problems. These include the possible existence of irrelevant variables that may distort the notion of similarity, or even excessive computational complexity for extremely large datasets. Still, for these large problems we can always use random samples to calculate the similarities.

Further readings on handling unknown values

The book *Data Preparation for Data Mining* by Pyle (1999) is an extensive source of information on all issues of preparing data for data mining, and includes handling missing values. The book *Predictive Data Mining* by Weiss and Indurkhya (1999) is another good source of information on data preparation in general, and unknown values in particular.

4.6   Obtaining Prediction Models

The main goal of this case study is to obtain predictions for the frequency values of the seven algae in a set of 140 water samples. Given that these frequencies are numbers, we are facing a regression task.[18] In simple words, this task consists of trying to obtain a model relating the values of a numerical variable with the values of a set of other explanatory variables. This model can be used either to predict the value of the target variable for future observations of the explanatory variables, or to provide a better understanding of the interactions among the variables in our problem. More extensive explanations of this instance of Predictive Analytics can be found in Section 3.4.5 (page 140).

In this section we will initially explore two different predictive models that could be applied to the algae domain: multiple linear regression and regression trees. Our choice was mainly guided by illustrative purposes in the context of this book, and not as a consequence of some formal model selection step. Still, these models are two good alternatives for regression problems as they are quite different in terms of their assumptions regarding the "shape" of the regression function being approximated and they are easy to interpret and fast to run on any computer. This does not mean that in a real data mining scenario we should not try other alternatives and then use some form of model selection to select one or more of them for the final predictions on our 140 test samples. In Section 4.7 we will do this for the current case study. For more information on model selection in general you should check Section 3.5 (page 172).

---

[18]Actually, as we want to predict seven values for each water sample, we can handle this problem as seven different regression problems.

The models we are going to try handle missing values in a different way. While the implementation of linear regression available in R is not able to use datasets with unknown values, the implementation of regression trees handles these values internally. As such, we will follow a different path concerning the preparation of the data before model construction. For linear regression we will use one of the techniques described in Section 4.5 for preprocessing the data so that we can use these models. Regarding regression trees we will use the original 200 water samples.[19]

In the analysis we are going to carry out, we will assume that we do not know the true values of the target variables for the 140 test samples. Still, we have these values and in the end we will use them to get a final feedback on the value of the models we are going to obtain.

4.6.1 Multiple Linear Regression

Multiple linear regression is among the most used statistical data analysis techniques. These models obtain an additive function relating a target variable to a set of predictor variables. This additive function is a sum of terms of the form $\beta_i \times X_i$, where X_i is a predictor variable and β_i is a number.

As mentioned before, there is no predefined way of handling missing values for this type of modeling technique. As such, we will use the data resulting from applying the method of exploring the similarities among the training cases to fill in the unknowns (*see* Section 4.5.4). Nevertheless, before we apply this method, we will remove water samples number 62 and 199 because, as mentioned before, they have six of the eleven predictor variables missing. The following code obtains a data frame without missing values:

```
> data(algae, package="DMwR2")
> algae <- algae[-manyNAs(algae), ]
> clean.algae <- knnImputation(algae, k = 10)
```

After executing this code we have a data frame, **clean.algae**, that has no missing variable values.

Let us start by learning how to obtain a linear regression model for predicting the frequency of one of the algae.

```
> lm.a1 <- lm(a1 ~ ., data = clean.algae[, 1:12])
```

The function **lm()** obtains a linear regression model. The first argument of this function[20] indicates the functional form of the model. In this example, it states that we want a model that predicts the variable *a1* using all other variables present in the data, which is the meaning of the dot character. For instance, if we wanted a model to predict *a1* as a function of the variables *mxPH* and *NH4*, we should have indicated the model as "**a1 ~ mxPH + NH4**". There are other variants of this model specification language, called formulas in R, as we have seen in previous chapters. The **data** parameter sets the data sample to be used to obtain the model.[21]

The result of the function is an object that contains the linear model information. We can obtain more details on the linear model with the following instruction:

---

[19] Actually, we will remove two of them because they have too many missing values.
[20] Actually, of most functions used to obtain models in R.
[21] We have indicated the 11 explanatory variables plus the column respecting algal *a1*.

```
> summary(lm.a1)


Call:
lm(formula = a1 ~ ., data = clean.algae[, 1:12])

Residuals:
    Min      1Q  Median      3Q     Max
-37.679 -11.893  -2.567   7.410  62.190

Coefficients:
              Estimate Std. Error t value Pr(>|t|)
(Intercept)  42.942055  24.010879   1.788  0.07537 .
seasonspring  3.726978   4.137741   0.901  0.36892
seasonsummer  0.747597   4.020711   0.186  0.85270
seasonwinter  3.692955   3.865391   0.955  0.34065
sizemedium    3.263728   3.802051   0.858  0.39179
sizesmall     9.682140   4.179971   2.316  0.02166 *
speedlow      3.922084   4.706315   0.833  0.40573
speedmedium   0.246764   3.241874   0.076  0.93941
mxPH         -3.589118   2.703528  -1.328  0.18598
mnO2          1.052636   0.705018   1.493  0.13715
Cl           -0.040172   0.033661  -1.193  0.23426
NO3          -1.511235   0.551339  -2.741  0.00674 **
NH4           0.001634   0.001003   1.628  0.10516
oPO4         -0.005435   0.039884  -0.136  0.89177
PO4          -0.052241   0.030755  -1.699  0.09109 .
Chla         -0.088022   0.079998  -1.100  0.27265
---
Signif. codes:  0 '***' 0.001 '**' 0.01 '*' 0.05 '.' 0.1 ' ' 1

Residual standard error: 17.65 on 182 degrees of freedom
Multiple R-squared:  0.3731,Adjusted R-squared:  0.3215
F-statistic: 7.223 on 15 and 182 DF,  p-value: 2.444e-12
```

Before we analyze the information provided by the function **summary**() when applied to linear models, let us say something about how R handled the three nominal variables. When using them as shown above, R will create a set of auxiliary variables.[22] Namely, for each factor variable with k levels, R will create $k - 1$ auxiliary variables. These variables have the values 0 or 1. A value of 1 means that the associated value of the factor is "present", and that will also mean that the other auxiliary variables will have the value 0. If all $k - 1$ variables are 0, then it means that the factor variable has the remaining kth value. Looking at the summary presented above, we can see that R has created three auxiliary variables for the factor *season* (**seasonspring**, **seasonsummer**, and **seasonwinter**). This means that if we have a water sample with the value "autumn" in the variable *season*, all three auxiliary variables will be set to zero.

The application of the function **summary**() to a linear model gives some diagnostic information concerning the obtained model. First of all, we have information concerning the residuals (i.e., the errors) of the fit of the linear model to the used data. These residuals should have a mean zero and should have a normal distribution (and obviously be as small as possible!).

For each coefficient (variable) of the multiple regression equation, R will show its value

---

[22]Often called *dummy* variables.

and also its standard error (an estimate of the variability of these coefficients). In order to check the importance of each coefficient, we can test the hypothesis that each of them is null, that is, $H0 : \beta_i = 0$. To test this hypothesis, the t-test is normally used. R calculates a t value, which is defined as the ratio between the coefficient value and its standard error, that is, $\frac{\beta_i}{s_{\beta_i}}$. R will show us a column (Pr(>|t|)) associated with each coefficient with the level at which the hypothesis that the coefficient is null is rejected. Thus a value of 0.0001 means that we are 99.99% confident that the coefficient is not null. R marks each test with a symbol corresponding to a set of common confidence levels used for these tests. In summary, only for the coefficients that have some symbol in front of them can we reject the hypothesis that they may be null with at least 90% confidence.

Another piece of relevant diagnostics information outputted by R are the R^2 coefficients (multiple and adjusted). These indicate the degree of fit of the model to the data, that is, the proportion of variance in the data that is explained by the model. Values near 1 are better (almost 100% explained variance) — while the smaller the values, the larger the lack of fit. The adjusted coefficient is more demanding as it takes into account the number of parameters of the regression model.

Finally, we can also test the null hypothesis that there is no dependence of the target variable on any of the explanatory variables, that is, $H0 : \beta_1 = \beta_2 = \ldots = \beta_m = 0$. The F-statistic can be used for this purpose by comparing it to a critical value. R provides the confidence level at which we are sure to reject this null hypothesis. Thus a p-level of 0.0001 means that we are 99.99% confident that the null hypothesis is not true. Usually, if the model fails this test (e.g., with a p value that is considered too high, for example, higher than 0.1), it makes no sense to look at the t-tests on the individual coefficients.

Some diagnostics may also be checked by plotting a linear model. In effect, we can issue a command like plot(lm.a1) to obtain a series of successive plots that help in understanding the performance of the model. One of the graphs simply plots each fitted target variable value against the respective residual (error) of the model. Larger errors are usually marked by adding the corresponding row number to the dot in the graph, so that you can inspect the observations if you wish. Another graph shown by R is a normal Q-Q plot of the errors that helps you check if they follow a normal distribution[23] as they should.

The proportion of variance explained by this model is not very impressive (around 32.0%). Still, we can reject the hypothesis that the target variable does not depend on the predictors (the p value of the F test is very small). Looking at the significance of some of the coefficients, we may question the inclusion of some of them in the model. There are several methods for simplifying regression models. In this section we will explore a method usually known as *backward elimination*.

We will start our study of simplifying the linear model using the anova() function. When applied to a single linear model, this function will give us a sequential analysis of variance of the model fit. That is, the reductions in the residual sum of squares (the total error of the model) as each term of the formula is added in turn. The result of this analysis for the model obtained above is shown below.

```
> anova(lm.a1)

Analysis of Variance Table

Response: a1
         Df Sum Sq Mean Sq F value    Pr(>F)
season    3     85    28.2  0.0905 0.9651944
size      2  11401  5700.7 18.3088 5.69e-08 ***
```

---

[23]Ideally, all errors would be in a straight line in this graph.

```
speed          2    3934   1967.2   6.3179 0.0022244 **
mxPH           1    1329   1328.8   4.2677 0.0402613 *
mnO2           1    2287   2286.8   7.3444 0.0073705 **
Cl             1    4304   4304.3  13.8239 0.0002671 ***
NO3            1    3418   3418.5  10.9789 0.0011118 **
NH4            1     404    403.6   1.2963 0.2563847
oPO4           1    4788   4788.0  15.3774 0.0001246 ***
PO4            1    1406   1405.6   4.5142 0.0349635 *
Chla           1     377    377.0   1.2107 0.2726544
Residuals    182   56668    311.4
---
Signif. codes:  0 '***' 0.001 '**' 0.01 '*' 0.05 '.' 0.1 ' ' 1
```

These results indicate that the variable *season* is the variable that least contributes to the reduction of the fitting error of the model. Let us remove it from the model:

```
> lm2.a1 <- update(lm.a1, . ~ . - season)
```

The **update()** function can be used to perform small changes to an existing linear model. In this case we use it to obtain a new model by removing the variable *season* from the **lm.a1** model. The summary information for this new model is given below:

```
> summary(lm2.a1)


Call:
lm(formula = a1 ~ size + speed + mxPH + mnO2 + Cl + NO3 + NH4 +
    oPO4 + PO4 + Chla, data = clean.algae[, 1:12])

Residuals:
    Min      1Q  Median      3Q     Max
-36.460 -11.953  -3.044   7.444  63.730

Coefficients:
              Estimate Std. Error t value Pr(>|t|)
(Intercept) 44.9532874 23.2378377   1.934  0.05458 .
sizemedium   3.3092102  3.7825221   0.875  0.38278
sizesmall   10.2730961  4.1223163   2.492  0.01358 *
speedlow     3.0546270  4.6108069   0.662  0.50848
speedmedium -0.2976867  3.1818585  -0.094  0.92556
mxPH        -3.2684281  2.6576592  -1.230  0.22033
mnO2         0.8011759  0.6589644   1.216  0.22561
Cl          -0.0381881  0.0333791  -1.144  0.25407
NO3         -1.5334300  0.5476550  -2.800  0.00565 **
NH4          0.0015777  0.0009951   1.586  0.11456
oPO4        -0.0062392  0.0395086  -0.158  0.87469
PO4         -0.0509543  0.0305189  -1.670  0.09669 .
Chla        -0.0841371  0.0794459  -1.059  0.29096
---
Signif. codes:  0 '***' 0.001 '**' 0.01 '*' 0.05 '.' 0.1 ' ' 1

Residual standard error: 17.57 on 185 degrees of freedom
Multiple R-squared:  0.3682,Adjusted R-squared:  0.3272
F-statistic: 8.984 on 12 and 185 DF,  p-value: 1.762e-13
```

The fit has improved a bit (32.8%) but it is still not too impressive. We can carry out a more formal comparison between the two models by again using the **anova()** function, but this time with both models as arguments:

```
> anova(lm.a1,lm2.a1)

Analysis of Variance Table

Model 1: a1 ~ season + size + speed + mxPH + mnO2 + Cl + NO3 + NH4 + oPO4 +
    PO4 + Chla
Model 2: a1 ~ size + speed + mxPH + mnO2 + Cl + NO3 + NH4 + oPO4 + PO4 +
    Chla
  Res.Df   RSS Df Sum of Sq      F Pr(>F)
1    182 56668
2    185 57116 -3   -447.62 0.4792 0.6971
```

This function performs an analysis of variance of the two models using an F-test to assess the significance of the differences. In this case, although the sum of the squared errors has decreased (-448), the comparison shows that the differences are not significant (a value of 0.6971 tells us that with only around 30% confidence we can say they are different). Still, we should recall that this new model is simpler. In order to check if we can remove more coefficients, we would again use the **anova()** function, applied to the **lm2.a1** model. This process would continue until we have no candidate coefficients for removal. However, to simplify our backward elimination process, R has a function that performs all process for us.

The following code creates a linear model that results from applying the backward elimination method to the initial model we have obtained (**lm.a1**):[24]

```
> final.lm <- step(lm.a1)
```

The function **step()** uses the Akaike Information Criterion to perform a model search. The search uses backward elimination by default, but with the parameter **direction** you may use other algorithms (check the help page of this function for further details).

We can obtain the information on the final model by

```
> summary(final.lm)


Call:
lm(formula = a1 ~ size + mxPH + Cl + NO3 + PO4, data = clean.algae[,
    1:12])

Residuals:
    Min      1Q  Median      3Q     Max
-28.874 -12.732  -3.741   8.424  62.926

Coefficients:
            Estimate Std. Error t value Pr(>|t|)
(Intercept) 57.28555   20.96132   2.733  0.00687 **
sizemedium   2.80050    3.40190   0.823  0.41141
sizesmall   10.40636    3.82243   2.722  0.00708 **
mxPH        -3.97076    2.48204  -1.600  0.11130
```

---

[24]We have omitted the output of the **step()** function for space reasons.

```
Cl            -0.05227    0.03165  -1.651   0.10028
NO3           -0.89529    0.35148  -2.547   0.01165 *
PO4           -0.05911    0.01117  -5.291 3.32e-07 ***
---
Signif. codes:  0 '***' 0.001 '**' 0.01 '*' 0.05 '.' 0.1 ' ' 1

Residual standard error: 17.5 on 191 degrees of freedom
Multiple R-squared:  0.3527,Adjusted R-squared:  0.3324
F-statistic: 17.35 on 6 and 191 DF,  p-value: 5.554e-16
```

The proportion of variance explained by this model is still not very interesting. This kind of proportion is usually considered a sign that the linearity assumptions of this modeling approach may be inadequate for the domain.

Further readings on multiple linear regression models

Linear regression is one of the most used statistics techniques. As such, most statistics books will include a chapter on this subject. Still, specialized books should be used for deeper analysis. Two extensive books are the ones by Drapper and Smith (1981) and Myers (1990). These books should cover most of the topics you will ever want to know about linear regression.

4.6.2   Regression Trees

Let us now look at a different kind of regression model available in R. Namely, we will learn how to obtain a regression tree (e.g., Breiman et al., 1984) to predict the value of the frequencies of algal *a1*. As these models handle data sets with missing values, we only need to remove samples 62 and 199 for the reasons mentioned before. In this section we will briefly describe the main concepts behind regression trees and how to apply these models to our case study data. Further information on tree-based models can be found in Section 3.4.5.2 (page 145) where they were described in more detail.

The instructions necessary to obtain a regression tree are presented below:

```
> library(rpart)
> data(algae, package="DMwR2")
> algae <- algae[-manyNAs(algae), ]
> rt.a1 <- rpart(a1 ~ ., data = algae[, 1:12])
```

The first instruction loads the **rpart** (Therneau and Atkinson, 2010) package that implements regression trees in R. The last instruction obtains the tree. Note that this function uses the same schema as the `lm()` function to describe the functional form of the model. The second argument of `rpart()` indicates which data to use to obtain the tree.

The content of the object `rt.a1` object is the following:

```
> rt.a1

n= 198

node), split, n, deviance, yval
      * denotes terminal node

 1) root 198 90401.290 16.996460
   2) PO4>=43.818 147 31279.120  8.979592
     4) Cl>=7.8065 140 21622.830  7.492857
```

```
    8) oPO4>=51.118 84  3441.149  3.846429 *
    9) oPO4< 51.118 56 15389.430 12.962500
     18) mnO2>=10.05 24  1248.673  6.716667 *
     19) mnO2< 10.05 32 12502.320 17.646870
       38) NO3>=3.1875 9   257.080  7.866667 *
       39) NO3< 3.1875 23 11047.500 21.473910
         78) mnO2< 8 13  2919.549 13.807690 *
         79) mnO2>=8 10  6370.704 31.440000 *
  5) Cl< 7.8065 7  3157.769 38.714290 *
 3) PO4< 43.818 51 22442.760 40.103920
  6) mxPH< 7.87 28 11452.770 33.450000
   12) mxPH>=7.045 18  5146.169 26.394440 *
   13) mxPH< 7.045 10  3797.645 46.150000 *
  7) mxPH>=7.87 23  8241.110 48.204350
   14) PO4>=15.177 12  3047.517 38.183330 *
   15) PO4< 15.177 11  2673.945 59.136360 *
```

A regression tree is a hierarchy of logical tests on some of the explanatory variables. Tree-based models automatically select the more relevant variables; thus, not all variables need to appear in the tree. A tree is read from the *root node* that is marked by R with the number 1. R provides some information about the data in this node. Namely, we can observe that we have 198 samples (the overall training data used to obtain the tree) at this node, that these 198 samples have an average value for the frequency of algal *a1* of 16.99, and that the deviance[25] from this average is 90401.29. Each node of a tree has two branches. These are related to the outcome of a test on one of the predictor variables. For instance, from the root node we have a branch (tagged by R with "2)") for the cases where the test "$PO4 \geq 43.818$" is true (147 samples); and also a branch for the 51 remaining cases not satisfying this test (marked by R with "3)"). From node 2 we have two other branches leading to nodes 4 and 5, depending on the outcome of a test on *Cl*. This testing goes on until a *leaf node* is reached. These nodes are marked with asterisks by R. At these leaves we have the predictions of the tree. This means that if we want to use a tree to obtain a prediction for a particular water sample, we only need to follow a branch from the root node to a leaf, according to the outcome of the tests for this sample. The average target variable value found at the leaf we have reached is the prediction of the tree.

We can also obtain a graphical representation of the tree. This can be done by successively applying the functions `plot()` and `text()` to the tree. These functions have several parameters to control the visualization of the tree. A much more practical alternative is to use the functions provided by package **rpart.plot** (Milborrow, 2015). This package includes the function `prp()` that produces nice and highly flexible graphical representation of the trees produced by the function `rpart()`. Applying it to the obtained tree (with some parameter tweaking), we obtain the result shown in Figure 4.10.

```
> library(rpart.plot)
> prp(rt.a1,extra=101,box.col="orange",split.box.col="grey")
```

The `summary()` function can also be applied to tree objects. This will produce a lot of information concerning the tests on the tree, the alternative tests that could be considered, and also the surrogate splits. These last splits are part of the strategy used in **rpart** regression trees to handle unknown values.

As we have mentioned in in Section 3.4.5.2, trees are usually obtained in two steps. Initially, a large tree is grown, and then this tree is pruned by deleting bottom nodes through

---

[25]The sum of squared differences from the average.

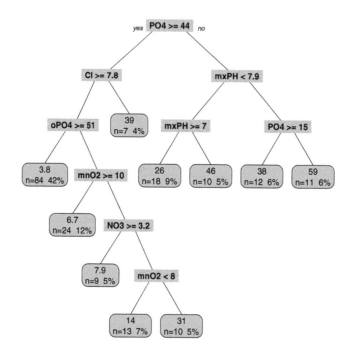

FIGURE 4.10: A regression tree for predicting algal *a1*.

a process of statistical estimation. This process has the goal of avoiding overfitting. This has to do with the fact that an overly large tree will fit the training data almost perfectly, but will be capturing spurious relationships of the given dataset (overfitting it), and thus will perform badly when faced with a new data sample for which predictions are required. The overfitting problem occurs in many modeling techniques, particularly when the assumptions regarding the function to approximate are more relaxed. These models, although having a wider application range (due to these relaxed criteria), suffer from this overfitting problem, thus requiring a posterior, statistically based estimation step to preclude this effect.

The function `rpart()` that we have used to obtain our tree only grows the tree, stopping when certain criteria are met. Namely, the tree stops growing whenever (1) the decrease in the deviance goes below a certain threshold; when (2) the number of samples in the node is less than another threshold; or when (3) the tree depth exceeds another value. These thresholds are controlled by the parameters `cp`, `minsplit`, and `maxdepth`, respectively. If we want to avoid the overfitting problem we should always check the validity of these default criteria. This can be carried out through a process of post-pruning the obtained tree.

The **rpart** package implements a pruning method called *cost complexity* pruning (Breiman et al., 1984). This method uses the values of the parameter `cp` that R calculates for each node of the tree. The pruning method tries to estimate the value of `cp` that ensures the best compromise between predictive accuracy and tree size. Given a tree obtained with the `rpart()` function, R can produce a set of sub-trees of this tree and estimate their predictive performance. This information can be obtained using the function `printcp()` :[26]

---

[26]You can obtain similar information in graphical form using `plotcp(rt.a1)`.

```
> printcp(rt.a1)
```

```
Regression tree:
rpart(formula = a1 ~ ., data = algae[, 1:12])
```

```
Variables actually used in tree construction:
[1] Cl    mnO2 mxPH NO3  oPO4 PO4
```

```
Root node error: 90401/198 = 456.57
```

```
n= 198
```

```
          CP nsplit rel error  xerror    xstd
1 0.405740      0   1.00000 1.00996 0.13033
2 0.071885      1   0.59426 0.70253 0.11269
3 0.030887      2   0.52237 0.69007 0.11504
4 0.030408      3   0.49149 0.71433 0.11890
5 0.027872      4   0.46108 0.72874 0.12022
6 0.027754      5   0.43321 0.71352 0.11833
7 0.018124      6   0.40545 0.70953 0.11719
8 0.016344      7   0.38733 0.72854 0.11454
9 0.010000      9   0.35464 0.75211 0.11483
```

The tree returned by the **rpart()** function is the last tree of this list (tree 9). This tree has a **cp** value of 0.01 (the default value of this parameter), includes nine tests, and has a relative error (compared to the root node) of 0.35464. However, R estimates, using an internal process of ten-fold cross-validation, that this tree will have an average relative error[27] of 0.75211 ± 0.11483. Using the information provided by these more reliable estimates of performance, which avoid the overfitting problem, we can observe that we would theoretically be better off with the tree number 3, which has a lower estimated relative error (0.69007). An alternative selection rule is to choose the best tree according to the 1-SE rule. This consists of looking at the cross-validation error estimates ("xerror" columns) and their standard deviations ("xstd" column). In this case the 1-SE tree is the smallest tree with error less than $0.69007+0.11504 = 0.80511$, which in this case is the tree number 2 with 1 test and an estimated error of 0.70253. If we prefer this tree to the one suggested by R, we can obtain it using the respective **cp** value:[28]

```
> rt2.a1 <- prune(rt.a1, cp = 0.08)
> rt2.a1
```

```
n= 198
```

```
node), split, n, deviance, yval
      * denotes terminal node
```

```
1) root 198 90401.29 16.996460
  2) PO4>=43.818 147 31279.12  8.979592 *
  3) PO4< 43.818 51 22442.76 40.103920 *
```

---

[27] It is important to note that you may have obtained different numbers on the columns 'xerror' and 'xstd'. The cross-validation estimates are obtained using a random sampling process, meaning that your samples will probably be different and thus the results will also differ.

[28] Actually, any value that is between its **cp** value and the one of the tree above it.

As we have mentioned before the book package includes the function `rpartXse()` that automates this process and takes as an argument the `se` value, defaulting to 1:

```
> (rt.a1 <- rpartXse(a1 ~ ., data = algae[, 1:12]))

n= 198

node), split, n, deviance, yval
      * denotes terminal node

1) root 198 90401.29 16.996460
  2) PO4>=43.818 147 31279.12  8.979592 *
  3) PO4< 43.818 51 22442.76 40.103920 *
```

R also allows a kind of interactive pruning of a tree through the function `snip.rpart()`. This function can be used to generate a pruned tree in two ways. The first consists of indicating the number of the nodes (you can obtain these numbers by printing a tree object) at which you want to prune the tree:

```
> first.tree <- rpart(a1 ~ ., data = algae[, 1:12])
> snip.rpart(first.tree, c(4, 7))

n= 198

node), split, n, deviance, yval
      * denotes terminal node

 1) root 198 90401.290 16.996460
  2) PO4>=43.818 147 31279.120  8.979592
    4) Cl>=7.8065 140 21622.830  7.492857 *
    5) Cl< 7.8065 7  3157.769 38.714290 *
  3) PO4< 43.818 51 22442.760 40.103920
    6) mxPH< 7.87 28 11452.770 33.450000
     12) mxPH>=7.045 18  5146.169 26.394440 *
     13) mxPH< 7.045 10  3797.645 46.150000 *
    7) mxPH>=7.87 23  8241.110 48.204350 *
```

Note that the function returns a tree object like the one returned by the `rpart()` function, which means that you can store your pruned tree using something like `my.tree <- snip.rpart(first.tree,c(4,7))`.

Alternatively, you can use `snip.rpart()` in a graphical way. First, you plot the tree, and then you call the function without the second argument. If you click the mouse on some node, R prints on its console some information about the node. If you click again on that node, R prunes the tree at that node.[29] You can go on pruning nodes in this graphical way. You finish the interaction by clicking the right mouse button. The result of the call is again a tree object. Please note that this graphical pruning procedure cannot unfortunately, be used with the `prp()` function. Instead you need to used the more "standard" (but not so nice) way of obtaining a graphical representation of the tree,

```
> plot(first.tree)
> text(first.tree)
> snip.rpart(first.tree)
```

---

[29]Note that the plot of the tree is not updated, so you will not see the pruning being carried out in the graphics window.

4.7 Model Evaluation and Selection

In Section 4.6 we saw two examples of prediction models that could be used in this case study. The obvious question is which one should we use for obtaining the predictions for the seven algae of the 140 test samples? To answer this question, one needs to specify some preference criteria over the space of possible models; that is, we need to specify how we will evaluate the performance of the models.

Several criteria exist for evaluating (and thus comparing) models. Among the most popular are criteria that calculate the predictive performance of the models. Still, other criteria exist such as the model interpretability, or even the model computational efficiency, that can be important for very large data mining problems.

The predictive performance of regression models is obtained by comparing the predictions of the models with the real values of the target variables, and calculating some average error measure from this comparison. One such measure is the mean absolute error (MAE). Let us see how to obtain this measure for our two models (linear regression and regression trees). The first step is to obtain the model predictions for the set of cases where we want to evaluate it. To obtain the predictions of any model in R, one uses the function `predict()`. This general function receives a model and a test dataset and retrieves the corresponding model predictions:

```
> lm.predictions.a1 <- predict(final.lm, clean.algae)
> rt.predictions.a1 <- predict(rt.a1, algae)
```

These two statements collect the predictions of the models obtained in Section 4.6 for alga *a1*. Note that we have used the `clean.algae` data frame with linear models, because of the missing values.

Having the predictions of the models, we can calculate their mean absolute error as follows:

```
> (mae.a1.lm <- mean(abs(lm.predictions.a1 - algae[["a1"]])))

[1] 13.10681

> (mae.a1.rt <- mean(abs(rt.predictions.a1 - algae[["a1"]])))

[1] 8.480619
```

Another popular error measure is the mean squared error (MSE). This measure can be obtained as follows:

```
> (mse.a1.lm <- mean((lm.predictions.a1 - algae[["a1"]])^2))

[1] 295.5407

> (mse.a1.rt <- mean((rt.predictions.a1 - algae[["a1"]])^2))

[1] 161.9202
```

This latter statistic has the disadvantage of not being measured in the same units as the target variable, and thus being less interpretable from the user perspective. Even if we use the MAE statistic, we can ask ourselves the question of whether the scores obtained by the models are good or bad. An alternative statistic that provides a reasonable answer to this question is the normalized mean squared error (NMSE). This statistic calculates a ratio between the performance of our models and that of a baseline predictor, usually taken as the mean value of the target variable:

```
> (nmse.a1.lm <- mean((lm.predictions.a1-algae[['a1']])^2)/
+                 mean((mean(algae[['a1']])-algae[['a1']])^2))

[1] 0.6473034

> (nmse.a1.rt <- mean((rt.predictions.a1-algae[['a1']])^2)/
+                 mean((mean(algae[['a1']])-algae[['a1']])^2))

[1] 0.3546432
```

The NMSE is a unitless error measure with values usually ranging from 0 to 1. If your model is performing better than this very simple baseline predictor, then the NMSE should clearly be less than 1. The smaller the NMSE, the better. Values greater than 1 mean that your model is performing worse than simply always predicting the average for all cases! Further details on evaluation metrics can be found in Section 3.4.5.1 (page 141).

It is also interesting to have some kind of visual inspection of the predictions of the models. A possibility is to use a scatter plot of the errors. Figure 4.11 shows an example of this type of analysis for the predictions of our two models, and it was produced with the following code:

```
> library(ggplot2)
> dg <- data.frame(lm.a1=lm.predictions.a1,
+                  rt.a1=rt.predictions.a1,
+                  true.a1=algae[["a1"]])
> ggplot(dg,aes(x=lm.a1,y=true.a1)) +
+     geom_point() + geom_abline(slope=1,intercept=0,color="red") +
+     ggtitle("Linear Model")
> ggplot(dg,aes(x=rt.a1,y=true.a1)) +
+     geom_point() + geom_abline(slope=1,intercept=0,color="red") +
+     ggtitle("Regression Tree")
```

Looking at Figure 4.11 we can observe that the models have rather poor performance in several cases. In the ideal scenario that they make correct predictions for all cases, all the points in the plots should lie on the red lines, which were obtained with the call to geom_abline(). These lines cross the origin of the plots and represent the points where the X-coordinate is equal to the Y-coordinate. Given that each point in the plots obtains its coordinates from the predicted and truth values of the target variable, if these values were equal, the points would all be placed on this ideal line. As we observe, that is not the case at all! We can check which is the sample number where a particularly bad prediction is made with the function identify(), which can be used to let the user interactively click on the dots in a graph. Unfortunately, this type of interaction is not possible with **ggplot2** graphs, so we resort to the standard graphics in this case,

```
> plot(lm.predictions.a1,algae[['a1']],main="Linear Model",
+      xlab="Predictions",ylab="True Values")
> abline(0,1,col="red")
> algae[identify(lm.predictions.a1,algae[['a1']]),]
```

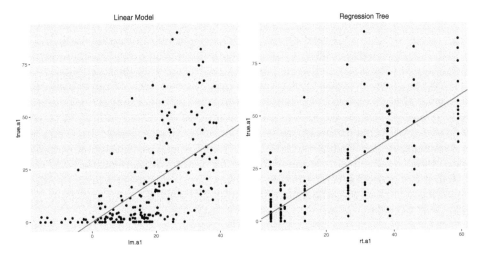

FIGURE 4.11: Errors scatter plot.

Using this code and after finishing the interaction with the graphics window by right-clicking on the graph, you should see the rows of the `algae` data frame corresponding to the clicked points — because we are using the vector returned by the `identify()` function to index the `algae` data frame.

Looking at Figure 4.11 (left) with the predictions of the linear model, we can see that this model predicts negative algae frequencies for some cases. In this application domain, it makes no sense to say that the occurrence of an alga in a water sample is negative (at most, it can be zero). As such, we can take advantage of this domain knowledge and use this minimum value as a form of improving the linear model performance:

```
> sensible.lm.predictions.a1 <- ifelse(lm.predictions.a1 < 0, 0, lm.predictions.a1)
> (mae.a1.lm <- mean(abs(lm.predictions.a1 - algae[["a1"]])))

[1] 13.10681

> (smae.a1.lm <- mean(abs(sensible.lm.predictions.a1 - algae[["a1"]])))

[1] 12.48276
```

We have used the function `ifelse()` to achieve this effect. This function has three arguments. The first is a logical condition, the second is the result of the function call when the condition is true, while the third argument is the result when the condition is false. Notice how this small detail has improved the performance of our model.

According to the performance measures calculated previously, one should prefer the regression tree to obtain the predictions for the 140 test samples as it obtained a lower NMSE. However, there is a trap in this reasoning. Our goal is to choose the best model for obtaining the predictions on the 140 test samples. As we do not know the target variable values for those samples, we have to estimate which of our models will perform better on these test samples. The key issue here is to obtain a reliable estimate of a model performance on data for which we do not know the true target value. Calculating the performance metrics using the training data (as we did before) is unreliable because the obtained estimates are biased. In effect, there are models that can easily obtain zero prediction error on the training data. However, this performance will hardly generalize over new samples for which the target variable value is unknown. This phenomenon is usually known as *overfitting* the training data, as mentioned previously. Thus, to select a model, one needs to obtain more reliable estimates of the model's performance on unseen data. k-fold cross-validation (k-fold CV) is among the most frequently used methods for obtaining these reliable estimates for small datasets like our case study. This method can be briefly described as follows. Obtain k equally sized and random subsets of the training data. For each of these k subsets, build a model using the remaining $k - 1$ sets and evaluate this model on the kth subset. Store the performance of the model and repeat this process for all remaining subsets. In the end, we have k performance measures, all obtained by testing a model on data not used for its construction, and that is the key issue. The k-fold cross-validation estimate is the average of these k measures. A common choice for k is 10. Sometimes we even repeat the overall k-fold CV process several times to get even more reliable estimates. Further details on this important issue of methodologies for obtaining reliable estimates of the predictive perfomance of a model were given in Section 3.5 (page 172).

In general, we can say that when facing a predictive task, we have to make the following decisions:

- Select the alternative models to consider (the models can actually be parameter variants of the same algorithm) for the predictive task(s) we want to address.

- Select the evaluation metrics that will be used to compare the models.

- Choose the experimental methodology for obtaining reliable estimates of these metrics.

As we have seen in Section 3.5, the package **performanceEstimation** (Torgo, 2014a) provides and infrastructure designed specifically for these model comparison and selection problems. It implements several different estimation methods, including cross-validation. The package includes the function `performanceEstimation()` that can be used to carry out this type of experiments. This function has three main parameters: (1) the predictive tasks to use in the comparison, (2) the alternative approaches to consider for these tasks, and (3) the estimation task specification. We will illustrate its use by comparing a linear model with several variants of regression trees, on the algae dataset.

We will assume that we want to use the NMSE as the evaluation metric of our regression trees and linear models. Moreover, we will use 5 repetitions of a 10-fold cross validation process to estimate the scores of this statistic of the different approaches we will consider. The following code runs this estimation process for 4 models: a linear regression model and 3 variants (different pruning levels) of a regression tree.

```
> library(performanceEstimation)
> res <- performanceEstimation(
+     PredTask(a1 ~ ., algae[, 1:12], "a1"),
+     c(Workflow(learner="lm",pre="knnImp",post="onlyPos"),
+       workflowVariants(learner="rpartXse",learner.pars=list(se=c(0,0.5,1)))),
+     EstimationTask(metrics="nmse",method=CV(nReps=5,nFolds=10))
+ )
```

As mentioned previously, the first argument should be a vector (or a single one, which is a vector of length 1) with the predictive tasks to be used in the experimental comparison. Each task is specified as `PredTask(<formula>,<data frame>,<label>)`, with `<label>` being an optional name to give to the task. The second argument of `performanceEstimation()` contains a vector of workflows. As mentioned before we call a workflow to a solution of a predictive task. This typically will include the call to some learning algorithm (e.g. a regression tree) but it can also include some data pre-processing steps, or any other steps that the user considers to be useful to solve the task. In package **performanceEstimation** there are two main types of workflows: (i) standard workflows; and (ii) user-defined workflows. The former are ready-to-use workflows that will cover most set-ups of the users of this package, whilst the latter are for specific set-ups where the user wants some specific solution to be applied. We will see examples of the user-defined workflows in the other case studies of this book. Here we are using standard workflows. A workflow is created with the constructor `Workflow()`. The first argument of this function is the name of the workflow to use, which can be omitted if this is the standard workflow provided by the package, as is done in the example above. This standard workflow (implemented through function `standardWF()`) accepts several arguments that can be used to specify your solution to the task. A key parameter is the `learner` where you can indicate the name of the R function implementing your learning algorithm. Standard workflows include other arguments that allow you to specify other settings of your approach, like the parameters to be used when calling the learning algorithm, eventual pre-processing functions to be applied to the data before learning, or even post-processing functions to be applied to the predictions of the learner. In the above code we see an example where we are using the standard workflow with the linear regression learning algorithm (function `lm()`), we are using the function `knnImp()` to fill in the unknown values of the data using a k-nearest neighbor approach, and we are post-processing the predictions of the linear model with the function `onlyPos()` that basically truncates any negative predicted value to zero, as we have done before, because we know algae frequencies can not be negative.

In the above code we have also used the function `workflowVariants()`. This auxiliary function facilitates the specification of several variants of a workflow without having to type in all their details. The result of this function is a set of workflows, each resulting from some variation of the parameters of a workflow. In this case we are generating these variants by saying that all are variants of the same learning algorithm (`rpartXse` in this case), with three different settings of the parameter `se` of this learner. This means the above function call will generate three workflows, each with a different value of the `se` learning parameter of the function `rpartXse()`. Any parameter that we provide with a vector as value will be assumed to be a source for variants generation. If more than one parameter is supplied with a vector, the function `workflowVariants()` will generate as many workflows as there are combinations of the values of the different parameters. Check the help page of function `workflowVariants()` to get more details and examples (or the PDF accompanying package **performanceEstimation**). In summary, the above call will carry out an experimental comparison involving 4 different workflows: a linear regression model and three variants of a regression tree (with different levels of pruning).

The final argument of the function `performanceEstimation()` specifies the estimation tasks. This involves essentially deciding which metrics are to be estimated and which estimation method should be used. The specification of this estimation task is done through function `EstimationTask()`.

The result of this call is a complex object containing all information concerning the experimental comparison. The package **performanceEstimation** provides several utility functions to explore this information. For instance, the following provides a summary of the results of the comparison:

```
> summary(res)


== Summary of a  Cross Validation Performance Estimation Experiment ==

Task for estimating  nmse  using
 5 x 10 - Fold Cross Validation
```

```
Run with seed =  1234

* Predictive Tasks ::  a1
* Workflows   ::  lm, rpartXse.v1, rpartXse.v2, rpartXse.v3

-> Task:  a1
  *Workflow: lm
              nmse
avg       0.7087223
std       0.1641574
med       0.6902144
iqr       0.1573738
min       0.4675652
max       1.2261698
invalid 0.0000000

   *Workflow: rpartXse.v1
              nmse
avg       0.6037975
std       0.2548283
med       0.5431126
iqr       0.3034833
min       0.1890749
max       1.3156177
invalid 0.0000000

   *Workflow: rpartXse.v2
              nmse
avg       0.6443387
std       0.2230355
med       0.6375429
iqr       0.3111928
min       0.2146359
max       1.1222208
invalid 0.0000000

   *Workflow: rpartXse.v3
              nmse
avg       0.6728360
std       0.2218169
med       0.6451861
iqr       0.3418516
min       0.2804985
max       1.1222208
invalid 0.0000000
```

As can be seen, one of the variants of the regression tree achieves the best average NMSE score. Whether the difference is statistically significant with respect to the other alternatives is a question we will address later in this section. We can also obtain a visualization (Figure 4.12) of these results as follows:

```
> plot(res)
```

The `performanceEstimation()` function assigns a label to each model variant. In case

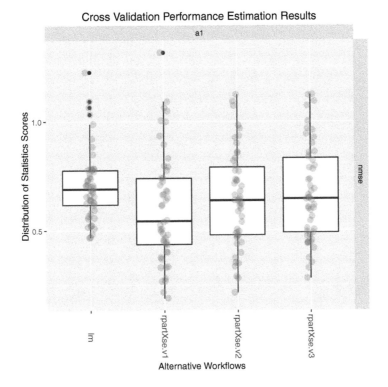

FIGURE 4.12: Visualization of the cross-validation results.

you want to know the specific parameter settings corresponding to any label, you can proceed as follows:

```
> getWorkflow("rpartXse.v1", res)

Workflow Object:
Workflow ID       ::  rpartXse.v1
Workflow Function ::  standardWF
     Parameter values:
 learner.pars  -> se=0
 learner  -> rpartXse
```

We can carry out a similar comparative experiment for all seven prediction tasks we are facing at the same time. The following code implements that idea:

```
> DSs <- sapply(names(algae)[12:18],
+          function(x,names.attrs) {
+            f <- as.formula(paste(x, "~ ."))
+            PredTask(f, algae[,c(names.attrs,x)], x, copy=TRUE)
+          },
+          names(algae)[1:11])
> res.all <- performanceEstimation(
+     DSs,
+     c(Workflow(learner="lm", pre="knnImp", post="onlyPos"),
+       workflowVariants(learner="rpartXse", learner.pars=list(se=c(0,0.5,1)))),
+     EstimationTask(metrics="nmse" ,method=CV(nReps=5, nFolds=10)))
```

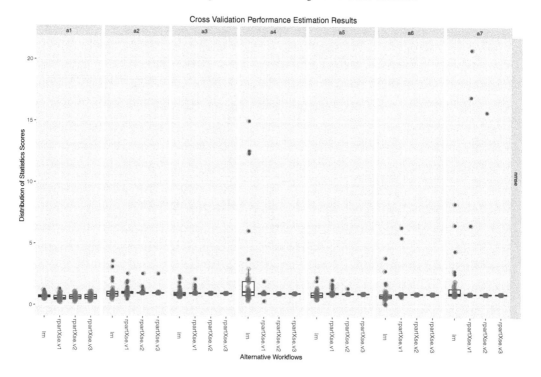

FIGURE 4.13: Visualization of the cross-validation results on all algae.

For space reasons we have omitted the output of the above commands. This code starts by creating the vector of predictive tasks to use in the comparisons, that is, the seven prediction tasks. For this we need to create a formula for each problem. We have obtained this formula creating a string by concatenating the name of the column of each target variable with the string "$\sim$.". The resulting string is then transformed into an R formula using the function `as.formula()`. With this formula we can create the respective **PredTask** object. You may have noticed the `copy=TRUE` argument in the call to the constructor. It is necessary because the data for each of the tasks is created on the fly and we do not have a separate object for each task, thus we need to copy the data into the **PredTask** object to keep it "permanent". Having created the vector of tasks we have used the function `performanceEstimation()` as before, with the single difference that this time we have carried out five repetitions of the tenfold cross-validation process for increased statistical significance of the results. Depending on the power of your computer, this code may take a while to run.

In Figure 4.13 we show the results of the models for the different algae on the CV process. The figure was obtained with,

```
> plot(res.all)
```

As we can observe, there are several very bad results; that is, NMSE scores clearly above 1, which is the baseline of being as competitive as predicting always the average target variable value for all test cases! If we want to check which is the best model for each problem, we can use the function `topPerformers()`:

```
> topPerformers(res.all)

$a1
        Workflow Estimate
nmse rpartXse.v1    0.604

$a2
        Workflow Estimate
nmse rpartXse.v3    1.034

$a3
        Workflow Estimate
nmse rpartXse.v2        1

$a4
        Workflow Estimate
nmse rpartXse.v2        1

$a5
     Workflow Estimate
nmse       lm   0.934

$a6
     Workflow Estimate
nmse       lm   0.936

$a7
        Workflow Estimate
nmse rpartXse.v3        1
```

The output of this function (a list with as many components as there are tasks) confirms that, with the exception of alga 1, the results are rather disappointing. The variability of the results (see Figure 4.13) provides good indications that this might be a good candidate for an ensemble approach. Ensembles are model construction methods that basically try to overcome some limitations of individual models by generating a large set of alternative models and then combining their predictions. There are many approaches to obtain ensembles that differ not only in the way the diversity of models is obtained (e.g., different training samples, different variables, different modeling techniques, etc.), but also in how the ensemble prediction is reached (e.g., voting, averaging, etc.). Further details on ensemble models were provided in Section 3.4.5.5 (page 165). Random forests (Breiman, 2001) are regarded as one of the more competitive examples of ensembles. They are formed by a large set of tree-based models (regression or classification trees). Each tree is fully grown (no post-pruning); and at each step of the tree growing process, the best split for each node is chosen from a random subset of attributes. Predictions for regression tasks are obtained by averaging the predictions of the trees in the ensemble. The R package `randomForest` (Liaw and Wiener, 2002) implements these ideas on the function `randomForest()`. The following code repeats the previous cross-validation experiment, this time including three variants of random forests, each with a different number of trees in the ensemble. We have again omitted the output for space reasons.

```
> library(randomForest)
> res.all <- performanceEstimation(
+       DSs,
```

```
+      c(Workflow(learner="lm", pre="knnImp",post="onlyPos"),
+        workflowVariants(learner="rpartXse",
+                         learner.pars=list(se=c(0,0.5,1))),
+        workflowVariants(learner="randomForest", pre="knnImp",
+                         learner.pars=list(ntree=c(200,500,700)))),
+      EstimationTask(metrics="nmse",method=CV(nReps=5,nFolds=10)))
```

Using the function **rankWorkflows()** we can confirm the advantages of the ensemble approach:

```
> rankWorkflows(res.all, top=3)

$a1
$a1$nmse
          Workflow  Estimate
1 randomForest.v1 0.5484773
2 randomForest.v2 0.5492354
3 randomForest.v3 0.5498515


$a2
$a2$nmse
          Workflow  Estimate
1 randomForest.v3 0.7759238
2 randomForest.v2 0.7763979
3 randomForest.v1 0.7839276


$a3
$a3$nmse
          Workflow  Estimate
1 randomForest.v3 0.9992762
2      rpartXse.v2 1.0000000
3      rpartXse.v3 1.0000000


$a4
$a4$nmse
          Workflow  Estimate
1 randomForest.v1 0.9847430
2 randomForest.v3 0.9884407
3 randomForest.v2 0.9940180


$a5
$a5$nmse
          Workflow  Estimate
1 randomForest.v3 0.7844936
2 randomForest.v2 0.7852387
3 randomForest.v1 0.7913406


$a6
$a6$nmse
          Workflow  Estimate
```

```
1 randomForest.v2 0.9095273
2 randomForest.v3 0.9103364
3 randomForest.v1 0.9208936


$a7
$a7$nmse
          Workflow Estimate
1      rpartXse.v3 1.000000
2 randomForest.v3 1.181581
3 randomForest.v2 1.183661
```

In effect, for most problems the best score is obtained by some variant of a random forest. Still, the results are not always very good, in particular for alga 7. The output of the function `rankWorkflows()` does not tell us whether the difference between the scores of these best models and the remaining alternatives is statistically significant; that is, what is the confidence that with another random sample of data we get a similar outcome? The function `pairedComparisons()` from the package **performanceEstimation** provides this information. It carries out a series of statistical tests that can be used to check the statistical validity of certain hypotheses concerning the observed differences among the performance of the different workflows. In the case of the above comparison, and according to the work by Demsar (2006), the adequate procedure when we have several workflows being compared on a series of tasks is to use the Friedman test to check that we can reject the null hypothesis that all workflows perform equally on a set of predictive tasks, and if this is rejected then proceed with a post-hoc test. If the goal is to compare all workflows against each other we use the post-hoc Nemenyi test, whilst if the objective is to compare a series of workflows against some baseline we use the post-hoc Bonferroni-Dunn test. More information on this topic was given in Section 3.5.4 (page 181).

The following code shows how to obtain the results of these tests using the infrastructure of package **performanceEstimation**,

```
> p <- pairedComparisons(res.all,baseline="randomForest.v3")
> p$nmse$F.test

$chi
[1] 27.35204

$FF
[1] 11.20376

$critVal
[1] 0.6524015

$rejNull
[1] TRUE

> p$nmse$BonferroniDunn.test

$critDif
[1] 3.046397

$baseline
[1] "randomForest.v3"
```

```
$rkDifs
                lm       rpartXse.v1      rpartXse.v2      rpartXse.v3
        3.8571429        4.7142857        3.2142857        2.3571429
randomForest.v1 randomForest.v2
        1.1428571        0.7142857


$signifDifs
                lm       rpartXse.v1      rpartXse.v2      rpartXse.v3
             TRUE             TRUE             TRUE            FALSE
randomForest.v1 randomForest.v2
            FALSE            FALSE
```

The function `pairedComparisons()` uses the information contained in the object with the outcome of the experimental comparisons to carry out a series of statistical tests. In case you also supply a baseline workflow, the tests are carried out "against" this baseline. In the above example we are setting this baseline to the variant of random forest that seems to be the best over all seven algae. Our idea is to check whether the difference between the performance of this random forest and the other alternative workflows is statistically significant or not. This means that we are comparing a baseline against a series of alternatives on a set of tasks. As such, we first use the Friedman test to check if we can reject the null hypothesis that there is no difference among the alternative worklows. The outcome of the function `pairedComparisons()` is a list with as many components as there are evaluation metrics (in this case a single one, *NMSE*). For each metric, we have another list whose components are the statistical tests. These tests in turn typically return as result another list with different values used in the test. For instance, the second statement above shows the outcome of the Friedman test (component name `F.test`) for the *NMSE* metric. This is a list with the values of the statistics used in the test, but most importantly, the outcome of the test, i.e. whether we can reject the null hypothesis or not. As we can observe in this case we can reject the null hypothesis that the performance of the workflows is not different. In this context, we can proceed to the post-hoc Bonferroni-Dunn test as we want to compare the other workflows against our baseline. The last statement above presents the outcome of this test. As we can see, the difference between the baseline random forest and other variants can not be considered statistically significant with 95% confidence (the default confidence level used by the function `pairedComparisons()`, which is changeable through parameter `p.value`). Still, we can reject with 95% confidence, the hypothesis that the performance of the baseline is the same as the performance of two of the regression trees and the linear regression model. In summary, we are confident enough to say that our baseline is better than the linear model and two of the regression trees on these seven regression tasks. Nevertheless, we can not reject the hypothesis that its performance is not better than that of the other workflows (at least with 95% confidence).

This type of analysis can also be carried out visually through CD diagrams. Figure 4.14 presents the Bonferroni-Dunn CD diagram corresponding to the statistical tests described before. The figure was obtained using function `CDdiagram.BD()` as follows:

```
> CDdiagram.BD(p)
```

The diagram presents each workflow with a different colored line, the baseline having the name in bold. The lines of the workflows lead to a position in the X axis corresponding to the average ranking position of the respective workflow across all tasks involved in the comparison. This means for instance that, in Figure 4.14 the workflow "randomforest.v1" has an average rank of ≈ 3 across the seven tasks. From the line corresponding to the baseline workflow we have a horizontal thick black line whose length corresponds to the

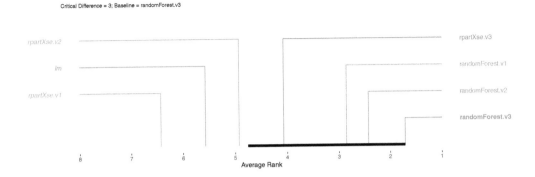

FIGURE 4.14: The CD Diagram for comparing all workflows against *randomforest.v3*.

critical difference in average ranks that, according to the Bonferroni-Dunn test, is necessary for being significantly different from the baseline. All lines that are outside of this length correspond to workflows whose average rank is considered significantly different from the baseline, and their names are presented in italics.

4.8 Predictions for the Seven Algae

In this section we will see how to obtain the predictions for the seven algae on the 140 test samples. Section 4.7 described how to proceed to choose the best models to obtain these predictions. The procedure used consisted of obtaining unbiased estimates of the NMSE for a set of models on all seven predictive tasks, by means of a cross-validation experimental process.

The main goal in this data mining problem is to obtain seven predictions for each of the 140 test samples. Each of these seven predictions will be obtained using the model that our cross-validation process has indicated as being the "best" for that task. This will be one of either the models shown by our call to the `rankWorkflows()` function in the previous section. Namely, it will be one of the random forest variants.

Let us start by obtaining these models using all the available training data so that we can apply them to the test set. The following code obtains the best workflows for each of the seven algae:

```
> wfs <- sapply(taskNames(res.all),
+               function(t) topPerformer(res.all,metric="nmse",task=t))
> wfs[["a1"]]

Workflow Object:
Workflow ID       ::  randomForest.v1
Workflow Function ::  standardWF
```

```
    Parameter values:
  learner.pars  -> ntree=200
  learner  -> randomForest
  pre  -> knnImp


> wfs[["a7"]]

Workflow Object:
Workflow ID       ::  rpartXse.v3
Workflow Function ::  standardWF
    Parameter values:
  learner.pars  -> se=1
  learner  -> rpartXse
```

We use the function `taskNames()` to obtain a vector with the names of the seven prediction tasks and then for each of these names we apply a function that essentially uses the function `topPerformer()` to obtain the workflow that is the best at a certain task on a given metric. As a result the object `wfs` will be a list with each 7 objects of class **Workflow**. Function `runWorkflow()` can be used to apply any of these workflows to some given train and test sets. As a result this function will return the outcome of this application, which depends on the author of the workflow. In our case we were using the standard workflows implemented by function `standardWF()` of the package **peformanceEstimation**. This workflow returns as a result a list with several components, among which the predictions of the learned model for the given test set.

We are now ready to obtain the matrix with the predictions of the best workflows for the entire test set:

```
> full.test.algae <- cbind(test.algae, algae.sols)
> pts <- array(dim = c(140,7,2),
+                 dimnames = list(1:140, paste0("a",1:7), c("trues","preds")))
> for(i in 1:7) {
+     res <- runWorkflow(wfs[[i]],
+                        as.formula(paste(names(wfs)[i],"~.")),
+                        algae[,c(1:11,11+i)],
+                        full.test.algae[,c(1:11,11+i)])
+     pts[,i,"trues"] <- res$trues
+     pts[,i,"preds"] <- res$preds
+ }
```

We start by putting the test cases and the respective solutions in a single data frame. Then we create an array (`pts`) with 3 dimensions that will store all information on the application of the models to make predictions for the seven algae. It is like having two matrices of 140 × 7 (where 140 is the number of test cases and 7 the number of algae predicted for each test case). The first of these matrices contains the true values of the algae, whilst the second contains the predictions of our workflows. For instance, if we wanted to know the prediction and true values for algae "a1" and "a3" on the first 3 test cases we could obtain them as follows:

```
> pts[1:3,c("a1","a3"),]

, , trues

   a1  a3
```

```
1 1.2 1.9
2 1.2 0.0
3 7.0 6.5

, , preds

         a1        a3
1  3.495208 4.707276
2 13.951108 3.450281
3 12.717983 6.846536
```

This array was filled in by successively applying the best workflows for each of the 7 algae using function `runWorkflow()`. For this we had to build an adequate formula for each predictive task as well as using the correct columns of the original data to obtain the model. The result of the call to `runWorkflow()` (actually a call to `standardWF()` that is the specific workflow we are using) is a list that contains, among others, the components `trues` and `preds`, with the true and predicted values, respectively.

Using the information stored in the array (`pts`) we can compare the predictions with the real values to obtain some feedback on the quality of our approach to this prediction problem. The following code calculates the NMSE scores of our models on the seven algae:

```
> avg.preds <- apply(algae[,12:18], 2, mean)
> apply((pts[,,"trues"] - pts[,,"preds"])^2, 2 ,sum) /
+     apply( (scale(pts[,,"trues"], avg.preds, FALSE))^2, 2, sum)

       a1        a2        a3        a4        a5        a6        a7
0.4739169 0.8608667 0.7749362 0.7259074 0.7154015 0.8113643 1.0000000
```

We first obtained the predictions of the baseline model used to calculate the NMSE, which in our case consists of predicting the average value of the target variable. Then we proceed to calculate the NMSEs for the seven models/algae. This is done on a single statement that may seem a bit complex at first but as soon as you understand it, we are sure you will be amazed by its simplicity and compactness. The `scale()` function can be used to normalize a data set. It works by subtracting the second argument from the first and then dividing the result by the third, unless this argument is FALSE, as is the case above. In this example we are thus using it to subtract a vector (the average target value of all seven algae) from each line of a matrix.

The results that we obtained are in accordance with the cross-validation estimates obtained previously. They confirm the difficulty in obtaining good scores for alga 7, while for the other problems the results are slightly more competitive, in particular for alga 1.

In summary, with a proper model selection phase, we were able to obtain interesting scores for these prediction problems.

4.9 Summary

The main goal of this first case study was to familiarize the reader with the use of R for data mining. For this purpose we used a small problem — at least by data mining standards. We described how to perform some of the most basic data analysis tasks in R.

If you are interested in knowing more about the international data analysis competition that was behind the data used in this chapter, you can browse through the competition Web page,[30] or read some of the papers of the winning solutions (Bontempi et al., 1999; Chan, 1999; Devogelaere et al., 1999; Torgo, 1999b) to compare the data analysis strategies followed by these authors.

In terms of data mining, this case study has provided information on

- Data visualization

- Descriptive statistics

- Strategies to handle unknown variable values

- Regression tasks

- Evaluation metrics for regression tasks

- Multiple linear regression

- Regression trees

- Model selection/comparison through k-fold cross-validation

- Model ensembles and random forests

We hope that by now you are more acquainted with the interaction with R, and also familiarized with some of its features. Namely, you should have learned some techniques for

- Loading data from text files

- How to obtain descriptive statistics of datasets

- Basic visualization of data

- Handling datasets with unknown values

- How to obtain some regression models

- How to use the obtained models to obtain predictions for a test set

Further cases studies will give you more details on these and other data mining techniques.

Chapter 5

Predicting Stock Market Returns

This second case study tries to move a bit further in terms of the use of data mining techniques. We will address some of the difficulties of incorporating data mining tools and techniques into a concrete business problem. The specific domain used to illustrate these problems is that of automatic stock trading systems. We will address the task of building a stock trading system based on prediction models obtained with daily stock quotes data. Several models will be tried with the goal of predicting the future returns of the S&P 500 market index. These predictions will be used together with a trading strategy to reach a decision regarding the market orders to generate. This chapter addresses several new data mining issues, among which are (1) how to handle prediction problems with a time ordering among data observations (also known as time series), and (2) an example of the challenges of translating model predictions into decisions and actions in real-world applications.

5.1 Problem Description and Objectives

Stock market trading is an application domain with a large potential for data mining. In effect, the existence of an enormous amount of historical data suggests that data mining can provide a competitive advantage over human inspection of these data. On the other hand, there are researchers claiming that the markets adapt so rapidly in terms of price adjustments that there is no space to obtain profits in a consistent way. This is usually known as the *efficient markets hypothesis*. This theory has been successively replaced by more relaxed versions that leave some space for trading opportunities due to temporary market inefficiencies.

The general goal of stock trading is to maintain a portfolio of assets based on buy and sell orders. The long-term objective is to achieve as much profit as possible from these trading actions. In the context of this chapter we will constrain a bit more this general scenario. Namely, we will only "trade" a single security, actually a market index. Given this security and an initial capital, we will try to maximize our profit over a future testing period by means of trading actions (Buy, Sell, Hold). Our trading strategy will use as a basis for decision making the indications provided by the result of a data mining process. This process will consist of trying to predict the future evolution of the index based on a model obtained with historical quotes data. Thus our prediction model will be incorporated in a trading system that generates its decisions based on the predictions of the model. Our overall evaluation criteria will be the performance of this trading system, that is, the profit/loss resulting from the actions of the system as well as some other statistics that are of interest to investors. This means that our main evaluation criteria will be the operational results of applying the knowledge discovered by our data mining process and not the predictive accuracy of the models developed during this process.

As it should be obvious, our goal is not to provide you with an automatic stock trading system that will make you rich! The concrete application is merely used as a vehicle for addressing relevant data mining problems and providing illustrations on how to solve these problems using R. At most, our proposals can be regarded as a good starting point if you are serious about trying to use data mining tools for trading in the stock markets.

5.2   The Available Data

In our case study we will concentrate on trading the S&P 500 market index. Daily data concerning the quotes of this security are freely available in many places, for example, the Yahoo finance site.[1]

The data we will use is available in the book package. Once again we will explore other means of getting the data as a form of illustrating some of the capabilities of R. Moreover, some of these other alternatives will allow you to apply the concepts learned in this chapter to data more recent than the one packaged at the time of writing this book.

In order to get the data through the book R package, it is enough to issue

```
> library(xts)
> data(GSPC, package="DMwR2")
> first(GSPC)

           GSPC.Open GSPC.High GSPC.Low GSPC.Close GSPC.Volume
1970-01-02     92.06     93.54    91.79         93     8050000
           GSPC.Adjusted
1970-01-02            93

> last(GSPC)

           GSPC.Open GSPC.High GSPC.Low GSPC.Close GSPC.Volume
2016-01-25   1906.28   1906.28  1875.97    1877.08  4401380000
           GSPC.Adjusted
2016-01-25       1877.08
```

The first statement loads the package **xts** (Ryan and Ulrich, 2014) that implements the time series classes we use to store the daily quotes data. We then load an object, GSPC,[2] of class **xts** that contains the daily quotes of S&P500. Finally, we show the first and last observations of our data, which tells us that we have roughly 45 years of daily quotes.

At the book Web site,[3] you can find these data in comma separated values (CSV) file format. For illustration purposes we will also illustrate how to read in this file into R. Nevertheless, for the purpose of replicating the solutions you will see in the next sections the easiest path is to use the procedure shown above of loading the data from the book package.

For the sake of completeness we will also mention yet another way of getting this data into R, which consists of downloading it directly from the Web. If you choose to follow this path, you should remember that you will probably be using a larger dataset than the one used in the analysis carried out in this book, which means that some results may be slightly different.

---

[1] http://finance.yahoo.com.

[2] ^GSPC is the ticker ID of S&P 500 at Yahoo finance from where the quotes were obtained.

[3] http://www.fc.dcc.up.pt/~ltorgo/DMwR2.

Whichever source you choose to use, the daily stock quotes data includes information regarding the following properties:

- Date of the stock exchange session

- Open price at the beginning of the session

- Highest price during the session

- Lowest price

- Closing price of the session

- Volume of transactions

- Adjusted close price[4]

5.2.1 Reading the Data from the CSV File

As we have mentioned before, at the book Web site you can find different sources containing the data to use in this case study. If you decide to use the CSV file, you will download a file whose first lines look like this:

```
"Index" "GSPC.Open" "GSPC.High" "GSPC.Low" "GSPC.Close" "GSPC.Volume" "GSPC.Adjusted"
1970-01-02 92.059998 93.540001 91.790001 93 8050000 93
1970-01-05 93 94.25 92.529999 93.459999 11490000 93.459999
1970-01-06 93.459999 93.809998 92.129997 92.82 11460000 92.82
1970-01-07 92.82 93.379997 91.93 92.629997 10010000 92.629997
1970-01-08 92.629997 93.470001 91.989998 92.68 10670000 92.68
```

Assuming you have downloaded the file and have saved it with the name "sp500.csv" on the current working directory of your R session, you can load it into R and create an **xts** object with the data, as follows:

```
> library(xts)
> GSPC <- as.xts(read.zoo("sp500.csv", header = TRUE))
```

The function **read.zoo()** of package **zoo**[5] (Zeileis and Grothendieck, 2005) reads a CSV file and transforms the data into a **zoo** object assuming that the first column contains the time tags. The function **as.xts()** coerces the resulting object into an object of class **xts**.

5.2.2 Getting the Data from the Web

Another alternative way of getting the S&P 500 quotes is to use the free service provided by Yahoo finance.

An easy way of downloading the daily quotes from this site is to use the function **getSymbols()** from package **quantmod** (Ryan, 2009). This is an extra package that you should install before using it. It provides several facilities related to financial data analysis that we will use throughout this chapter. Function **getSymbols()** in conjunction with other functions of this package provide a rather simple but powerful way of getting quotes data from different data sources. Let us see some examples of its use:

---

[4]This is basically the closing price adjusted for stock splits, dividends/distributions, and rights offerings.

[5]You may wonder why we did not load the package **zoo** with a call to the **library()** function. The reason is that this was already done when we loaded the package **xts** because it depends on the package **zoo**.

```
> library(quantmod)
> GSPC <- getSymbols("^GSPC",auto.assign=FALSE)
```

The function `getSymbols()` receives on the first argument a set of symbol names and will fetch the quotes of these symbols from different web sources or even local databases, returning by default an `xts` object with the same name as the symbol,[6] which will silently be created in the working environment. If you want to decide the name of the object storing the data you may proceed as above, where we assigned the function result to this object and used `auto.assign=FALSE`. The function has many parameters that allow more control over some of these issues. As you can verify, the returned object does not cover the same period as the data coming with our book package. The get the same data period we can do:

```
> GSPC <- getSymbols("^GSPC",from="1970-01-02",to="2016-01-25",auto.assign=FALSE)
```

The package **quantmod** provides several other functions that allow you to download, for instance, exchange rate data, or financial information of companies. Explore the help page of the package for information on this and other facilities.

5.3 Defining the Prediction Tasks

Generally speaking, our goal is to have good forecasts of the future price of the S&P 500 index so that profitable orders can be placed on time. This general goal should allow us to easily define what to predict with our models—it should resort to forecast the future values of the price time series. However, it is easy to see that even with this simple task we immediately face several questions, namely, (1) which of the daily quotes? or (2) for which time in the future? Answering these questions may not be easy and usually depends on how the predictions will be used for generating trading orders.

5.3.1 What to Predict?

The trading strategies we will describe in Section 5.5.1 assume that we obtain a prediction of the tendency of the market in the next few days. Based on this prediction, we will place orders that will be profitable if the tendency is confirmed in the future.

Let us assume that if the prices vary more than $p\%$, we consider this worthwhile in terms of trading (e.g., covering transaction costs). In this context, we want our prediction models to forecast whether this margin is attainable in the next k days.[7] Please note that within these k days we can actually observe prices both above and below this percentage. This means that predicting a particular quote for a specific future time $t + k$ might not be the best idea. In effect, what we want is to have a prediction of the overall dynamics of the price in the next k days, and this is not captured by a particular price at a specific time. For instance, the closing price at time $t + k$ may represent a variation much lower than $p\%$, but it could have been preceded by a period of prices representing variations much higher than $p\%$ within the window $t \cdots t + k$. So, what we want in effect is to have a good prediction of the overall tendency of the prices in the next k days.

We will describe a variable, calculated with the quotes data, that can be seen as an

---

[6]Eventually pruned from invalid characters for R object names.
[7]We obviously do not want to be waiting years to obtain the profit margin.

indicator (a value) of the tendency in the next k days. The value of this indicator should be related to the confidence we have that the target margin p will be attainable in the next k days. At this stage it is important to note that when we mention a variation of $p\%$, we mean above or below the current price. The idea is that positive variations will lead us to buy, while negative variations will trigger sell actions. The indicator we are proposing resumes the tendency as a single value, positive for upward tendencies, and negative for downward price tendencies.

Let the daily average price be approximated by

$$\bar{P}_i = \frac{C_i + H_i + L_i}{3} \tag{5.1}$$

where C_i, H_i and L_i are the close, high, and low quotes for day i, respectively.

Let V_i be the set of k percentage variations (often called arithmetic returns) of today's close to the following k days average prices :

$$V_i = \left\{ \frac{\bar{P}_{i+j} - C_i}{C_i} \right\}_{j=1}^{k} \tag{5.2}$$

Our indicator variable is the total sum of the variations in this set whose absolute value is above our target margin $p\%$:

$$T_i = \sum \{v \in V_i : v > p\% \lor v < -p\%\} \tag{5.3}$$

The general idea of the variable T is to signal k-days periods that have several days with average daily prices clearly above the target variation. High positive values of T mean that there are several average daily prices that are $p\%$ higher than today's close. Such situations are good indications of potential opportunities to issue a buy order, as we have good expectations that the prices will rise. On the other hand, highly negative values of T suggest sell actions, given the prices will probably decline. Values around zero can be caused by periods with "flat" prices or by conflicting positive and negative variations that cancel each other.

The following function implements this simple indicator:

```
> T.ind <- function(quotes, tgt.margin = 0.025, n.days = 10) {
+     v <- apply(HLC(quotes), 1, mean)
+     v[1] <- Cl(quotes)[1]

+     r <- matrix(NA, ncol = n.days, nrow = NROW(quotes))
+     for (x in 1:n.days) r[, x] <- Next(Delt(v, k = x), x)

+     x <- apply(r, 1, function(x) sum(x[x > tgt.margin | x < -tgt.margin]))

+     if (is.xts(quotes)) xts(x, time(quotes)) else x
+ }
```

The function starts by obtaining the average price calculated according to Equation 5.1. The function HLC() extracts the High, Low, and Close quotes from a quotes object. We then obtain the returns of the next n.days days with respect to the current close price. The Next() function allows one to shift the values of a time series in time (both forward or backward). The Delt() function can be used to calculate percentage or log returns of a series of prices. Finally, the T.ind() function sums up the large absolute returns, that is, returns above the target variation margin, which we have set by default to 2.5%.

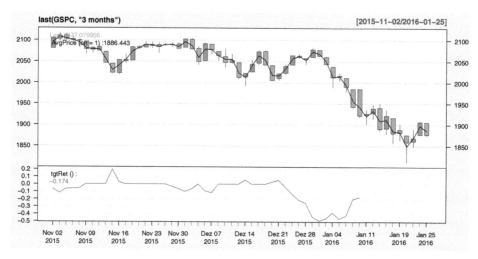

FIGURE 5.1: S&P500 on the last 3 months and our T indicator.

We can get a better idea of the behavior of this indicator in Figure 5.1, which was produced with the following code:

```
> candleChart(last(GSPC,'3 months'),theme='white', TA=NULL)
> avgPrice <- function(p) apply(HLC(p),1,mean)
> addAvgPrice <- newTA(FUN=avgPrice,col=1,legend='AvgPrice')
> addT.ind <- newTA(FUN=T.ind,col='red', legend='tgtRet')
> addAvgPrice(on=1)
> addT.ind()
```

The function **candleChart()** draws candlestick graphs of stock quotes. These graphs represent the daily quotes by a colored box and a vertical bar. The bar represents the High and Low prices of the day, while the box represents the Open-Close amplitude. The color of the box indicates if the top of the box is the Open or the Close price, that is, if the prices declined (orange in Figure 5.1) or rose (green in our graphs) across the daily session. We have added to the candlestick graph two indicators: the average price (on the same graph as the candlesticks because it has a similar scale) and our T indicator (below). The function **newTA()** can be used to create new plotting functions for indicators that we wish to include in candlestick graphs. The return value of this function is a plotting function![8] This means that the objects **addT.ind** and **addAvgPrice** can be called like any other R function. This is done on the last two instructions. Each of them adds an indicator to the initial graph produced by the **candleChart()** function. The function **addAvgPrice()** was called with the parameter **on** set to 1, which means that the indicator will be plotted on the first graph window; that is, the graph where the candlesticks are. The function **addT.ind()** was not called with this argument, leading to a new graph below the candlesticks. This is what makes sense in the case of our indicator, given the completely different scale of values.

As you can observe in Figure 5.1, the T indicator achieves the highest values when there is a subsequent period of positive variations. Obviously, to obtain the value of the indicator for time i, we need to have the quotes for the following 10 days, so we are not saying that T anticipates these movements. This is not the goal of the indicator. Its goal

---

[8]You can confirm that by issuing **class(addT.ind)** or by typing the name of the object (without the parenthesis) to obtain its contents.

is to summarize the observed future behavior of the prices into a single value and not to predict this behavior!

In our approach to this problem we will assume that the correct trading action at time t is related to what our expectations are concerning the evolution of prices in the next k days. Moreover, we will describe this future evolution of the prices by our indicator T. The correct trading signal at time t will be "buy" if the T score is higher than a certain threshold, and will be "sell" if the score is below another threshold. In all other cases, the correct signal will be do nothing (i.e., "hold"). In summary, we want to be able to predict the correct signal for time t. On historical data we will fill in the correct signal for each day by calculating the respective T scores and using the thresholding method just outlined above.

5.3.2   Which Predictors?

We have defined an indicator (T) that summarizes the behavior of the price time series in the next k days. Our data mining goal will be to predict this behavior. The main assumption behind trying to forecast the future behavior of financial markets is that it is possible to do so by observing the past behavior of the market. More precisely, we are assuming that if in the past a certain behavior p was followed by another behavior f, and if that causal chain happened frequently, then it is plausible to assume that this will occur again in the future; and thus if we observe p now, we predict that we will observe f next. We are approximating the future behavior (f), by our indicator T. We now have to decide on how we will describe the recent prices pattern (p in the description above). Instead of using again a single indicator to describe these recent dynamics, we will use several indicators, trying to capture different properties of the price time series to facilitate the forecasting task.

The simplest type of information we can use to describe the past are the recent observed prices. Informally, that is the type of approach followed in several standard time series modeling approaches. These approaches develop models that describe the relationship between future values of a time series and a window of past q observations of this time series. We will try to enrich our description of the current dynamics of the time series by adding further features to this window of recent prices.

Technical indicators are numeric summaries that reflect some properties of the price time series. Despite their debatable use as tools for deciding when to trade, they can nevertheless provide interesting summaries of the dynamics of a financial time series. The amount of technical indicators available can be overwhelming. In R we can find a very good sample of them, thanks to the package **TTR** (Ulrich, 2009).

The indicators usually try to capture some properties of the prices series, such as if they are varying too much, or following some specific trend, etc. In our approach to this problem, we will not carry out an exhaustive search for the indicators that are most adequate to our task. Still, this is a relevant research question, and not only for this particular application. It is usually known as the feature selection problem, and can informally be defined as the task of finding the most adequate subset of available input variables for a modeling task. The existing approaches to this problem can usually be cast in two groups: (1) feature filters and (2) feature wrappers. The former are independent of the modeling tool that will be used after the feature selection phase. They basically try to use some statistical properties of the features (e.g., correlation) to select the final set of features. The wrapper approaches include the modeling tool in the selection process. They carry out an iterative search process where at each step a candidate set of features is tried with the modeling tool and the respective results are recorded. Based on these results, new tentative sets are generated using some search operators, and the process is repeated until some convergence criteria are met that will define the final set.

We will use a simple approach to select the features to include in our model. The idea is to illustrate this process with a concrete example and not to find the best possible solution to this problem, which would require other time and computational resources. We will define an initial set of features and then use a technique to estimate the importance of each of these features. Based on these estimates we will select the most relevant features.

We will center our analysis on the Close quote, as our buy/sell decisions will be made at the end of each daily session. The initial set of features will be formed by several past returns on the Close price. The h-days (arithmetic) returns,[9] or percentage variations, can be calculated as

$$R_{i-h} = \frac{C_i - C_{i-h}}{C_{i-h}} \tag{5.4}$$

where C_i is the Close price at session i.

We have included in the set of candidate features ten of these returns by varying h from 1 to 10. Next, we have selected an illustrative set of technical indicators, from those available in the package **TTR** — namely, the Average True Range (ATR), which is an indicator of the volatility of the series; the Stochastic Momentum Index (SMI), which is a momentum indicator; the Welles Wilder's Directional Movement Index (ADX); the Aroon indicator that tries to identify starting trends; the Bollinger Bands that compare the volatility over a period of time; the Chaikin Volatility; the Close Location Value (CLV) that relates the session Close to its trading range; the Arms' Ease of Movement Value (EMV); the MACD oscillator; the Money Flow Index (MFI); the Parabolic Stop-and-Reverse; and the Volatility indicator. More details and references on these and other indicators can be found in the respective help pages of the functions implementing them in the package **TTR**. Most of these indicators produce several values that together are used for making trading decisions. As mentioned before, we do not plan to use these indicators for trading. As such, we have carried out some post-processing of the output of the TTR functions to obtain a single indicator score for each one. The following functions implement this process:

```
> library(TTR)
> myATR       <- function(x) ATR(HLC(x))[,'atr']
> mySMI       <- function(x) SMI(HLC(x))[, "SMI"]
> myADX       <- function(x) ADX(HLC(x))[,'ADX']
> myAroon     <- function(x) aroon(cbind(Hi(x),Lo(x)))$oscillator
> myBB        <- function(x) BBands(HLC(x))[, "pctB"]
> myChaikinVol <- function(x) Delt(chaikinVolatility(cbind(Hi(x),Lo(x))))[, 1]
> myCLV       <- function(x) EMA(CLV(HLC(x)))[, 1]
> myEMV       <- function(x) EMV(cbind(Hi(x),Lo(x)),Vo(x))[,2]
> myMACD      <- function(x) MACD(Cl(x))[,2]
> myMFI       <- function(x) MFI(HLC(x),  Vo(x))
> mySAR       <- function(x) SAR(cbind(Hi(x),Cl(x))) [,1]
> myVolat     <- function(x) volatility(OHLC(x),calc="garman")[,1]
```

The variables we have just described form our initial set of predictors for the task of forecasting the future value of the T indicator. We will try to reduce this set of 22 variables using a feature selection method. Random forests (Breiman, 2001) were used in Section 4.7 to obtain predictions of algae occurrences. Random forests can also be used to estimate the importance of the variables involved in a prediction task. Informally, this importance can be estimated by calculating the percentage increase in the error of the random forest if we remove each variable in turn. In a certain way this resembles the idea of wrapper filters as

---

[9]Alternatively you could use log returns defined as $\log(C_i/C_{i-h})$.

it includes a modeling tool in the process of selecting the features. However, this is not an iterative search process and moreover, we will use other predictive models to forecast T, which means that the set of variables selected by this process is not optimized for these other models, and in this sense we are going to use this method more like a filter approach.

In our approach to this application, we will split the available data into two separate sets: (1) one used for constructing the trading system; and (2) other to test it. The first set will be formed by the first 35 years of quotes of S&P 500. We will leave the remaining data (around 10 years) for the final test of our trading system. In this context, we must leave this final test set out of this feature selection process to ensure unbiased results.

We will use a period between 1995 and 2005 (the last 10 years of the training data) for this feature selection process. The code to obtain the respective random forest is the following:

```
> library(randomForest)
> data.model <- specifyModel(T.ind(GSPC) ~ Delt(Cl(GSPC),k=1:10) +
+          myATR(GSPC) + mySMI(GSPC) + myADX(GSPC) + myAroon(GSPC) +
+          myBB(GSPC)  + myChaikinVol(GSPC) + myCLV(GSPC) +
+          CMO(Cl(GSPC)) + EMA(Delt(Cl(GSPC))) + myEMV(GSPC) +
+          myVolat(GSPC)  + myMACD(GSPC) + myMFI(GSPC) + RSI(Cl(GSPC)) +
+          mySAR(GSPC) + runMean(Cl(GSPC)) + runSD(Cl(GSPC)))
> set.seed(1234)
> rf <- buildModel(data.model,method='randomForest',
+               training.per=c("1995-01-01","2005-12-30"),
+               ntree=1000, importance=TRUE)
```

The code given above starts by specifying and obtaining the data to be used for modeling using the function **specifyModel()**. This function creates a **quantmod** object that contains the specification of a certain abstract model (described by a formula). This specification may refer to data coming from different types of **quantmod** data sources, some of which may even not be currently in the memory of the computer. The function will take care of these cases using **getSymbols()** to obtain the necessary data. This results in a very handy form of specifying and getting the data necessary for your subsequent modeling stages. Moreover, for symbols whose source is the Web, you can later use the obtained object (**data.model** in our case) as an argument to the function **getModelData()**, to obtain a refresh of the object including any new quotes that may be available at that time. Again, this is quite convenient if you want to maintain a trading system that should be updated with new quotes information.

The function **buildModel()** uses the resulting model specification and obtains a model with the corresponding data and a concrete learning system. Through parameter **training.per**, you can specify the data that should be used to obtain the model. This function currently contains wrappers for several learning tools,[10] among which are random forests. In case you wish to use a model not contemplated by **buildModel()**, you may obtain the data using the function **modelData()**, and use it with your favorite modeling function, as shown in the following illustrative example:

```
> ex.model <- specifyModel(T.ind(IBM) ~ Delt(Cl(IBM), k = 1:3))
> data <- modelData(ex.model, data.window = c("2009-01-01",  "2009-08-10"))
```

The obtained **data** object is a standard **zoo** object, which can be easily cast into a matrix or data frame, for use as a parameter of any modeling function, as the following artificial[11] example illustrates:

---

[10]Check its help page to know which ones.
[11]Do not run it as this is a "fake" modeling tool.

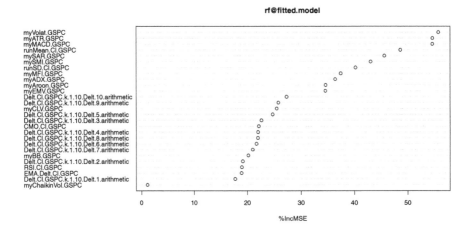

FIGURE 5.2: Variable importance according to the random forest.

```
> m <- myFavouriteModellingTool(ex.model@model.formula, as.data.frame(data))
```

Notice how we have indicated the model formula. The "real" formula is not exactly the same as the one provided in the argument of function `specifyModel()`. This latter formula is used to fetch the data, but the "real" formula should use whichever columns and respective names the `specifyModel()` call has generated. This information is contained in the slot `model.formula` of the `quantmod` object generated by that function.

Notice that on this small artificial example we have mentioned a ticker (IBM) for which we currently had no data in memory. The `specifyModel()` function takes care of that by silently fetching the quotes data from the Web using the `getSymbols()` function. All this is done in a transparent way to the user and you may even include symbols in your model specification that are obtained from different sources.

Returning to our feature selection problem, notice that we have included the parameter `importance=TRUE` so that the random forest estimates the variable importance. For regression problems, the R implementation of random forests estimates variable importance with two alternative scores. The first is the percentage increase in the error of the forest if we remove each variable in turn. This is measured by calculating the increase in the mean squared error of each tree on an out-of-bag sample when each variable is removed. This increase is averaged over all trees in the forest and normalized with the standard error. The second score has to do with the decrease in node impurity that is accountable with each variable, again averaged over all the trees. We will use the first score as it is the one mentioned in the original paper on random forests (Breiman, 2001). After obtaining the model, we can check the importance of the variables as follows:

```
> varImpPlot(rf@fitted.model, type = 1)
```

The result of this function call is given in Figure 5.2. The arguments to the `varImpPlot()` function are the random forest and the score we wish to plot (if omitted both are plotted) - in this case we have selected (with `type=1`) the percentage increase in the error of the forest. The generic function `buildModel()` returns the obtained model as a slot (`fitted.model`) of the `quantmod` object it produces as a result.

At this stage we need to decide on a threshold of the importance score to select only a subset of the features. Looking at the results in the figure and given that this is a simple illustration of the concept of using random forests for selecting features, we will use the value of 30 as the threshold as there seems to be a clear difference in scores of the features above and below this value:

```
> imp <- importance(rf@fitted.model, type = 1)
> rownames(imp)[which(imp > 30)]

 [1] "myATR.GSPC"     "mySMI.GSPC"     "myADX.GSPC"
 [4] "myAroon.GSPC"   "myEMV.GSPC"     "myVolat.GSPC"
 [7] "myMACD.GSPC"    "myMFI.GSPC"     "mySAR.GSPC"
[10] "runMean.Cl.GSPC" "runSD.Cl.GSPC"
```

The function **importance()** obtains the concrete scores (in this case the first score) for each variable, which we then filter with our threshold to obtain the names of the variables that we will use in our modeling attempts. Using this information we can obtain our final dataset as follows:

```
> data.model <- specifyModel(T.ind(GSPC) ~ myATR(GSPC) + mySMI(GSPC) +  myADX(GSPC) +
+                            myAroon(GSPC) + myEMV(GSPC) + myVolat(GSPC) +
+                            myMACD(GSPC) + myMFI(GSPC) + mySAR(GSPC) +
+                            runMean(Cl(GSPC)) + runSD(Cl(GSPC)))
```

5.3.3 The Prediction Tasks

In the previous section we have obtained a **quantmod** object (**data.model**) containing the specification of the data we plan to use with our predictive models. This data has as a target the value of the T indicator and as predictors a series of other variables that resulted from a feature selection process. We have seen in Section 5.3.1 that our real goal is to predict the correct trading signal at any time t. How can we do that, given the data we have generated in the previous section? We will explore two paths to obtain predictions for the correct trading signal.

The first alternative is to use the T value as the target variable and try to obtain models that forecast this value using the predictor's information. This is a multiple regression task similar to the ones we considered in the previous chapter. If we follow this path, we will then have to "translate" our model predictions into trading signals. This means to decide upon the thresholds on the predicted T values that will lead to either of the three possible trading actions. We will carry out this transformation using the following values:

$$
signal = \begin{cases} sell & \text{if } T < -0.1 \\ hold & \text{if } -0.1 \le T \le 0.1 \\ buy & \text{if } T > 0.1 \end{cases} \tag{5.5}
$$

The selection of the values 0.1 and -0.1 is purely heuristic and we can also use other thresholds. Still, these values mean that during the 10-day period used to generate the T values, there were at least four average daily prices that are 2.5% above the current close ($4 \times 0.025 = 0.1$). If you decide to use other values, you should consider that too high absolute values will originate fewer signals, while too small values may lead us to trade on too small variations of the market, thus incurring a larger risk. Function **trading.signals()**, available in the book package, can carry out this transformation of the numeric T values into a factor with three possible values: "s", "h", and "b", for sell, hold and buy actions, respectively.

The second alternative prediction task we will consider consists of predicting the signals directly. This means to use as a target variable the "correct" signal for day d. How do we obtain these correct signals? Again using the T indicator and the same thresholds used in Equation 5.5. For the available historical data, we obtain the signal of each day by calculating the T value using the following 10 days and using the thresholds in Equation 5.5 to decide on the signal. The target variable in this second task is nominal. This type of prediction problem is known as a classification task.[12]

The **xts** package infrastructure is geared toward numeric data. The data slots of **xts** objects must be either vectors or matrices, thus single mode data. This means it is not possible to have one of the columns of our training data as a nominal variable (a factor in R), together with all the numeric predictors. We will overcome this difficulty by carrying out all modeling steps outside the **xts** framework. This is easy and not limiting, as we will see. The infrastructure provided by **xts** is mostly used for data sub-setting and plotting, but the modeling stages do not need these facilities.

The following code creates all the data structures that we will use in the subsequent sections for obtaining predictive models for the two tasks.

```
> ## The regression task
> Tdata.train <- as.data.frame(modelData(data.model,
+                               data.window=c('1970-01-02','2005-12-30')))
> Tdata.eval <- na.omit(as.data.frame(modelData(data.model,
+                               data.window=c('2006-01-01','2016-01-25'))))
> Tform <- as.formula('T.ind.GSPC ~ .')
> ## The classification task
> buy.thr <- 0.1
> sell.thr <- -0.1
> Tdata.trainC <- cbind(Signal=trading.signals(Tdata.train[["T.ind.GSPC"]],
+                                       buy.thr,sell.thr),
+                       Tdata.train[,-1])
> Tdata.evalC <-  cbind(Signal=trading.signals(Tdata.eval[["T.ind.GSPC"]],
+                                       buy.thr,sell.thr),
+                       Tdata.eval[,-1])
> TformC <- as.formula("Signal ~ .")
```

The `Tdata.train` and `Tdata.eval` (and their classification variants) are data frames with the data to be used for the training and evaluation periods, respectively. We have used data frames as the basic data structures to allow for mixed mode data that is required in the classification tasks. For these tasks we replace the target value column with the corresponding signals that were generated using the `trading.signals()` function. The evaluation data frames will be left out of all model selection and comparison processes we will carry out. They will be used in the final evaluation of the "best" models we select. The call to `na.omit()` is necessary to avoid NAs at the end of the data frames caused by lack of future data to calculate the T indicator.

5.3.4 Evaluation Criteria

The prediction tasks described in the previous section can be used to obtain models that will output some form of indication regarding the future market direction. This indication will be a number in the case of the regression tasks (the predicted value of T), or a direct signal in the case of classification tasks. Even in the case of regression tasks, we have seen that we will cast this number into a signal by a thresholding mechanism. In Section 5.5 we

---

[12]Some statistics schools use the term "discrimination tasks" instead.

will describe several trading strategies that use these predicted signals to act on the market, i.e. that will transform these predicted signals into concrete market orders.

In this section we will address the question of how to evaluate the signal predictions of our models. We will not consider the evaluation of the numeric predictions of the T indicator. Due to the way we are using these numeric predictions, this evaluation is a bit irrelevant. One might even question whether it makes sense to have these regression tasks, given that we are only interested in the trading signals. We have decided to maintain these numeric tasks because different trading strategies could take advantage of the numeric predictions, for instance, to decide which amount of money to invest when opening a position. For example, T values much higher than our thresholds for acting ($T > 0.1$ for buying and $T < -0.1$ for selling) could lead to stronger investments.

The evaluation of the signal predictions could be carried out by measuring the error rate, defined as

$$err = \frac{1}{N} \sum_{i=1}^{N} L_{0/1}(y_i, \hat{y}_i) \tag{5.6}$$

where $\hat{y}_i$ is the prediction of the model for test case i, which has true class label y_i, and $L_{0/1}$ is known as the 0/1 loss function:

$$L_{0/1}(y_i, \hat{y}_i) = \begin{cases} 1 & \text{if } \hat{y}_i \neq y_i \\ 0 & \text{if } \hat{y}_i = y_i \end{cases} \tag{5.7}$$

One often uses the complement of this measure, known as accuracy, given by $acc = 1 - err$.

These two statistics basically compare the model predictions to what really happened to the markets in the k future days.

The problem with accuracy (or error rate) is that it turns out not to be a good measure for this type of problem. In effect, there will be a very strong imbalance between the three possible outcomes, with a strong prevalence of hold signals over the other two, as big movements in prices are rare phenomena in financial markets.[13] This means that the accuracy scores will be dominated by the performance of the models on the most frequent outcome that is *hold*. This is not very interesting for trading. We want to have models that are accurate at the rare signals (*buy* and *sell*). These are the ones that lead to market actions and thus potential profit—the final goal of this application.

Financial markets forecasting is an example of an application driven by rare events. Event-based prediction tasks are usually evaluated by the precision and recall metrics that focus the evaluation on the events, disregarding the performance of the common situations (in our case, the hold signals). *Precision* can be informally defined as the proportion of event signals produced by the models that are correct. *Recall* is defined as the proportion of events occurring in the domain that are signaled as such by the models. These metrics can be easily calculated with the help of confusion matrices that sum up the results of a model in terms of the comparison between its predictions and the true values for a particular test set. Table 5.1 shows an example of a confusion matrix for our domain, where for instance, the entry $n_{b,h}$ is the number of times on the test set a model predicted a hold signal when the true value was a buy.

With the help of Table 5.1 we can formalize the notions of precision and recall for this problem, as follows:

$$Prec = \frac{n_{s,s} + n_{b,b}}{N_{.,s} + N_{.,b}} \tag{5.8}$$

---

[13]This obviously depends on the target profit margin you establish; but to cover the trading costs, this margin should be large enough, and this rarity will be a fact.

TABLE 5.1: A Confusion Matrix for the Prediction of Trading Signals.

		Predictions			
		sell	hold	buy	
True	sell	$n_{s,s}$	$n_{s,h}$	$n_{s,b}$	$N_{s,.}$
Values	hold	$n_{h,s}$	$n_{h,h}$	$n_{h,b}$	$N_{h,.}$
	buy	$n_{b,s}$	$n_{b,h}$	$n_{b,b}$	$N_{b,.}$
		$N_{.,s}$	$N_{.,h}$	$N_{.,b}$	N

$$Rec = \frac{n_{s,s} + n_{b,b}}{N_{s,.} + N_{b,.}} \tag{5.9}$$

We can also calculate these statistics for particular signals by obtaining the precision and recall for sell and buy signals, independently; for example,

$$Prec_b = \frac{n_{b,b}}{N_{.,b}} \tag{5.10}$$

$$Rec_b = \frac{n_{b,b}}{N_{b,.}} \tag{5.11}$$

Precision and recall are often "merged" into a single statistic, called the $F-measure$ (Rijsbergen, 1979), given by

$$F = \frac{(\beta^2 + 1) \cdot Prec \cdot Rec}{\beta^2 \cdot Prec + Rec} \tag{5.12}$$

where $0 \leq \beta \leq 1$, controls the relative importance of recall to precision.

5.4 The Prediction Models

In this section we will explore some models that can be used to address the prediction tasks defined in the previous section. The selection of models was mainly guided by the fact that these techniques are well known by their ability to handle highly nonlinear modeling tasks. That is the case in our domain. Still, many other methods could have been applied to this problem. Any thorough approach to this domain would necessarily require a larger comparison of more alternatives. In the context of this book, such exploration does not make sense due to its costs in terms of space and computation power required.

5.4.1 How Will the Training Data Be Used?

Complex time series problems frequently exhibit different regimes, such as periods with strong variability followed by more "stable" periods, or periods with some form of systematic tendency. These types of phenomena are often called non-stationarities and can cause serious problems to several modeling techniques due to their underlying assumptions. It is reasonably easy to see, for instance by plotting the price time series, that this is the case of our data. There are several strategies we can follow to try to overcome the negative impact of these effects. For instance, several transformation techniques can be applied to the original time series to eliminate some of the effects. The use of percentage variations (returns) instead of the original absolute price values is such an example. Other approaches include using the available data in a more selective way. Let us suppose we are given the task of obtaining a model using a certain period of training data and then testing it in a subsequent period. The standard approach would use the training data to develop the model that would then be applied to obtain predictions for the testing period. If we have strong reasons to believe that there are regime shifts, using the same model during all testing period may not be the best idea, particularly if during this period there is some regime change that can seriously damage the performance of the model. In these cases it is often better to change or adapt the model using more recent data that better captures the current regime of the data.

In time series problems there is an implicit (time) ordering among the test cases. In this context, it makes sense to assume that when we are obtaining a prediction for time i, all test cases with time tag $k < i$ already belong to the past. This means that it is safe to assume that we already know the values of the time series of these past test cases and, moreover, that we can safely use this information. So, if at some time m of the testing period we are confident that there is a regime shift in the time series, then we can incorporate the information of all test cases occurring before m into the initial training data, and with this refreshed training set that contains observations of the "new" regime, somehow update our predictive model to improve the performance on future test cases. One form of updating the model could be to change it in order to take into account the new training cases. These approaches are usually known as incremental learners as they adapt the current model to new evidence instead of starting from scratch. There are not so many modeling techniques that can be used in this way, particularly in R. In this context, we will follow the other approach to the updating problem, which consists of re-learning a new model with the new updated training set. This is obviously more expensive in computational terms and may even be inadequate for applications where the data arrives at a very fast pace and for which models and decisions are required almost in real-time. This is rather frequent in applications addressed in a research area usually known as data streams. In our application, we are making decisions on a daily basis after the market closes, so speed is not a key issue.[14] Assuming that we will use a re-learn approach, we have essentially two forms of incorporating the new cases into our training set. The growing window approach simply adds them to the current training set, thus constantly increasing the size of this set. The eventual problem of this approach lies in the fact that as we are assuming that more recent data is going to be helpful in producing better models, we may also consider whether the oldest part of our training data may already be too outdated and in effect, contributing to decreasing the accuracy of the models. Based on these considerations, the sliding window approach deletes the oldest data of the training set at the same time it incorporates the fresher observations, thus maintaining a training set of constant size.

Both the growing and the sliding window approaches involve a key decision: when to change or adapt the model by incorporating fresher data. There are essentially two ways of answering this question. The first involves estimating this time by checking if the performance of our current model is starting to degrade. If we observe a sudden decrease in this performance, then we can take this as a good indication of some form of regime shift. The main challenge of these approaches lies in developing proper estimates of these changes in performance. We want to detect the change as soon as possible but we do not want to over-react to some spurious test case that our model missed. Another simpler approach consists of updating the model on a regular time basis, that is, every w test cases, we obtain a new model with fresher data. In this case study we follow this simpler method.

Summarizing, for each model that we will consider, we will apply it using three different

---

[14]It could be if we were trading in real-time, that is, intra-day trading.

approaches: (1) single model for all test period, (2) growing window with a fixed updating step of w days, and (3) sliding window with the same updating step w. Figure 5.3 illustrates the three approaches.

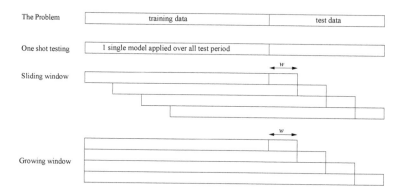

FIGURE 5.3: Three forms of obtaining predictions for a test period.

Further readings on regime changes

The problem of detecting changes of regime in time series data is a subject studied for a long time in an area known as statistic process control (e.g., Oakland, 2007), which uses techniques like control charts to detect break points in the data. This subject has been witnessing an increased interest with the impact of data streams (e.g., Gama and Gaber, 2007) in the data mining field. Several works (e.g., Gama et al., 2004; Kifer et al., 2004; Klinkenberg, 2004) have addressed the issues of how to detect the changes of regime and also how to learn models in the presence of these changes. A good survey on this area is the work by Gama et al. (2014).

5.4.2 The Modeling Tools

In this section we briefly describe the modeling techniques we will use to address our prediction tasks and illustrate how to use them in R.

5.4.2.1 Artificial Neural Networks

Artificial neural networks (ANNs) are frequently used in financial forecasting (e.g., De-boeck, 1994) because of their ability to deal with highly nonlinear problems. The package **nnet** (Venables and Ripley, 2002) is one of the several packages in R that implements feed-forward neural nets. This type of neural network is among the most used and also what we will be applying.

ANNs are formed by a set of computing units (the neurons) linked to each other. Each neuron executes two consecutive calculations: a linear combination of its inputs, followed by a nonlinear computation of the result to obtain its output value that is then fed to other neurons in the network. Each of the neuron connections has an associated weight. Constructing an artificial neural network consists of establishing an architecture for the network and then using an algorithm to find the weights of the connections between the neurons.

Feed-forward artificial neural networks have their neurons organized in layers. The first layer contains the input neurons of the network. The training observations of the problem are presented to the network through these input neurons. The final layer contains the predictions of the neural network for any case presented at its input neurons. In between, we usually have one or more "hidden" layers of neurons. The weight updating algorithms, such as the back-propagation method, try to obtain the connection weights that optimize a certain error criterion, that is, trying to ensure that the network outputs are in accordance with the cases presented to the model. This is accomplished by an iterative process of presenting several times the training cases at the input nodes of the network, and after obtaining the prediction of the network at the output nodes and calculating the respective prediction error, updating the weights in the network to try to improve its prediction error. This iterative process is repeated until some convergence criterion is met. A more detailed explanation of ANNs was given at Section 3.4.5.4 (page 158).

Feed-forward ANNs with one hidden layer can be easily obtained in R using a function of the package **nnet** (Venables and Ripley, 2002). The networks obtained by this function can be used for both classification and regression problems and thus are applicable to both our prediction tasks (*see* Section 5.3.3).

ANNs are known to be sensitive to different scales of the variables used in a prediction problem. In this context, it makes sense to transform the data before giving them to the network, in order to avoid eventual negative impacts on the performance. In our case we will standardize the data with the goal of making all variables have a mean value of zero and a standard deviation of one. As we have seen before, this can be easily accomplished by subtracting the values of each variable by the respective sample mean and dividing the result by the sample standard deviation.

The function **scale()** can be used to carry out this transformation for our data. Below you can find a very simple illustration of how to obtain and use this type of ANN in R:

```
> set.seed(1234)
> library(nnet)
> ## The first column is the target variable
> norm.data <- data.frame(T.ind.GSPC=Tdata.train[[1]],scale(Tdata.train[,-1]))
> nn <- nnet(Tform, norm.data[1:1000, ], size = 5, decay = 0.01,
+            maxit = 1000, linout = TRUE, trace = FALSE)
> preds <- predict(nn, norm.data[1001:2000, ])
```

By default, the function **nnet()** sets the initial weights of the links between neurons with random values in the interval $[-0.5 \cdots 0.5]$. This means that two successive runs of the function with exactly the same arguments can actually lead to different solutions. To ensure you get the same results as we present below, we have added a call to the function **set.seed()** that initializes the random number generator to some seed number. This ensures that you will get exactly the same ANN as the one we report here. In this illustrative example we have used the first 1,000 cases to obtain the network and tested the model on the following 1,000. After normalizing our training data, we call the function **nnet()** to obtain the model. The first two parameters are the usual of any modeling function in R: the functional form of the model specified by a formula, and the training sample used to obtain the model. We have also used some of the parameters of the **nnet()** function. Namely, the parameter **size** allows us to specify how many nodes the hidden layer will have. There is no magic recipe on which value to use here. One usually tries several values to observe the network behavior. Still, one frequently uses a value smaller than the number of predictors of the problem. The parameter **decay** controls the weight updating rate of the back-propagation algorithm. Again, trial and error is your best friend here. Finally, the parameter **maxit** controls the maximum number of iterations the weight convergence process is allowed to use, while the **linout=TRUE** setting tells the function that we are handling a regression problem. The **trace=FALSE** is used to avoid some of the output of the function regarding the optimization process.

The function **predict()** can be used to obtain the predictions of the neural network for a set of test data.

Let us evaluate the results of the ANN for predicting the correct signals for the test set.

We do this by transforming the numeric predictions into signals and then evaluate them using the statistics presented in Section 5.3.4.

```
> sigs.nn <- trading.signals(preds,0.1,-0.1)
> true.sigs <- trading.signals(Tdata.train[1001:2000, "T.ind.GSPC"], 0.1, -0.1)
> sigs.PR(sigs.nn,true.sigs)

      precision    recall
s     0.2809917 0.1931818
b     0.3108108 0.2857143
s+b   0.2973978 0.2373887
```

Function `trading.signals()` transforms numeric predictions into signals, given the buy and sell thresholds, respectively. The function `sigs.PR()`, also from our book package, obtains a matrix with the precision and recall scores of the two types of events, and overall. These scores show that the performance of the ANN is not brilliant. In effect, you get rather low precision scores, and also not so interesting recall values. The latter are not so serious as they basically mean lost opportunities and not costs. On the contrary, low precision scores mean that the model gave wrong signals rather frequently. If these signals are used for trading, this may lead to serious losses of money.

ANNs can also be used for classification tasks. For these problems the main difference in terms of network topology is that instead of a single output unit, we will have as many output units as there are values of the target variable (sometimes known as the classes). Each of these output units will produce a probability estimate of the respective class value. This means that for each test case, an ANN can produce a set of probability values, one for each possible class value.

The use of the `nnet()` function for these tasks is very similar to its use for regression problems. The following code illustrates this, using our training data:

```
> set.seed(1234)
> library(nnet)
> norm.data <- data.frame(Signal=Tdata.trainC$Signal,scale(Tdata.trainC[,-1]))
> nn <- nnet(Signal ~ ., norm.data[1:1000, ], size = 10, decay = 0.01,
+             maxit = 1000, trace = FALSE)
> preds <- predict(nn, norm.data[1001:2000, ], type = "class")
```

The `type="class"` argument is used to obtain a single class label for each test case instead of a set of probability estimates. With the network predictions we can calculate the model precision and recall as follows:

```
> sigs.PR(preds, norm.data[1001:2000, 1])

      precision    recall
s     0.3607595 0.3238636
b     0.3267974 0.3105590
s+b   0.2250804 0.2077151
```

The precision and recall scores are similar to the ones obtained in the regression task.

Further readings on neural networks in financial markets

The book by Zirilli (1997) is a good and easy reading book. The collection of papers entitled "Artificial Neural Networks Forecasting Time Series" (Rogers and Vemuri, 1994) is another example of a good source of references. Part I of the book by Deboeck (1994) provides several chapters devoted to the application of neural networks to trading.

5.4.2.2 Support Vector Machines

Support vector machines (SVMs)[15] are modeling tools that, as ANNs, can be applied to both regression and classification tasks. SVMs have been witnessing increased attention from different research communities based on their successful application to several domains and also their strong theoretical background. Vapnik (1995, 1998) and Cristianini and Shawe-Taylor (2000) are essential references for SVMs. Smola and Schölkopf (2004, 1998) published an excellent tutorial giving an overview of the basic ideas underlying SVMs for regression. In R we have several implementations of SVMs available, among which we can refer to the package **kernlab** by Karatzoglou et al. (2004) with several functionalities available, and also the function `svm()` on package **e1071** by Dimitriadou et al. (2009).

The basic idea behind SVMs is that of mapping the original data into a new, high-dimensional space, where it is possible to apply linear models to obtain a separating hyper plane, for example, separating the classes of the problem, in the case of binary classification tasks. The mapping of the original data into this new space is carried out with the help of the so-called kernel functions. These functions are interesting because when applied to any pair of cases in the original space produce a value that is equal to the dot product of these cases in the new (and extremely large) space. Dot products play an essential role in the optimization process that SVMs use to obtain their solution. Calculating dot products in these high-dimensionality spaces where SVMs project the data, is computationally expensive. In this context, the equivalence provided by kernel functions is very interesting because it allows avoiding these extra computation costs.[16] SVMs are thus linear machines operating on this new and very large space where linear separation is possible. Section 3.4.5.3 (page 151) provides a more detailed explanation of SVMs for both regression and classification tasks.

We will now provide very simple examples of the use of this type of models in R. We start with the regression task for which we will use the function provided in the package **e1071**:

```
> set.seed(1234)
> library(e1071)
> sv <- svm(Tform, Tdata.train[1:1000, ], gamma = 0.001, cost = 100)
> s.preds <- predict(sv, Tdata.train[1001:2000, ])
> sigs.svm <- trading.signals(s.preds, 0.1, -0.1)
> true.sigs <- trading.signals(Tdata.train[1001:2000, "T.ind.GSPC"], 0.1, -0.1)
> sigs.PR(sigs.svm, true.sigs)

      precision       recall
s         0.375 0.017045455
b           NaN 0.000000000
s+b       0.375 0.008902077
```

In this example we have used the `svm()` function with most of its default parameters with the exception of the parameters `gamma` and `cost`. In this context, the function uses a radial basis kernel function

$$K(\mathbf{x}, \mathbf{y}) = \exp\left(-\gamma \times \|\mathbf{x} - \mathbf{y}\|^2\right) \tag{5.13}$$

where γ is a user parameter that in our call we have set to 0.001 (function `svm()` uses as default `1/ncol(data)`).

The parameter `cost` indicates the cost of the violations of the margin[17]. You may wish to explore the help page of the function to learn more details on these and other parameters.

---

[15]Extensive information on this class of models can be obtained at http://www.kernel-machines.org.

[16]Using kernel functions in place of the expensive dot products is usually known as the *kernel trick*.

[17]Check Section 3.4.5.3 for explanations of this concept of margin.

As we can observe, the SVM model achieves a considerably better score than the ANN in terms of precision, although with a much lower recall. Moreover, the SVM model never predicted a buy signal and thus the errors in calculating the precision for these signals and the zero in the respective recall.

Next, we consider the classification task, this time using the **kernlab** package for illustration purposes:

```
> library(kernlab)
> ksv <- ksvm(Signal ~ ., Tdata.trainC[1:1000, ], C = 10)
> ks.preds <- predict(ksv, Tdata.trainC[1001:2000, ])
> sigs.PR(ks.preds, Tdata.trainC[1001:2000, 1])

    precision    recall
s   0.2386364 0.2386364
b   0.3421053 0.1614907
s+b 0.2698413 0.2017804
```

We have used the `C` parameter of the `ksvm()` function of package **kernlab**, to specify a different cost of constraints violations, which by default is 1. Apart from this we have used the default parameter values, which for classification involves, for instance, using the radial basis kernel. Once again, more details can be obtained in the help pages of the `ksvm()` function.

5.4.2.3 Multivariate Adaptive Regression Splines

Multivariate adaptive regression splines (Friedman, 1991) are an example of an additive regression model (Hastie and Tibshirani, 1990). The main idea behind generalized additive models is that a complex function may be decomposed in an additive way such that each term has a simpler form. The main advantage/motivation of this decomposition lies on the fact that additive models are generally considered very interpretable as you can easily understand the contribution of each term towards the predictions of the model. Generalized additive models can be described by the following general equation,

$$r(\mathbf{x}) = \alpha + \sum_{i=1}^{a} f_i(X_i) \qquad (5.14)$$

where the f_i's are univariate functions.

These models can be further generalized over functions with more than one variable. The model parameters are frequently obtained through the *backfitting* algorithm (Friedman and Stuetzle, 1981).

Multivariate adaptive regression splines (MARS) models are an instance of these approaches. A MARS model has the following general form:

$$mars(\mathbf{x}) = c_0 + \sum_{i=1}^{k} c_i \times B_i(\mathbf{x}) \qquad (5.15)$$

where the c_i's are constants and the B_i's are basis functions.

The basis functions usually take one of the following forms: (i) the constant 1 (for the intercept); (ii) a hinge function with the form $\max(0, X - k)$ or $\max(0, k - X)$, where k are constants; or (iii) a product of two or more hinge functions, which try to capture the interactions between two or more variables. Figure 5.4 shows an example of two hinge functions.

MARS models are built in two phases: the forward and backward passes. In the forward

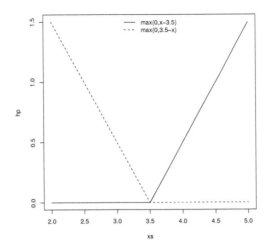

FIGURE 5.4: An example of two hinge functions with the same threshold.

pass the algorithm tries to add new terms to the model. It starts with an intercept (mean of the target variable) and then iteratively keeps adding new basis function terms until a certain termination criterion is met. In the backward pass the algorithm tries to remove each term in turn, using a cross validation criterion to compare and select alternatives.

MARS models have been implemented in at least two packages within R. Package **mda** (Leisch et al., 2009) contains the function `mars()`, while package **earth** (Milborrow, 2009) has the function `earth()` that also implements this methodology. This latter function has the advantage of following a more standard R schema in terms of modeling functions, by providing a formula-based interface. It also implements several other facilities not present in the other package and thus it will be our selection.

The following code applies the function `earth()` to the financial regression task we have been using:

```
> library(earth)
> e <- earth(Tform, Tdata.train[1:1000, ])
> e.preds <- predict(e, Tdata.train[1001:2000, ])
> sigs.e <- trading.signals(e.preds, 0.1, -0.1)
> true.sigs <- trading.signals(Tdata.train[1001:2000, "T.ind.GSPC"], 0.1, -0.1)
> sigs.PR(sigs.e, true.sigs)

    precision    recall
s   0.2894737 0.2500000
b   0.3504274 0.2546584
s+b 0.3159851 0.2522255
```

The results are slightly better than the ones obtained with SVMs for classification, with precision scores around 30%, and recall approximately 25%.

You can also have more information on the obtained model using the function `summary()`,

```
> summary(e)

Call: earth(formula=Tform, data=Tdata.train[1:1000,])
```

```
                            coefficients
(Intercept)                    0.5241811
h(myATR.GSPC-2.56817)          1.2724353
h(-61.825-mySMI.GSPC)          0.0594203
h(myADX.GSPC-40.6215)         -0.0104803
h(50.657-myADX.GSPC)          -0.0025279
h(myADX.GSPC-50.657)           0.0823181
h(0.204717-myVolat.GSPC)      -0.5105416
h(myVolat.GSPC-0.204717)      -5.6100523
h(myVolat.GSPC-0.271459)       5.6725474
h(mySAR.GSPC-74.7031)         -0.0693496
h(87.944-mySAR.GSPC)          -0.0575104
h(mySAR.GSPC-87.944)           0.0800171
h(runMean.Cl.GSPC-79.265)      0.2074780
h(81.942-runMean.Cl.GSPC)      0.1058493
h(runMean.Cl.GSPC-81.942)     -0.2185753

Selected 15 of 18 terms, and 6 of 11 predictors
Termination condition: Reached nk 23
Importance: myVolat.GSPC, runMean.Cl.GSPC, myATR.GSPC, mySMI.GSPC, ...
Number of terms at each degree of interaction: 1 14 (additive model)
GCV 0.01470628    RSS 13.86568    GRSq 0.3536668    RSq 0.38939
```

This gives you an idea of the functional form (involving the hinge functions) of the obtained model as well as some diagnostic measures (for which you can obtain even more detail with the function **plot()** applied to the model). Finally, you may get more detailed information on the importance assigned by the algorithm to the variables with the following:

```
> evimp(e, trim=FALSE)
```

```
                        nsubsets   gcv    rss
myVolat.GSPC               13    100.0  100.0
runMean.Cl.GSPC            13    100.0  100.0
myATR.GSPC                12     96.7   96.4
mySMI.GSPC                11     81.5   82.4
mySAR.GSPC                 7     44.1   47.7
myADX.GSPC                 5     57.8>  58.5>
myAroon.GSPC-unused        0      0.0    0.0
myEMV.GSPC-unused          0      0.0    0.0
myMACD.GSPC-unused         0      0.0    0.0
myMFI.GSPC-unused          0      0.0    0.0
runSD.Cl.GSPC-unused       0      0.0    0.0
```

You get the variables ordered by decreasing importance and, with **trim=FALSE**, you can also see which variables are completely discarded from the model (the ones with their named appended by "unused").

MARS is only applicable to regression problems so we do not show any example for the classification task.[18]

Further readings on multivariate adaptive regression splines

---

[18]Actually, as you may see in one of the package vignettes that come with the package **earth** that you can plugin the **earth()** function into the **fda()** function of package **mda** to solve a kind of non-linear discriminant (which is a classification method), but we will not use this approach here.

The definitive reference on MARS is the original journal article by Friedman (1991). This is a very well-written article providing all details concerning the motivation for the development of MARS, that curiously have to do with problems with tree-based models, as well as the techniques used in the system. The article also includes quite an interesting discussion section by other scientists that provides other views of this work.

5.5   From Predictions into Actions

This section will address the issue of how will we use the signal predictions obtained with the modeling techniques described previously. Given a set of signals output by some model there are many ways we can use them to act on the market.

5.5.1   How Will the Predictions Be Used?

In our case study we will assume we will be trading in future markets. These markets are based on contracts to buy or sell a commodity on a certain date in the future at the price determined by the market at that future time. The technical details of these contracts are beyond the scope of this book. Still, in objective terms, this means that our trading system will be able to open two types of trading positions: long and short. Long positions are opened by buying a commodity at time t and price p, and selling it at a later time $t + x$. It makes sense to open such positions when we have the expectation that the price will rise in the future, thus allowing us to make some profit with that transaction. On short positions, we sell the security at time t with price p with the obligation of buying it in the future. This is possible thanks to a borrowing schema whose details you can find in appropriate documents (e.g., Wikipedia). These types of positions allow us to make profit when the prices decline as we will buy the security at a time later than t. Informally, we can say that we will open short positions when we believe the prices are going down, and open long positions when we believe the prices are going up.

Given a set of signals, there are many ways we can use them to trade in future markets. We will describe a few plausible trading strategies that we will be using and comparing in our experiments with the models. Due to space and time constraints, it is not possible to explore this important issue further. Still, the reader is left with some plausible strategies and with the means to develop and try other possibilities.

The mechanics of the first trading strategy we are going to use are the following. First, all decisions will be taken at the end of the day, that is, after knowing all daily quotes of the current session. Suppose that at the end of day t, our models provide evidence that the prices are going down, that is, predicting a low value of T or a sell signal. If we already have a position opened, the indication of the model will be ignored. If we currently do not hold any opened position, we will open a short position by issuing a sell order. When this order is carried out by the market at a price pr sometime in the future, we will immediately post two other orders. The first is a buy limit order with a limit price of $pr - p\%$, where $p\%$ is a target profit margin. This type of order is carried out only if the market price reaches the target limit price or below. This order expresses what our target profit is for the short position just opened. We will wait 10 days for this target to be reached. If the order is not carried out by this deadline, we will buy at the closing price of the 10th day. The second order is a buy stop order with a price limit $pr + l\%$. This order is placed with the goal of limiting our eventual losses with this position. The order will be executed if the market reaches the price $pr + l\%$, thus limiting our possible losses to $l\%$.

If our models provide indications that the prices will rise in the near future, with high predicted T values or buy signals, we will consider opening a long position. This position will only be opened if we are currently out of the market. With this purpose we will post a buy order that will be accomplished at a time t and price pr. As before, we will immediately post two new orders. The first will be a sell limit order with a target price of $pr + p\%$, which will only be executed if the market reaches a price of $pr + p\%$ or above. This sell limit order will have a deadline of 10 days, as before. The second order is a sell stop order with price $pr - l\%$, which will again limit our eventual losses to $l\%$.

This first strategy can be seen as a bit conservative as it will only have a single position opened at any time. Moreover, after 10 days of waiting for the target profit, the positions are immediately closed. We will also consider a more "risky" trading strategy. This other strategy is similar to the previous one, with the exception that we will always open new positions if there are signals with that indication, and if we have sufficient money for that. Moreover, we will wait forever for the positions to reach either the target profit or the maximum allowed loss.

We will only consider these two main trading strategies with slight variations on the used parameters (e.g., holding time, expected profit margin, or amount of money invested on each position). As mentioned, these are simply chosen for illustrative purposes.

5.5.2   Trading-Related Evaluation Criteria

The metrics described in Section 5.3.4 do not translate directly to the overall goal of this application, which has to do with economic performance. Factors like the economic results and the risk exposure of some financial instrument or tool are of key importance in this context. This is an area that alone could easily fill this chapter. The R package PerformanceAnalytics (Carl and Peterson, 2014) implements many of the existing financial metrics for analyzing the returns of some trading algorithm as the one we are proposing in this chapter. We will use some of the functions provided by this package to collect information on the economic performance of our proposals. Our evaluation will be focused on the overall results of the methods, on their risk exposure, and on the average results of each position hold by the models. In the final evaluation of our proposed system to be described in Section 5.7, we will carry out a more in-depth analysis of its performance using tools provided by this package.

With respect to the overall results, we will use (1) the simple net balance between the initial capital and the capital at the end of the testing period (sometimes called the profit/loss), (2) the percentage return that this net balance represents, and (3) the excess return over the buy and hold strategy. This strategy consists of opening a long position at the beginning of the testing period and waiting until the end to close it. The return over the buy and hold measures the difference between the return of our trading strategy and this simple strategy.

Regarding risk-related measures, we will use the Sharpe ratio coefficient, which measures the return per unit of risk, the latter being measured as the standard deviation of the returns. We will also calculate the maximum draw-down, which measures the maximum cumulative successive loss of a model. This is an important risk measure for traders, as any system that goes over a serious consecutive draw-down is probably doomed to be without money to run, as investors will most surely be scared by these successive losses and redraw their money.

Finally, the performance of the positions held during the test period will be evaluated by their number, the average return per position, and the percentage of profitable positions, as well as other less relevant metrics.

5.5.3 Putting Everything Together: A Simulated Trader

This section describes how to implement the ideas we have sketched regarding trading with the signals of our models. Our book package provides the function `trading.simulator()`, which can be used to put all these ideas together by carrying out a trading simulation with the signals of any model. The main parameters of this function are the market quotes for the simulation period and the model signals for this period. Two other parameters are the name of the user-defined trading policy function and its list of parameters. Finally, we can also specify the cost of each transaction and the initial capital available for the trader. The simulator will call the user-provided trading policy function at the end of each daily section, and the function should return the orders that it wants the simulator to carry out. The simulator carries out these orders on the market and records all activity on several data structures. The result of the simulator is an object of class `tradeRecord` containing the information of this simulation. This object can then be used in other functions to obtain economic evaluation metrics or graphs of the trading activity, as we will see.

Before proceeding with an example of this type of simulation, we need to provide further details on the trading policy functions that the user needs to supply to the simulator. These functions should be written using a certain protocol, that is, they should be aware of how the simulator will call them, and should return the information this simulator is expecting.

At the end of each daily session d, the simulator calls the trading policy function with four main arguments plus any other parameters the user has provided in the call to the simulator. These four arguments are (1) a vector with the predicted signals until day d, (2) the market quotes (up to d), (3) the currently opened positions, and (4) the money currently available to the trader. The current position is a matrix with as many rows as there are open positions at the end of day d. This matrix has four columns: "pos.type" that can be 1 for a long position or -1 for a short position; "N.stocks", which is the number of stocks of the position; "Odate", which is the day on which the position was opened (a number between 1 and d); and "Oprice", which is the price at which the position was opened. The row names of this matrix contain the IDs of the positions that are relevant when we want to indicate to the simulator that a certain position is to be closed.

All this information is provided by the simulator to ensure the user can define a broad set of trading policy functions. The user-defined functions should return a data frame with a set of orders that the simulator should carry out. This data frame should include the following information (columns): "order", which should be 1 for buy orders and -1 for sell orders; "order.type", which should be 1 for market orders that are to be carried out immediately (actually at next day open price), 2 for limit orders or 3 for stop orders; "val", which should be the quantity of stocks to trade for opening market orders, `NA` for closing market orders, or a target price for limit and stop orders; "action", which should be "open" for orders that are opening a new position or "close" for orders closing an existing position; and finally, "posID", which should contain the ID of the position that is being closed, if applicable.

The following is an illustration of a user-defined trading policy function:

```
> policy.1 <- function(signals,market,opened.pos,money,
+                       bet=0.2,hold.time=10,
+                       exp.prof=0.025, max.loss= 0.05
+                       )
+   {
+      d <- NROW(market) # this is the ID of today
+      orders <- NULL
+      nOs <- NROW(opened.pos)
+      # nothing to do!
```

```
+      if (!nOs && signals[d] == 'h') return(orders)

+      # First lets check if we can open new positions
+      # i) long positions
+      if (signals[d] == 'b' && !nOs) {
+        quant <- round(bet*money/Cl(market)[d],0)
+        if (quant > 0)
+          orders <- rbind(orders,
+                data.frame(order=c(1,-1,-1),order.type=c(1,2,3),
+                          val = c(quant,
+                                  Cl(market)[d]*(1+exp.prof),
+                                  Cl(market)[d]*(1-max.loss)
+                                  ),
+                          action = c('open','close','close'),
+                          posID = c(NA,NA,NA)
+                          )
+                )

+      # ii) short positions
+      } else if (signals[d] == 's' && !nOs) {
+        # this is the nr of stocks we already need to buy
+        # because of currently opened short positions
+        need2buy <- sum(opened.pos[opened.pos[,'pos.type']==-1,
+                              "N.stocks"])*Cl(market)[d]
+        quant <- round(bet*(money-need2buy)/Cl(market)[d],0)
+        if (quant > 0)
+          orders <- rbind(orders,
+                data.frame(order=c(-1,1,1),order.type=c(1,2,3),
+                          val = c(quant,
+                                  Cl(market)[d]*(1-exp.prof),
+                                  Cl(market)[d]*(1+max.loss)
+                                  ),
+                          action = c('open','close','close'),
+                          posID = c(NA,NA,NA)
+                          )
+                )
+      }

+      # Now lets check if we need to close positions
+      # because their holding time is over
+      if (nOs)
+        for(i in 1:nOs) {
+          if (d - opened.pos[i,'Odate'] >= hold.time)
+            orders <- rbind(orders,
+                  data.frame(order=-opened.pos[i,'pos.type'],
+                            order.type=1,
+                            val = NA,
+                            action = 'close',
+                            posID = rownames(opened.pos)[i]
+                            )
+                  )
+        }

+    orders
+  }
```

This `policy.1()` function implements the first trading strategy we described in Section 5.5.1. The function has four parameters that we can use to tune this strategy. These are the `bet` parameter, which specifies the percentage of our current money, that we will invest each time we open a new position; the `exp.prof` parameter, which indicates the profit margin we wish for our positions and is used when posting the limit orders; the `max.loss`, which indicates the maximum loss we are willing to admit before we close the position, and is used in stop orders; and the `hold.time` parameter, which indicates the number of days we are willing to wait to reach the profit margin. If the holding time is reached without achieving the wanted margin, the positions are closed.

Notice that whenever we open a new position, we send three orders back to the simulator: a market order to open the position, a limit order to specify our target profit margin, and a stop order to limit our losses.

Equivalently, the following function implements our second trading strategy:

```r
> policy.2 <- function(signals,market,opened.pos,money,
+                      bet=0.2,exp.prof=0.025, max.loss= 0.05
+                      )
+   {
+     d <- NROW(market) # this is the ID of today
+     orders <- NULL
+     nOs <- NROW(opened.pos)
+     # nothing to do!
+     if (!nOs && signals[d] == 'h') return(orders)
+
+     # First lets check if we can open new positions
+     # i) long positions
+     if (signals[d] == 'b') {
+       quant <- round(bet*money/Cl(market)[d],0)
+       if (quant > 0)
+         orders <- rbind(orders,
+               data.frame(order=c(1,-1,-1),order.type=c(1,2,3),
+                     val = c(quant,
+                             Cl(market)[d]*(1+exp.prof),
+                             Cl(market)[d]*(1-max.loss)
+                         ),
+                     action = c('open','close','close'),
+                     posID = c(NA,NA,NA)
+                 )
+             )
+
+     # ii) short positions
+     } else if (signals[d] == 's') {
+       # this is the money already committed to buy stocks
+       # because of currently opened short positions
+       need2buy <- sum(opened.pos[opened.pos[,'pos.type']==-1,
+                             "N.stocks"])*Cl(market)[d]
+       quant <- round(bet*(money-need2buy)/Cl(market)[d],0)
+       if (quant > 0)
+         orders <- rbind(orders,
+             data.frame(order=c(-1,1,1),order.type=c(1,2,3),
+                     val = c(quant,
+                             Cl(market)[d]*(1-exp.prof),
+                             Cl(market)[d]*(1+max.loss)
+                         ),
```

```
+                              action = c('open','close','close'),
+                              posID = c(NA,NA,NA)
+                          )
+                      )
+          }

+      orders
+  }
```

This function is very similar to the previous one. The main difference lies in the fact that in this trading policy we allow for more than one position to be opened at the same time, and also there is no aging limit for closing the positions.

Having defined the trading policy functions, we are ready to try our trading simulator. For illustration purposes we will select a small sample of our data to obtain an SVM, which is then used to obtain predictions for a subsequent period. We call our trading simulator with these predictions to obtain the results of trading using the signals of the SVM in the context of a certain trading policy.

```
> ## Train and test periods
> start <- 1
> len.tr <- 1000
> len.ts <- 500
> tr <- start:(start+len.tr-1)
> ts <- (start+len.tr):(start+len.tr+len.ts-1)
> ## getting the quotes for the testing period
> data(GSPC)
> date <- rownames(Tdata.train[start+len.tr,])
> marketTP <- GSPC[paste(date,'/',sep='')][1:len.ts]
> ## learning the model and obtaining its signal predictions for the test period
> library(e1071)
> s <- svm(Tform, Tdata.train[tr,], cost=10,gamma=0.01)
> p <- predict(s, Tdata.train[ts,])
> sig <- trading.signals(p, 0.1, -0.1)
> ## now using the simulated trader during the testing period
> t1 <- trading.simulator(marketTP, signals=sig, policy.func='policy.1',
+                         policy.pars=list(exp.prof=0.05,bet=0.2,hold.time=30))
```

Please note that for this code to work, you have to previously create the objects with the data for modeling, using the instructions given in Section 5.3.3.

In our call to the trading simulator we have selected the first trading policy and have provided some different values for some of its parameters. We have used the default values for transaction costs (five monetary units) and for the initial capital (1 million monetary units). The result of the call is an object of class **tradeRecord**. We can check its contents as follows:

```
> t1


Object of class tradeRecord with slots:

 trading: <xts object with a numeric  500 x 5  matrix>
 positions: <numeric  8 x 7  matrix>
 init.cap :   1e+06
 trans.cost :   5
```

```
policy.func :  policy.1
policy.pars : <list with  3  elements>

> summary(t1)


== Summary of a Trading Simulation with  500  days ==

Trading policy function :  policy.1
Policy function parameters:
 exp.prof  =  0.05
 bet  =  0.2
 hold.time  =  30

Transaction costs :  5
Initial Equity    :  1e+06
Final Equity      :  1019712   Return :  1.97 %
Number of trading positions:  8

Use function "tradingEvaluation()" for further stats on this simulation.
```

The function **tradingEvaluation()** can be used to obtain a series of economic indicators of the performance during this simulation period:

```
> tradingEvaluation(t1)

    NTrades        NProf     PercProf          PL        Ret    RetOverBH
       8.00         5.00        62.50    19712.54       1.97        -4.88
       MaxDD SharpeRatio      AvgProf     AvgLoss      AvgPL      MaxProf
    25630.72         0.04         5.11       -5.00       1.32         5.26
     MaxLoss
       -5.00
```

We can also obtain a graphical overview of the performance of the trader using the function **plot()** as follows:

```
> plot(t1,marketTP, theme = "white",  name = "SP500")
```

The result of this command is shown in Figure 5.5.

The results of this trader are not very interesting. Would the scenario be different if we had used the second trading policy? Let us check:

```
> t2 <- trading.simulator(marketTP, sig, "policy.2", list(exp.prof = 0.05, bet = 0.3))
> summary(t2)


== Summary of a Trading Simulation with  500  days ==

Trading policy function :  policy.2
Policy function parameters:
 exp.prof  =  0.05
 bet  =  0.3

Transaction costs :  5
Initial Equity    :  1e+06
```

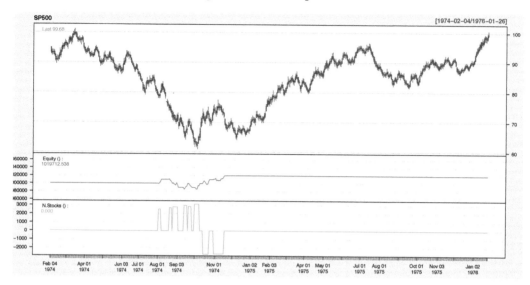

FIGURE 5.5: The results of trading using Policy 1 based on the signals of an SVM.

```
Final Equity       :  1152332   Return :  15.23 %
Number of trading positions:  37

Use function "tradingEvaluation()" for further stats on this simulation.

> tradingEvaluation(t2)

    NTrades       NProf    PercProf          PL         Ret    RetOverBH
      37.00       26.00       70.27   152332.30       15.23         8.38
      MaxDD SharpeRatio     AvgProf     AvgLoss       AvgPL      MaxProf
   67492.23        0.06        4.99       -4.89        2.05         5.26
    MaxLoss
      -5.00
```

Using the same exact signals (i.e. not changing anything in the modeling stages), but with a different trading policy, we got a completely different result! Let us repeat the experiment with different training and testing periods:

```
> start <- 2000
> len.tr <- 1000
> len.ts <- 500
> tr <- start:(start + len.tr - 1)
> ts <- (start + len.tr):(start + len.tr + len.ts - 1)
> data(GSPC)
> date <- rownames(Tdata.train[start+len.tr,])
> marketTP <- GSPC[paste(date,'/',sep='')][1:len.ts]
> s <- svm(Tform, Tdata.train[tr, ], cost = 10, gamma = 0.01)
> p <- predict(s, Tdata.train[ts, ])
> sig <- trading.signals(p, 0.1, -0.1)
> t2 <-  trading.simulator(marketTP, sig,
+                   "policy.2", list(exp.prof = 0.05, bet = 0.3))
> summary(t2)
```

```
== Summary of a Trading Simulation with  500  days ==

Trading policy function :  policy.2
Policy function parameters:
 exp.prof  =  0.05
 bet  =  0.3

Transaction costs :  5
Initial Equity     :  1e+06
Final Equity       :  215220.1   Return :  -78.48 %
Number of trading positions:  231

Use function "tradingEvaluation()" for further stats on this simulation.

> tradingEvaluation(t2)
```

NTrades	NProf	PercProf	PL	Ret	RetOverBH
231.00	29.00	12.55	-784779.95	-78.48	-111.74
MaxDD	SharpeRatio	AvgProf	AvgLoss	AvgPL	MaxProf
973177.31	0.02	5.19	-2.59	-1.62	5.56
MaxLoss					
-4.89					

This trader, obtained by the same modeling technique and using the same trading strategy, scored considerably worse. The major lesson to be learned here is: we need reliable statistical estimates. Do not be fooled by a few repetitions of some experiments, even if it includes a 2-year testing period. We need more repetitions under different conditions to ensure some statistical reliability of our results. This is particularly true for time series models that have to handle different regimes (e.g., periods with rather different volatility or trend). This is the topic of the next section.

5.6 Model Evaluation and Selection

In this section we will consider how to obtain reliable estimates of the selected evaluation criteria. These estimates will allow us to properly compare and select among different alternative trading systems.

5.6.1 Monte Carlo Estimates

Time series problems like the one we are addressing bring new challenges in terms of obtaining reliable estimates of our evaluation metrics. This is caused by the fact that all data observations have an attached time tag that imposes an ordering among them. This ordering should be respected with the risk of obtaining estimates that are not reliable. In Chapter 4 we used the cross-validation method to obtain reliable estimates of some evaluation statistics. As we have seen in Section 3.5.2 (page 177), this methodology includes a random re-sampling step that changes the original ordering of the observations. This means that cross-validation should not be applied to time series problems. Applying this method could mean to test models on observations that are older than the ones used to obtain them. This is not feasible in reality, and thus the estimates obtained by this process are unreliable and possibly overly optimistic, as it is easier to predict the past given the future than the opposite.

All other experimental methodologies described in Section 3.5 involve some random step that may break the implicit ordering of the available dataset. Any estimation process using time series data should ensure that the models are always tested on data that is more recent than the data used to obtain the models. This means no random re-sampling of the observations or any other process that changes the time ordering of the given data. However, as we have discussed in Section 3.5, any proper estimation process should include some random choices to ensure the statistical reliability of the obtained estimates. This involves repeating the estimation process several times under different conditions, preferably randomly selected. Given a time series dataset spanning from time t to time $t + N$, how can we ensure this? First, we have to choose the train+test setup for which we want to obtain estimates. This means deciding what is the size of both the train and test sets to be used in the estimation process. The sum of these two sizes should be smaller than N to ensure that we are able to randomly generate different experimental scenarios with the data that was provided to us. However, if we select too small a training size, we may seriously impair the performance of our models. Similarly, small test sets will also be less reliable, particularly if we suspect there are regime shifts in our problem and we wish to test the models under these circumstances.

Our dataset includes roughly 35 years of daily quotes. We will evaluate all alternatives by estimating their performance on a test set of 5 years of quotes, when given 10 years of training data. This ensures train and test sizes that are sufficiently large; and, moreover, it leaves space for different repetitions of this testing process as we have 35 years of data.

In terms of experimental methodology, we will use a Monte Carlo experiment to obtain reliable estimates of our evaluation metrics. Monte Carlo methods rely on random sampling to obtain their results. We are going to use this sampling process to choose a set of R points in our 35-year period of quotes. For each randomly selected time point r, we will use the previous 10 years of quotes to obtain the models and the subsequent 5 years to test them. At the end of these R iterations we will have R estimates for each of our evaluation metrics. Each of these estimates is obtained on a randomly selected window of 15 years of data, the first 10 years used for training and the remaining 5 years for testing. This ensures that our experiments always respect the time ordering of the time series data. Repeating the process R times will ensure sufficient variability on the train+test conditions, which increases the reliability of our estimates. Moreover, if we use the same set of R randomly selected points for evaluating different alternatives, we can carry out paired comparisons to obtain statistical confidence levels on the observed differences of mean performance. Figure 5.6 summarizes the Monte Carlo experimental method. Notice that as we have to ensure that for every random point r there are 10 years of data before and 5 years after, this eliminates some of the data from the random selection of the R points.

The function `performanceEstimation()`, which was used in Chapter 4 for carrying out k-fold cross-validation experiments, can also be used for this type of Monte Carlo experiments. In the next section we will use it to obtain reliable estimates of the selected evaluation metrics for several alternative trading systems.

5.6.2 Experimental Comparisons

This section describes a set of Monte Carlo experiments designed to obtain reliable estimates of the evaluation criteria mentioned in Sections 5.3.4 and 5.5.2. The base data used in these experiments are the datasets created at the end of Section 5.3.3.

Each of the alternative predictive models considered in these experiments will be used in three different model updating setups. These were already described in Section 5.4.1

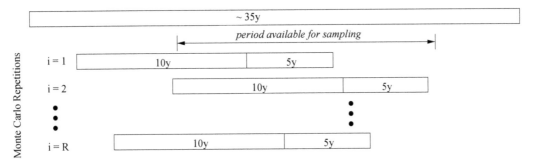

FIGURE 5.6: The Monte Carlo experimental process.

and consist of using a single model for all 5-year testing periods, using a sliding window, or a growing window. Although package **performanceEstimation** contains a pre-defined standard workflow (named `timeseriesWF()`) that implements these strategies, we will be writing our own workflow function. The main reason lies on the fact that we will need several steps that are specific to this concrete application. For instance, we will need to transform the predictions into trading signals, then decide what to do with these signals (the trading policy), and finally actually trading on the market using our simulator to get the results of our workflow in terms of the financial metrics we have selected. All these steps require specific code so we will need to develop our own workflow, and then supply it to the function `performanceEstimation()`.

The following code implements our approach (workflow) given a certain train+test period that will be generated by the `performanceEstimation()` function. The function implements different variants of our approach (e.g. slide and growing windows) that can be selected through specific parameter values of the workflow function. The function will be called from within the Monte Carlo routines of package **performanceEstimation** with different train and test periods according to the schema described in Figure 5.6. When creating your own workflow functions for using with this package, the main requirements are: (i) the function should accept in the first three arguments a formula, a training data frame and a testing data frame; and (ii) should return the result of applying a certain modeling approach (implemented in the workflow) to these datasets.

```
> tradingWF <- function(form, train, test,
+                        quotes, pred.target="signals",
+                        learner, learner.pars=NULL,
+                        predictor.pars=NULL,
+                        learn.test.type='fixed', relearn.step=30,
+                        b.t, s.t,
+                        policy, policy.pars,
+                        trans.cost=5, init.cap=1e+06)
+ {
+     ## obtain the model(s) and respective predictions for the test set
+     if (learn.test.type == 'fixed') {  # a single fixed model
+         m <- do.call(learner,c(list(form,train),learner.pars))
+         preds <- do.call("predict",c(list(m,test),predictor.pars))
+     } else {  # either slide or growing window strategies
+         data <- rbind(train,test)
+         n <- NROW(data)
+         train.size <- NROW(train)
+         sts <- seq(train.size+1,n,by=relearn.step)
```

```
+            preds <- vector()
+            for(s in sts) {  # loop over each relearn step
+                tr <- if (learn.test.type=='slide') data[(s-train.size):(s-1),]
+                      else data[1:(s-1),]
+                ts <- data[s:min((s+relearn.step-1),n),]

+                m <- do.call(learner,c(list(form,tr),learner.pars))
+                preds <- c(preds,do.call("predict",c(list(m,ts),predictor.pars)))
+            }
+        }

+        ## Getting the trading signals
+        if (pred.target != "signals") { # the model predicts the T indicator
+            predSigs <- trading.signals(preds,b.t,s.t)
+            tgtName <- all.vars(form)[1]
+            trueSigs <- trading.signals(test[[tgtName]],b.t,s.t)
+        } else { # the model predicts the signals directly
+            tgtName <- all.vars(form)[1]
+            if (is.factor(preds))
+                predSigs <- preds
+            else {
+                if (preds[1] %in% levels(train[[tgtName]]))
+                    predSigs <- factor(preds,labels=levels(train[[tgtName]]),
+                                       levels=levels(train[[tgtName]]))
+                else
+                    predSigs <- factor(preds,labels=levels(train[[tgtName]]),
+                                       levels=1:3)
+            }
+            trueSigs <- test[[tgtName]]
+        }

+        ## obtaining the trading record from trading with the signals
+        date <- rownames(test)[1]
+        market <- get(quotes)[paste(date,"/",sep='')][1:length(preds),]
+        tradeRec <- trading.simulator(market,predSigs,
+                                      policy.func=policy,policy.pars=policy.pars,
+                                      trans.cost=trans.cost,init.cap=init.cap)

+        return(list(trueSigs=trueSigs,predSigs=predSigs,tradeRec=tradeRec))
+ }
```

The first part of the workflow takes care of obtaining the model(s) that make the predictions for the test period. This can be a single model that is applied throughout the full test period, or can be several models using either growing or sliding windows at a step controlled by the **relearn.step** parameter. After this stage we need to get the signals for this testing period. If the models already had as target the trading signals (parameter **pred.target="signals"**) this is trivial, otherwise we need to convert the predicted T indicator values into signals. Finally, using these signals, we trade on the simulator during the test period. The outcome of the workflow is a list with the true and predicted signals as well as the trading record. These are the elements that are necessary for calculating the evaluation metrics.

Associated with this user-defined workflow we will also write our own function to obtain the evaluation metrics that we want to use in our problem. Once again the motivation is the specificity of our problem that demands for some special metrics not implemented in the package **performanceEstimation**. The following function implements our required evaluation metrics when called with the outcome of the above trading workflow:

```
> tradingEval <- function(trueSigs,predSigs,tradeRec,...)
+ {
+     ## Signals evaluation
+     st <- sigs.PR(predSigs,trueSigs)
+     dim(st) <- NULL
+     names(st) <- paste(rep(c('prec','rec'),each=3),c('s','b','sb'),sep='.')
+
+     ## Trading record evaluation
+     tradRes <- tradingEvaluation(tradeRec)
+     return(c(st,tradRes))
+ }
```

This function calculates the precision and recall of the signals of the model, and also some trading-related metrics using function **tradingEvaluation()** that we have seen before. All these functions were fully described and exemplified in Section 5.5.3.

Having defined specific workflow and evaluation functions we are ready to run our comparative experiments. The following code runs the Monte Carlo experiments. We recommend that you think twice before running this code. Even on rather fast computers, it will take several days to complete. On the book web page we provide the objects resulting from running the experiments so that you can replicate the results analysis that will follow, without having to run these experiments on your computer.

```
> library(performanceEstimation)
> library(e1071)
> library(earth)
> library(nnet)
> LEARNERS <- c('svm','earth','nnet')
> EST.TASK <- EstimationTask(method=MonteCarlo(nReps=20,
+                                              szTrain=2540,szTest=1270,
+                                              seed=1234),
+                            evaluator="tradingEval")
> VARS <- list()
>
> VARS$svm <- list(learner.pars=list(cost=c(10,50,150),
+                                     gamma=c(0.01,0.05)))
> VARS$earth <- list(learner.pars=list(nk=c(10,17),
+                                       degree=c(1,2),
+                                       thresh=c(0.01,0.001)))
> VARS$nnet <-  list(learner.pars=list(linout=TRUE, trace=FALSE,
+                                       maxit=750,
+                                       size=c(5,10),
+                                       decay=c(0.001,0.01,0.1)))
>
> VARS$learning <- list(learn.test.type=c("fixed","slide","grow"), relearn.step=120)
> VARS$trading  <- list(policy=c("policy.1","policy.2"),
+                       policy.pars=list(bet=c(0.2,0.5),exp.prof=0.05,max.loss=0.05),
+                       b.t=c(0.01,0.05),s.t=c(-0.01,-0.05))
>
> ## Regression (forecast T indicator) Workflows
> for(lrn in LEARNERS) {
+     objName <- paste(lrn,"res","regr",sep="_")
```

```
+        assign(objName,
+               performanceEstimation(PredTask(Tform,Tdata.train,"SP500"),
+                                     do.call("workflowVariants",
+                                             c(list("tradingWF",
+                                                    varsRootName=paste0(lrn,"Regr"),
+                                                    quotes="GSPC",
+                                                    learner=lrn,
+                                                    pred.target="indicator"),
+                                               VARS[[lrn]],
+                                               VARS$learning,
+                                               VARS$trading)
+                                             ),
+                                     EST.TASK,
+                                     cluster=TRUE) # for parallel computation
+                     )
+        save(list=objName,file=paste(objName,'Rdata',sep='.'))
+ }
>
> ## Specific settings to make nnet work as a classifier
> VARS$nnet$learner.pars$linout <-  FALSE
> VARS$nnet$predictor.pars <-  list(type="class")
>
> ## Classification (forecast signal) workflows
> for(lrn in c("svm","nnet")) { # only these because MARS is only for regression
+        objName <- paste(lrn,"res","class",sep="_")
+        assign(objName,
+               performanceEstimation(PredTask(TformC,Tdata.trainC,"SP500"),
+                                     do.call("workflowVariants",
+                                             c(list("tradingWF",
+                                                    varsRootName=paste0(lrn,"Class"),
+                                                    quotes="GSPC",
+                                                    learner=lrn,
+                                                    pred.target="signals"),
+                                               VARS[[lrn]],
+                                               VARS$learning,
+                                               VARS$trading)
+                                             ),
+                                     EST.TASK,
+                                     cluster=TRUE) # for parallel computation
+                     )
+        save(list=objName,file=paste(objName,'Rdata',sep='.'))
+ }
```

The first part of the above code (before the first **for** loop) sets up a series of data structures holding information on: (i) the learning systems that will be tried; (ii) the estimation experiment to be carried out; and (iii) the different variants of the workflow parameters that are to be considered. This last item is obviously far from exhaustive and many more alternatives could have been considered. In terms of learners we considered SVMs, MARS and ANNs (again just for illustrative purposes). Regarding experimental settings we used 20 repetitions of a Monte Carlo experiment with 10 years ($\sim$ 2540 daily sessions) of data used for model development and the subsequent 5 years ($\sim$ 1270 daily sessions) for testing. Note that we specify our previously defined **tradingEval()** function to be used for calculating the evaluation metrics that we are estimating with the experiment.

The first **for** loop runs the experiments for the workflows based on regression models, i.e. models that try to forecast the T indicator. We run them in a loop to separate the calls to each learner. This is done purely due to computation reasons. As the code takes too long to run we want to avoid some problem with one of the learners to "abort" all experiments. This way we run one learner at a time and at the end of each learner we save its results in a separate file[19]. After finishing this loop we will have 3 files named "smv_res_regr.Rdata", "earth_res_regr.Rdata" and "nnet_res_regr.Rdata". Note that these file names and the objects they store (whose name is the same without the extension) were obtained programmatically from the content of the variable that controls the loop (`lrn`). Because of this the assignment that stores the results of the call to `performanceEstimation()` is also "special". The left side of an assignment operator must contain the name of the variable where to store the content calculated in the right side. However, in this case the name of this variable is contained in a variable (`objName`) that was constructed programmatically. In this context, we need to resort to function `assign()` to carry out the assignment. This function allows us to specify the name of the left side as the content of another variable (`objName` in our case). Also noteworthy is the call to the function `workflowVariants()` that generates the different variants of the workflows to be considered for each learner. Again this is done programmatically through the function `do.call()` that allows us to "construct" the call to any function. In this case we are using this function to "attach" the proper arguments to the `workflowVariants()` call. These calls to `workflowVariants()` will generate a large set of workflow variants (and thus the high computational cost of this code that we have mentioned above). For instance, for the SVM we will have 3×2 parameter variants, but each of these 6 variants is then combined with 3 learning variants and $2 \times 2 \times 2 \times 2$ trading variants, for a total of 288 workflows involving SVMs in regression tasks. Each of these 288 workflows is applied 20 times with different train and test data splits. And this is just SVM for regression! So, you are probably starting to understand why this code takes a bit long to run. You may have noticed that we are calling the function `performanceEstimation()` with a fourth argument: `cluster=TRUE`. This optional parameter allows you to use some of the parallel computation facilities of R. In this case, the computational speed-ups will come from running the different repetitions of the Monte Carlo experiment in parallel on each of the cores of your local CPU (assuming you have a multi-core machine which is rather standard nowadays). There are other possible configurations, like for instance using clusters of computers. Check the documentation of package **performanceEstimation** for more information on these ways of trying to speed-up large experimental comparisons.

In spite of the large set of alternatives we are considering, we should remark that this is a tiny sample of all possibilities of tuning that we have mentioned during the description of our approach to this problem. There were far too many "small" decisions where we could have followed other paths (e.g., the buy/sell thresholds, other learning systems, etc.). This means that any serious attempt at this domain of application will require massive computation resources to carry out a proper model selection. This is clearly outside the scope of this book. Our aim here is to provide the reader with proper methodological guidance and not to help find the best trading system for this particular data.

The second `for` loop follows the same structure but for the approaches that directly forecast the trading signals through a classification model. This requires a slight change on the neural network parameters and it also means skipping the MARS models that are not directly applicable to classification tasks.

---

[19]We could even run the code for each learner on different computers.

5.6.3 Results Analysis

The code provided in the previous section generates five data files with the objects containing the results of all variants involving the five learning approaches we have tried. These data files are named "svm_res_regr.Rdata", "svm_res_class.Rdata", "earth_res_regr.Rdata", "nnet_res_regr.Rdata", and "nnet_res_class.Rdata". Each of them contains an object with the same name as the file, except for the extension. These objects are the result of running the function `performanceEstimation()` and thus are of class **ComparisonResults**. Package **performanceEstimation** contains several functions that can be used to explore the results they store.

Because you probably did not run the experiments yourself, you can find the files on the book web page. Download them to your current working directory in your computer and then use the following commands to load the objects into R:

```
> load("svm_res_regr.Rdata")
> load("nnet_res_regr.Rdata")
> load("earth_res_regr.Rdata")
> load("svm_res_class.Rdata")
> load("nnet_res_class.Rdata")
> allResults <- mergeEstimationRes(svm_res_regr, earth_res_regr, nnet_res_regr,
+                                  svm_res_class, nnet_res_class,
+                                  by="workflows")
> rm(svm_res_regr, earth_res_regr, nnet_res_regr, svm_res_class, nnet_res_class)
```

After loading each of the individual **ComparisonResults** objects that resulted from the experiments we have carried out, we merge them into a single object containing the results of all workflows with the function **mergeEstimationRes()**. This is possible because the individual objects share the same structure, with the exception of the workflows involved, i.e. they use the same estimation procedure to obtain scores of the same metrics, on the same tasks. In this context, we merge them by workflows. The function also allows other types of merges, for instance of objects where we have the same workflows ran separately on different tasks (though using the same estimation procedure and metrics) and then merge them by tasks. After merging the objects we may spare some computer memory by removing the individual objects using function **rm()**.

For each trading system variant, we have measured several statistics of performance. Some are related to the performance in terms of predicting the correct signals, while others are related to the economic performance when using these signals to trade. Deciding which are the best models according to our experiments involves a balance between all these scores. The selected model(s) may vary depending on which criteria we value the most.

We are going to select a few of them as more important for us and then use them as the main criteria for comparing the models. Obviously, other selections would be possible and would probably lead to other conclusions in terms of model selection. Among the signal prediction statistics, precision is clearly more important than recall for this application. In effect, precision has to do with the predicted signals, and these drive the trading decisions as they are the causes for opening positions. Low precision scores are caused by wrong signals, which means opening positions at the wrong timings. This will most surely lead to high losses. Recall does not have this cost potential. Recall measures the ability of the models to capture trading opportunities. If this score is low, it means lost opportunities, but not high costs caused by wrong decisions. In this context, we will be particularly interested in the scores of the models for metric "prec.sb", which measures the overall precision of the buy and sell signals. Still, we must remember that according to our trading policies (outlined in Section 5.5.1) not all trading signals will be used, particularly for the first policy, so the precision scores may not be too high and still reasonable economic results are obtained.

In terms of economic performance, the return of the systems is important (metric named "Ret" in our experiments), as well as the return over the buy and hold strategy ("RetOverBH" in our experiments). Also important is the percentage of profitable trades, which should be clearly above 50% (metric "PercProf"). In terms of risk analysis, it is relevant to look at both the value of the Sharpe Ratio and the Maximum Draw-Down ("MaxDD").

The function `summary()` can be applied to the `ComparisonResults` objects. However, given the number of workflows and performance metrics, the output would be overwhelming in this case.

An alternative is to use the function `rankWorkflows()` provided by the package **performanceEstimation**. With this function we can obtain the top workflows for the evaluation metrics in which we are interested:

```
> tgtStats <- c('NTrades','prec.sb','Ret','RetOverBH','PercProf',
+               'MaxDD','SharpeRatio')
> toMax <- c(rep(TRUE,5),FALSE,TRUE)
> rankWorkflows(subset(allResults,
+                      metrics=tgtStats,
+                      partial=FALSE),
+               top=3,
+               maxs=toMax)
```

```
$SP500
$SP500$NTrades
      Workflow Estimate
1  svmRegr.v24   985.35
2 svmRegr.v168   960.15
3  svmRegr.v23   958.95

$SP500$prec.sb
       Workflow  Estimate
1  nnetClass.v1 0.3199433
2 nnetClass.v19 0.3199433
3 nnetClass.v37 0.3199433

$SP500$Ret
       Workflow Estimate
1 svmRegr.v138 155.1225
2  svmRegr.v60  82.7015
3 svmRegr.v204  81.3495

$SP500$RetOverBH
       Workflow Estimate
1 svmRegr.v138  63.1045
2  svmRegr.v60  -9.3155
3 svmRegr.v204 -10.6670

$SP500$PercProf
       Workflow Estimate
1 nnetRegr.v169   63.876
2 nnetRegr.v175   62.751
3 nnetRegr.v176   62.640

$SP500$MaxDD
```

```
        Workflow Estimate
1    nnetClass.v1 12594.36
2   nnetClass.v73 12594.36
3  nnetClass.v145 12594.36


$SP500$SharpeRatio
        Workflow Estimate
1  nnetRegr.v177    0.0400
2  nnetRegr.v167    0.0395
3  nnetRegr.v171    0.0385
```

The function subset() can be applied to **ComparisonResults** objects to select a part of the information stored in these objects. In this case we are selecting only a subset of the estimated metrics. Note the use of partial=FALSE. This makes the subset function match the exact name of the statistics. Without it the function uses partial matching and we could eventually catch other metrics with similar names. Finally, we use the function rankWorkflows() to obtain the top three scores among all trading systems for the metrics we have selected. The notion of best score varies with each metric. Sometimes we want the largest values, while for others we want the lowest values. This can be set up by the parameter maxs of function rankWorkflows(), which lets you specify the metrics for which best means maximum possible score.

The first thing we notice when looking at these top three results is that all of them involve either the svm or nnet algorithm, and most of them regression approaches, i.e. approaches that first predict the T indicator instead of predicting directly the signal. The exceptions occur on the precision of the signals and on the maximum draw down metrics, where the classification approaches emerge as the best. If we are curious about the characteristics of any workflow we may use function getWorkflow() by providing its name in the first argument and the name of the object with the experiments results in the second:

```
> getWorkflow("svmRegr.v138",analysisSet)

Workflow Object:
Workflow ID        ::   svmRegr.v138
Workflow Function ::   tradingWF
     Parameter values:
 learner.pars  ->   cost=150 gamma=0.05
 policy.pars   ->   bet=0.5 exp.prof=0.0  ...
 quotes   ->  GSPC
 learner  ->  svm
 pred.target  ->  indicator
 learn.test.type  ->  slide
 relearn.step  ->  120
 policy  ->  policy.2
 b.t  ->   0.05
 s.t  ->  -0.01
```

With the goal of making our results analysis more manageable we will create a new **ComparisonResults** object with only a subset of the workflows, namely the top 100 workflows according to the previously mentioned main metrics:

```
> best <- rankWorkflows(subset(allResults,
+                      metrics=tgtStats,
+                      partial=FALSE),
```

```
+                   top=100,
+                   maxs=toMax)
> bestWFs <- unique(as.vector(sapply(best$SP500,function(x) x$Workflow)))
> analysisSet <- subset(allResults, workflows=bestWFs, partial=FALSE)
> rm(allResults)
```

Let us take a closer look at the best performers for each of the more important metrics:

```
> (tps <- topPerformers(subset(analysisSet,metrics=tgtStats,partial=FALSE),
+                       maxs=toMax))
```

```
$SP500
                   Workflow  Estimate
NTrades         svmRegr.v24    985.35
prec.sb         nnetClass.v1      0.32
Ret            svmRegr.v138   155.123
RetOverBH      svmRegr.v138    63.104
PercProf        nnetRegr.v169   63.876
MaxDD          nnetClass.v1 12594.359
SharpeRatio    nnetRegr.v177      0.04
```

Function `topPerformers()` gives us a table with the best workflows for each metric. We can use this information to obtain more detailed information about these workflows on some of the metrics.

```
> summary(subset(analysisSet,
+                workflows=tps$SP500[c("prec.sb","Ret","PercProf","MaxDD"),
+                "Workflow"],
+                metrics=tgtStats[-c(1,4,7)],
+                partial=FALSE))
```

```
== Summary of a  Monte Carlo Performance Estimation Experiment ==

Task for estimating all metrics of the selected evaluation function using
20  repetitions Monte Carlo Simulation using:
 seed =  1234
 train size =  2540  cases
 test size =  1270  cases

* Predictive Tasks ::  SP500
* Workflows  ::  nnetClass.v1, svmRegr.v138, nnetRegr.v169, nnetClass.v1

-> Task:  SP500
  *Workflow: nnetClass.v1
            prec.sb       Ret PercProf      MaxDD
avg       0.3199433  0.198500  21.7040  12594.36
std       0.2134790  2.048353  28.8249  20844.75
med       0.2329298  0.000000   0.0000      0.00
iqr       0.2459596  0.000000  43.5525  16435.03
min       0.0000000 -4.180000   0.0000      0.00
max       0.6250000  6.280000  75.0000  64942.07
invalid  12.0000000  0.000000   0.0000      0.00

  *Workflow: svmRegr.v138
```

```
          prec.sb       Ret  PercProf      MaxDD
avg     0.22493318  155.1225  52.384500  2081116.6
std     0.06968098  390.1813   4.616856  1352582.7
med     0.21721373   16.3600  51.975000  1652147.9
iqr     0.08365744  195.7275   7.060000  1439520.3
min     0.10979548  -92.3400  45.860000   789925.2
max     0.35475352 1519.3300  62.350000  6537727.0
invalid 0.00000000    0.0000   0.000000        0.0


   *Workflow: nnetRegr.v169
          prec.sb       Ret  PercProf     MaxDD
avg     0.29545145   25.83700  63.87600  248605.8
std     0.09640889   31.57113  10.47377  158502.6
med     0.33147567   21.38500  66.22500  235386.7
iqr     0.15400154   37.89000  12.34750  175996.6
min     0.11247803  -45.33000  40.25000   69260.9
max     0.41073826   77.11000  77.50000  601398.2
invalid 0.00000000    0.00000   0.00000       0.0


   *Workflow: nnetClass.v1
          prec.sb       Ret  PercProf      MaxDD
avg     0.3199433   0.198500  21.7040   12594.36
std     0.2134790   2.048353  28.8249   20844.75
med     0.2329298   0.000000   0.0000       0.00
iqr     0.2459596   0.000000  43.5525   16435.03
min     0.0000000  -4.180000   0.0000       0.00
max     0.6250000   6.280000  75.0000   64942.07
invalid 12.0000000  0.000000   0.0000       0.00
```

As you can observe, most of these workflows achieve good performance on one of the metrics but then are disappointing on others. For instance, while "svmRegr.v138" is the best in terms of average return it achieves bad scores in terms of maximum draw down and precision of the signals. Moreover, even in terms of return the results are rather unstable across the different repetitions with a very high variance (and actually the median return is significantly lower than the average return).

In this context, we will add some constraints on some of the metrics for a workflow to be considered as a reasonable candidate solution. Moreover, given the observed instability of the performance over the different repetitions, we will carry out our model selection looking at the median performance instead of the mean, as the former is more robust to outlying scores in some of the repetitions. In terms of constraints, we will require a minimum of 120 trades (roughly two per month on the 5 years testing periods) for a workflow to be considered. Then we will look at the return and percentage of profitable trades and will select the top 15 in terms of these metrics. Finally, we will select a small set of workflows that are either in the top 3 of one of these metrics or are part of the top 15 of both. Here is the code for finding these workflows:

```
> ms <- metricsSummary(subset(analysisSet,
+                          metrics=c("NTrades","Ret","PercProf"),
+                          partial=FALSE),
+                   summary="median")[["SP500"]]
> candidates <- subset(analysisSet,
+                 workflows=colnames(ms)[which(ms["NTrades",] > 120)],
+                 partial=FALSE)
> ms <- metricsSummary(subset(candidates,
```

```
+                            metrics=c("Ret","PercProf"),
+                            partial=FALSE),
+                    summary="median")[["SP500"]]
> (sms <- apply(ms,1,function(x) names(x[order(x,decreasing=TRUE)][1:15])))

        Ret              PercProf
 [1,] "nnetRegr.v200" "nnetRegr.v169"
 [2,] "svmRegr.v168"  "nnetRegr.v167"
 [3,] "svmRegr.v204"  "nnetRegr.v179"
 [4,] "svmRegr.v102"  "nnetRegr.v177"
 [5,] "svmRegr.v30"   "svmRegr.v169"
 [6,] "svmRegr.v24"   "svmRegr.v175"
 [7,] "svmRegr.v174"  "nnetRegr.v203"
 [8,] "nnetRegr.v211" "nnetRegr.v175"
 [9,] "nnetRegr.v213" "nnetRegr.v176"
[10,] "svmRegr.v60"   "nnetRegr.v205"
[11,] "nnetRegr.v202" "nnetRegr.v172"
[12,] "svmRegr.v246"  "nnetRegr.v173"
[13,] "svmRegr.v36"   "nnetRegr.v178"
[14,] "nnetRegr.v175" "nnetRegr.v213"
[15,] "nnetRegr.v203" "nnetRegr.v215"

> (winners <- unique(c(intersect(sms[,1],sms[,2]),sms[1:3,1],sms[1:3,2])))

[1] "nnetRegr.v213" "nnetRegr.v175" "nnetRegr.v203" "nnetRegr.v200"
[5] "svmRegr.v168"  "svmRegr.v204"  "nnetRegr.v169" "nnetRegr.v167"
[9] "nnetRegr.v179"

> winnersResults <- subset(analysisSet,
+                          metrics=tgtStats,workflows=winners,
+                          partial=FALSE)
```

We have used the function `metricsSummary()` to obtain the median score for the metrics we have chosen to filter the best workflows. We do a first filtering step on the number of trades (minimum of 120), creating object `candidates`. Then we proceed to obtain the names of the top 15 in terms of median return or median percentage of profitable trades. Finally, we do the last filtering selecting the best three on each of these two metrics and also all workflows that are part of the best 15 on both these two metrics, which leads to 9 selected workflows, all using a regression approach to the problem.

If we apply the summary function to the `winnersResults` object we may notice that when compared to the basic Buy and Hold strategy the results are rather disappointing. Moreover, all 9 approaches achieved a negative return on at least one of the repetitions (all minimum returns are negative). This means that overall even these best workflows do not seem very promising and are a bit risky in terms of using them for investment decisions. In a realistic scenario the recommendation from this model selection stage should be not to use any of these models.

Nevertheless, we can identify a few workflows that are more interesting than the others, depending on the profile of the investors. If they follow a more risky strategy they may eventually prefer "nnetRegr.v200" or "svmRegr.v168", that have more interesting performance in terms of return. More conservative decision makers may prefer "nnetRegr.v175" or "nnetRegr.v169", both showing a more consistent performance in terms of percentage of profitable trades and maximum draw down.

It is also worth considering the question of whether the differences between these workflows and the remaining alternatives are statistically significant or not. Let us first check whether the apparent advantage of "nnetRegr.v200" in terms of return is statistically significant:

```
> p <- pairedComparisons(winnersResults,baseline="nnetRegr.v200",maxs=toMax)
> p$Ret$WilcoxonSignedRank.test

, , SP500

              MedScore DiffMedScores   p.value
nnetRegr.v200  56.685            NA        NA
nnetRegr.v213  39.210        17.475 0.1893482
nnetRegr.v175  35.535        21.150 0.3883762
nnetRegr.v203  35.460        21.225 0.3883762
svmRegr.v168   49.105         7.580 0.6215134
svmRegr.v204   48.900         7.785 0.7011814
nnetRegr.v169  21.385        35.300 0.6476555
nnetRegr.v167  33.480        23.205 0.4090977
nnetRegr.v179  30.735        25.950 0.4980087
```

Function `pairedComparisons()` allows us to carry out a series of statistical tests based on the outcome of the experiments. Among these different tests, the one that is more adequate for our setup (one single predictive task with different workflows being applied to the same train+test partitions), is the Wilcoxon signed rank test (c.f. Section 3.5.4, page 181). We have specified "nnetRegr.v200" as the baseline model against which all others are compared (paired comparisons). The result of the function is a list with many components with the results of different tests for each metric. The second statement above presents the results of the Wilcoxon test. The first row shows the result (median value across the repetitions) of the baseline in terms of the selected metric (return). The remaining rows show the results of each alternative, the difference to the median score of the baseline and also the p-value of the paired comparison against that baseline. As we can observe these p values are too high which means that we can not reject the hypothesis that the performance of the other workflows is similar to that of the baseline.

We can carry out a similar test with the representative of the more conservative selection ("nnetRegr.v175"), looking this time at the maximum drawdown that is an important measure of the risk of the workflows,

```
> p <- pairedComparisons(winnersResults,"nnetRegr.v175",maxs=toMax)
> p$MaxDD$WilcoxonSignedRank.test

, , SP500

               MedScore DiffMedScores       p.value
nnetRegr.v175  190874.9            NA            NA
nnetRegr.v213  299346.4    -108471.47  1.678467e-04
nnetRegr.v203  402566.6    -211691.76  8.506775e-04
nnetRegr.v200  550732.9    -359857.96  4.768372e-05
svmRegr.v168   429145.4    -238270.56  7.076263e-04
svmRegr.v204   777845.6    -586970.71  1.335144e-05
nnetRegr.v169  235386.7     -44511.78  8.983173e-01
nnetRegr.v167  289129.3     -98254.37  3.998947e-02
nnetRegr.v179  250383.0     -59508.14  3.117943e-01
```

As we can observe there are several statistically significant differences. We can use the `signifDiffs()` function to filter the results of the `pairedComparisons()` function, showing only the differences above a certain confidence,

```
> sds <- signifDiffs(p,p.limit=0.05,metrics="MaxDD")
> sds$MaxDD$WilcoxonSignedRank.test$SP500

              MedScore DiffMedScores     p.value
nnetRegr.v175 190874.9            NA          NA
nnetRegr.v213 299346.4    -108471.47 1.678467e-04
nnetRegr.v203 402566.6    -211691.76 8.506775e-04
nnetRegr.v200 550732.9    -359857.96 4.768372e-05
svmRegr.v168  429145.4    -238270.56 7.076263e-04
svmRegr.v204  777845.6    -586970.71 1.335144e-05
nnetRegr.v167 289129.3     -98254.37 3.998947e-02
```

The outcome of this function tells us that this workflow is significantly better than most of the other workflows in terms of maximum drawdown.

Let us check the characteristics of these two workflows that are based both on a regression approach using neural networks,

```
> getWorkflow("nnetRegr.v200", winnersResults)

Workflow Object:
Workflow ID        ::  nnetRegr.v200
Workflow Function ::  tradingWF
     Parameter values:
 learner.pars  -> linout=TRUE maxit=750 size=10 decay=0.001
 policy.pars  -> bet=0.5 exp.prof=0.05 max.loss=0.05
 quotes  -> GSPC
 learner  -> nnet
 pred.target  -> indicator
 learn.test.type  -> fixed
 relearn.step  -> 120
 policy  -> policy.2
 b.t  -> 0.01
 s.t  -> -0.05
```

```
> getWorkflow("nnetRegr.v175", winnersResults)

Workflow Object:
Workflow ID        ::  nnetRegr.v175
Workflow Function ::  tradingWF
     Parameter values:
 learner.pars  -> linout=TRUE maxit=750 size=5 decay=0.001
 policy.pars  -> bet=0.2 exp.prof=0.05 max.loss=0.05
 quotes  -> GSPC
 learner  -> nnet
 pred.target  -> indicator
 learn.test.type  -> grow
 relearn.step  -> 120
 policy  -> policy.2
 b.t  -> 0.01
 s.t  -> -0.05
```

As we can observe, both use the same trading policy function ("policy.2") with the same buy and sell thresholds. However, while one uses a fixed model strategy, i.e. applying a single model over all testing window, the other uses a growing window strategy.

In summary, given these results, particularly the lack of statistical significance of the observed differences, the outcome of this model selection stage should be either to give up on these models or to invest more time on model tuning to try to obtain workflows with more convincing results. Given the scope of this book and the main objectives of this case study we will skip this further tuning step and will select two workflows for the final test on the 10 years we have left apart with this goal. The idea is to trade using these systems that represent two different trader profiles (more or less risky) in this final period. Workflow "nnetRegr.v200" will be used as the representative of a more risky attitude with the goal of trying to maximize return, while "nnetRegr.v175" will be selected as more adequate for a more conservative trader in terms of risk.

5.7   The Trading System

This section presents the results obtained by the "best" models in the final evaluation period, which was left out of the model comparison and selection stages. This period is formed by 10 years of quotes, and we will apply the selected workflows to trade during this period using our simulator.

5.7.1   Evaluation of the Final Test Data

In order to apply any of the selected workflows to the evaluation period, we need the last 10 years before this evaluation period. The reason is that all workflows were obtained using 10 years of data so we want to have for this final test similar conditions as the ones used for model selection. This means that the models associated with the workflows will be obtained with these 10 years of data before the start of the evaluation period and then will be asked to make their signal predictions for this latter period. These predictions may actually involve obtaining more models in the case of workflows using windowing schemes.

The following code obtains the evaluation statistics of all 9 workflows we have identified as the best in the previous section. This is just for illustration purposes as the model selection stage has identified just two of these as our best bets, so in principle we would apply only these two during a real test,

```
> set.seed(1234)
> data <- tail(Tdata.train, 2540) # the last 10 years of the training dataset
> results <- list()
> wfsOut <- list()
> for (name in winners) {
+     sys <- getWorkflow(name, analysisSet)
+     wfsOut[[name]] <- runWorkflow(sys, Tform, data, Tdata.eval)
+     results[[name]] <- do.call("tradingEval",wfsOut[[name]])
+ }
> results <- t(as.data.frame(results))
```

We start by obtaining the data to be used for training the models (i.e. the last 10 years of the training set). We then loop over the best workflows and apply them using this training data and testing on the evaluation period (`Tdata.eval`). This is done using the function `runWorkflow()` that can be used to apply a workflow to a prediction task which is identified

by a formula, a training set, and a test set. After obtaining the result of this application
we use it to calculate our metrics by means of the function **tradingEval()**. In the end of
the loop we transform the list containing the results of all workflows into a data frame for
easier visualization. Let us inspect the values of some of the main statistics:

```
> results[, c("NTrades","Ret","RetOverBH","PercProf","MaxDD")]

              NTrades    Ret RetOverBH PercProf      MaxDD
nnetRegr.v213     436 -18.45    -69.94    53.21   471735.8
nnetRegr.v175     579  16.82    -34.66    50.43   410526.5
nnetRegr.v203     666  68.94     17.45    56.31   769322.9
nnetRegr.v200     537 -63.82   -115.31    51.21   836981.2
svmRegr.v168     1473 -36.99    -88.47    50.58   570007.6
svmRegr.v204      997 -79.07   -130.56    50.15  1062361.4
nnetRegr.v169     518 -32.13    -83.61    45.75   385862.8
nnetRegr.v167     548 -15.12    -66.61    49.64   289180.9
nnetRegr.v179     541   8.97    -42.52    56.93   408308.2
```

As you can confirm, only three of the workflows obtain a positive return over this 10
year evaluation period. Moreover, the workflow our model selection process has identified
as the best in terms of return ("nnetRegr.v200") has obtained bad results from all possible
perspectives. Still, the results of the more conservative workflow ("nnetRegr.v175") were
more reasonable. This somehow confirms the uncertainty we have identified in the model
selection stage, with differences not being statistically significant and high variances across
the different repetitions of the process.

Among the selected workflows "nnetRegr.v203" achieved the best scores on this evaluation period. Here are its characteristics:

```
> getWorkflow("nnetRegr.v203", analysisSet)

Workflow Object:
Workflow ID        ::   nnetRegr.v203
Workflow Function ::    tradingWF
     Parameter values:
 learner.pars  -> linout=TRUE maxit=750 size=5 decay=0.1
 policy.pars   -> bet=0.5 exp.prof=0.05 max.loss=0.05
 quotes   -> GSPC
 learner   -> nnet
 pred.target  -> indicator
 learn.test.type  -> fixed
 relearn.step  -> 120
 policy  -> policy.2
 b.t   -> 0.01
 s.t   -> -0.05
```

This workflow is very similar to "nnetRegr.v200". It also uses "policy.2", and has similar
characteristics in terms of learning parameters (for instance, it also uses a fixed window).
Yet, the results on this 10 year testing period are considerably different showing how small
details may result on a big difference on this application. In effect, timing is key in this
domain and a difference of a single trading signal may have a large economic impact.

We will now illustrate how we can proceed with a deeper analysis of the performance of
this best trading system across the evaluation period.

Figure 5.7 plots the trading record of the system during the evaluation period, and was
obtained as follows:

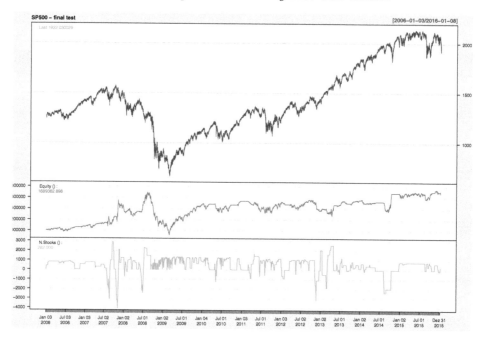

FIGURE 5.7: The results on the final evaluation period of the "nnetRegr.v203" workflow.

```
> date <- rownames(Tdata.eval)[1]
> market <- GSPC[paste(date, "/", sep = "")][1:nrow(Tdata.eval), ]
> plot(wfsOut[["nnetRegr.v203"]]$tradeRec, market,
+        theme = "white", name = "SP500 - final test")
```

The analysis of Figure 5.7 reveals that the system was very active during all trading period, and with the exception of the period of the 2008 crash, its results were mostly interesting. It is also interesting to note that in spite of a fast growing market a large part of the time, the workflow has managed to obtain better performance than the buy and hold strategy.

The package **PerformanceAnalytics**(Carl and Peterson, 2014) provides an overwhelming set of tools for analyzing the performance of any trading system. Here we provide a glance at some of these tools to obtain better insight into the performance of our trading system. The tools of this package work on the returns of the strategy under evaluation. The returns of our strategy can be obtained as follows:

```
> library(PerformanceAnalytics)
> equityWF <- as.xts(wfsOut[["nnetRegr.v203"]]$tradeRec@trading$Equity)
> rets <- Return.calculate(equityWF)
```

Please note that the function **Return.calculate()** does not calculate the percentage returns we have been using up to now, yet these returns are equivalent to ours by a factor of 100.

Figure 5.8 shows the cumulative returns of the strategy across all testing period. The figure was obtained using

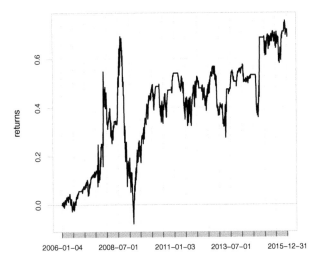

Cumulative returns of the strategy

FIGURE 5.8: The cumulative returns on the final evaluation period of the "nnetRegr.v203" system.

```
> chart.CumReturns(rets, main="Cumulative returns of the workflow", ylab = "returns")
```

With very short exceptions the workflow consistently achieves positive cumulative returns during all 10 years.

It is frequently useful to obtain information regarding the returns on an annual or even monthly basis. The package **PerformanceAnalytics** provides some tools to help with this type of analysis, namely, the function `yearlyReturn()`:

```
> yearlyReturn(equityWF)
```

```
           yearly.returns
2006-12-29     0.07006971
2007-12-31     0.33175485
2008-12-31    -0.18488113
2009-12-31     0.25897205
2010-12-31     0.05322307
2011-12-30    -0.02519987
2012-12-31    -0.08888908
2013-12-31     0.14347341
2014-12-31     0.06562536
2015-12-31     0.02583409
2016-01-08    -0.01205078
```

As we can see, in spite of the overall interesting return, the fact is that this system had negative returns on 3 years (the last negative value is irrelevant given that very few days have passed from 2016). Moreover, two of these years were consecutive (2011 and 2012), which is not very good, as most investors would be "scared" by such performance of a trading system.

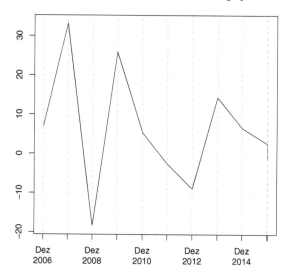

FIGURE 5.9: Yearly percentage returns of the "nnetRegr.v203" system.

Figure 5.9 presents this information graphically and it was obtained as follows,

```
> plot(100*yearlyReturn(equityWF),
+       main='Yearly percentage returns of the trading system')
```

The package **PerformanceAnalytics** also includes similar functions for other type of periodicity (e.g. monthly returns).

Finally, we present an illustration of some of the tools provided by the package **PerformanceAnalytics** concerning the risk analysis of the strategy using the function `table.DownsideRisk()`:

```
> table.DownsideRisk(rets)
```

	NA
Semi Deviation	0.0061
Gain Deviation	0.0086
Loss Deviation	0.0089
Downside Deviation (MAR=210%)	0.0113
Downside Deviation (Rf=0%)	0.0061
Downside Deviation (0%)	0.0061
Maximum Drawdown	0.4144
Historical VaR (95%)	-0.0139
Historical ES (95%)	-0.0230
Modified VaR (95%)	-0.0099
Modified ES (95%)	-0.0099

This function returns information on several risk measures, among which we find the percentage maximum draw-down, and also the semi-deviation that is currently accepted as a better risk measure than the more frequent Sharpe ratio. More information on these statistics can be found on the help pages of the package **PerformanceAnalytics**.

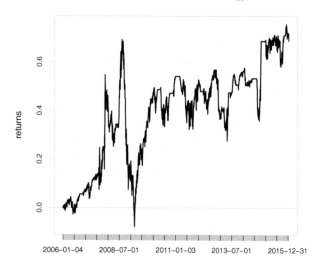

FIGURE 5.8: The cumulative returns on the final evaluation period of the "nnetRegr.v203" system.

```
> chart.CumReturns(rets, main="Cumulative returns of the workflow", ylab = "returns")
```

With very short exceptions the workflow consistently achieves positive cumulative returns during all 10 years.

It is frequently useful to obtain information regarding the returns on an annual or even monthly basis. The package **PerformanceAnalytics** provides some tools to help with this type of analysis, namely, the function `yearlyReturn()`:

```
> yearlyReturn(equityWF)
```

	yearly.returns
2006-12-29	0.07006971
2007-12-31	0.33175485
2008-12-31	-0.18488113
2009-12-31	0.25897205
2010-12-31	0.05322307
2011-12-30	-0.02519987
2012-12-31	-0.08888908
2013-12-31	0.14347341
2014-12-31	0.06562536
2015-12-31	0.02583409
2016-01-08	-0.01205078

As we can see, in spite of the overall interesting return, the fact is that this system had negative returns on 3 years (the last negative value is irrelevant given that very few days have passed from 2016). Moreover, two of these years were consecutive (2011 and 2012), which is not very good, as most investors would be "scared" by such performance of a trading system.

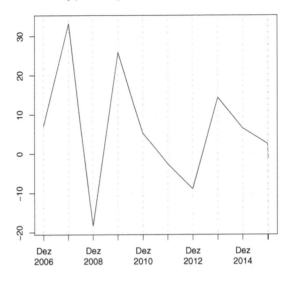

FIGURE 5.9: Yearly percentage returns of the "nnetRegr.v203" system.

Figure 5.9 presents this information graphically and it was obtained as follows,

```
> plot(100*yearlyReturn(equityWF),
+       main='Yearly percentage returns of the trading system')
```

The package **PerformanceAnalytics** also includes similar functions for other type of periodicity (e.g. monthly returns).

Finally, we present an illustration of some of the tools provided by the package **PerformanceAnalytics** concerning the risk analysis of the strategy using the function `table.DownsideRisk()`:

```
> table.DownsideRisk(rets)
```

	NA
Semi Deviation	0.0061
Gain Deviation	0.0086
Loss Deviation	0.0089
Downside Deviation (MAR=210%)	0.0113
Downside Deviation (Rf=0%)	0.0061
Downside Deviation (0%)	0.0061
Maximum Drawdown	0.4144
Historical VaR (95%)	-0.0139
Historical ES (95%)	-0.0230
Modified VaR (95%)	-0.0099
Modified ES (95%)	-0.0099

This function returns information on several risk measures, among which we find the percentage maximum draw-down, and also the semi-deviation that is currently accepted as a better risk measure than the more frequent Sharpe ratio. More information on these statistics can be found on the help pages of the package **PerformanceAnalytics**.

Overall, the analysis we have carried out shows that the best workflows according to our model selection process performed generally bad on the 10 years of the final evaluation period. The single exception was workflow "nnetRegr.v203" that achieved a more reasonable performance, although nothing particularly remarkable. Still, we must say that this was expected. This is a rather difficult problem with far too many variants/possibilities, some of which we have illustrated in this chapter. It would be rather surprising if the small set of possibilities we have tried led to a highly successful trading system.[20] This was not the goal of this case study. Our goal was to provide the reader with procedures that are methodologically sound, and not to carry out an in-depth search for the best trading system using these methodologies.

5.7.2 An Online Trading System

Let us suppose we are happy with the trading system we have developed. How could we use it in real-time to trade on the market? In this section we present a brief sketch of a system with this functionality.

The mechanics of the system we are proposing here are the following. At the end of each day, the system will be automatically called. The system should (1) obtain whichever new data is available, (2) carry out any modeling steps that it may require, and (3) generate a set of orders as output of its call.

Let us assume that the code of the system we want to develop is to be stored on a script file named "trader.R". The method to call this program at the end of each day depends on the operating system you are using. On Unix-based systems there is usually a table named "crontab" to which we can add entries with programs that should be run on a regular basis by the operating system. Editing this table can be done at the command line by issuing the command:

```
shell> crontab -e
```

The syntax of the entries in this table is reasonably simple and is formed by a set of fields that describe the periodicity and finally the command to run. Below you can find an example that should run our "trader.R" program every weekday by 19:00:

```
0 19 * * 1-5 /usr/bin/R --vanilla --quiet < /home/xpto/trader.R
```

The first two entries represent the minute and the hour. The third and fourth are the day of the month and month, respectively, and an asterisk means that the program should be run for all instances of these fields. The fifth entry is the weekday, with a 1 representing Mondays, and the '-' allowing for the specification of intervals. Finally, we have the program to be run that in this case is a call to R with the source code of our trader.

The general algorithm to be implemented in the "trader.R" program is the following:

```
- Read in the current state of the trader
- Get all new data available
- Check if it is necessary to re-learn the model (e.g. windowing approaches)
- Obtain the predicted signal for today
- With this signal, call the policy function to obtain the orders
- Output the orders of today
```

The current state of the trader should be a set of data structures that stores information

---

[20]And it would also be surprising if we were to publish such a system!

that is required to be memorized across the daily runs of the trader. In our case this should include the current neural network model, the learning parameters and the training data used to obtain the model and the associated data model specification, the "age" of the model (important to know when to re-learn it if using a windowing strategy), and the information on the trading record of the system until today, as well as its currently open positions. Please note that the information on the open positions needs to be updated from outside the system as it is the market that drives the timings for opening and closing positions, contrary to our simulator where we assumed that all orders are accomplished at the beginning of the next day. This means that there must be another script program that will change the current state of the trader as a result of the orders that are executed in the "real" market (things like the actual price at which an order was carried out, etc.).

Getting the new available data is easy if we have the data model specification. Function `getModelData()` can be used to refresh our dataset with the most recent quotes, as mentioned in Section 5.3.2.

The model will need to be re-learned if the age goes above the `relearn.step` parameter that should be memorized in conjunction with all model parameters.

Finally, we have to get a prediction for the signal of today. This means calling the `predict()` function with the current model to obtain a prediction for the last row of the training set, that is, today. Having this prediction, we can call the trading policy function with the proper parameters to obtain the set of orders to output for today. This should be the final result of the program.

This brief sketch should provide you with sufficient information for implementing such an online trading system.

5.8 Summary

The main goal of this chapter was to introduce the reader to a more real application of data mining. The concrete application that was described involved several new challenges, namely, (1) handling time series data, (2) dealing with a very dynamic system with possible changes of regime, and (3) moving from model predictions into concrete actions in the application domain.

In methodological terms we have introduced you to a few new topics:

- Time series modeling

- Handling regime shifts with windowing mechanisms

- Artificial neural networks

- Support vector machines

- Multivariate adaptive regression splines

- Evaluating time series models with the Monte Carlo method

- Several new evaluation statistics related either to the prediction of rare events or with financial trading performance

From the perspective of learning R we have illustrated

- How to handle time series data

- How to read data from different sources

- How to obtain several types of models (SVMs, ANNs, and MARS)

- How to use several packages specifically dedicated to financial modeling

- How to use package **performanceEstimation** to carry out large scale experimental comparisons between many different model variants

Chapter 6

Detecting Fraudulent Transactions

The third case study is an instance of the general problem of detecting unusual observations of a phenomena, that is, finding rare and quite different observations. The driving application has to do with transactions of a set of products that are reported by the salespeople of some company. The goal is to find "strange" transaction reports that may indicate fraud attempts by some of the salespeople. The outcome of the data mining process will support posterior auditing activities by the company. Given the limited amount of resources that can be allocated to this inspection activity, we want to provide a kind of fraud probability ranking as outcome of the process. These rankings should allow the company to apply its inspection resources in an optimal way. This general resource-bounded inspection activity is frequent in many fields, such as credit card transactions, tax declarations inspection, etc. This chapter addresses several new data mining tasks, namely, (1) outlier or anomaly detection, (2) clustering, and also (3) semi-supervised prediction models.

6.1   Problem Description and Objectives

Fraud detection is an important area for potential application of data mining techniques given the economic and social consequences that are usually associated with these illegal activities. From the perspective of data analysis, frauds are typically associated with unusual observations as these are activities that are supposed to be deviations from the norm. These deviations from normal behavior are frequently known as outliers in several data analysis disciplines. In effect, a standard definition of an outlier is that it is "an observation which deviates so much from other observations as to arouse suspicions that it was generated by a different mechanism" (Hawkins, 1980). Further information on methods for detecting anomalous observations in a dataset can be found in Section 3.4.4 (page 131).

The data we will be using in this case study refers to the transactions reported by the salespeople of some company. These salespeople sell a set of products of the company and report these sales with a certain periodicity. The data we have available concerns these reports over a short period of time. The salespeople are free to set the selling price according to their own policy and market. At the end of each month, they report back to the company their transactions. The goal of this data mining application is to help in the task of verifying the veracity of these reports given past experience of the company that has detected both errors and fraud attempts in these transaction reports. The help we provide will take the form of a ranking of the reports according to their probability of being fraudulent. This ranking will allow to allocate the limited inspection resources of the company to the reports that our system signals as being more "suspicious".

6.2   The Available Data

The data we have available is of an undisclosed source and has been anonymized. Each of the 401,146 rows of the data table includes information on one report by some salesman. This information includes his ID, the product ID, and the quantity and total value reported by the salesman. This data has already gone through some analysis at the company. The result of this analysis is shown in the last column, which has the outcome of the inspection of some transactions by the company. Summarizing, the dataset we will be using has the following columns:

- **ID** – a factor with the ID of the salesman.

- **Prod** – a factor indicating the ID of the sold product.

- **Quant** – the number of reported sold units of the product.

- **Val** – the reported total monetary value of the sale.

- **Insp** – a factor with three possible values: `ok` if the transaction was inspected and considered valid by the company, `fraud` if the transaction was found to be fraudulent, and `unkn` if the transaction was not inspected at all by the company.

6.2.1   Loading the Data into R

The dataset is available in our book package. To load it is enough to do:

```
> library(dplyr)
> data(sales, package="DMwR2")
```

The result is a (large) data frame table (*tibble*) named **sales** whose first few rows are shown below:

```
> sales

# A tibble: 401,146 × 5
        ID    Prod Quant    Val   Insp
     <fctr> <fctr> <int>  <dbl> <fctr>
1       v1     p1    182   1665   unkn
2       v2     p1   3072   8780   unkn
3       v3     p1  20393  76990   unkn
4       v4     p1    112   1100   unkn
5       v3     p1   6164  20260   unkn
6       v5     p2    104   1155   unkn
7       v6     p2    350   5680   unkn
8       v7     p2    200   4010   unkn
9       v8     p2    233   2855   unkn
10      v9     p2    118   1175   unkn
# ... with 401,136 more rows
```

6.2.2 Exploring the Dataset

To get an initial overview of the statistical properties of the data, we can use the function `summary()`:[1]

```
> summary(sales)
```

```
       ID              Prod             Quant                Val
 v431   : 10159   p1125  :  3923   Min.    :      100   Min.   :   1005
 v54    :  6017   p3774  :  1824   1st Qu.:      107   1st Qu.:   1345
 v426   :  3902   p1437  :  1720   Median :      168   Median :   2675
 v1679  :  3016   p1917  :  1702   Mean    :     8442   Mean   :  14617
 v1085  :  3001   p4089  :  1598   3rd Qu.:      738   3rd Qu.:   8680
 v1183  :  2642   p2742  :  1519   Max.    :473883883   Max.   :4642955
 (Other):372409   (Other):388860   NA's    :13842   NA's   :1182
   Insp
 ok   : 14462
 unkn :385414
 fraud:  1270
```

We have a significant number of products and salespeople, as we can confirm using the function `nlevels()`:

```
> nlevels(sales$ID)
```

```
[1] 6016
```

```
> nlevels(sales$Prod)
```

```
[1] 4548
```

The result of the `summary()` function reveals several important facts on this data. First there are a considerable number of unknown values in the columns `Quant` and `Val`. This can be particularly problematic if both happen at the same time, as this would represent a transaction report without the crucial information on the quantities involved in the sale. We can easily check if there are such situations:

```
> filter(sales,is.na(Quant),is.na(Val))
```

```
# A tibble: 888 × 5
      ID    Prod Quant   Val   Insp
   <fctr> <fctr> <int> <dbl> <fctr>
1    v29   p808    NA    NA   unkn
2   v453   p921    NA    NA   unkn
3   v431  p1035    NA    NA   unkn
4   v431     p1    NA    NA   unkn
5   v431     p1    NA    NA   unkn
6  v1039  p1101    NA    NA   unkn
7  v1158  p1101    NA    NA   unkn
```

[1]An interesting alternative can be obtained using the function `describe()` from the extra package `Hmisc`. Try it!

```
8     v1183  p1103    NA    NA    unkn
9      v709  p1125    NA    NA      ok
10     v426  p1190    NA    NA    unkn
# ... with 878 more rows
```

As you can see, this is a reasonable number of transactions. Given the large total amount of transactions, one can question whether it would not be better to simply delete these reports. We will consider this and other alternatives in Section 6.2.3.

Another interesting observation from the results of the `summary()` function is the distribution of the values in the inspection column. In effect, and as expected, the proportion of frauds is relatively low, even if we only take into account the reports that were inspected, which are also a small proportion overall:

```
> table(sales$Insp)/nrow(sales) * 100


      ok        unkn       fraud
 3.605171  96.078236    0.316593
```

Figure 6.1 shows the number of reports per salesperson. As you can confirm, the numbers are rather diverse across the salespeople. Figure 6.2 shows the same number but per product. Again we observe a strong variability. Both figures were obtained with the following code:

```
> library(ggplot2)
> ggplot(group_by(sales,ID) %>% summarize(nTrans=n()),aes(x=ID,y=nTrans)) +
+     geom_bar(stat="identity") +
+     theme(axis.text.x = element_blank(), axis.ticks.x=element_blank()) +
+     xlab("Salesmen") + ylab("Nr. of Transactions") +
+     ggtitle("Nr. of Transactions per Salesman")
> ggplot(group_by(sales,Prod) %>% summarize(nTrans=n()),aes(x=Prod,y=nTrans)) +
+     geom_bar(stat="identity") +
+     theme(axis.text.x = element_blank(), axis.ticks.x=element_blank()) +
+     xlab("Product") + ylab("Nr. of Transactions") +
+     ggtitle("Nr. of Transactions per Product")
```

The descriptive statistics of **Quant** and **Val** show a rather marked variability. This suggests that the products may be very different from each other and thus it may make sense to handle them separately. In effect, if the typical prices of the products are too different, then a transaction report can only be considered abnormal in the context of the reports of the same product. Still, these two quantities may not be the ideal ones from which to draw this conclusion. In effect, given the different quantity of products that are sold on each transaction, it is more correct to carry out this analysis over the unit price instead. This price can be added as a new column of our data frame:

```
> sales <- mutate(sales,Uprice=Val/Quant)
```

The unit price should be relatively constant over the transactions of the same product. When analyzing transactions over a short period of time, one does not expect strong variations of the unit price of the products.

If we check the distribution of the unit price, using for example,

Nr. of Transactions per Salesman

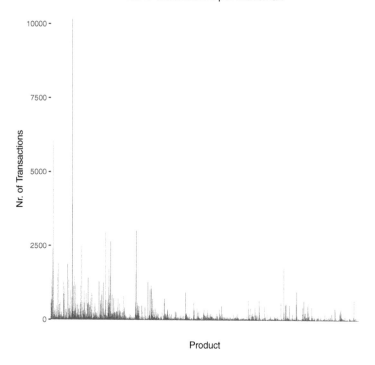

FIGURE 6.1: The number of transactions per salesperson.

Nr. of Transactions per Product

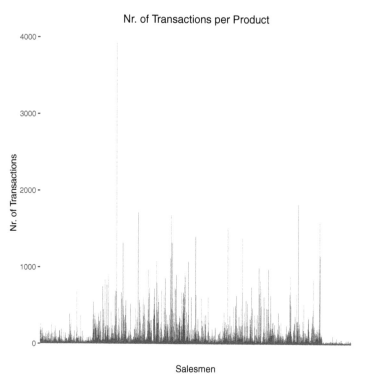

FIGURE 6.2: The number of transactions per product.

```
> summary(sales$Uprice)
```

```
   Min.  1st Qu.   Median    Mean  3rd Qu.      Max.      NA's
   0.00     8.46    11.89   20.30   19.11  26460.00     14136
```

we again observe a rather marked variability.

Given these facts, it seems inevitable that we should analyze the set of transactions of each product individually, looking for suspicious transactions on each of these sets. One problem with this approach is that some products have very few transactions. In effect, of the 4,548 products, 982 have less than 20 transactions. Declaring a report as unusual based on a sample of less than 20 reports may be too risky.

It may be interesting to check what are the top most expensive and cheap products. We will use the median unit price to represent the typical price at which a product is sold to avoid unwanted influence of outlying transaction reports (which may be potential frauds). The following code obtains the information we are looking for:

```
> prods <- group_by(sales,Prod)
> mpProds <- summarize(prods,medianPrice=median(Uprice,na.rm=TRUE))
> bind_cols(mpProds %>% arrange(medianPrice) %>% slice(1:5),
+           mpProds %>% arrange(desc(medianPrice)) %>% slice(1:5))
```

```
# A tibble: 5 × 4
     Prod medianPrice    Prod medianPrice
   <fctr>       <dbl> <fctr>       <dbl>
1   p560  0.01688455  p3689  9204.1954
2   p559  0.01884438  p2453   456.0784
3  p4195  0.03025914  p2452   329.3137
4   p601  0.05522265  p2456   304.8515
5   p563  0.05576406  p2459   283.8119
```

After grouping the transactions by product ID using the **group_by()** function we obtain the median price for each group (i.e. for each product ID). Finally, we obtain the table with the top and bottom 5 products in terms of median price using the function **bind_cols()**. This function is used to "glue" together the top 5 and the bottom 5 products. To obtain these products we have sorted the previously calculated median price per product both in ascending and descending order, picking the first 5 of these two lists using the **slice()** function that allows us to select specific rows of data frame table objects.

We can confirm the completely different price distribution of the cheapest and most expensive products using a box plot of their unit prices:

```
> library(ggplot2)
> library(forcats)
> ggplot(filter(sales,Prod %in% c("p3689","p560")),aes(x=fct_drop(Prod),y=Uprice)) +
+     geom_boxplot() + scale_y_log10() +
+     xlab("") + ylab("log10(UnitPrice)")
```

The **%in%** operator tests if a value belongs to a set. We have used the function **fct_drop()** from package **forcats** (Wickham, 2016) to focus the graph only on the two selected products. Without it as the column **Prod** resulting from the filtering is still a factor with many possible values, we would get one **boxplot()** for each level of the factor. You may wish to check function **droplevels()** that has similar objectives. The scales of the prices of the most expensive and cheapest products are rather different. Because of

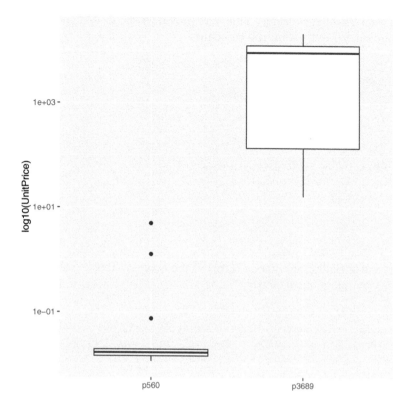

FIGURE 6.3: The distribution of the unit prices of the cheapest and most expensive products.

this, we have used a log scale in the Y-axis of the graph to avoid the values of the cheapest product becoming indistinguishable. This effect is obtained by the call to the function `scale_y_log10()`, which indicates that the Y-axis is on log scale. The result of this code is shown in Figure 6.3.

We can carry out a similar analysis to discover which salespeople are the ones who bring more (less) money to the company,

```
> ids <- group_by(sales,ID)
> tvIDs <- summarize(ids,totalVal=sum(Val,na.rm=TRUE))
> bind_cols(tvIDs %>% arrange(totalVal) %>% slice(1:5),
+            tvIDs %>% arrange(desc(totalVal)) %>% slice(1:5))

# A tibble: 5 × 4
       ID totalVal       ID   totalVal
   <fctr>    <dbl> <fctr>      <dbl>
1   v3355     1050   v431  211489170
2   v6069     1080    v54  139322315
3   v5876     1115    v19   71983200
4   v6058     1115  v4520   64398195
5   v4515     1125   v955   63182215
```

It may be interesting to note that the top 100 salespeople on this list account for almost 40% of the income of the company, while the bottom 2,000 out of the 6,016 salespeople generate less than 2% of the income. This may provide some insight into eventual changes that need to be carried out within the company:

```
> arrange(tvIDs,desc(totalVal)) %>% slice(1:100) %>%
+     summarize(t100=sum(totalVal)) /
+     (summarize(tvIDs,sum(totalVal))) * 100

      t100
1 38.33277

> arrange(tvIDs,totalVal) %>% slice(1:2000) %>%
+     summarize(b2000=sum(totalVal)) /
+     (summarize(tvIDs,sum(totalVal))) * 100

     b2000
1 1.988716
```

If we carry out a similar analysis in terms of the quantity that is sold for each product, the results are even more unbalanced:

```
> prods <- group_by(sales,Prod)
> qtProds <- summarize(prods,totalQty=sum(Quant,na.rm=TRUE))
> bind_cols(qtProds %>% arrange(desc(totalQty)) %>% slice(1:5),
+           qtProds %>% arrange(totalQty) %>% slice(1:5))

# A tibble: 5 × 4
    Prod totalQty   Prod totalQty
  <fctr>    <int> <fctr>    <int>
1  p2516 535301953  p2442        0
2  p3599 474050752  p2443        0
3   p314 367166615  p1653      108
4   p569 107686551  p4101      202
5   p319  86818285  p3678      405


> arrange(qtProds,desc(totalQty)) %>% slice(1:100) %>%
+     summarize(t100=sum(as.numeric(totalQty))) /
+     (summarize(qtProds,sum(as.numeric(totalQty)))) * 100

      t100
1 74.63478

> arrange(qtProds,totalQty) %>% slice(1:4000) %>%
+     summarize(b4000=sum(as.numeric(totalQty))) /
+     (summarize(qtProds,sum(as.numeric(totalQty)))) * 100

     b4000
1 8.944681
```

You may have noticed in the code above the use of the function **as.numeric()**. This is required in this case because the sum of the quantities generates too large a number to be stored as an integer, the original type of the column **totalQty**. This function will convert the result to a double thus overcoming this overflow problem.

From the 4,548 products, 4,000 represent less than 10% of the sales volume, with the top 100 representing nearly 75%. Notice that this information is only useful in terms of the production of the products. In particular, it does not mean that the company should consider stopping the production of the products that sell too few units. In effect, these may be more profitable if they have a larger profit margin. Because we do not have any information on the production costs of the products, we cannot draw any conclusion in terms of the usefulness in continuing to produce these products that sell so few units, which may not be the case in terms of consequences of the similar analysis we have carried out for each salesman.

One of the main assumptions we will be making in our analysis to find abnormal transaction reports is that the unit price of any product should follow a near-normal distribution. This means that we expect that the transactions of the same product will have roughly the same unit price with some small variability, possibly caused by some strategies of the salespeople to achieve their commercial goals. In this context, there are some basic statistical tests that can help us in finding deviations from this normality assumption. An example is the box plot rule. This rule serves as the basis of outlier identification in the context of box plots that we have already seen several times in this book. The rule states that an observation should be tagged as an anomaly high (low) value if it is above (below) the high (low) whisker, defined as $Q_3 + 1.5 \times IQR$ ($Q_1 - 1.5 \times IQR$), where Q_1 is the first quartile, Q_3 the third quartile, and $IQR = Q_3 - Q_1$ the inter-quartile range. This simple rule works rather well for normally distributed variables, and it is robust to the presence of a few outliers being based on robust statistics like the quartiles. The following code determines the number of outliers (according to the above definition) of each product:

```
> nouts <- function(x) length(boxplot.stats(x)$out)
> noutsProds <- summarise(prods,nOut=nouts(Uprice))
```

The `boxplot.stats()` function obtains several statistics that are used in the construction of box plots. It returns a list with this information. The `out` component of this list contains the observations that, according to the box plot rule, are considered outliers. The above code calculates their number for the transactions of each product. Note that you could also have used the function `bpRule()` we have defined in Section 3.4.1.1. The products with more outliers are the following:

```
> arrange(noutsProds,desc(nOut))

# A tibble: 4,548 × 2
      Prod   nOut
    <fctr> <int>
1    p1125   376
2    p1437   181
3    p2273   165
4    p1917   156
5    p1918   156
6    p4089   137
7     p538   129
8    p3774   125
9    p2742   120
10   p3338   117
# ... with 4,538 more rows
```

Using this very simple method, 29,446 transactions are considered outliers, which corresponds to approximately 7% of the total number of transactions,

```
> summarize(noutsProds,totalOuts=sum(nOut))

# A tibble: 1 × 1
  totalOuts
      <int>
1     29446

> summarize(noutsProds,totalOuts=sum(nOut))/nrow(sales)*100

  totalOuts
1   7.34047
```

One might question whether this simple rule for identifying outliers would be sufficient to provide the kind of help we want in this application. In Section 6.4.1.1 we will evaluate the performance of a small variant of this rule adapted to our application.

There is a caveat to some of the conclusions we have drawn in this section. We have been using the data independently of the fact that some of the reports were found to be fraudulent and some others may also be fraudulent although not yet detected. This means that some of these "conclusions" may be biased by data that is wrong. The problem is that for the transactions that are tagged as frauds, we do not know the correct values. Theoretically, the only transactions that we are sure correct are the ones for which the column Insp has the value OK, but these are just 3.6% of the data. So, although the analysis is correct, the conclusions may be impaired by low-quality data. This should be taken into account in a real-world situation so as not to provide advice to the company based on data that includes errors. Because a complete inspection of the data is impossible, this risk will always exist. At most we can avoid using the small number of transactions already found to be errors in all exploratory analysis of the data. Another thing one can do is present the results to the company and if some result is unexpected to them, carry out a closer analysis of the data that leads to that surprising result. This means that this sort of analysis usually requires some form of interaction with the domain experts, particularly when there are doubts regarding data quality, as is the case in this problem. Moreover, this type of exploratory analysis is of key importance with low-quality data as many of the problems can be easily spotted at these stages.

6.2.3 Data Problems

This section tries to address some data quality problems that can be an obstacle to the application of the techniques we will use later in this chapter.

6.2.3.1 Unknown Values

We start by addressing the problem of unknown variable values. As mentioned in Section 4.5 (page 205), there are three main alternative ways of dealing with this problem: (1) remove the cases, (2) fill in the unknowns using some strategy, or (3) use tools that handle datasets with this type of value. Considering the tools we will be using in this chapter, only the first two will be considered.

As mentioned before, the main concern is transactions that have both the value of Quant and Val missing. Removing all 888 cases may be problematic if this leads to removing most transactions of some product or salesperson. Let us check this.

We can obtain the salespeople with a larger proportion of transactions with unknowns on both Val and Quant as follows:

```
> prop.naQandV <- function(q,v) 100*sum(is.na(q) & is.na(v))/length(q)
> summarise(ids,nProbs=prop.naQandV(Quant,Val)) %>% arrange(desc(nProbs))

# A tibble: 6,016 × 2
        ID    nProbs
     <fctr>     <dbl>
1    v1237  13.793103
2    v4254   9.523810
3    v4038   8.333333
4    v5248   8.333333
5    v3666   6.666667
6    v4433   6.250000
7    v4170   5.555556
8    v4926   5.555556
9    v4664   5.494505
10   v4642   4.761905
# ... with 6,006 more rows
```

We have created an auxiliary function that given the values of `Quant` and `Val` of the transactions of a salesman, will calculate the percentage of these that are both `NA`. Looking at the results, it seems reasonable to delete these transactions, at least from the perspective of the salespeople, as they represent a small proportion of their transactions. Moreover, the alternative of trying to fill in both columns seems much more risky.

With respect to the products, these are the numbers:

```
> summarise(prods,nProbs=prop.naQandV(Quant,Val)) %>% arrange(desc(nProbs))

# A tibble: 4,548 × 2
       Prod    nProbs
     <fctr>     <dbl>
1     p2689  39.28571
2     p2675  35.41667
3     p4061  25.00000
4     p2780  22.72727
5     p4351  18.18182
6     p2686  16.66667
7     p2707  14.28571
8     p2690  14.08451
9     p2691  12.90323
10    p2670  12.76596
# ... with 4,538 more rows
```

There are several products that would have more than 20% of their transactions removed; and in particular, product **p2689** would have almost 40% of them removed. This seems clearly to be too much. On the other hand, if we decide to fill in these unknown values, the only reasonable strategy is to use the information on the "complete" transactions of the same product. This would mean to fill in 40% of the transactions of a product using the information of the remaining 60% (or less if some of these have either `Quant` or `Val` unknown). This also seems unreasonable. Luckily, looking at the similarity between the unit price distribution of the products (see Section 6.2.3.2), we will observe that these products are, in effect, rather similar to other products. In this context, if we conclude that they have too few transactions after the removal, we can always join their transactions with the ones from similar products to increase the statistical reliability of any outlier detection tests. In summary, the option of removing all transactions with unknown values on both the quantity and the value is the best option we have:

```
> sales <- filter(sales,!(is.na(Quant) & is.na(Val)))
```

Let us now analyze the remaining reports with unknown values in either the quantity or the value of the transaction. We start by calculating the proportion of transactions of each product that have the quantity unknown:

```
> prop.nas <- function(x) 100*sum(is.na(x))/length(x)
> summarise(prods,propNA.Q=prop.nas(Quant)) %>% arrange(desc(propNA.Q))
```

```
# A tibble: 4,548 × 2
      Prod  propNA.Q
    <fctr>     <dbl>
1    p2442 100.00000
2    p2443 100.00000
3    p1653  90.90909
4    p4101  85.71429
5    p4243  68.42105
6     p903  66.66667
7    p3678  66.66667
8    p4061  66.66667
9    p3955  64.28571
10   p4313  63.63636
# ... with 4,538 more rows
```

The first function we have created will be used for calculating the proportion of unknowns on a given set of values. It is used in the call to **summarise()** with the value of the quantities of the transactions of each product. There are two products (**p2442** and **p2443**) that have all their transactions with unknown values of the quantity. Without further information it is virtually impossible to do anything with the transactions of these products because we are unable to calculate their typical unit price. They are 54 reports, and two of them are tagged as frauds while another was found to be OK,

```
> filter(sales, Prod %in% c("p2442","p2443")) %>%
+     group_by(Insp) %>% count()
```

```
# A tibble: 3 × 2
     Insp     n
   <fctr> <int>
1      ok     1
2    unkn    51
3   fraud     2
```

This must mean that either the inspectors had more information than given in this dataset, or we are probably facing typing errors as it seems unfeasible to conclude anything on these transactions. In this context, we will delete them:

```
> sales <- droplevels(filter(sales,!(Prod %in% c("p2442", "p2443"))))
```

Given that we have removed two products from our dataset, we have used the function **droplevels()** to update the levels of the **Prod** factor to reflect this new situation where the two products removed do not exist any more in the dataset.

Are there salespeople with all the transactions with an unknown quantity?

```
> summarise(ids,propNA.Q=prop.nas(Quant)) %>% arrange(desc(propNA.Q))

# A tibble: 6,016 × 2
        ID  propNA.Q
    <fctr>     <dbl>
1    v2925 100.00000
2    v4356 100.00000
3    v5537 100.00000
4    v5836 100.00000
5    v6044 100.00000
6    v6058 100.00000
7    v6065 100.00000
8    v2923  90.00000
9    v4368  88.88889
10   v2920  85.71429
# ... with 6,006 more rows
```

As you can see, there are several salespeople who have not filled in the information on the quantity in all their reports. However, in this case the problem is not so serious as with the products. In effect, as long as we have other transactions of the same products reported by other salespeople, we can try to use this information to fill in these unknowns using the assumption that the unit price should be similar. Because of this, we will not delete these transactions.

We will now carry out a similar analysis for the transactions with an unknown value in the Val column. First, the proportion of transactions of each product with unknown value in this column:

```
> summarise(prods,propNA.V=prop.nas(Val)) %>% arrange(desc(propNA.V))

# A tibble: 4,548 × 2
      Prod  propNA.V
    <fctr>     <dbl>
1    p2689  39.28571
2    p2675  35.41667
3    p1110  25.00000
4    p4061  25.00000
5    p2780  22.72727
6    p4351  18.18182
7    p4491  18.18182
8    p2707  17.85714
9    p1462  17.77778
10   p1022  17.64706
# ... with 4,538 more rows
```

The numbers are reasonable so it does not make sense to delete these transactions as we may try to fill in these holes using the other transactions. With respect to the salesperson, the numbers are as follows:

```
> summarise(ids,propNA.V=prop.nas(Val)) %>% arrange(desc(propNA.V))

# A tibble: 6,016 × 2
        ID  propNA.V
    <fctr>     <dbl>
1    v5647 37.500000
```

```
2      v74 22.222222
3     v5946 20.000000
4     v5290 15.384615
5     v4022 13.953488
6     v1237 13.793103
7     v4472 12.500000
8      v975  9.574468
9     v4254  9.523810
10    v2814  9.090909
# ... with 6,006 more rows
```

Once again, the proportions are not too high.

At this stage we have removed all reports that had insufficient information to be subject to a fill-in strategy. For the remaining unknown values, we will apply a method based on the assumption that transactions of the same products should have a similar unit price. We will start by obtaining this typical unit price for each product. We will skip the prices of transactions that were found to be frauds in the calculation of the typical price. For the remaining transactions we will use the median unit price of the transactions as the typical price of the respective products:

```
> tPrice <- filter(sales, Insp != "fraud") %>%
+         group_by(Prod) %>%
+         summarise(medianPrice = median(Uprice,na.rm=TRUE))
```

Having a typical unit price for each product, we can use it to calculate any of the two possibly missing values (**Quant** or **Val**). This is possible because we currently have no transactions with both values missing. The following code fills in all the remaining unknown values:

```
> noQuantMedPrices <- filter(sales, is.na(Quant)) %>%
+     inner_join(tPrice) %>%
+     select(medianPrice)
> noValMedPrices <- filter(sales, is.na(Val)) %>%
+     inner_join(tPrice) %>%
+     select(medianPrice)
>
> noQuant <- which(is.na(sales$Quant))
> noVal <- which(is.na(sales$Val))
> sales[noQuant,'Quant'] <- ceiling(sales[noQuant,'Val'] /noQuantMedPrices)
> sales[noVal,'Val'] <- sales[noVal,'Quant'] * noValMedPrices
```

In case you missed it, we have just filled in 12,900 unknown quantity values plus 294 total values of transaction. If you are like me, I am sure you appreciate the compactness of the above code that carries out all these operations. It is all about indexing! We have used the function **ceiling()** to avoid non-integer values of **Quant**. This function returns the smallest integer not less than the number given as argument.

Given that we now have all **Quant** and **Val** values, we can recalculate the **Uprice** column to fill in the previously unknown unit prices:

```
> sales$Uprice <- sales$Val/sales$Quant
```

After all these pre-processing steps, we have a dataset free of unknown values. For future analysis, it makes sense that you save this current state of the **sales** data frame so that you can restart your analysis from this point, without having to repeat all the steps. You can save the data frame as follows:

```
> save(sales, file = "salesClean.Rdata")
```

The `save()` function can be used to save any set of objects in a file specified in the `file` parameter. Objects saved in these files can be loaded back into R using the `load()` function, as shown in Section 6.2.1.

6.2.3.2 Few Transactions of Some Products

There are products with very few transactions. This is a problem because we need to use the information on these transactions to decide if any of them are unusual. If we have too few, it is difficult to make this decision with the required statistical significance. In this context, it makes sense to question whether we can analyze the transactions of some products together to avoid this problem.

Despite the complete lack of information on the eventual relationships between products, we can try to infer some of these relationships by observing the similarity between their distributions of unit price. If we find products with similar prices, then we can consider merging their respective transactions and analyze them together to search for unusual values. One way of comparing two distributions is to visually inspect them. Given the number of products we have, this is unfeasible. An alternative is to compare some statistical properties that summarize the distributions. Two important properties of continuous variables distributions are their central tendency and spread. As mentioned before, it is reasonable to assume that the distribution of the unit price of any product is approximately normal. This means that although variations in the price occur, they should be nicely packed around the most common price. However, we have to assume that there will be outlying values, most probably caused by fraud attempts or errors. In this context, it makes more sense to use the median as the statistic of centrality and the inter-quartile range (IQR) as the statistic of spread. These statistics are more robust to the presence of outliers when compared to the more frequently used mean and standard deviation. We can obtain both statistics for all transactions of each product as follows:

```
> ms <- filter(sales,Insp != "fraud") %>%
+     group_by(Prod) %>%
+     summarize(median=median(Uprice,na.rm=TRUE),
+               iqr=IQR(Uprice,na.rm=TRUE),
+               nTrans=n(),
+               fewTrans=ifelse(nTrans>20,FALSE,TRUE))
> ms
```

```
# A tibble: 4,546 × 5
     Prod     median         iqr nTrans fewTrans
   <fctr>      <dbl>       <dbl>  <int>    <lgl>
1      p1 11.346154   8.5635799    196    FALSE
2      p2 10.877863   5.6097315     81    FALSE
3      p3 10.000000   4.8090920     31    FALSE
4      p4  9.911243   5.9985297    111    FALSE
5      p5 10.957447   7.1366009    161    FALSE
6      p6 13.223684   6.6851852     63    FALSE
7      p7  4.851453   0.5474666     52    FALSE
8      p8  3.850211   0.7282168     11     TRUE
9      p9  1.941457   0.3431872     38    FALSE
```

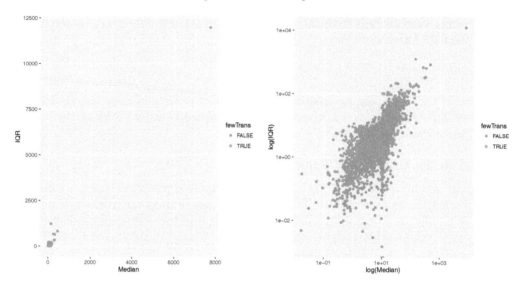

FIGURE 6.4: Some properties of the distribution of unit prices.

```
10      p10 42.232846 33.0267925      38      FALSE
# ... with 4,536 more rows
```

You may have noticed that we have also calculated the number of transactions for each product and have also added a logical value that is true if the product has few transactions (we have considered the threshold of 20).

The left graph on Figure 6.4 plots each product according to its respective median and IQR. The graph is difficult to read because a few products have very large values for these statistics. In particular, product **p3689** (the dot at the top right) is clearly different from all other products of the company. We can overcome this visualization problem using log scales (right graph in Figure 6.4). On both graphs we have associated the color to the property of being a product with small number of transactions or not. The figures were obtained as follows, where the functions `scale_y_log10()` and `scale_x_log10()` were used to set log scales on both axes of the graph:

```
> ggplot(ms,aes(x=median,y=iqr,color=fewTrans)) +
+      geom_point() +
+      xlab("Median") + ylab("IQR")
> ggplot(ms,aes(x=median,y=iqr,color=fewTrans)) +
+      geom_point() +
+      scale_y_log10() + scale_x_log10() +
+      xlab("log(Median)") + ylab("log(IQR)")
```

The first thing to note in the right graph of Figure 6.4 is that there are many products that have approximately the same median and IQR, even taking into account that we are looking at a log scale. This provides good indications of the similarity of their distributions of unit price. Moreover, we can see that among the products with few transactions (blue dots), there are many that are very similar to other products. However, there are also several products that not only have few transactions but also have a rather distinct distribution of unit prices. These are clearly the products for which we will have more difficulty in declaring a transaction as fraudulent.

Despite the virtues of the visual inspection of the distribution properties of the unit prices, formal tests are required to obtain more precision when comparing the distributions of two products. We will use a nonparametric test to compare the distributions of unit prices, as these tests are more robust to the presence of outliers. The Kolmogorov-Smirnov test can be used to compare any two samples to check the validity of the null hypothesis that both come from the same distribution. This test works by calculating a statistic that measures the maximum difference between the two empirical cumulative distribution functions. If the two distributions are similar, this distance should be rather small.

For each of the products that has less than 20 transactions, we will search for the product with the most similar unit price distribution and then use a Kolmogorov-Smirnov test to check if the similarity is statistically significant. Carrying out this task for all combinations of products would be computationally too demanding. Instead, we have decided to take advantage of the information given by the distribution properties we calculated before (median and IQR). Namely, for each of the products with few transactions, we have searched for the product with the most similar median and IQR. Given this similar product, we have carried out a Kolmogorov-Smirnov test between their respective unit price distributions, storing the results of this test. The following code obtains a matrix (**similar**) with the information on this type of test for each of the products with less than 20 transactions. It uses the **ms** object we obtained before with the information on the medians and IQRs of the unit prices of each product.

```
> ms <- mutate(ms,smedian=scale(median),siqr=scale(iqr))
> smalls <- which(ms$fewTrans)
> nsmalls <- as.character(ms$Prod[smalls])
> similar <- matrix(NA,length(smalls),7,
+      dimnames=list(nsmalls,
+          c("RowSimProd", "ks.stat", "ks.p", "medP", "iqrP", "medS","iqrS")))
> xprods <- tapply(sales$Uprice, sales$Prod, list)
> for(i in seq_along(smalls)) {
+      d <- scale(ms[,c("smedian","siqr")],
+                  c(ms$smedian[smalls[i]],ms$siqr[smalls[i]]),
+                  FALSE)
+      d <- sqrt(drop(d^2 %*% rep(1, ncol(d))))
+      stat <- ks.test(xprods[[nsmalls[i]]], xprods[[order(d)[2]]])
+      similar[i, ] <- c(order(d)[2], stat$statistic, stat$p.value,
+                      ms$median[smalls[i]],ms$iqr[smalls[i]],
+                      ms$median[order(d)[2]],ms$iqr[order(d)[2]])
+ }
```

The code starts by normalizing the data in the object **ms** to avoid negative scale effects when calculating the distances. After a few initializations, we have the main loop that goes over all the products with few transactions. The first two statements in this loop calculate the distances between the distribution properties of the product under analysis (the current value of **i**) and all other products. The resulting object (**d**) has the values of all these distances. The second smallest distance is the product that is most similar to the product being considered. It is the second because the first is the product itself. We note again that the similarity between the products is being calculated using the information on the median and IQR of the respective unit prices. The next step is to carry out the Kolmogorov-Smirnov test to compare the two distributions of unit prices. This is done with a call to the **ks.test()** function. This function returns a significant amount of information, among which we have "extracted" the value of the statistic of the test and the respective significance level. The value of the statistic is the maximum difference between the two cumulative distribution functions. Values of the confidence level near 1 indicate strong statistical significance of the null hypothesis that both distributions are equal. Below we show the first few lines of the resulting **similar** object:

```
> head(similar)

    RowSimProd   ks.stat      ks.p      medP      iqrP      medS      iqrS
p8        2827 0.4339623 0.06470603 3.850211 0.7282168 3.868306 0.7938557
p18        213 0.2568922 0.25815859 5.187266 8.0359968 5.274884 7.8207052
p38       1044 0.3650794 0.11308315 5.490758 6.4162095 5.651818 6.2436224
p39       3418 0.2214286 0.81418197 7.986486 1.4229755 8.005181 1.5625650
p40       1335 0.3760000 0.04533293 9.674797 1.6104511 9.711538 1.6505602
p47       1387 0.3125000 0.48540576 2.504092 2.5625835 2.413498 2.6402087
```

The row names indicate the product for which we are obtaining the most similar product. The first column has information on this latter product. For instance, if we want the product that is most similar to the first of the products with few transactions we can do the following:

```
> bind_rows(filter(ms,Prod==rownames(similar)[1]),
+           ms[similar[1,1],])

# A tibble: 2 × 7
    Prod   median       iqr nTrans fewTrans     smedian        siqr
  <fctr>    <dbl>     <dbl>  <int>    <lgl>       <dbl>       <dbl>
1     p8 3.850211 0.7282168     11     TRUE -0.09361149 -0.06746071
2  p2829 3.868306 0.7938557     51    FALSE -0.09345463 -0.06709663
```

After the columns with the Kolmogorov-Smirnov statistic and confidence level, we have the medians and IQRs of the product and the most similar product, respectively.

We can check how many products have a product whose unit price distribution is significantly similar with 90% confidence:

```
> nrow(similar[similar[, "ks.p"] >= 0.9, ])

[1] 140
```

Or more efficiently,

```
> sum(similar[, "ks.p"] >= 0.9)

[1] 140
```

As you see from the 985 products with less than 20 transactions, we have only managed to find similar products for 140 of them. Nevertheless, this is useful information when it comes to analyzing which transactions are abnormal. For these 140 products we can include more transactions into the decision process to increase the statistical significance of our tests. We will save the **similar** object in case we decide to use this similarity between products later:

```
> save(similar, file = "similarProducts.Rdata")
```

6.3   Defining the Data Mining Tasks

The main goal of this application is to use data mining to provide guidance in the task of deciding which transaction reports should be considered for inspection as a result of strong suspicion of being fraudulent. Given the limited and varying resources available for this auditing task, such guidance should take the form of a ranking of fraud probability.

6.3.1   Different Approaches to the Problem

The available dataset has a column (`Insp`) that has information on previous inspection activities. The main problem we have is that the majority of the available reports have not been audited. From the perspective of the task of deciding whether or not a report is fraudulent, the value `unkn` in the `Insp` variable has the meaning of an unknown variable value. This value represents the absence of information on whether the transaction is OK or a fraud. This means that we have two types of observations in our dataset. We have a (small) set of labeled observations for which we have the description of their characteristics plus the result of their inspection. We have another (large) set of unlabeled observations that have not been inspected, that is, have the value `unkn` in the `Insp` column. In this context, there are different types of modeling approaches that can be applied to these data, depending on which observations we use for obtaining the models.

6.3.1.1   Unsupervised Techniques

In the reports that were not inspected, the column `Insp` is in effect irrelevant as it carries no information. For these observations we only have descriptors of the transactions. This means that these sales reports are only described by a set of variables. This is the type of data used by unsupervised learning techniques. These methods are named this way because their goal is not to learn some "concept" with the help of a "teacher" as in supervised methods. The data used by these latter methods are examples of the concepts being learned (e.g., the concept of fraud or normal transaction). This requires that the data is preclassified (labeled) by a domain expert into one of the target concepts. This is not the case for the set of reports with unknown inspection results. We are thus facing a descriptive data mining task as opposed to a predictive task, which is the goal of supervised methods.

Clustering is an example of a descriptive data mining technique. Clustering methods try to find the "natural" groupings of a set of observations by forming clusters of cases that are similar to each other. The notion of similarity usually requires the definition of a metric over the space defined by the variables that describe the observations. This metric is a distance function that measures how far an observation is from another. Cases that are near to each other are usually considered part of the same natural group of data. More details on clustering methods was provided in Section 3.4.3 (page 119).

Outlier detection can also be viewed as a descriptive data mining task. Some outlier detection methods assume a certain expected distribution of the data, and tag as outliers any observations that deviate from this distribution. Another common outlier detection strategy is to assume a metric over the space of variables and use the notion of distance to tag as outliers observations that are "too far" from others. Methods for detecting anomalies/outliers were described in Section 3.4.4 (page 131).

From the above descriptions we can see that there are strong relationships between clustering and outlier detection. This is particularly true in methodologies based on the notion of distance between observations. Outliers are, by definition, rather different cases and thus they should not fit well in groups with other observations because they are too distant from them. This means that a good clustering of a dataset should not include outliers in large groups of data. At most, one can expect outliers to be similar to other outliers but by definition these are rare observations and thus should not form big groups of cases.

The use of unsupervised techniques in our problem involves some restrictions. In effect, our goal is to obtain an outlier ranking for a set of observations. This ranking is to serve as a basis for the inspection decisions within the company. This means that the unsupervised tools we select must be able to identify outliers and also rank them. Section 6.4.1 describes the unsupervised techniques we have selected to address this data mining task.

6.3.1.2 Supervised Techniques

The set of transactions that were labeled normal or fraudulent (i.e., have been inspected) can be used with other types of modeling approaches. Supervised learning methods use this type of labeled data. The goal of these approaches is to obtain a model that relates a target variable (the concept being learned) with a set of independent variables (predictors, attributes). This model can be regarded as an approximation of an unknown function $Y = f(X_1, X_2, \cdots, X_p)$ that describes the relationship between the target variable Y and the predictors $X_1, X_2, \cdots, X_p$. The task of the modeling technique is to obtain the model parameters that optimize a certain selected criterion, for example, minimize the prediction error of the model. This search task is carried out with the help of a sample of observations of the phenomena under study, that is, it is based on a dataset containing examples of the concept being learned. These examples are particular instances of the variables $X_1, X_2, \cdots, X_p, Y$. If the target variable Y is continuous, we have a (multiple) regression problem. If Y is a nominal variable, we have a classification problem. Predictive analytics, which we have described in Section 3.4.5 (page 140), has to do with solving these tasks.

In the case of our dataset, the target variable is the result of the inspection task and can take two possible values: ok and fraud. This means that our goal is to learn the concepts of fraudulent and normal reports. We are thus facing a (binary) classification problem. Notice that the transactions that were not inspected cannot be used in these tasks because we are unsure whether or not they are frauds. This means that if we want to use a classification technique to obtain a model to predict whether a given report is or is not a fraud, we can only use 15,732 of the 401,146 available reports as the training sample.

The classification problem we are facing has a particularity that can impact both the way we will evaluate the performance of the models and also the models themselves. This particularity is the fact that among the two possible class values, one is much more frequent than the other. In effect, from the 15,732 inspected reports, 14,462 are normal transactions and only the remaining 1,270 ($\sim 8\%$) are examples of frauds. Moreover, this less frequent concept is, in effect, the most important in this problem as it is related to the aim of the application: detect frauds. This means that we have to select evaluation criteria that are able to correctly measure the performance of the models on this less frequent class, and we should select modeling techniques that are able to cope with datasets with a strong class imbalance.

The use of classification tools in our problem involves a few adaptations. In effect, we are interested in obtaining a ranking of the transactions according to their probability of being frauds. This means that given a test set with new reports, we will use the model to decide which are the reports to be audited. Some classification algorithms are only able to output the class label when given a test case. This is not enough for our problem because it does not establish a ranking among the cases classified as frauds. If these are too many for the available inspection resources, we are unable to decide which ones to handle. What we need is a probabilistic classification, that is, the model should not only predict a class label, but also an associated probability of this label. These probabilities allow us to obtain a ranking of the test cases according to the estimated probability that they are frauds.

6.3.1.3 Semi-Supervised Techniques

Semi-supervised methods are motivated by the observation that for many applications it is costly to find labeled data—that is, cases for which we have the value of the target variable. This information usually requires the work of domain experts, which increases the costs of data collection. On the other hand, unlabeled data is frequently easy to obtain, particularly with the widespread use of sensors and other types of automatic data collection devices. In this context, one frequently faces problems with a large proportion of data that is unlabeled, together with a small amount of labeled data. This is the case of our application, as we have seen before.

Semi-supervised methods are named this way exactly because they can handle this type of datasets with both labeled and unlabeled cases. There are usually two different types of semi-supervised methods. On the one hand, there are semi-supervised classification methods that try to improve the performance of standard supervised classification algorithms with the help of the extra information provided by the unlabeled cases. The alternative approach is given by semi-supervised clustering methods that try to bias the clustering process by incorporating some form of constraints based on the labeled data in the criteria used to form the groups.

In semi-supervised clustering, the idea is to use the available labels to bias the clustering process to include the cases with the same label in the same groups (*must-link* constraints), or to keep cases with different labels in different groups (*cannot-link* constraints). In search-based semi-supervised clustering, the criteria used to form the clusters is changed to bias the methods to find the appropriate groups of cases. In similarity-based semi-supervised approaches, the metric used by the algorithms is optimized to satisfy the constraints imposed by the labeled data. This means that the notion of distance is "distorted" to reflect the *must-link* and *cannot-link* constraints.

With respect to semi-supervised classification there are many alternative methodologies. A well-known method is self-training. This is an iterative approach that starts by obtaining a classification model with the given labeled data. The next step is to use this model to classify the unlabeled data. The cases for which the model has very high confidence on the classification are added together with the predicted label to the initial training set, thus augmenting it. Using this new set, a new model is obtained and the overall process is repeated until some convergence criterion is reached or until no classification has sufficient confidence to be added to the current training set. Another example of semi-supervised classification models are transductive support vector machines (TSVMs). The goal of TSVMs is to obtain labels for a set of unlabeled data, such that a linear boundary achieves the maximum margin on both the original labeled data and on the unlabeled data (see Section 5.4.2.2 on page 127 for more details on SVMs).

Once again we should consider the particular restrictions of our application, namely in terms of obtaining outlier rankings. This can be accomplished using the same strategies outlined in the previous sections for unsupervised and supervised methods, depending on whether we use semi-supervised clustering or semi-supervised classification, respectively.

Further readings on semi-supervised methods

Semi-supervised learning has been receiving an increasing interest by the research community. Good surveys of the existing work are given in Zhu (2006), Seeger (2002), or Zhu (2005). The book by Chapelle et al. (2006) is a good reference on this area.

6.3.2 Evaluation Criteria

In this section we discuss how to evaluate the models we will develop for this data mining task. When given a test set of transaction reports, each model will produce a ranking of these reports that is supposed to provide advice on auditing priorities. This section discusses how to evaluate this ranking. We will also describe the experimental methodology that will be used to obtain reliable estimates of the selected evaluation metrics.

Our dataset has the particularity of including both labeled and unlabeled data. In this application the two situations translate into inspected and non-inspected transaction reports. This increases the difficulty of comparing the models because supervised and unsupervised methods are usually evaluated differently. The rankings obtained by the models will most probably include both labeled and unlabeled observations, although for a real test set (one formed with data collected in the future) they will all be unlabeled. Regarding labeled data, it is easy to evaluate whether or not their inclusion in the set of reports to inspect is correct. In the case of unlabeled cases, this evaluation is more difficult because we cannot be sure whether or not these cases are frauds until we actually audit them.

6.3.2.1 Precision and Recall

In this domain, if we are to apply a model to a subset of our available data taken as a test set, the known frauds within this test set should appear at the top positions of the auditing ranking suggested by the model. Fraudulent reports are a minority in our data. Given a number k of reports that our auditing resources allow to inspect, we would like that among the k top-most positions of the obtained ranking, we only have either frauds or non-inspected reports. Moreover, we would like to include in these k positions all of the known fraud cases that exist in the test set.

As we have seen in Sections 5.3.4 (page 252) and 3.4.5.1 (page 141), when our aim is to predict a small set of rare events (in this case frauds), precision and recall are the adequate evaluation metrics. Given the inspection effort limit k, we can calculate the precision and recall of the k top-most positions of the ranking produced by a model[2]. This k limit determines which reports are to be inspected according to the model. From a supervised classification perspective, this is equivalent to considering the top k positions as predictions of the class `fraud`, while the remaining are normal reports. The value of precision will tell us what proportion of these k top-most reports are, in effect, labeled as frauds. The value of recall will measure the proportion of frauds in the test set that are included in these k top-most positions. We should note that the obtained values are pessimistic. In effect, if the k top-most positions include unlabeled reports, they will not enter the calculation of precision and recall. However, if they are inspected, we may find that they are, in effect, frauds and thus the real values of precision and recall could be higher.

Usually there is a trade-off between precision and recall. For instance, it is quite easy to achieve 100% recall if all test cases are predicted as events. However, such a strategy will inevitably also lead to a very low precision. Still, our current application has some particularities. Given the fact that there will be constraints on the resources invested in inspection activities, what we really want is to maximize the use of these resources. This means that if we can spend x hours inspecting reports and in these x hours we are able to capture all the frauds, we are happy—even if in these x hours we actually inspect several normal reports, that is, even with a low precision in our ranking. Recall is actually the key issue in this application. What we want is to be able to achieve 100% recall with the resources we have available.

---

[2]Sometimes known as precision@k and recall@k.

6.3.2.2 Lift Charts and Precision/Recall Curves

In the previous section we mentioned calculating the values of precision and recall for a given inspection effort. It is interesting to check the performance of the models at different effort levels. Different models may prevail at different levels and this may be useful information when comparing them. This is particularly interesting in application scenarios where the available auditing effort may vary along time. Under these settings we may be interested in studying the behavior of the models across a range of operating scenarios instead of a single setup.

Precision/recall (PR) curves are visual representations of the performance of a model in terms of the precision and recall statistics. The curves are obtained by proper interpolation of the values of the statistics at different working points. These working points can be given by different cut-off limits on a ranking of the class of interest provided by the model. In our case this would correspond to different effort limits applied to the outlier ranking produced by the models. Iterating over different limits (i.e., inspect more or less reports), we get different values of precision and recall. PR curves allow this type of analysis.

The package **ROCR** (Sing et al., 2009) contains several functions that are very useful for evaluating binary classifiers (i.e., classifiers for two classes problems like ours). This is an extra package that you should install before trying the code below. The package implements many evaluation metrics and it includes methods to obtain a wide range of curves. PR curves can be easily obtained with the functions in this package. The use of this package is rather simple. We start by obtaining an object of the class `prediction` using the predictions of the model and the true values of the test set. This is done with the `prediction()` function. The resulting object can be passed as an argument to the function `performance()` to obtain several evaluation metrics. Finally, the result of this latter function can be used with the function `plot()` to obtain different performance curves. The following code is an illustration of this process using some example data included in the package:

```
> library(ROCR)
> data(ROCR.simple)
> pred <- prediction(ROCR.simple$predictions, ROCR.simple$labels)
> perf <- performance(pred, "prec", "rec")
> plot(perf)
```

This code plots a PR curve that is shown on the left-most graph of Figure 6.5. The PR curves produced by the **ROCR** package have a sawtooth shape. This is usually considered not too clear and there are methods to overcome this effect. Namely, we can calculate the interpolated precision $Prec_{int}$ for a certain recall level r as the highest precision value found for any recall level greater than or equal to r:

$$Prec_{int}(r) = \max_{r' \geq r} Prec(r') \qquad (6.1)$$

where $Prec(x)$ is the precision at a certain recall level x.

If we take a close look at the object returned by the `performance()` function, we will see that it has a slot named `y.values` with the values of the y axis of the graph, that is, the precision values that are plotted. We can obtain a PR curve without the sawtooth effect by simply substituting this slot with the values of the interpolated precision according to Equation 6.1. The following function implements this idea for the general case:

```
> PRcurve <- function(preds, trues, ...) {
+       require(ROCR, quietly = TRUE)
+       pd <- prediction(preds, trues)
```

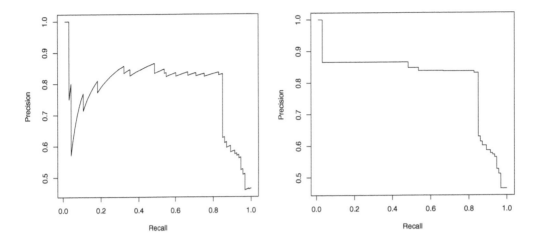

FIGURE 6.5: Smoothed (right) and non-smoothed (left) precision/recall curves.

```
+       pf <- performance(pd, "prec", "rec")
+       pf@y.values <- lapply(pf@y.values, function(x) rev(cummax(rev(x))))
+       plot(pf, ...)
+ }
```

The code uses the function `lapply()` because the slot `y.values` is, in effect, a list as it can include the results of several iterations of an experimental process. We will take advantage of this fact later on this chapter. For each vector of precision values, we calculate the interpolated precision using the functions `cummax()` and `rev()`. The latter simply reverses a vector, while the `cummax()` function obtains the cumulative maximum of a set of numbers. Try it with a vector of numbers if you have difficulty understanding the concept. The `PRcurve()` function is actually included in our book package, so you do not need to type the above code to use it.

We can apply the `PRcurve()` function to the example data given above, producing the right-most graph of Figure 6.5.

```
> PRcurve(ROCR.simple$predictions, ROCR.simple$labels)
```

How can we evaluate our outlier ranking models with these types of curves? We will have a test set with a variable `Insp` with possible values `unkn`, `ok`, and `fraud`, and a ranking of the observations in this set, produced by some model. We will require our models to obtain an outlier score for each observation in the test set. The higher the score, the higher the confidence of the model that an observation is a fraud. This score is the source of information for obtaining the ranking of the observations. If we order the test set observations by decreasing outlier score, we can calculate different values of precision and recall, depending on where we put our inspection effort limit. Setting this limit is equivalent to choosing a threshold on the outlier score above which we will consider the observations as fraudulent. Let us see a small example. Suppose we have seven test cases with the values $\{ok, ok, fraud, unknown, fraud, fraud, unknown\}$ in the `Insp` column. Imagine a certain model produces as outlier scores for these observations the values $\{0.2, 0.1, 0.7, 0.5, 0.4, 0.3, 0.25\}$, respectively. If we rank the observations by these scores, we obtain $\{fraud, unknown, fraud, fraud, unknown, ok, ok\}$. If

TABLE 6.1: A Confusion Matrix for the Illustrative Example.

		Predictions		
		ok	fraud	
True	ok	3	1	4
Values	fraud	2	1	3
		5	2	7

our inspection limit only allows us to inspect two observations, it would be equivalent to a model "predicting" $\{fraud, fraud, ok, ok, ok, ok, ok\}$ for the true values $\{fraud, unknown, fraud, fraud, unknown, ok, ok\}$. This, in turn, corresponds to the confusion matrix in Table 6.1 and to the following values of precision and recall calculated according to that matrix:

$$Prec = \frac{1}{1+1} = 0.5 \qquad Rec = \frac{1}{2+1} = 0.3333$$

Notice that as mentioned in Section 6.3.2.1, we have followed a pessimistic estimate of precision and recall with respect to the reports that have not been inspected. Because of this, the prediction of **fraud** for the report in the second position of the ranking, which has the value **unkn**, is considered an error as we are not sure whether or not it is a fraud.

We will use this type of post-processing of the outlier rankings to obtain their scores in terms of precision and recall as well as the respective PR curves. The curves can be obtained by varying the inspection threshold, i.e. using the simple example above by inspecting only the first, second, third, ..., and so on, positions of the ranking produced by the outlier scores of the model, and for each of these thresholds calculating the respective precision and recall scores.

Lift charts provide a different perspective of the model predictions. These graphs give more importance to the values of recall and thus are, in a way, more adequate to our objectives, as mentioned in the end of Section 6.3.2.1. The x-axis of these graphs is the value of the rate of positive predictions (RPP), which is the probability that the model predicts a positive class. This is estimated by the proportion of positive class predictions divided by the total number of test cases. In the example of Table 6.1, this would have the value of $(1 + 1)/7$. In the context of our application, we can look at this statistic as the proportion of reports selected for inspection. The y-axis of lift charts is the value of recall divided by the value of RPP.

Lift charts can be obtained with the infrastructure provided by the **ROCR** package. The following is an illustrative example of its use with the corresponding lift chart shown in the left-most graph of Figure 6.6:

```
> pred <- prediction(ROCR.simple$predictions, ROCR.simple$labels)
> perf <- performance(pred, "lift", "rpp")
> plot(perf, main = "Lift Chart")
```

Despite their usefulness lift charts are not exactly what we search for in our particular application. A more interesting graph would be one that shows the recall values in terms of the inspection effort that is captured by the RPP. We will call this type of graph the *cumulative recall chart*; it can be implemented by the following function thanks to the **ROCR** package:

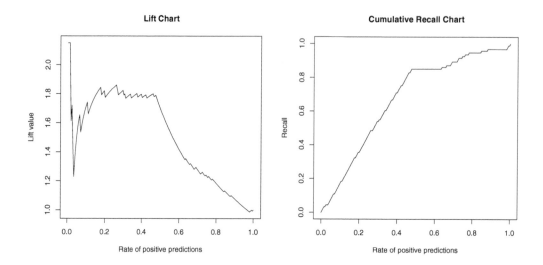

FIGURE 6.6: Lift (left) and cumulative recall (right) charts.

```
> CRchart <- function(preds, trues, ...) {
+     require(ROCR, quietly = T)
+     pd <- prediction(preds, trues)
+     pf <- performance(pd, "rec", "rpp")
+     plot(pf, ...)
+ }
```

Using again the artificial example, we obtain the right-most graph of Figure 6.6:

```
> CRchart(ROCR.simple$predictions, ROCR.simple$labels,
+         main='Cumulative Recall Chart')
```

For cumulative recall charts, the nearer the curve of a model is to the top-left corner of the graph, the better. The `CRchart()` function is also included in our book package so you can use it at any time, provided you load the package.

6.3.2.3   Normalized Distance to Typical Price

The measures we have seen in previous sections only evaluate the quality of the rankings in terms of the labeled reports. They are supervised classification evaluation metrics. The rankings obtained by the models will most probably also contain unlabeled reports in the top positions. Are these unlabeled cases correctly positioned in the ranking? We cannot be sure about this as we have not inspected them. Nevertheless, we can say something about them. For instance, we can compare their unit price with the typical price of the reports of the same product. We would expect that the difference between these prices is high, as this is an indication that something is wrong with the report. In this context, the distance between the unit price of a report and the typical unit price of the respective product is a good indicator of the quality of the outlier ranking obtained by a model.

Different products have a different scale of unit prices, as we have seen in Figure 6.4. To avoid the effects of these differences in our proposed measure of outlier ranking quality, we will normalize the distance to the typical unit price. We use the IQR to normalize this distance:

$$NDTP_p(u) = \frac{|u - \widetilde{U_p}|}{IQR_p} \tag{6.2}$$

where $\widetilde{U_p}$ is the typical unit price of the product p, measured by the median unit price of its transactions, and IQR_p is the respective inter-quartile range of the unit prices of that product.

In our experiments we will use the average value of $NDTP_p$ as one of the evaluation metrics to characterize the performance of the models. The following function calculates the value of this statistic:

```
> avgNDTP <- function(toInsp,train,stats) {
+    if (missing(train) && missing(stats))
+        stop('Provide either the training data or the product stats')
+    if (missing(stats)) {
+        stats <- as.matrix(filter(train,Insp != 'fraud') %>%
+                        group_by(Prod) %>%
+                        summarise(median=median(Uprice),iqr=IQR(Uprice)) %>%
+                        select(median,iqr))
+        rownames(stats) <- levels(train$Prod)
+        stats[which(stats[,'iqr']==0),'iqr'] <- stats[which(stats[,'iqr']==0),'median']
+    }

+    return(mean(abs(toInsp$Uprice-stats[toInsp$Prod,'median']) /
+                stats[toInsp$Prod,'iqr']))
+ }
```

The function receives, as the main argument, the set of transactions that a model selects for inspection. Then it must receive either the training set to obtain the median and IQR of each product, or an already prepared data structure with this information, to increase the computational efficiency of repeated calls to this function. If the training data is received, the function calculates the median and IQR values of the nonfraudulent transactions of each product in the training set. It may happen that the IQR is zero, particularly in products with very few transactions. To avoid division by zero in calculating $NDTP_p$, we have set the IQR of these cases to the value of the median.

6.3.3   Experimental Methodology

The dataset we are using has a very reasonable size. In this context, it makes sense to select the Holdout method for our experimental comparisons. This method consists of randomly splitting the available dataset in two partitions (typically in 70%/30% proportions). One of the partitions is used for obtaining the models, while the other is used for testing them. The process can eventually be repeated a few times to ensure more reliability, if necessary, leading to what is usually known as random subsampling. The size of our dataset ensures that the values we obtain are statistically reliable. If we select 30% of the cases for the test set, this corresponds to 120,343 reports.

One additional difficulty in this situation is the imbalance between the distributions of the different types of reports, namely on the labeled cases. A normal re-sampling strategy may lead to a test set with a different distribution of the normal/fraudulent reports. Whenever we have this type of imbalanced class distributions, it is recommended to use a stratified sampling strategy. This strategy consists of randomly sampling from bags with the observations of the different classes, ensuring that the obtained sample respects the distribution of the initial dataset. For instance, if we have 10% of cases of class X and the remaining 90% of another class Y, we will put these observations in two separate bags. If we want a random stratified sample with 100 cases, we will randomly pick ten cases from the bag with the X class cases, and the remaining 90 from the bag with the Ys, thus respecting the original proportions of the classes.

As we have seen in Section 3.5 (page 172), package **performanceEstimation** provides an experimental infrastructure that also includes the Holdout estimation procedure. We can use this method by specifying it in the third argument of the `performanceEstimation()` function, where we indicate the metrics and the estimation method. By including a call to the function `Holdout()` in the `method` parameter of the `EstimationTask()` constructor we obtain this type of estimate. Parameters `nReps` and `hldSz` of the `Holdout()` function can be used to indicate the number of repetitions (thus choosing random subsampling if greater than one) and the size of the holdout, respectively. This function also includes an extra parameter (`strat`) that if set to `TRUE` ensures the procedure uses stratified sampling. We will use these facilities of package **performanceEstimation** to obtain reliable estimates of our selected evaluation metrics. These are precision, recall, and the average $NDTP$. Given the specificity of the $NDTP$ metric we need to write our own evaluation function:

```
> evalOutlierRanking <- function(testSet,rankOrder,Threshold,statsProds,...)
+ {
+    ordTS <- testSet[rankOrder,]
+    N <- nrow(testSet)
+    nF <- if (Threshold < 1) as.integer(Threshold*N) else Threshold
+    cm <- table(c(rep('fraud',nF),rep('ok',N-nF)),ordTS$Insp)
+    prec <- cm['fraud','fraud']/sum(cm['fraud',])
+    rec <- cm['fraud','fraud']/sum(cm[,'fraud'])
+    AVGndtp <- avgNDTP(ordTS[1:nF,],stats=statsProds)
+    return(c(Precision=prec,Recall=rec,avgNDTP=AVGndtp))
+ }
```

The function requires the user to supply the test set, the ranking proposed by the model for this set, a threshold specifying the inspection limit effort (either as a percentage or as a number of reports), and the statistics (median and IQR) of the products.

In Section 6.2.3.2 we observed that the products are rather different, and that some products have, in effect, few transactions. In this context, we may question whether it makes sense to analyze the transactions of all products together. An argument in favor of checking them together is that there is a variable (the product ID) that can be used to discriminate among the products, and thus the modeling techniques can use the variable if necessary. Moreover, by putting all transactions together, the models can take advantage of some eventual relationships among products. Nevertheless, an alternative would be to analyze each product in turn, ranking its transactions by some outlier score. This would require an extra step of obtaining the final global ranking from the individual product rankings but this should be simple. We will experiment with modeling approaches that follow a different strategy with respect to this issue. From the perspective of the experimental methodology, we will put all products together. With these transactions we will randomly select a test set using a stratified holdout strategy. This test set will be given to different modeling techniques that should return a ranking of these transactions according to their estimated probability of being frauds. Internally, the models may decide to analyze the products individually or all together.

6.4 Obtaining Outlier Rankings

This section describes the different models we will try with the goal of obtaining outlier rankings. For each attempt we will estimate its results using a stratified 70%/30% holdout strategy.

6.4.1 Unsupervised Approaches

6.4.1.1 The Modified Box Plot Rule

In Section 6.2.2 we described the box plot rule, which can be used to detect outliers of a continuous variable provided it follows a near-normal distribution. This is the case of the unit price of the products. In this context, one can think of this simple rule as the baseline method that we can apply to our data.

The application of the box plot rule to detect unusual unit price values of the transactions of each product will result in the identification of some values as potential outliers. We can use this rule on each set of transactions of the products appearing in a given test set. In the end we will have a set of potential outliers for each of the products. We have to decide how to move from these sets into an outlier ranking of all test sets. This means we have to distinguish the outliers to be able to rank them. A possibility is to use the idea of the normalized distance to the typical (median) unit price ($NDTP$) that we described in Section 6.3.2.3. This measure can be seen as a variation of the box plot rule because both use a kind of distance from the central values to decide on the "outlyingness" of a value. The advantage of the $NDTP$ is that it is a unitless metric and thus we can mix together the values for the different products and thus produce a global ranking of all test cases.

The idea outlined above can be implemented by the following function that receives a set of transactions and obtains their ranking order and score:

```
> BPrule.wf <- function(form,train,test,...) {
+     require(dplyr, quietly=TRUE)
+     ms <- as.matrix(filter(train,Insp != 'fraud') %>%
+                     group_by(Prod) %>%
+                     summarise(median=median(Uprice),iqr=IQR(Uprice)) %>%
+                     select(median,iqr))
+     rownames(ms) <- levels(train$Prod)
+     ms[which(ms[,'iqr']==0),'iqr'] <- ms[which(ms[,'iqr']==0),'median']
+     ORscore <- abs(test$Uprice-ms[test$Prod,'median']) /
+               ms[test$Prod,'iqr']
+     rankOrder <- order(ORscore,decreasing=TRUE)
+     res <- list(testSet=test,rankOrder=rankOrder,
+               probs=matrix(c(ORscore,ifelse(test$Insp=='fraud',1,0)),
+                       ncol=2))
+     res
+ }
```

This workflow function will be called from the **performanceEstimation()** function. As any user-defined workflow function this needs to follow some protocol in terms of the parameters that accepts and also the return value of its execution. In terms of parameters the **performanceEstimation()** function requires all user-defined wrokflow functions to accept as the first three parameters a formula, a training set, and a test set. All remaining parameters are specific to the workflow function and there can exist as many as the author of the function needs. In the above example the formula parameter is useless as the solution we are implementing does not use the values of the target variable, i.e. it is unsupervised. In the workflow we use the training data to calculate the median and IQR values per product. These statistics are then used to obtain the outlier score using the formula of Equation (6.2). You might eventually feel tempted to think that these statistics could be obtained once using all available data, but this would be wrong. We are writing a workflow (a solution to a predictive task) whose solution is based on these statistics. Whatever the result of an approach to a task, it should only depend on the given training data. If this rule of thumb is broken then the results of this workflow will inevitably be biased as they would be based on more information than what was given for training. The above workflow returns a list with the score mentioned above and the rank order of the test set observations, according to this score. Given that this method uses the $NDTP$ values to obtain its ranking, it is foreseeable that it will score very well in terms of the average value of this metric, which means that it will be a hard baseline to beat!

As a side note, we should remark that this is the place where we could have used the information on the similarity between products. In effect, for products with very few transactions, we could consider checking if there is a product that has a distribution of unit prices that is significantly similar. If there is such a product, we could add its transactions and thus obtain the estimate of the median and IQR statistics using a larger sample. This would mean that instead of calculating the median and IQR per product we would need to "unify" the transactions of products with few transactions with the ones of their most similar products. This would need to be done before the call to **summarise()** that calculates these statistics. We leave this as an exercise for the reader.

We will now evaluate this simple method using the holdout experimental methodology. To be more precise we will use three repetitions of holdout which correspond to random subsampling, though we will use the more common holdout term to refer to our approach. We start by calculating the values of the median and IQR for each product required for the evaluation of the candidate solutions to this task by the average $NDTP$ score. We will use all available data for this calculation, as our goal is to have the most precise estimate of these values to correctly evaluate the outlier ranking capabilities of the models. Because this global information is not passed to the modeling techniques, this cannot be regarded as giving information from the test data to the models. It is just a form of obtaining more reliable estimates of the ability of our models for detecting unusual values — we are using it for evaluating the models and not for obtaining them.

```
> library(dplyr)
> globalStats <- as.matrix(filter(sales,Insp != 'fraud') %>%
+                          group_by(Prod) %>%
+                          summarise(median=median(Uprice),iqr=IQR(Uprice)) %>%
+                          select(median,iqr))
> rownames(globalStats) <- levels(sales$Prod)
> globalStats[which(globalStats[,'iqr']==0),'iqr'] <-
+     globalStats[which(globalStats[,'iqr']==0),'median']
> head(globalStats,3)

      median       iqr
p1 11.34615 8.563580
p2 10.87786 5.609731
p3 10.00000 4.809092
```

With this information we are ready to run the **performanceEstimation()** function to obtain the holdout estimates of the selected statistics for the **BPrule.wf** workflow. As estimation settings we will use a 70%/30% division of the full dataset using a stratified sampling strategy, and calculate the precision/recall statistics for a predefined inspection limit effort of 10% of the test set. This last setting is somewhat arbitrary and any other threshold could have been selected. The estimates will be obtained based on three repetitions of this process. A more global perspective of the performance of the system over different inspection effort limits will be given by the PR and cumulative recall curves.

```
> library(performanceEstimation)
> bp.res <- performanceEstimation(
+       PredTask(Insp ~ ., sales),
+       Workflow("BPrule.wf"),
+       EstimationTask(metrics=c("Precision","Recall","avgNDTP"),
+                      method=Holdout(nReps=3, hldSz=0.3, strat=TRUE),
+                      evaluator="evalOutlierRanking",
+                      evaluator.pars=list(Threshold=0.1, statsProds=globalStats))
+ )
```

Instead of using the standard workflows provided by the package **performanceEstimation**, we have specified our own **BPrule.wf** function that implements the box-plot rule. Moreover, we are also specifying our own evaluator function (**evalOutlierRanking**) as we want special purpose metrics to be calculated. We are using the parameter **evaluator.pars** to specify some parameters that should be passed to this evaluator function any time it is called, in this case the inspection effort (parameter **Threshold**) and the median and IQR of the products (parameter **statsProds**) that are necessary to calculate the average normalized distance to typical price. Notice the specification of the estimation method described above through function **Holdout()**, in particular the indication of a stratified sampling mechanism through parameter **strat**.

The summary of the results of this experiment can be obtained as follows:

```
> summary(bp.res)


== Summary of a  Hold Out Performance Estimation Experiment ==

Task for estimating  Precision,Recall,avgNDTP  using
Stratified  3 x70 %/ 30 % Holdout
 Run with seed =  1234

* Predictive Tasks ::  sales.Insp
* Workflows   ::  BPrule.wf

-> Task:  sales.Insp
   *Workflow: BPrule.wf
            Precision      Recall      avgNDTP
avg      0.0166583375 0.52631579 11.1748886
std      0.0006505289 0.02055329  0.9004590
med      0.0163251707 0.51578947 10.7913476
iqr      0.0005830418 0.01842105  0.8369579
min      0.0162418791 0.51315789 10.5297012
max      0.0174079627 0.55000000 12.2036171
invalid 0.0000000000 0.00000000  0.0000000
```

The results of precision and recall are rather low. On average, only 52% of the known frauds are included in the top 10% reports of the rank produced by the *BPrule* approach.

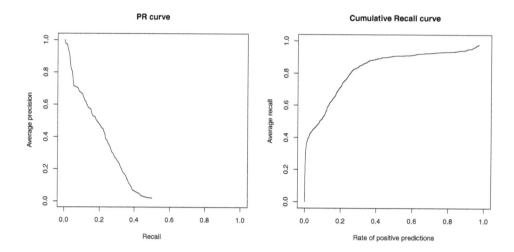

FIGURE 6.7: The PR (left) and cumulative recall (right) curves of the *BPrule* method.

The low values of recall could mean that the 10% effort was not enough for including all frauds, but that is not possible given the proportion of frauds in the test set and also the low values in precision. The extremely low value of precision means that this method is putting on the top 10% positions mostly **unkn** or **ok** cases. In the case of **unkn** reports, this is not necessarily bad, as these may actually be fraudulent reports. Given the relatively high score of $NDTP$, we can at least be sure that the unit price of these top reports is rather different from the typical price of the respective products. In effect, an average value of 11.1 for $NDTP$ means that the difference between the unit price of these top ranked reports and the median price of the reports of the same product is around 11 times the value of the IQR of these prices. Given that the IQR includes 50% of the reports, this means that the unit prices of these transactions are rather unusual. In summary, in spite of the poor results in terms of precision and recall, the score on avgNTPD seems to indicate that this simple method is able to suggest the inspection of highly unusual transaction reports.

To obtain the PR and cumulative recall charts, we need access to the actual outlier scores of the method on each holdout repetition, as well as the true "class" labels. The workflow function we have created (**BPrule.wf()**) returns these values in the component **probs**. All information returned by the workflows for all iterations of the estimation process is stored by package **performanceEstimation** functions on the returned results objects. This allows for posterior inspection/usage as we are planning to do here to produce the charts. Below you can find an example of this using function `getIterationsInfo()`. This function can be used to inspect the results returned on each iteration which are a list. We extract from the component **probs** of these lists the information necessary to produce our charts that are shown in Figure 6.7,

```
> ps.bp <- sapply(getIterationsInfo(bp.res),function(i) i$probs[,1])
> ts.bp <- sapply(getIterationsInfo(bp.res),function(i) i$probs[,2])
> PRcurve(ps.bp,ts.bp,main="PR curve",avg="vertical")
> CRchart(ps.bp,ts.bp,main='Cumulative Recall curve',avg='vertical')
```

Both curves are obtained by vertically averaging the curves of each of the three repetitions of the holdout process. The cumulative recall chart gives a more global perspective of the performance of the method. We can observe that the method obtains around 40% of recall with a very low inspection effort. However, to achieve values around 80%, we need to inspect roughly 30% of the reports.

6.4.1.2 Local Outlier Factors (*LOF*)

Outlier ranking is a well-studied research topic. Breunig et al. (2000) have developed the local outlier factor (*LOF*) system that is usually considered a state-of-the-art outlier ranking method. The main idea of this method is to try to obtain an outlyingness score for each case by estimating its degree of isolation with respect to its local neighborhood. The method is based on the notion of the local density of the observations. Cases in regions with very low density are considered outliers. The estimates of the density are obtained using the distances between cases. This method was described in detail in Section 3.4.4.2 (page 133).

Our book package includes an implementation of the *LOF* algorithm based on the work by (Acuna et al., 2009). Namely, we provide the function `lofactor()` that receives as arguments a dataset and the value of k that specifies the size of the neighborhood used in calculating the *LOF* of the observations. This implementation of the *LOF* system is limited to datasets described by numeric variables. This is, in effect, a frequent limitation for many modeling algorithms. As we have seen, our dataset includes several nominal variables. This means that we cannot apply this function directly to our dataset. There are several ways of overcoming this issue. A first alternative would be to change the source code of the implementation of *LOF* so that a mixed-mode distance function is used. There are several distance functions that can calculate the distance between observations described by variables of different types. An example is given by the function `daisy()` in the `cluster` package (Maechler et al., 2015). Another alternative consists of re-coding the nominal variables so that the observations are described by continuous variables only. Any nominal variable with n possible values can be re-coded into $n - 1$ binary (0/1) variables. These variables, frequently called dummy variables, indicate the presence (absence) of any of the n values. The application of this method to our dataset has a problem. The `ID` variable has 6,016 possible values while the variable `Prod` has 4,546. This means that if we use this strategy, we will obtain a dataset with 10,566 variables. This is an absurd increase in the dimensionality of the original data. This method is inadequate for this problem. The third alternative consists of handling each product individually, as we have done with the *BPrule* method. By proceeding this way, not only do we decrease significantly the computational requirements to handle this problem, but we also eliminate the need for the variable `Prod`. Moreover, handling the products separately was always a plausible approach, given the observed differences between them (see Section 6.2.3.2). Nevertheless, we still have to decide what to do with the information on the salespeople (the variable `ID`). Eliminating also this variable would mean assuming the fact that we consider some report unusual is independent of the salesman reporting it. This assumption does not seem too risky. The fact is that even if some salesperson is more prone to fraud, this should also be reflected in the unit prices that the person reports. In this context, the alternative of eliminating both columns and treating the products separately seems clearly more reasonable than the option of re-coding the variables. Summarizing, we will apply the *LOF* algorithm to a dataset of reports described only by the unit price. The following function implements a workflow using the *LOF* algorithm to produce the rankings of a set of transaction reports:

```
> LOF.wf <- function(form, train, test, k, ...) {
+     require(DMwR2, quietly=TRUE)
+     ntr <- nrow(train)
+     all <- as.data.frame(rbind(train,test))
+     N <- nrow(all)
+     ups <- split(all$Uprice,all$Prod)
```

```
+        r <- list(length=ups)
+        for(u in seq(along=ups))
+            r[[u]] <- if (NROW(ups[[u]]) > 3)
+                            lofactor(ups[[u]],min(k,NROW(ups[[u]]) %/% 2))
+                        else if (NROW(ups[[u]])) rep(0,NROW(ups[[u]]))
+                        else NULL
+        all$lof <- vector(length=N)
+        split(all$lof,all$Prod) <- r
+        all$lof[which(!(is.infinite(all$lof) | is.nan(all$lof)))] <-
+            SoftMax(all$lof[which(!(is.infinite(all$lof) | is.nan(all$lof)))])

+        res <- list(testSet=test,
+                    rankOrder=order(all[(ntr+1):N,'lof'],decreasing=TRUE),
+                    probs=as.matrix(cbind(all[(ntr+1):N,'lof'],
+                                    ifelse(test$Insp=='fraud',1,0))))
+        res
+ }
```

The workflow starts by merging the train and test datasets and use *LOF* to rank this full set of reports. From the ranking obtained we then select the outlier scores of the cases belonging to the test set. We could have ranked only the test set but this would not use the information in the training data. The alternative of ranking only the training data would also not make sense because this is an unsupervised method whose result cannot be used to make "predictions" for a test set.

The function split() was used to divide the unit prices of this full dataset by product. The result is a list whose components are the unit prices of the respective products. The for loop goes over each of these sets of prices and applies the *LOF* method to obtain an outlier factor for each of the prices. These factors are collected in a list (r) also organized by product. We only used the *LOF* method if there were at least three reports; otherwise all values were tagged as normal (score 0). After the main loop, the outlier factors obtained are "attached" to the respective transactions in the data frame all, again using the split() function. The next statement has the goal of changing the outlier factors into a 0..1 scale. It uses the function SoftMax() from our book package for this purpose. This function "squashes" a range of values into this scale. Due to the fact that the lofactor() function produced some Inf and NaN values for some transactions, we had to constrain the application of the SoftMax() function.

The next step is to use a holdout process to obtain the estimates of our evaluation metrics, as done before for the *BPrule* method. We will use the same settings as before and, in particular, will use the same random number generator seed to ensure that the same data partitions are used. All estimation method specification functions of the package **performanceEstimation** have a parameter named seed that allows you to set a random number generator seed. We are using its default value and thus all runs using different workflows will be applied to the same exact data partitions. We have set the value of the k parameter of the lofactor() function to 7. Further experiments could be carried out to tune this parameter. A word of warning before you execute the following code: depending on your hardware, this may start to take a bit too long, although still on the minutes scale.

```
> lof.res <- performanceEstimation(
+     PredTask(Insp ~ . , sales),
+     Workflow("LOF.wf", k=7),
+     EstimationTask(metrics=c("Precision","Recall","avgNDTP"),
+                    method=Holdout(nReps=3, hldSz=0.3, strat=TRUE),
+                    evaluator="evalOutlierRanking",
```

```
+                     evaluator.pars=list(Threshold=0.1, statsProds=globalStats))
+      )
```

The results of the *LOF* method were the following:

```
> summary(lof.res)


== Summary of a  Hold Out Performance Estimation Experiment ==

Task for estimating  Precision,Recall,avgNDTP  using
Stratified  3 x 70 % / 30 % Holdout
 Run with seed =  1234

* Predictive Tasks ::  sales.Insp
* Workflows   ::  LOF.wf

-> Task:  sales.Insp
  *Workflow: LOF.wf
            Precision      Recall    avgNDTP
avg      0.0221000611 0.69824561 8.7661376
std      0.0006251502 0.01975146 0.9362724
med      0.0220722972 0.69736842 8.4358879
iqr      0.0006246877 0.01973684 0.8915197
min      0.0214892554 0.67894737 8.0397428
max      0.0227386307 0.71842105 9.8227821
invalid 0.0000000000 0.00000000 0.0000000
```

As you may observe, the values of precision and recall for this 10% inspection effort are higher than the values obtained by the *BPrule* method. In particular, the value of recall has increased from 52% to 69%. However, the value of *NDTP* has decreased, though a value near 9 is still an interesting assertion on the degree of outlyingness of the unit prices of the reports put up front by the *LOF* method.

A more global perspective can be obtained with the PR and cumulative recall curves. To enable a better comparison with the *BPrule* method, we have also plotted the curves of this method, using the argument **add=TRUE** to make more than one curve appear on the same graph (Figure 6.8):

```
> ps.lof <- sapply(getIterationsInfo(lof.res), function(i) i$probs[,1])
> ts.lof <- sapply(getIterationsInfo(lof.res), function(i) i$probs[,2])
> PRcurve(ps.bp,ts.bp,main="PR curve",lty=1,
+         xlim=c(0,1),ylim=c(0,1),avg="vertical")
> PRcurve(ps.lof,ts.lof,add=TRUE,lty=2,avg='vertical')
> legend('topright',c('BPrule','LOF'),lty=c(1,2))
>
> CRchart(ps.bp,ts.bp,main='Cumulative Recall curve',
+         lty=1,xlim=c(0,1),ylim=c(0,1),avg='vertical')
> CRchart(ps.lof,ts.lof,add=TRUE,lty=2,avg='vertical')
> legend('bottomright',c('BPrule','LOF'),lty=c(1,2))
```

The analysis of the PR curves (left graph of Figure 6.8), shows that for smaller recall values, the *BPrule* generally achieves a considerably higher precision. For values of recall above 40%, the tendency is inverse although with not so marked differences. In terms of recall achieved by inspection effort (Figure 6.8, right), we can say that generally the *LOF*

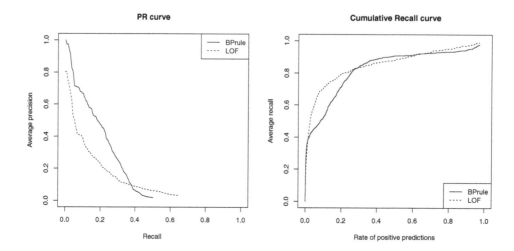

FIGURE 6.8: The PR (left) and cumulative recall (right) curves of the LOF, and $BPrule$ models.

method dominates the $BPrule$ for inspection efforts below 25% - 30%. For higher inspection efforts, the differences are not so clear, and the results are rather comparable. Given that the interest of the company is obviously on lower inspection efforts to decrease its costs (provided a good recall is achieved), we would say that the LOF method is more interesting. In effect, with an effort around 15% to 20%, one can capture roughly 70% to 80% of the frauds. Moreover, we should note that the values of $NDTP$ of LOF were interesting at this inspection effort of 10%.

6.4.1.3 Clustering-Based Outlier Rankings (OR_h)

The next outlier ranking method we consider is based on the results of a clustering algorithm. The OR_h method (Torgo, 2007) uses a hierarchical agglomerative clustering algorithm to obtain a dendrogram of the given data. Dendrograms are visual representations of the merging process of these clustering methods. The function `hclust()` of the base package `stats` implements several variants of this type of clustering. The object returned by this function includes a data structure (`merge`) that includes information on which cases are involved in each merging step. The OR_h method uses the information in this data structure as the basis for obtaining outlier rankings. The basic idea is that outliers should offer greater resistance to be merged and thus, when they are finally merged, the size difference between the group to which they belong and the group to which they are being merged should be very large. This reflects the idea that outliers are rather different from other observations, and thus their inclusion in groups with more "normal" observations should clearly decrease the homogeneity of the resulting group. Occasionally, outliers are merged at initial stages with other observations, but only if these are similar outliers. Otherwise, they will only be merged at later stages of the clustering process and usually with a much larger group of cases. This is the general idea that is captured by the OR_h method. More details on this methodology were given in Section 3.4.4.2 (page 133).

The function `outliers.ranking()` of our book package implements this method. The following function implements a workflow that uses the OR_h method to obtain the outlier scores of a test set of reports:

```
> ORh.wf <- function(form, train, test, ...) {
+     require(DMwR2, quietly=TRUE)
+     ntr <- nrow(train)
+     all <- as.data.frame(rbind(train,test))
+     N <- nrow(all)
+     ups <- split(all$Uprice,all$Prod)
+     r <- list(length=ups)
+     for(u in seq(along=ups))
+         r[[u]] <- if (NROW(ups[[u]]) > 3)
+                      outliers.ranking(ups[[u]])$prob.outliers
+                   else if (NROW(ups[[u]])) rep(0,NROW(ups[[u]]))
+                   else NULL
+     all$orh <- vector(length=N)
+     split(all$orh,all$Prod) <- r
+     all$orh[which(!(is.infinite(all$orh) | is.nan(all$orh)))] <-
+         SoftMax(all$orh[which(!(is.infinite(all$orh) | is.nan(all$orh)))])
+     res <- list(testSet=test,
+                 rankOrder=order(all[(ntr+1):N,'orh'],decreasing=TRUE),
+                 probs=as.matrix(cbind(all[(ntr+1):N,'orh'],
+                                 ifelse(test$Insp=='fraud',1,0))))
+     res
+ }
```

The function is very similar to the one presented previously for the *LOF* method. Once again we have used the approach of handling the products individually, primarily for the same reasons described for the *LOF* method. Nevertheless, the `outliers.ranking()` function can receive as argument a distance matrix of the observations being ranked, instead of the dataset. This means that we can obtain this matrix using any distance function that handles mixed-mode data (e.g., function `daisy()` in package `cluster`). However, if you decide to try this you will need large computation resources as clustering such a large dataset will require a large amount of main memory and also a fast processor. Even using this approach of handling each product separately, the following code that runs the full holdout experiments will surely take a while to run on any normal computer.

As with *LOF*, we have not carried out any thorough exploration of the several parameter values that the OR_h method accepts, simply using its defaults:

```
> orh.res <- performanceEstimation(
+     PredTask(Insp ~ . , sales),
+     Workflow("ORh.wf"),
+     EstimationTask(metrics=c("Precision","Recall","avgNDTP"),
+                    method=Holdout(nReps=3, hldSz=0.3, strat=TRUE),
+                    evaluator="evalOutlierRanking",
+                    evaluator.pars=list(Threshold=0.1, statsProds=globalStats))
+ )
```

A summary of the results of the OR_h method is shown below:

```
> summary(orh.res)


== Summary of a  Hold Out Performance Estimation Experiment ==

Task for estimating  Precision,Recall,avgNDTP  using
```

```
Stratified  3 x70 %/ 30 % Holdout
 Run with seed =  1234


* Predictive Tasks ::  sales.Insp
* Workflows  ::  ORh.wf


-> Task:  sales.Insp
  *Workflow: ORh.wf
             Precision      Recall    avgNDTP
avg      0.0215725471 0.681578947 8.8744953
std      0.0001442654 0.004558028 0.3911522
med      0.0214892554 0.678947368 8.9422496
iqr      0.0001249375 0.003947368 0.3867260
min      0.0214892554 0.678947368 8.4538922
max      0.0217391304 0.686842105 9.2273443
invalid 0.0000000000 0.000000000 0.0000000
```

The results of the OR_h-based workflow are very similar to the scores obtained with *LOF*.

The PR and cumulative recall curves of this method are shown in Figure 6.9, together with the curves of the other unsupervised methods we have tried previously. The following code was used to generate these graphs:

```
> ps.orh <- sapply(getIterationsInfo(orh.res), function(i) i$probs[,1])
> ts.orh <- sapply(getIterationsInfo(orh.res), function(i) i$probs[,2])
> PRcurve(ps.bp,ts.bp,main="PR curve",lty=1,
+         xlim=c(0,1),ylim=c(0,1),avg="vertical")
> PRcurve(ps.lof,ts.lof,add=TRUE,lty=2,avg='vertical')
> PRcurve(ps.orh,ts.orh,add=TRUE,lty=1,col='grey', avg='vertical')
> legend('topright',c('BPrule','LOF','ORh'),lty=c(1,2,1),
+        col=c('black','black','grey'))
>
> CRchart(ps.bp,ts.bp,main='Cumulative Recall curve',
+         lty=1,xlim=c(0,1),ylim=c(0,1),avg='vertical')
> CRchart(ps.lof,ts.lof,add=TRUE,lty=2,avg='vertical')
> CRchart(ps.orh,ts.orh,add=TRUE,lty=1,col='grey',avg='vertical')
> legend('bottomright',c('BPrule','LOF','ORh'),lty=c(1,2,1),
+        col=c('black','black','grey'))
```

As you can see, the results of the OR_h method are comparable to those of *LOF* in terms of the cumulative recall curve. However, regarding the PR curve, the OR_h system clearly dominates the score of *LOF*, with a smaller advantage over *BPrule*.

6.4.2   Supervised Approaches

In this section we explore several supervised classification approaches to our problem. Given our goal of obtaining a ranking for a set of transaction reports, we will have to constrain the selection of models. We will use only systems that are able to produce probabilistic classifications. For each test case, these methods output the probability of belonging to each of the possible classes. This type of information will allow us to rank the test reports according to their probability of belonging to our "target" class: the fraudulent reports.

Before describing a few concrete classification algorithms that we will use, we address a particular problem of our dataset: the imbalanced distribution of the class labels.

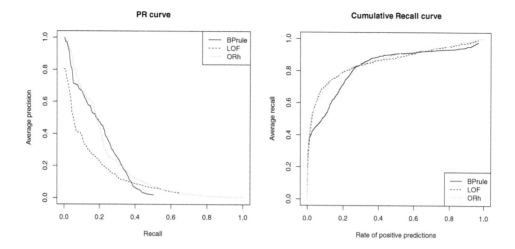

FIGURE 6.9: The PR (left) and cumulative recall (right) curves of the OR_h, LOF, and *BPrule* models.

6.4.2.1   The Class Imbalance Problem

Our dataset has a very imbalanced proportion of normal and fraudulent reports. The latter are a clear minority, roughly 8.1% of the inspected reports (i.e., supervised cases). Problems of this type can create all sorts of difficulties in the task of obtaining predictive models (Branco et al., 2016b). First, they require proper evaluation metrics as it is well known that the standard accuracy (or its complement error rate) is clearly inadequate for these domains. In effect, for our application it would be easy to obtain around 90% accuracy by predicting that all reports are normal. Given the prevalence of this class, this would get us to this apparently very high accuracy level. Another problem with class imbalance is that it has a strong impact on the performance of the learning algorithms that tend to disregard the minority class given its lack of statistical support. This is particularly problematic in situations where this minority class is exactly the most relevant class, as is the case in our domain.

There are several techniques that have been developed with the purpose of helping the learning algorithms overcome the problems raised by class imbalance. They generally group in two main families: (1) methods that bias the learning process by using specific evaluation metrics that are more sensitive to minority class examples; and (2) sampling methods that manipulate the training data to change the class distribution. In our attempt to use supervised classification methods in our problem, we will use a method belonging to this second category.

Several sampling methods have been proposed to change the class imbalance of a dataset. Under-sampling methods select a small part of the majority class examples and add them to the minority class cases, thereby building a dataset with a more balanced class distribution. Over-sampling methods work the other way around, using some process to replicate the minority class examples. Many variants of these two general sampling approaches exist. A successful example is the SMOTE method (Chawla et al., 2002). The general idea of this method is to artificially generate new examples of the minority class using the nearest neighbors of these cases. Furthermore, the majority class examples are also under-sampled, leading to a more balanced dataset.

Package **UBL** (Branco et al., 2016a) implements many alternative methods for addressing imbalanced target variable distributions for both classification and regression tasks. We will use the functions provided by this package in our task. Below you may find a simple illustration of using the implementation of SMOTE provided in this package.

```
> library(UBL)
> data(iris)
> data <- iris[, c(1, 2, 5)]
> data$Species <- factor(ifelse(data$Species == "setosa", "rare","common"))
> table(data$Species)


common    rare
   100      50

> newData <- SmoteClassif(Species ~ ., data, C.perc = "balance")
> table(newData$Species)


common    rare
    75      75

> newData2 <- SmoteClassif(Species ~ ., data, C.perc = list(common = 1,rare = 6))
> table(newData2$Species)


common    rare
   100     300
```

This small example uses the **iris** data to create an artificial dataset with two predictor variables (for easier visualization) and a new target variable that has an unbalanced class distribution. The code includes two example calls to the function SmoteClassif() from package **UBL**. The function takes in the first two arguments a formula (used to know which is the target variable) and the imbalanced data. The parameter C.per of the function controls the way the under- and over-sampling takes place. In the first example we have set it to the value "balance". With this value the function tries to balance the classes of the problem. In the second example we have indicated, for each class, the percentage of over- or under-sampling we want. If the value is above one the function oversamples the respective class, otherwise the class is under-sampled.

We can get a better idea of what was done by plotting the original and SMOTE'd datasets. This is the purpose of the following code, with the results shown in Figure 6.10:

```
> library(ggplot2)
> ggplot(data,aes(x=Sepal.Length,y=Sepal.Width,color=Species)) +
+     geom_point() + ggtitle("Original Data")
> ggplot(newData2,aes(x=Sepal.Length,y=Sepal.Width,color=Species)) +
+     geom_point() + ggtitle("SMOTE'd Data")
```

In our experiments with supervised classification algorithms, we will try variants of the methods using training sets balanced by this SMOTE method.

Further readings on class imbalance

Class imbalance is a well-studied subject. Examples of this research can be found in several workshops on this specific topic, such as the AAAI'2000 and ICML'2003 Workshops on Imbalanced datasets, or the special issue on Learning from Imbalanced Datasets in SIGKDD (Chawla et al., 2004). A recent survey of existing work can be found in Branco et al. (2016b). Class imbalance has implications in several relevant subjects of predictive

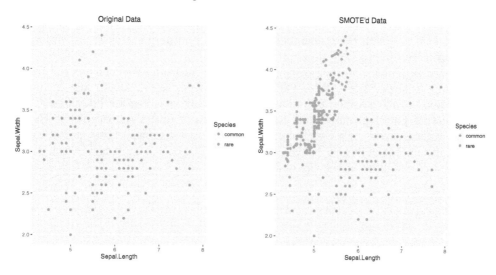

FIGURE 6.10: Using SMOTE to create more rare class examples.

modeling. Examples include the evaluation of prediction models (e.g., Provost and Fawcett (1997, 2001); Provost et al. (1998)), or cost sensitive learning (e.g., Domingos (1999); Drummond and Holte (2006); Elkan (2001)). Regarding sampling-based approaches to class imbalance, some reference works include Kubat and Matwin (1997), Japkowicz (2000), and Weiss and F.Provost (2003), among others. Specifically on SMOTE, the main references are Chawla et al. (2002) and Chawla et al. (2003).

6.4.2.2 Naive Bayes

Naive Bayes is a probabilistic classifier based on the Bayes theorem that uses very strong assumptions on the independence between the predictors. These assumptions rarely hold for real-world problems — and thus the name naive. Nevertheless, this method has been successfully applied to a large number of real-world applications.

The Bayes theorem specifies that $P(A|B) = \frac{P(B|A)P(A)}{P(B)}$. Using this theorem, the Naive Bayes classifier calculates the probability of each class for a given test case as

$$P(c|X_1, \cdots, X_p) = \frac{P(c)P(X_1, \cdots, X_p|c)}{P(X_1, \cdots, X_p)} \tag{6.3}$$

where c is a class and $X_1, \cdots, X_p$ are the observed values of the predictors for the given test case.

The probability $P(c)$ can be seen as the prior expectation of the class c. $P(X_1, \cdots, X_p|c)$ is the likelihood of the test case given the class c. Finally, the denominator is the probability of the observed evidence. This equation is calculated for all possible class values to determine the most probable class of the test case. This decision depends only on the numerator of the equation, as the denominator will be constant over all classes. This means that the most probable class for a given test case is the class c that maximizes the expression $P(c)P(X_1, \cdots, X_p|c)$.

Using some statistical definitions on conditional probabilities and assuming (naively) conditional independence between the predictors, we reduce the numerator of the fraction to

$$P(c)P(X_1, \cdots, X_p|c) = P(c) \prod_{i=1}^{p} P(X_i|c) \tag{6.4}$$

Naive Bayes implementations estimate these probabilities from the training sample using relative frequencies. Using these estimates, the method outputs the class probabilities for each test case according to Equation 6.3.

R has several implementations of the Naive Bayes method. We will use the function `naiveBayes()` from package **e1071**. Package **klaR** (Weihs et al., 2005) also includes an implementation of this classifier, together with interesting visualization functions.

The following function implements a workflow for our task that uses Naive Bayes to obtain the ranking scores of a test set of reports. It uses the inspected reports from the given training sample to obtain a Naive Bayes model. The outlier ranking is obtained using the estimated probabilities of the class being `fraud`:

```
> NB.wf <- function(form,train,test,...) {
+     require(e1071,quietly=TRUE)
+     sup <- which(train$Insp != 'unkn')
+     data <- as.data.frame(train[sup,c('ID','Prod','Uprice','Insp')])
+     data$Insp <- factor(data$Insp,levels=c('ok','fraud'))
+     model <- naiveBayes(Insp ~ .,data, ...)
+     preds <- predict(model,test[,c('ID','Prod','Uprice','Insp')], type='raw')
+     rankOrder <- order(preds[,'fraud'], decreasing=TRUE)
+     rankScore <- preds[,'fraud']
+     res <- list(testSet=test,
+                    rankOrder=rankOrder,
+                 probs=as.matrix(cbind(rankScore,
+                            ifelse(test$Insp=='fraud',1,0))))
+     res
+ }
```

We can obtain the results of this workflow using a call similar to the ones used with the previous workflows:

```
> nb.res <- performanceEstimation(
+     PredTask(Insp ~ . , sales),
+     Workflow("NB.wf"),
+     EstimationTask(metrics=c("Precision","Recall","avgNDTP"),
+                    method=Holdout(nReps=3,hldSz=0.3,strat=TRUE),
+                 evaluator="evalOutlierRanking",
+                 evaluator.pars=list(Threshold=0.1,
+                            statsProds=globalStats))
+     )
```

The results of the Naive Bayes model for the 10% inspection effort are the following:

```
> summary(nb.res)


== Summary of a  Hold Out Performance Estimation Experiment ==

Task for estimating  Precision,Recall,avgNDTP  using
Stratified  3 x70 %/ 30 % Holdout
 Run with seed =  1234

* Predictive Tasks ::  sales.Insp
* Workflows  ::  NBsm.wf
```

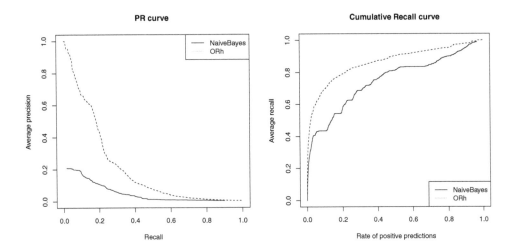

FIGURE 6.11: The PR (left) and cumulative recall (right) curves of the Naive Bayes and *ORh* methods.

```
-> Task:   sales.Insp
   *Workflow: NBsm.wf
            Precision      Recall     avgNDTP
avg        0.013743128  0.43421053  6.3672930
std        0.001082792  0.03421053  0.7743854
med        0.013743128  0.43421053  5.9861039
iqr        0.001082792  0.03421053  0.7004955
min        0.012660336  0.40000000  5.8573920
max        0.014825920  0.46842105  7.2583829
invalid    0.000000000  0.00000000  0.0000000
```

The scores are considerably worse than the scores obtained previously with the unsupervised methods. They are the worse scores we got till now with any of the methods we have tried.

Next we obtain the usual curves to get a better overall perspective of the performance of the model. We compare Naive Bayes with one of the best unsupervised models, OR_h:

```
> ps.nb <- sapply(getIterationsInfo(nb.res), function(i) i$probs[,1])
> ts.nb <- sapply(getIterationsInfo(nb.res), function(i) i$probs[,2])
> PRcurve(ps.nb,ts.nb,main="PR curve",lty=1,
+         xlim=c(0,1),ylim=c(0,1),avg="vertical")
> PRcurve(ps.orh,ts.orh,add=TRUE,lty=2,avg='vertical')
> legend('topright',c('NaiveBayes','ORh'),lty=1,col=c('black','grey'))
>
> CRchart(ps.nb,ts.nb,main='Cumulative Recall curve',
+         lty=1,xlim=c(0,1),ylim=c(0,1),avg='vertical')
> CRchart(ps.orh,ts.orh,add=TRUE,lty=2,avg='vertical')
> legend('bottomright',c('NaiveBayes','ORh'),lty=1,col=c('black','grey'))
```

The graphs of Figure 6.11 show very clearly that the Naive Bayes method is inferior to the OR_h method for this particular application. Both curves indicate that OR_h dominates over all possible setups.

A possible cause for the poor performance of the Naive Bayes may be the class imbalance of this problem. In Section 6.4.2.1 we discussed several methods for addressing this problem and, in particular, the SMOTE algorithm. We will now apply the Naive Bayes classifier using a training set pre-processed using SMOTE. This idea is implemented in the following workflow function:

```
> NBsm.wf <- function(form,train,test,C.perc="balance",dist="HEOM",...) {
+      require(e1071,quietly=TRUE)
+      require(UBL,quietly=TRUE)

+      sup <- which(train$Insp != 'unkn')
+      data <- as.data.frame(train[sup,c('ID','Prod','Uprice','Insp')])
+      data$Insp <- factor(data$Insp,levels=c('ok','fraud'))
+      newData <- SmoteClassif(Insp ~ .,data,C.perc=C.perc,dist=dist,...)
+      model <- naiveBayes(Insp ~ .,newData)
+      preds <- predict(model,test[,c('ID','Prod','Uprice','Insp')],type='raw')
+      rankOrder <- order(preds[,'fraud'],decreasing=T)
+      rankScore <- preds[,'fraud']

+      res <- list(testSet=test,
+                  rankOrder=rankOrder,
+                  probs=as.matrix(cbind(rankScore,
+                                        ifelse(test$Insp=='fraud',1,0))))
+      res
+ }
```

The following statement obtains the hold-out estimates for this SMOTE'd version of Naive Bayes:

```
> nbs.res <- performanceEstimation(
+     PredTask(Insp ~ ., sales),
+     Workflow("NBsm.wf"),
+     EstimationTask(metrics=c("Precision","Recall","avgNDTP"),
+                    method=Holdout(nReps=3,hldSz=0.3,strat=TRUE),
+                    evaluator="evalOutlierRanking",
+                    evaluator.pars=list(Threshold=0.1,
+                                        statsProds=globalStats))
+     )
```

The results of this version of the Naive Bayes model for the 10% inspection effort are the following:

```
> summary(nbs.res)


== Summary of a  Hold Out Performance Estimation Experiment ==

Task for estimating  Precision,Recall,avgNDTP  using
Stratified  3 x 70 % / 30 % Holdout
 Run with seed =  1234

* Predictive Tasks ::  sales.Insp
* Workflows   ::   NBsm.wf

-> Task:  sales.Insp
  *Workflow: NBsm.wf
```

```
           Precision     Recall    avgNDTP
avg        0.013909712 0.43947368 6.4017351
std        0.001332667 0.04210526 0.8850754
med        0.013909712 0.43947368 6.0882813
iqr        0.001332667 0.04210526 0.8424183
min        0.012577045 0.39736842 5.7160437
max        0.015242379 0.48157895 7.4008803
invalid 0.000000000 0.00000000 0.0000000
```

These results are almost indistinguishable from the results of the "normal" Naive Bayes. The scores are only slightly superior but still very far from the best results of the unsupervised models. It seems that despite the over-sampling of the minority class carried out by SMOTE, Naive Bayes is still not able to correctly predict which are the fraudulent reports. Let us check the graphs for a more global perspective of the performance of this variant:

```
> ps.nbs <- sapply(getIterationsInfo(nbs.res), function(i) i$probs[,1])
> ts.nbs <- sapply(getIterationsInfo(nbs.res), function(i) i$probs[,2])
> PRcurve(ps.nb,ts.nb,main="PR curve",lty=1,
+         xlim=c(0,1),ylim=c(0,1), avg="vertical")
> PRcurve(ps.orh,ts.orh,add=TRUE,lty=2, avg='vertical')
> PRcurve(ps.nbs,ts.nbs,add=TRUE,lty=1, col='grey',avg='vertical')
> legend('topright',c('NaiveBayes','ORh','smoteNaiveBayes'),lty=c(1,2,1),
+         col=c('black','black','grey'))
>
> CRchart(ps.nb,ts.nb,main='Cumulative Recall curve',
+         lty=1,xlim=c(0,1),ylim=c(0,1),avg='vertical')
> CRchart(ps.orh,ts.orh,add=TRUE,lty=2,avg='vertical')
> CRchart(ps.nbs,ts.nbs,add=TRUE,lty=1,col='grey',avg='vertical')
> legend('bottomright',c('NaiveBayes','ORh','smoteNaiveBayes'),lty=c(1,2,1),
+         col=c('black','black','grey'))
```

The graphs of Figure 6.12 confirm the disappointing results of the SMOTE'd version of Naive Bayes. In effect, it shows the same poor results as the standard Naive Bayes when compared to OR_h and, moreover, its performance is almost always surpassed by the standard version.

Given these results, we might question whether the fact that we have not split the model construction by product, as done in the unsupervised methods, may be causing difficulties with this model. As an exercise you can try to follow this approach with Naive Bayes. You need to adapt the code used for the unsupervised models that splits the transactions by product to the Naive Bayes model. An additional difficulty that you will meet, if you decide to carry out this exercise, is the fact that you will have very few supervised reports by product. In effect, even without the restriction of being labeled, we have observed that several products have too few transactions. If we add the restriction of only using the labeled transactions, this problem will surely increase.

Further readings on Naive Bayes

Naive Bayes is a well-known classification algorithm studied in many research areas. Some interesting additional references on this topic include the works by Domingos and Pazzani (1997), Rish (2001), Hand and Yu (2001); and Kononenko (1991).

6.4.2.3 AdaBoost

AdaBoost (Freund and Shapire, 1996) is a learning algorithm that belongs to the class of ensemble models. These types of models are, in effect, formed by a set of base models

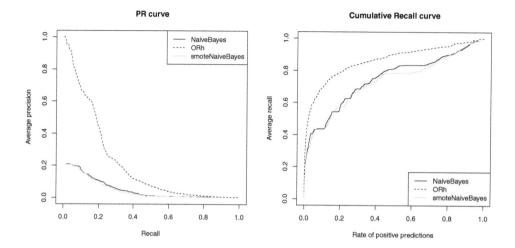

FIGURE 6.12: The PR (left) and cumulative recall (right) curves for the two versions of Naive Bayes and *ORh* methods.

that contribute to the prediction of the algorithm using some form of aggregation. *AdaBoost* uses an adaptive boosting method to obtain the set of base models. Boosting is a general method that can be used to improve the performance of any base algorithm provided it is better than the random classifier. The construction of the *AdaBoost* model is obtained sequentially. Each new member of the sequence is obtained by improving on the errors of the previous model of the sequence. The improvements are obtained using a weighting schema that increases the weights of the cases that are incorrectly classified by the previous model. This means that the base learner is used on different distributions of the training data. After some number of iterations of this process, the result is a set of base models obtained on different training samples. This ensemble can be used to obtain predictions for test cases of the original problem. The predictions are obtained by a weighted average of the predictions of the individual base models. These weights are defined so that larger values are given to the last models in the sequence (theoretically the ones with lower error).

The case weighting schema used by *AdaBoost* is interesting from the perspective of learning with imbalance class distributions. Even if at the initial iterations the cases of the minority class are disregarded by the models, their weight is increased and the models are "forced" to focus on learning them. Theoretically, this should lead the resulting ensemble to be more accurate at predicting these rare cases.

Further details on ensembles in general and boosting in particular, including *AdaBoost*, were given in Section 3.4.5.5 (page 165).

AdaBoost.M1 is a particular instantiation of the *AdaBoost* method. It uses as base learners classification trees with a small number of nodes. This method is implemented in function `boosting()` of the extra package **adabag** (Alfaro et al., 2013). Another alternative is to use an implementation available in the Weka[3] data mining software. Weka is an open source software for data mining and machine learning. This excellent tool provides many learning algorithms with a nice graphical user interface. Compared to R, it offers several algorithms that are not available in R, and it offers an easy and nice user interface. R, on the other hand, offers much more flexibility in terms of software development/prototyping and many more available modeling tools spanning a much wider set of research areas. Thanks

---

[3]http://www.cs.waikato.ac.nz/ml/weka/.

to the R extra package **RWeka** (Hornik et al., 2009), we can easily use most Weka facilities within R. Installing this package will also install Weka on your computer, provided you already have Java installed on it. The installation process will complain and give you clear instructions on what to do if that is not your case. We strongly suggest that after installing the package, you read its help pages to get an idea of the many methods that are available through RWeka.

The function `AdaBoostM1()` provided in package **RWeka** obtains *AdaBoost.M1* classification models using the Weka implementation of this algorithm. Compared to the implementation of the package **adabag**, this function is significantly faster to run, which in reasonably large datasets like ours may pay off depending on the setup. By default, the Weka implementation uses decision stumps as the base learners. These models are a special type of classification trees formed by a single test node. That is not the case of the **adabag** implementation that uses full trees, and that may explain the differences in computational efficiency. Several parameters of the function can be changed if required. The function `WOW()` allows you to check which parameters are available for a particular Weka learning algorithm. The following is an example of its use for our target model:

```
> library(RWeka)
> WOW(AdaBoostM1)

-P <num>
        Percentage of weight mass to base training on.  (default
        100, reduce to around 90 speed up)
Number of arguments: 1.
-Q      Use resampling for boosting.
-S <num>
        Random number seed.  (default 1)
Number of arguments: 1.
-I <num>
        Number of iterations.  (default 10)
Number of arguments: 1.
-W      Full name of base classifier.  (default:
        weka.classifiers.trees.DecisionStump)
Number of arguments: 1.
-output-debug-info
        If set, classifier is run in debug mode and may output
        additional info to the console
-do-not-check-capabilities
        If set, classifier capabilities are not checked before
        classifier is built (use with caution).

Options specific to classifier weka.classifiers.trees.DecisionStump:

-output-debug-info
        If set, classifier is run in debug mode and may output
        additional info to the console
-do-not-check-capabilities
        If set, classifier capabilities are not checked before
        classifier is built (use with caution).
```

The value of some parameter can be changed when we call the respective function with the help of the parameter `control` and the function `Weka_control()`. Here is a small illustrative example of applying `AdaBoostM1()` to the well-known `iris` dataset, using 100 iterations instead of the default 10:

```
> data(iris)
> idx <- sample(150,100)
> model <- AdaBoostM1(Species ~ .,iris[idx,], control=Weka_control(I=100))
> preds <- predict(model,iris[-idx,])
> head(preds)

[1] setosa setosa setosa setosa setosa setosa
Levels: setosa versicolor virginica

> table(preds,iris[-idx,'Species'])
```

```
preds         setosa versicolor virginica
  setosa          18          0         0
  versicolor       0         15         1
  virginica        0          0        16
```

The following function implements a workflow using the *AdaBoost.M1* algorithm. As with the Naive Bayes algorithm, we will apply the *AdaBoost.M1* method to all transactions — and not individually by product.

```
> ab.wf <- function(form,train,test,ntrees=100,...) {
+      require(RWeka,quietly=TRUE)
+      sup <- which(train$Insp != 'unkn')
+      data <- as.data.frame(train[sup,c('ID','Prod','Uprice','Insp')])
+      data$Insp <- factor(data$Insp,levels=c('ok','fraud'))
+      model <- AdaBoostM1(Insp ~ .,data,
+                          control=Weka_control(I=ntrees))
+      preds <- predict(model,test[,c('ID','Prod','Uprice','Insp')],
+                       type='probability')
+      rankOrder <- order(preds[,"fraud"],decreasing=TRUE)
+      rankScore <- preds[,"fraud"]

+      res <- list(testSet=test,
+                  rankOrder=rankOrder,
+                  probs=as.matrix(cbind(rankScore,
+                                  ifelse(test$Insp=='fraud',1,0))))
+      res
+ }
```

Finally, we have the code to run the hold-out experiments for this workflow:

```
> ab.res <- performanceEstimation(
+      PredTask(Insp ~ .,sales),
+      Workflow("ab.wf"),
+      EstimationTask(metrics=c("Precision","Recall","avgNDTP"),
+                     method=Holdout(nReps=3,hldSz=0.3,strat=TRUE),
+                     evaluator="evalOutlierRanking",
+                     evaluator.pars=list(Threshold=0.1,
+                                    statsProds=globalStats))
+      )
```

The results of *AdaBoost* for the 10% effort are the following:

```
> summary(ab.res)


== Summary of a  Hold Out Performance Estimation Experiment ==

Task for estimating  Precision,Recall,avgNDTP  using
Stratified  3 x70 %/ 30 % Holdout
 Run with seed =  1234


* Predictive Tasks ::  sales.Insp
* Workflows  ::  ab.wf


-> Task:  sales.Insp
  *Workflow: ab.wf
            Precision      Recall    avgNDTP
avg      0.0204897551 0.64736842 7.0543305
std      0.0004997501 0.01578947 0.3744884
med      0.0204897551 0.64736842 6.9309492
iqr      0.0004997501 0.01578947 0.3589210
min      0.0199900050 0.63157895 6.7571001
max      0.0209895052 0.66315789 7.4749422
invalid 0.0000000000 0.00000000 0.0000000
```

These results are among the best we have seen thus far. In effect, these scores compare well with the best scores we have obtained with both LOF and OR_h. Moreover, we note that this model is using only a very small part of the given reports (the inspected ones) to obtain its rankings. Despite this, it achieved a robust 64% of recall with a good 7 score in terms of average $NDTP$.

The PR and cumulative recall curves can be obtained as before:

```
> ps.ab <- sapply(getIterationsInfo(ab.res), function(i) i$probs[,1])
> ts.ab <- sapply(getIterationsInfo(ab.res), function(i) i$probs[,2])
> PRcurve(ps.nb,ts.nb,main="PR curve",lty=1,
+         xlim=c(0,1),ylim=c(0,1), avg="vertical")
> PRcurve(ps.orh,ts.orh,add=TRUE,lty=1, color='grey', avg='vertical')
> PRcurve(ps.ab,ts.ab,add=TRUE,lty=2,avg='vertical')
> legend('topright',c('NaiveBayes','ORh','AdaBoostM1'),
+        lty=c(1,1,2),col=c('black','grey','black'))
>
> CRchart(ps.nb,ts.nb,main='Cumulative Recall curve',
+         lty=1,xlim=c(0,1),ylim=c(0,1),avg='vertical')
> CRchart(ps.orh,ts.orh,add=TRUE,lty=1,color='grey',avg='vertical')
> CRchart(ps.ab,ts.ab,add=TRUE,lty=2,avg='vertical')
> legend('bottomright',c('NaiveBayes','ORh','AdaBoostM1'),
+        lty=c(1,1,2),col=c('black','grey','grey'))
```

The graphs in Figure 6.13 confirm the excellent performance of the *AdaBoost.M1* algorithm, particularly in terms of the cumulative recall curve. This curve shows that for most effort levels, *AdaBoost.M1* matches the score obtained by OR_h. In terms of precision/recall, the performance of *AdaBoost.M1* is not that interesting, particularly for low levels of recall. However, for higher recall levels, it clearly matches the precision of the best scores we have obtained thus far. Moreover, we note that these higher recall levels are exactly what matters for this application.

Summarizing, we have seen that *AdaBoost.M1* is a very competitive algorithm for this

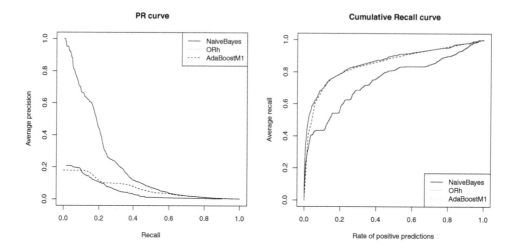

FIGURE 6.13: The PR (left) and cumulative recall (right) curves of the Naive Bayes, *ORh*, and *AdaBoost.M1* methods.

application. Despite the difficulties of class imbalance, this ensemble method has managed to achieve top performance with the rankings it produces.

Further readings on boosting

The *AdaBoost.M1* algorithm is an example of a wider class of boosting algorithms that try to obtain good predictive performance using an ensemble of weak learners (learners that are marginally better than random guessing). The reference work on *AdaBoost* is the paper by Freund and Shapire (1996). Other important historical references on boosting are the works by Shapire (1990) and Freund (1990). Some important analyses can also be found in Breiman (1998), Friedman (2002), and Rätsch et al. (2001). A very good description of boosting can be found in Chapter 10 of the book by Hastie et al. (2001).

6.4.3   Semi-Supervised Approaches

This section describes an attempt to use both inspected and non-inspected reports to obtain a classification model to detect fraudulent reports. This means we need some form of semi-supervised classification method (*see* Section 6.3.1.3).

Self-training (e.g., Rosenberg et al. (2005); Yarowsky (1995)) is a well-known form of semi-supervised classification. This approach consists of building an initial classifier using the given labeled cases. This classifier is then used to predict the labels of the unlabeled cases in the given training set. The cases for which the classifier has very high confidence in the predicted label are added to the labeled set, together with their predicted labels. With this larger dataset, a new classifier is obtained and so on. This iterative process is continued until some criteria are met. The last classifier is the result of the learning process. This methodology can be applied to any base classification algorithm, provided it is able to output some indication of its confidence in the predictions. This is the case of probabilistic classifiers like the two we described in Section 6.4.2. The self-training method has three relevant parameters: (1) the base learner, (2) the threshold on the confidence of classifications that determines which cases are added to the new training set, and (3) the criteria to decide when to terminate the self-training process. In our book package we have included a general function (`SelfTrain()`) that can be used with any probabilistic classifier to learn a model based on a training set with both labeled and unlabeled cases.

Below you can find a simple example that illustrates its use with the *Iris* dataset. We have artificially created a few unlabeled examples in this dataset to make semi-supervised classification potentially useful:

```
> library(DMwR2)
> library(e1071)
> data(iris)
> set.seed(1234)
> idx <- sample(150, 100)
> tr <- iris[idx, ]
> ts <- iris[-idx, ]
> nb <- naiveBayes(Species ~ ., tr)
> table(predict(nb, ts), ts$Species)


            setosa versicolor virginica
  setosa        12          0         0
  versicolor     0         21         1
  virginica      0          0        16

> trST <- tr
> nas <- sample(100, 90)
> trST[nas, "Species"] <- NA
> func <- function(m, d) {
+     p <- predict(m, d, type = "raw")
+     data.frame(cl = colnames(p)[ apply(p, 1, which.max) ],
+                p = apply(p, 1, max))
+ }
> nbSTbase <- naiveBayes(Species ~ ., trST[-nas, ])
> table(predict(nbSTbase, ts), ts$Species)


            setosa versicolor virginica
  setosa        12          0         0
  versicolor     0         18         2
  virginica      0          3        15

> nbST <- SelfTrain(Species ~ ., trST,
+                   learner="naiveBayes", learner.pars=list(),
+                   pred="func")
> table(predict(nbST, ts), ts$Species)


            setosa versicolor virginica
  setosa        12          0         0
  versicolor     0         20         2
  virginica      0          1        15
```

The above code obtains three different Naive Bayes models. The first (nb) is obtained with a sample of 100 labeled cases. This set of 100 cases is then transformed in another set where 90 of the cases were unlabeled by setting the target variable to NA. Using the remaining ten labeled cases we obtain the second Naive Bayes model (nbSTbase). Finally, the dataset with the mixed labeled and unlabeled cases is given to the SelfTrain() function and another model (nbST) obtained. As you can observe, in this small example, the self-trained model is able to almost reach the same level of performance as the initial model obtained with all 100 labeled cases.

In order to use `SelfTrain()`, the user must create a function (`func()` on the code above) that given a model and a test set is able to return a data frame with two columns and the same number of rows as the test set. The first column of this data frame contains the labels predicted for the cases, while the second column has the respective probability of that classification. This needs to be defined outside the `SelfTrain()` function because not all `predict` methods use the same syntax to obtain probabilistic classifications.

The `SelfTrain()` function has several parameters that control the iterative process. Parameter `thrConf` (defaulting to 0.9) sets the required probability for an unlabeled case to be merged into the labeled set. Parameter `maxIts` (default value of 10) allows the user to indicate a maximum number of self-training iterations, while parameter `percFull` (default value of 1) indicates that the process should stop if the labeled set reaches a certain percentage of the given dataset. The self-training iterative process finishes if either there are no classifications that reach the required probability level, if the maximum number of iterations is reached, or if the size of the current labeled training set is already the target percentage of the given dataset. A final note on the fact that the `SelfTrain()` function requires that the unlabeled cases be signaled as such by having the value `NA` on the target variable.

We have applied this self-training strategy with the Naive Bayes model as base classifier. The following functions implement a workflow using this self-trained Naive Bayes model and run the hold-out experiments with this workflow. A word of warning is in order concerning the computational resources that are necessary for carrying out these experiments. Depending on your hardware, this can take some time, although always on the order of minutes (at least on my average computer):

```
> pred.nb <- function(m,d) {
+     p <- predict(m,d,type='raw')
+     data.frame(cl=colnames(p)[apply(p,1,which.max)],
+                p=apply(p,1,max)
+                )
+ }
>
> nb.st.wf <- function(form,train,test,...) {
+     require(e1071,quietly=TRUE)
+     require(DMwR2, quietly=TRUE)
+     train <- as.data.frame(train[,c('ID','Prod','Uprice','Insp')])
+     train[which(train$Insp == 'unkn'),'Insp'] <- NA
+     train$Insp <- factor(train$Insp,levels=c('ok','fraud'))
+     model <- SelfTrain(form,train,
+                        learner='naiveBayes', learner.pars=list(),
+                        pred='pred.nb')
+     preds <- predict(model,test[,c('ID','Prod','Uprice','Insp')],
+                      type='raw')

+     rankOrder <- order(preds[,'fraud'],decreasing=TRUE)
+     rankScore <- preds[,"fraud"]

+     res <- list(testSet=test,
+                 rankOrder=rankOrder,
+                 probs=as.matrix(cbind(rankScore,
+                                 ifelse(test$Insp=='fraud',1,0))))
+     res
```

```
+ }


> nb.st.res <- performanceEstimation(
+      PredTask(Insp ~ .,sales),
+      Workflow("nb.st.wf"),
+      EstimationTask(metrics=c("Precision","Recall","avgNDTP"),
+                     method=Holdout(nReps=3,hldSz=0.3,strat=TRUE),
+                     evaluator="evalOutlierRanking",
+                     evaluator.pars=list(Threshold=0.1,
+                                         statsProds=globalStats))
+      )
```

The results of this self-trained model are the following:

```
> summary(nb.st.res)


== Summary of a  Hold Out Performance Estimation Experiment ==

Task for estimating  Precision,Recall,avgNDTP  using
Stratified  3 x70 %/ 30 % Holdout
 Run with seed =  1234

* Predictive Tasks ::  sales.Insp
* Workflows   ::  nb.st.wf

-> Task:  sales.Insp
   *Workflow: nb.st.wf
             Precision      Recall    avgNDTP
avg      0.013521017 0.42719298 7.0820716
std      0.001130846 0.03572879 0.7413338
med      0.013659837 0.43157895 6.7859004
iqr      0.001124438 0.03552632 0.6955485
min      0.012327170 0.38947368 6.5346088
max      0.014576045 0.46052632 7.9257057
invalid 0.000000000 0.00000000 0.0000000
```

These results are rather disappointing. They are very similar to the results obtained with a Naive Bayes model learned only on the labeled data. With the exception of the average $NDTP$, which has improved slightly, all other statistics are roughly the same, and thus still far from the best scores we have obtained so far.

Figure 6.14 shows the PR and cumulative recall curves of this model as well as those of the standard Naive Bayes and OR_h methods. They were obtained with the following code:

```
> ps.nb.st <- sapply(getIterationsInfo(nb.st.res), function(i) i$probs[,1])
> ts.nb.st <- sapply(getIterationsInfo(nb.st.res), function(i) i$probs[,2])
> PRcurve(ps.nb,ts.nb,main="PR curve",lty=1,
+         xlim=c(0,1),ylim=c(0,1), avg="vertical")
> PRcurve(ps.orh,ts.orh,add=TRUE,lty=1, color='grey', avg='vertical')
> PRcurve(ps.nb.st,ts.nb.st,add=TRUE,lty=2,avg='vertical')
> legend('topright',c('NaiveBayes','ORh','NaiveBayes-ST'),
+         lty=c(1,1,2),col=c('black','grey','black'))
>
```

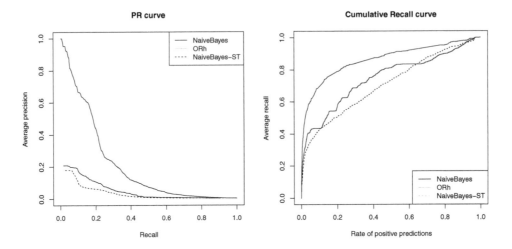

FIGURE 6.14: The PR (left) and cumulative recall (right) curves of the self-trained Naive Bayes, together with the standard Naive Bayes and *ORh* methods.

```
> CRchart(ps.nb,ts.nb,main='Cumulative Recall curve',
+        lty=1,xlim=c(0,1),ylim=c(0,1),avg='vertical')
> CRchart(ps.orh,ts.orh,add=TRUE,lty=1,color='grey',avg='vertical')
> CRchart(ps.nb.st,ts.nb.st,add=TRUE,lty=2,avg='vertical')
> legend('bottomright',c('NaiveBayes','ORh','NaiveBayes-ST'),
+        lty=c(1,1,2),col=c('black','grey','grey'))
```

The graphs confirm the disappointing performance of the self-trained Naive Bayes classifier. For this particular problem, this semi-supervised classifier is clearly not competitive even with the standard Naive Bayes model obtained with a considerable smaller dataset.

We have also used the self-training approach with the *AdaBoost.M1* algorithm. The following code describes the workflow function and the respective experiments:

```
> pred.ada <- function(m,d) {
+     p <- predict(m,d,type='probability')
+     data.frame(cl=colnames(p)[apply(p,1,which.max)],
+                p=apply(p,1,max)
+                )
+ }
>
> ab.st.wf <- function(form,train,test,ntrees=100,...) {
+     require(RWeka,quietly=TRUE)
+     require(DMwR2,quietly=TRUE)
+     train <- as.data.frame(train[,c('ID','Prod','Uprice','Insp')])
+     train[which(train$Insp == 'unkn'),'Insp'] <- NA
+     train$Insp <- factor(train$Insp,levels=c('ok','fraud'))
+     model <- SelfTrain(form,train,
+                   learner='AdaBoostM1',
+                   learner.pars=list(control=Weka_control(I=ntrees)),
+                   pred='pred.ada')
+     preds <- predict(model,test[,c('ID','Prod','Uprice','Insp')],
+                   type='probability')
```

```
+       rankOrder <- order(preds[,'fraud'],decreasing=T)
+       rankScore <- preds[,"fraud"]

+       res <- list(testSet=test,
+                   rankOrder=rankOrder,
+                   probs=as.matrix(cbind(rankScore,
+                                         ifelse(test$Insp=='fraud',1,0))))
+       res
+ }


> ab.st.res <- performanceEstimation(
+       PredTask(Insp ~ .,sales),
+       Workflow("ab.st.wf"),
+       EstimationTask(metrics=c("Precision","Recall","avgNDTP"),
+                       method=Holdout(nReps=3,hldSz=0.3,strat=TRUE),
+                       evaluator="evalOutlierRanking",
+                       evaluator.pars=list(Threshold=0.1,
+                                           statsProds=globalStats))
+       )
```

The results of the self-trained *AdaBoost* for the 10% effort are the following:

```
> summary(ab.st.res)


== Summary of a  Hold Out Performance Estimation Experiment ==

Task for estimating  Precision,Recall,avgNDTP   using
Stratified  3 x70 %/ 30 % Holdout
 Run with seed =   1234

* Predictive Tasks ::  sales.Insp
* Workflows   ::  ab.st.wf

-> Task:  sales.Insp
  *Workflow: ab.st.wf
            Precision      Recall     avgNDTP
avg       0.021294908  0.67280702  7.9596032
std       0.001087055  0.03434521  0.8194148
med       0.021655839  0.68421053  7.8507389
iqr       0.001041146  0.03289474  0.8139729
min       0.020073297  0.63421053  7.2000624
max       0.022155589  0.70000000  8.8280083
invalid   0.000000000  0.00000000  0.0000000
```

Although not impressive, these scores represent a slight improvement over the *AdaBoost.M1* model obtained using only the labeled data. While precision stayed basically the same, there were small improvements in recall and average *NDTP*.

Figure 6.15 shows the curves of this self-trained model, together with the standard *AdaBoost.M1* and OR_h methods. The curves were obtained as usual.

```
> ps.ab.st <- sapply(getIterationsInfo(ab.st.res), function(i) i$probs[,1])
> ts.ab.st <- sapply(getIterationsInfo(ab.st.res), function(i) i$probs[,2])
```

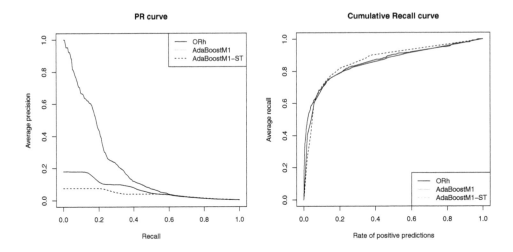

FIGURE 6.15: The PR (left) and cumulative recall (right) curves of *AdaBoost.M1* with self-training together with *ORh* and standard *AdaBoost.M1* methods.

```
> PRcurve(ps.orh,ts.orh,main="PR curve",lty=1,
+         xlim=c(0,1),ylim=c(0,1), avg="vertical")
> PRcurve(ps.ab,ts.ab,add=TRUE,lty=1, color='grey', avg='vertical')
> PRcurve(ps.ab.st,ts.ab.st,add=TRUE,lty=2,avg='vertical')
> legend('topright',c('ORh','AdaBoostM1','AdaBoostM1-ST'),
+         lty=c(1,1,2),col=c('black','grey','black'))
>
> CRchart(ps.orh,ts.orh,main='Cumulative Recall curve',
+         lty=1,xlim=c(0,1),ylim=c(0,1),avg='vertical')
> CRchart(ps.ab,ts.ab,add=TRUE,lty=1,color='grey',avg='vertical')
> CRchart(ps.ab.st,ts.ab.st,add=TRUE,lty=2,avg='vertical')
> legend('bottomright',c('ORh','AdaBoostM1','AdaBoostM1-ST'),
+         lty=c(1,1,2),col=c('black','grey','grey'))
```

The cumulative recall curve confirms that the self-trained *AdaBoost.M1* is among the best models from the ones we have considered for this fraud detection problem. In particular, for inspection efforts above 15% it dominates the other systems in terms of the proportion of frauds that it detects. In terms of precision, the scores are not that interesting, but as we mentioned before, this is not necessarily bad if the unlabeled reports that the model puts on higher positions in the ranking are confirmed as frauds after being audited.

6.5   Summary

The main goal of this chapter was to introduce the reader to a new class of data mining problems: outliers ranking. In particular, we have used a data set that enabled us to tackle this task from different perspectives. Namely, we used supervised, unsupervised and semi-supervised approaches to the problem. The application used in this chapter can be regarded as an instantiation of the general problem of finding unusual observations of a phenomenon having a limited amount of resources. Several real-world applications map into this general framework, such as detecting frauds in credit card transactions, telecommunications, tax declarations, etc. In the area of security, there are also several applications of this general concept of outlier ranking.

In methodological terms we have introduced the reader to a few new topics:

- Outlier detection and ranking

- Clustering methods

- Semi-supervised learning

- Semi-supervised classification through self-training

- Imbalanced class distributions and methods for handling this type of problems

- Naive Bayes classifiers

- *AdaBoost* classifiers

- Precision/recall and cumulative recall curves

- Holdout experiments

From the perspective of learning R, we have illustrated,

- How to obtain several evaluation statistics and how to visualize them using the `ROCR` package

- How to obtain holdout estimates of evaluation metrics

- How to obtain local outlier factors with the LOF method

- How to obtain outlier rankings using the OR_h method

- How to fight class imbalance through SMOTE

- How to obtain Naive Bayes classification models

- How to obtain *AdaBoost.M1* classifiers

- How to use methods from the Weka data mining system with the `RWeka` package

- How to apply a classifier to a semi-supervised dataset using self-training

Chapter 7

Classifying Microarray Samples

The fourth case study is from the area of bioinformatics. Namely, we will address the problem of classifying microarray samples into a set of alternative classes. More specifically, given a microarray probe that describes the gene expression levels of a patient, we aim to classify this patient into a pre-defined set of genetic mutations of acute lymphoblastic leukemia. This case study addresses several new data mining topics. The main focus, given the characteristics of this type of dataset, is on feature selection, that is, how to reduce the number of features that describe each observation. In our approach to this particular application we will illustrate several general methods for feature selection. Other new data mining topics addressed in this chapter include k-nearest neighbors classifiers, bootstrap estimates, and some new variants of ensemble models.

7.1 Problem Description and Objectives

Bioinformatics is one of the main areas of application of R. There is even an associated project based on R, with the goal of providing a large set of analysis tools for this domain. The project is called Bioconductor.[1] This case study will use the tools provided by this project to address a supervised classification problem.

7.1.1 Brief Background on Microarray Experiments

One of the main difficulties faced by someone coming from a background outside the biological sciences is the huge amount of "new" terms used in bioinformatics. In this very brief background section, we try to introduce the reader to some of the "jargon" in this field and also to provide some mapping to more "standard" data mining terminology.

The analysis of differential gene expression is one of the key applications of DNA microarray experiments. Gene expression microarrays allow us to characterize a set of samples (e.g., individuals) according to their expression levels on a large set of genes. In this area a sample is thus an observation (case) of some phenomenon under study. Microarray experiments are the means used to measure a set of "variables" for these observations. The variables here are a large set of genes. For each variable (gene), these experiments measure an expression value. In summary, a dataset is formed by a set of samples (the cases) for which we have measured expression levels on a large set of genes (the variables). If these samples have some disease state associated with them, we may try to approximate the unknown function that maps gene expression levels into disease states. This function can be approximated using a dataset of previously analyzed samples. This is an instantiation of supervised classification tasks, where the target variable is the disease type. The observations

---

[1]http://www.bioconductor.org.

353

in this problem are samples (microarrays, individuals), and the predictor variables are the genes for which we measure a value (the expression level) using a microarray experiment. The key hypothesis here is thus that different disease types can be associated with different gene expression patterns and, moreover, that by measuring these patterns using microarrays we can accurately predict what the disease type of an individual is.

There are several types of technologies created with the goal of obtaining gene expression levels on some sample. Short oligonucleotide arrays are an example of these technologies. The output of oligonucleotide chips is an image that after several pre-processing steps can be mapped into a set of gene expression levels for quite a large set of genes. The bioconductor project has several R packages devoted to these pre-processing steps that involve issues like the analysis of the images resulting from the oligonucleotide chips, normalization tasks, and several other steps that are necessary until we reach a set of gene expression scores. In this case study we do not address these initial steps. The interested reader is directed to several informative sources available at the bioconductor site as well as several books (e.g., Hahne et al. (2008)).

In this case study, our starting point will be a matrix of gene expression levels that results from these pre-processing steps. This is the information on the predictor variables for our observations. As we will see, there are usually many more predictor variables being measured than samples; that is, we have more predictors than observations. This is a typical characteristic of microarray datasets. Another particularity of these expression matrices is that they appear transposed when compared to what is "standard" for datasets. This means that the rows will represent the predictors (i.e., genes), while the columns are the observations (the samples). For each of the samples we will also need the associated classification. In our case this will be an associated type of mutation of a disease. There may also exist information on other covariates (e.g., sex and age of the individuals being sampled, etc.).

7.1.2 The ALL Dataset

The dataset we will use comes from a study on acute lymphoblastic leukemia (Chiaretti et al., 2004; Li, 2009). The data consists of microarray samples from 128 individuals with this type of disease. Actually, there are two different types of tumors among these samples: T-cell ALL (33 samples) and B-cell ALL (95 samples).

We will focus our study on the data concerning the B-cell ALL samples. Even within this latter group of samples we can distinguish different types of mutations. Namely, ALL1/AF4, BCR/ABL, E2A/PBX1, p15/p16 and also individuals with no cytogenetic abnormalities. In our analysis of the B-cell ALL samples we will discard the p15/p16 mutation as we only have one sample. Our modeling goal is to be able to predict the type of mutation of an individual given its microarray assay. Given that the target variable is nominal with 4 possible values, we are facing a supervised classification task.

7.2 The Available Data

The ALL dataset is part of the bioconductor set of packages. To use it, we need to install at least a set of basic packages from bioconductor. We have not included the dataset in our book package because the dataset is already part of the R "universe".

To install a set of basic bioconductor packages and the ALL dataset, we need to carry out the following instructions that assume we have a working Internet connection:

```
> source("http://bioconductor.org/biocLite.R")
> biocLite()
> biocLite("ALL")
```

This only needs to be done for the first time. Once you have these packages installed, if you want to use the dataset, you simply need to do

```
> library(Biobase)
> library(ALL)
> data(ALL)
```

These instructions load the **Biobase** (Gentleman et al., 2004) and the **ALL** (Gentleman et al., 2010) packages. We then load the **ALL** dataset, that creates an object of a special class (**ExpressionSet**) defined by Bioconductor. This class of objects contains significant information concerning a microarray dataset. There are several associated functions to handle this type of object. If you ask R about the content of the **ALL** object, you get the following information:

```
> ALL

ExpressionSet (storageMode: lockedEnvironment)
assayData: 12625 features, 128 samples
  element names: exprs
protocolData: none
phenoData
  sampleNames: 01005 01010 ... LAL4 (128 total)
  varLabels: cod diagnosis ... date last seen (21 total)
  varMetadata: labelDescription
featureData: none
experimentData: use 'experimentData(object)'
  pubMedIds: 14684422 16243790
Annotation: hgu95av2
```

The information is divided in several groups. First we have the assay data with the gene expression levels matrix. For this dataset we have 12,625 genes and 128 samples. The object also contains a lot of meta-data about the samples of the experiment. This includes the **phenoData** part with information on the sample names and several associated co-variates. It also includes information on the features (i.e., genes) as well as annotations of the genes from biomedical databases. Finally, the object also contains information that describes the experiment.

There are several functions that facilitate access to the information in the **Expression-Set** objects. We give a few examples below. We start by obtaining some information on the co-variates associated to each sample:

```
> pD <- phenoData(ALL)
> varMetadata(pD)
```

	labelDescription
cod	Patient ID
diagnosis	Date of diagnosis
sex	Gender of the patient
age	Age of the patient at entry
BT	does the patient have B-cell or T-cell ALL

remission	Complete remission(CR), refractory(REF) or NA. Derived from CR
CR	Original remisson data
date.cr	Date complete remission if achieved
t(4;11)	did the patient have t(4;11) translocation. Derived from citog
t(9;22)	did the patient have t(9;22) translocation. Derived from citog
cyto.normal	Was cytogenetic test normal? Derived from citog
citog	original citogenetics data, deletions or t(4;11), t(9;22) status
mol.biol	molecular biology
fusion protein	which of p190, p210 or p190/210 for bcr/able
mdr	multi-drug resistant
kinet	ploidy: either diploid or hyperd.
ccr	Continuous complete remission? Derived from f.u
relapse	Relapse? Derived from f.u
transplant	did the patient receive a bone marrow transplant? Derived from f.u
f.u	follow up data available
date last seen	date patient was last seen

```
> table(ALL$BT)
```

```
 B B1 B2 B3 B4  T T1 T2 T3 T4
 5 19 36 23 12  5  1 15 10  2
```

```
> table(ALL$mol.biol)
```

```
ALL1/AF4  BCR/ABL E2A/PBX1     NEG   NUP-98  p15/p16
      10       37        5      74        1        1
```

```
> table(ALL$BT, ALL$mol.bio)
```

	ALL1/AF4	BCR/ABL	E2A/PBX1	NEG	NUP-98	p15/p16
B	0	2	1	2	0	0
B1	10	1	0	8	0	0
B2	0	19	0	16	0	1
B3	0	8	1	14	0	0
B4	0	7	3	2	0	0
T	0	0	0	5	0	0
T1	0	0	0	1	0	0
T2	0	0	0	15	0	0
T3	0	0	0	9	1	0
T4	0	0	0	2	0	0

The first two statements obtain the names and descriptions of the existing co-variates. We then obtain some information on the distribution of the samples across the two main co-variates: the BT variable that determines the type of acute lymphoblastic leukemia, and the mol.bio variable that describes the cytogenetic abnormality found on each sample (NEG represents no abnormality).

We can also obtain some information on the genes and samples:

```
> featureNames(ALL)[1:10]
```

```
 [1] "1000_at"   "1001_at"   "1002_f_at" "1003_s_at" "1004_at"
 [6] "1005_at"   "1006_at"   "1007_s_at" "1008_f_at" "1009_at"
```

```
> sampleNames(ALL)[1:5]
```

```
[1] "01005" "01010" "03002" "04006" "04007"
```

This code shows the names of the first 10 genes and the names of the first 5 samples.

As mentioned before, we will focus our analysis of this data on the B-cell ALL cases and in particular on the samples with a subset of the mutations, which will be our target class. The code below obtains the subset of data that we will use:

```
> tgt.cases <- which(ALL$BT %in% levels(ALL$BT)[1:5] &
+                    ALL$mol.bio %in% levels(ALL$mol.bio)[1:4])
> ALLb <- ALL[,tgt.cases]
> ALLb
```

```
ExpressionSet (storageMode: lockedEnvironment)
assayData: 12625 features, 94 samples
  element names: exprs
protocolData: none
phenoData
  sampleNames: 01005 01010 ... LAL5 (94 total)
  varLabels: cod diagnosis ... date last seen (21 total)
  varMetadata: labelDescription
featureData: none
experimentData: use 'experimentData(object)'
  pubMedIds: 14684422 16243790
Annotation: hgu95av2
```

The first statement obtains the set of cases that we will consider. These are the samples with specific values of the BT and mol.bio variables. Check the calls to the table() function we have shown before to see which ones we are selecting. We then subset the original ALL object to obtain the 94 samples that will enter our study. This subset of samples only contains some of the values of the BT and mol.bio variables. In this context, we should update the available levels of these two factors on our new ALLb object:

```
> ALLb$BT <- factor(ALLb$BT)
> ALLb$mol.bio <- factor(ALLb$mol.bio)
```

The ALLb object will be the dataset we will use throughout this chapter. It may eventually be a good idea to save this object in a local file on your computer, so that you do not need to repeat these pre-processing steps in case you want to start the analysis from scratch:

```
> save(ALLb, file = "myALL.Rdata")
```

7.2.1 Exploring the Dataset

The function exprs() allows us to access the gene expression levels matrix:

```
> es <- exprs(ALLb)
> dim(es)
```

```
[1] 12625    94
```

The matrix of our dataset has 12,625 rows (the genes/features) and 94 columns (the samples/cases).

In terms of dimensionality, the main challenge of this problem is the fact that there are far too many variables (12,625) for the number of available cases (94). With these dimensions, most modeling techniques will have a hard time obtaining any meaningful result. In this context, one of our first goals will be to reduce the number of variables, that is, eliminate some genes from our analysis. To help in this task, we start by exploring the expression levels data.

The following instruction tells us that most expression values are between 4 and 7:

```
> summary(as.vector(es))

  Min. 1st Qu.  Median    Mean 3rd Qu.    Max.
 1.985   4.122   5.469   5.624   6.829  14.040
```

A better overview of the distribution of the expression levels can be obtained graphically. We will use a function from package **genefilter** (Gentleman et al., 2010). This package must be installed before using it. Please notice that this is a Bioconductor package, and these packages are not installed from the standard R repository. The easiest way to install a Bioconductor package is through the script provided by this project for this effect:

```
> source("http://bioconductor.org/biocLite.R")
> biocLite("genefilter")
```

The first instruction loads the script and then we use it to download and install the package. We can now proceed with the above-mentioned graphical display of the distribution of the expression levels, whose results are shown in Figure 7.1,

```
> library(genefilter)
> library(ggplot2)
> exprVs <- data.frame(exprVal=as.vector(es))
> ds <- data.frame(Stat=c("1stQ","Median","3rdQ","Shorth"),
+                   Value=c(quantile(exprVs$exprVal,
+                           probs=c(0.25, 0.5, 0.75)),
+                           shorth(exprVs$exprVal)),
+                   Color=c("red","green","red","yellow"))
> ggplot(exprVs,aes(x=exprVal)) + geom_histogram(fill="lightgrey") +
+     geom_vline(data=ds,aes(xintercept=Value,color=Color)) +
+     geom_text(data=ds,aes(x=Value-0.2,y=0,label=Stat,colour=Color),
+               angle=90,hjust="left") +
+     xlab("Expression Levels") + guides(colour="none", fill="none")
```

We start by obtaining a data frame containing a few statistics that we will add to a histogram of the expression levels. Namely, the 1st and 3rd quartiles, the median and the shorth. This last statistic is a robust estimator of the centrality of a continuous distribution that is implemented by the function **shorth()** of package **genefilter**. It is calculated as the mean of the values in a central interval containing 50% of the observations (i.e., the inter-quartile range). We use **geom_histogram()** to obtain the histogram of the expression levels and then use **geom_vline()** and **geom_text()** to add vertical lines and text labels for each statistic, respectively. As we can observe from the figure, the gene expression levels are reasonably packaged around the centrality statistics, with a few large values.

Are the distributions of the gene expression levels of the samples with a particular mutation different from each other? The following code answers this question:

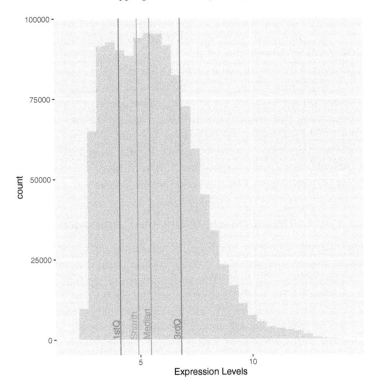

FIGURE 7.1: The distribution of the gene expression levels.

```
> sapply(levels(ALLb$mol.bio),
+        function(x) summary(as.vector(es[, which(ALLb$mol.bio == x)])))
```

```
          ALL1/AF4 BCR/ABL E2A/PBX1    NEG
Min.        2.266   2.195    2.268   1.985
1st Qu.     4.141   4.124    4.152   4.111
Median      5.454   5.468    5.497   5.470
Mean        5.621   5.627    5.630   5.622
3rd Qu.     6.805   6.833    6.819   6.832
Max.       14.030  14.040   13.810  13.950
```

As we see, things are rather similar across these subsets of samples and, moreover, they are similar to the global distribution of expression levels. As an exercice you may try to produce a graph that shows several plots similar to that shown in Figure 7.1, one for each mutation, using **ggplot** facets.

7.3   Gene (Feature) Selection

Feature selection is an important task in many data mining problems. The general problem is to select the subset of features (variables) of a problem that is more relevant for the analysis of the data we plan to carry out. This can be regarded as an instantiation of the more general problem of deciding the weights (importance) of the features in the subsequent modeling stages. Generally, there are two types of approaches to feature selection: (1) filters and (2) wrappers. As mentioned in Section 3.3.4.2 (page 82) the former use statistical properties of the features to select the final set, while the latter include the data mining tools in the selection process. Filter approaches are carried out in a single step, while wrappers typically involve a search process where we iteratively look for the set of features that is more adequate for the data mining tools we are applying. Feature wrappers have a clear overhead in terms of computational resources. They involve running the full filter+model+evaluate cycle several times until some convergence criteria are met. This means that for very large data mining problems, they may not be adequate if time is critical. Yet, they will find a solution that is theoretically more adequate for the used modeling tools. The strategies we use and describe in this section can be seen as filter approaches.

7.3.1 Simple Filters Based on Distribution Properties

The first gene filtering methods we describe are based on information concerning the distribution of the expression levels. This type of experimental data usually includes several genes that are not expressed at all or show very small variability. The latter property means that these genes can hardly be used to differentiate among samples. Moreover, this type of microarray usually has several control probes that can be safely removed from our analysis. In the case of this study, which uses Affymetrix U95Av2 microarrays, these probes have their names starting with the letters "AFFX". In our analysis we will need annotation data of this Affymetrix set so we need package **hgu95av2.db** (Carlson, 2016) from the Bioconductor project, which can be installed as follows

```
> source("https://bioconductor.org/biocLite.R")
> biocLite("hgu95av2.db")
```

We can get an overall idea of the distribution of the expression levels of each gene across all individuals with the following graph. We will use the median and inter-quartile range (IQR) as the representatives of these distributions. The following code obtains these scores for each gene and plots their resulting values on the graph shown in Figure 7.2:

```
> rowIQRs <- function(em)
+     rowQ(em,ceiling(0.75*ncol(em))) - rowQ(em,floor(0.25*ncol(em)))
> library(ggplot2)
> dg <- data.frame(rowMed=rowMedians(es), rowIQR=rowIQRs(es))
> ggplot(dg,aes(x=rowMed, y=rowIQR)) + geom_point() +
+     xlab("Median expression level") + ylab("IQR expression level") +
+     ggtitle("Main Characteristics of Genes Expression Levels")
```

The function `rowMedians()` from package **Biobase** obtains a vector of the medians per row of a matrix. This is an efficient implementation of this task. A less efficient alternative would be to use the function `apply()`.[2] The `rowQ()` function is another efficient implementation provided by this package with the goal of obtaining quantiles of a distribution from the rows of a matrix. The second argument of this function is an integer ranging from 1 (that would give us the minimum) to the number of columns of the matrix (that would result in the maximum). In this case we are using this function to obtain the IQR by subtracting the 3rd quartile from the 1st quartile. These statistics correspond to 75% and 25% of the data, respectively. We have used the functions `floor()` and `ceiling()` to obtain the corresponding order in the number of values of each row. Both functions take the integer

---

[2]As an exercise, time both alternatives using function `system.time()` to observe the difference.

Main Characteristics of Genes Expression Levels

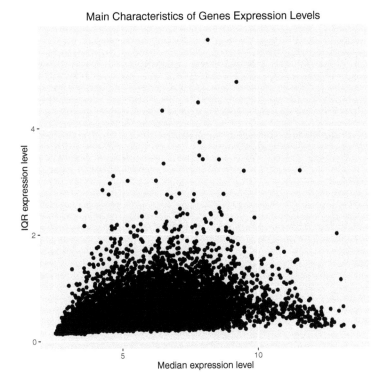

FIGURE 7.2: The median and IQR of the gene expression levels.

part of a floating point number, although with different rounding procedures. Experiment with both to see the difference. Using the function `rowQ()`, we have created the function `rowIQRs()` to obtain the IQR of each row.

Figure 7.2 provides interesting information. Namely, we can observe that a large proportion of the genes have very low variability (IQRs near 0). As mentioned above, if a gene has a very low variability across all samples, then it is reasonably safe to conclude that it will not be useful in discriminating among the different types of mutations of B-cell ALL. This means that we can safely remove these genes from our classification task. We should note that there is a caveat on this reasoning. In effect, we are looking at the genes individually. This means that there is some risk that some of these genes with low variability, when put together with other genes, could actually be useful for the classification task. Still, the gene-by-gene approach that we will follow is the most common for these problems as exploring the interactions among genes with datasets of this dimension is not easy. Nevertheless, there are methods that try to estimate the importance of features, taking into account their dependencies. That is the case of the RELIEF method (Kira and Rendel, 1992; Kononenko et al., 1997) for which you may find an implementation in package **CORElearn** (Robnik-Sikonja and Savicky, 2015). More information on this and other packages was given in Section 3.3.4.2 (page 82).

We will use a heuristic threshold based on the value of the IQR to eliminate some of the genes with very low variability. Namely, we will remove any genes with a variability that is smaller than 1/5 of the global IQR. The function `nsFilter()` from the package **genefilter** can be used for this type of filtering:

```
> library(genefilter)
> resFilter <- nsFilter(ALLb,
+                   var.func=IQR,
+                   var.cutoff=IQR(as.vector(es))/5,
+                   feature.exclude="^AFFX")
> resFilter

$eset
ExpressionSet (storageMode: lockedEnvironment)
assayData: 3943 features, 94 samples
  element names: exprs
protocolData: none
phenoData
  sampleNames: 01005 01010 ... LAL5 (94 total)
  varLabels: cod diagnosis ... mol.bio (22 total)
  varMetadata: labelDescription
featureData: none
experimentData: use 'experimentData(object)'
  pubMedIds: 14684422 16243790
Annotation: hgu95av2


$filter.log
$filter.log$numDupsRemoved
[1] 2858


$filter.log$numLowVar
[1] 4654


$filter.log$numRemoved.ENTREZID
[1] 1151


$filter.log$feature.exclude
[1] 19
```

As you see, we are left with only 3,943 genes from the initial 12,625. This is a rather significant reduction. Nevertheless, we are still far from a dataset that is "manageable" by most classification models, given that we only have 94 observations.

The result of the **nsFilter()** function is a list with several components. Among these we have several containing information on the removed genes, and also the component **eset** with the "filtered" **ExpressionSet** class object. We can update our **ALLb** and **es** objects with the filtered object:

```
> ALLb <- resFilter$eset
> es <- exprs(ALLb)
> dim(es)

[1] 3943    94
```

7.3.2   ANOVA Filters

If a gene has a distribution of expression values that is similar across all possible values of the target variable, then it will not be very useful to discriminate among these values. Our next approach builds on this idea. We will compare the mean expression level of genes across the subsets of samples belonging to a certain B-cell ALL mutation, that is, the mean conditioned on the target variable values. Genes for which we have high statistical confidence of having the same mean expression level across the groups of samples belonging to each mutation will be discarded from further analysis.

Comparing means across more than two groups can be carried out using an ANOVA statistical test. In our case study, we have four groups of cases, one for each of the gene mutations of B-cell ALL we are considering. Filtering of genes based on this test is rather easy in R, thanks to the facilities provided by the **genefilter** package. We can carry out this type of filtering as follows:

```
> f <- Anova(ALLb$mol.bio, p = 0.01)
> ff <- filterfun(f)
> selGenes <- genefilter(exprs(ALLb), ff)
> sum(selGenes)

[1] 746
```

The function `Anova()` creates a new function for carrying out ANOVA filtering. It requires a factor that determines the subgroups of our dataset and a statistical significance level. The resulting function is stored in the variable f. The `filterfun()` function works in a similar manner. It generates a filtering function that can be applied to an expression matrix. This application is carried out with the `genefilter()` function that produces a vector with as many elements as there are genes in the given expression matrix. The vector contains logical values. Genes that are considered useful according to the ANOVA statistical test have the value TRUE. As you can see, there are only 746. Finally, we can use this vector to filter our **ExpressionSet** object.

Next we update our data structures to include only these selected genes:

```
> ALLb <- ALLb[selGenes, ]
> ALLb

ExpressionSet (storageMode: lockedEnvironment)
assayData: 746 features, 94 samples
  element names: exprs
protocolData: none
phenoData
  sampleNames: 01005 01010 ... LAL5 (94 total)
  varLabels: cod diagnosis ... mol.bio (22 total)
  varMetadata: labelDescription
featureData: none
experimentData: use 'experimentData(object)'
  pubMedIds: 14684422 16243790
Annotation: hgu95av2

> es <- exprs(ALLb)
> dim(es)

[1] 746   94
```

Figure 7.3 shows the median and IQR of the genes selected by the ANOVA test. The figure was obtained as follows:

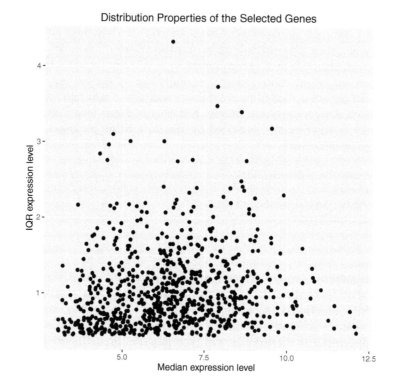

FIGURE 7.3: The median and IQR of the final set of genes.

```
> dg <- data.frame(rowMed=rowMedians(es), rowIQR=rowIQRs(es))
> ggplot(dg,aes(x=rowMed, y=rowIQR)) + geom_point() +
+     xlab("Median expression level") + ylab("IQR expression level") +
+     ggtitle("Distribution Properties of the Selected Genes")
```

The variability in terms of IQR and the median that we can observe in Figure 7.3 provides evidence that the genes are expressed in different scales of values. Several modeling techniques are influenced by problems where each case is described by a set of variables using different scales. Namely, any method relying on distances between observations will suffer from this type of problem as distance functions typically sum up the differences between variable values. In this context, variables with a higher average value will end up having a larger influence on the distance between observations. To avoid this effect, it is usual to standardize the data. This transformation consists of subtracting the typical value of the variables and dividing the result by a measure of spread. Given that not all modeling techniques are affected by this data characteristic we will leave this transformation to the modeling stages, making it depend on the tool to be used.

7.3.3 Filtering Using Random Forests

The expression level matrix resulting from the ANOVA filter is already of manageable size, although we still have many more features than observations. In effect, in our modeling attempts described in Section 7.4, we will apply the selected models to this matrix. Nevertheless, one can question whether better results can be obtained with a dataset with a more "standard" dimensionality. In this context, we can try to further reduce the number of features and then compare the results obtained with the different datasets.

Random forests can be used to obtain a ranking of the features in terms of their usefulness for a classification task. In Section 5.3.2 (page 112) we saw an example of using random forests to obtain a ranking of importance of the variables in the context of a prediction problem.

Random forests can be used to obtain a ranking of the genes as follows,

```
> library(randomForest)
> dt <- data.frame(t(es), Mut = ALLb$mol.bio)
> dt$Mut <- droplevels(dt$Mut)
> set.seed(1234)
> rf <- randomForest(Mut ~ ., dt, importance = TRUE)
> imp <- importance(rf)
> rf.genes <- rownames(imp)[order(imp[,"MeanDecreaseAccuracy"],
+                                 decreasing = TRUE)[1:30]]
```

We construct a training set by adding the mutation information to the transpose of the expression matrix.[3] We then obtain a random forest with the parameter **importance** set to **TRUE** to obtain estimates of the importance of the variables. The function **importance()** is used to obtain the relevance of each variable. This function actually returns several scores on different columns, according to different criteria and for each class value. We select the column with the variable scores measured as the estimated mean decrease in classification accuracy when each variable is removed in turn. We order the values of this score in decreasing order and select the highest 30 of these scores, obtaining the names of the corresponding genes.

We may be curious about the expression level distribution of theses 30 genes across the different mutations. We can obtain the median level for these top 30 genes as follows:

```
> sapply(rf.genes, function(g) tapply(dt[, g], dt$Mut, median))
```

	X1635_at	X40504_at	X1467_at	X37015_at	X1674_at	X34699_at
ALL1/AF4	7.302814	3.218079	3.708985	3.752649	3.745752	4.253504
BCR/ABL	8.693082	4.924310	4.239306	4.857105	5.833510	6.315966
E2A/PBX1	7.562676	3.455316	3.411696	6.579530	3.808258	6.102031
NEG	7.324691	3.541651	3.515020	3.765741	4.244791	6.092511

	X39837_s_at	X37027_at	X37225_at	X40202_at	X40480_s_at	X34850_at
ALL1/AF4	6.633188	9.118515	5.220668	8.550639	6.414368	5.426653
BCR/ABL	7.374046	9.421987	3.460902	9.767293	8.208263	6.898979
E2A/PBX1	6.708400	6.688977	7.445655	7.414635	6.722296	5.928574
NEG	6.878846	7.408175	3.387552	7.655605	7.362318	6.327281

	X34210_at	X1307_at	X36873_at	X41470_at	X40454_at	X41237_at
ALL1/AF4	5.641130	3.368915	7.040593	9.616743	4.007171	10.94079
BCR/ABL	9.204237	4.945270	3.490262	5.205797	3.910912	12.11895
E2A/PBX1	8.198781	4.678577	3.634471	3.931191	7.390283	11.35610
NEG	8.791774	4.863930	3.824670	4.157748	3.807652	11.93624

	X40795_at	X32378_at	X1914_at	X37951_at	X37981_at	X37579_at
ALL1/AF4	3.867134	8.703860	7.066848	3.418433	6.170311	7.614200
BCR/ABL	4.544239	9.694933	3.935540	3.881780	6.882755	8.231081
E2A/PBX1	4.151637	10.066073	3.761856	3.461861	8.080002	9.494368
NEG	3.909532	9.743168	4.032755	3.419113	7.423079	8.455750

	X36617_at	X32434_at	X41191_at	X36275_at	X36638_at	X37105_at

---

[3]Remember that expression matrices have genes (variables) on the rows.

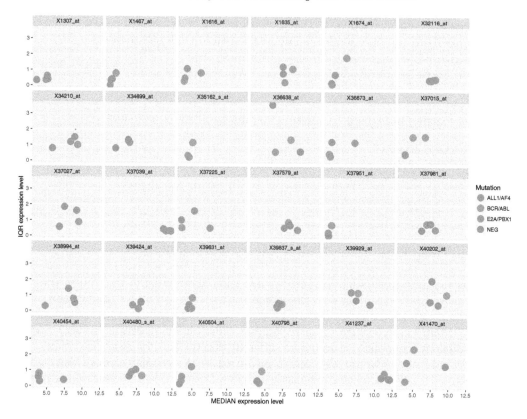

FIGURE 7.4: The median and IQR of the gene expression levels across the mutations.

ALL1/AF4	6.438007	3.317480	6.314058	3.618819	9.811828	6.845719
BCR/ABL	7.480436	5.339625	4.459709	6.259073	8.486446	6.493001
E2A/PBX1	6.627934	3.668714	4.325834	3.635956	6.259730	6.740213
NEG	6.561701	3.226766	4.369366	3.749953	5.856580	6.298859

We can observe several interesting differences between the median expression level across the types of mutations, which provides a good indication of the discriminative power of these genes. We can obtain even more detail by graphically inspecting the median and inter-quartile ranges of the expression levels of these genes for the 94 samples:

```
> library(tidyr)
> library(dplyr)
> d <- gather(dt[,c(rf.genes,"Mut")],Gene,ExprValue,1:length(rf.genes))
> dat <- group_by(d,Mut,Gene) %>%
+     summarise(med=median(ExprValue), iqr=IQR(ExprValue))
> ggplot(dat, aes(x=med,y=iqr,color=Mut)) +
+     geom_point(size=6) + facet_wrap(~ Gene) +
+     labs(x="MEDIAN expression level",y="IQR expression level",color="Mutation")
```

The graph obtained with this code is shown in Figure 7.4. We observe that there are several genes with marked differences in expression level across the different mutations. For instance, there are obvious differences in expression level at gene X41470_at (bottom right panel) between ALL1/AF4 and the other mutations. The same happens with gene X4045_at for mutation E2A/PBX1, among other less marked differences. To obtain this graph we used the function `gather()` of the **tidyr** package. This function puts the original expression data in a format that is easier for summarization using package **dplyr**.

7.3.4 Filtering Using Feature Clustering Ensembles

The approach described in this section uses a clustering algorithm to obtain 30 groups of variables that are supposed to be similar. These 30 variable clusters will then be used to obtain an ensemble classification model where m models will be obtained with 30 variables, each one randomly chosen from one of the 30 clusters.

Ensembles are learning methods that build a set of predictive models and then classify new observations using some form of averaging of the predictions of these models. They are known for often outperforming the individual models that form the ensemble. Ensembles are based on some form of diversity among the individual models. There are many forms of creating this diversity. It can be through different model parameter settings or by different samples of observations used to obtain each model, for instance. Another alternative is to use different predictors for each model in the ensemble. The ensembles we use in this section follow this latter strategy. This approach works better if the pool of predictors from which we obtain different sets is highly redundant. We will assume that there is some degree of redundancy on our set of features generated by the ANOVA filter. We will try to model this redundancy by clustering the variables. Clustering methods are based on distances, in this case distances between variables. Two variables are near (and thus similar) to each other if their expression values across the 94 samples are similar. By clustering the variables we expect to find groups of genes that are similar to each other. The **Hmisc** package contains a function that uses a hierarchical clustering algorithm to cluster the variables of a dataset. The name of this function is `varclus()`. We can use it as follows:

```
> library(Hmisc)
> vc <- varclus(t(es))
> clus30 <- cutree(vc$hclust, 30)
> table(clus30)

clus30
 1  2  3  4  5  6  7  8  9 10 11 12 13 14 15 16 17 18 19 20 21 22 23 24 25
18 34 30 22 34 35 19 16 40 52 19 22 17 24 30 26 20 17 18 21 43 30 32 14 23
26 27 28 29 30
28 18 17 11 16
```

We used the function `cutree()` to obtain a clustering formed by 30 groups of variables. We then checked how many variables (genes) belong to each cluster. Based on this clustering we can create sets of predictors by randomly selecting one variable from each cluster. The reasoning is that members of the same cluster will be similar to each other and thus somehow redundant.

The following function facilitates the process by generating one set of variables via randomly sampling from the selected number of clusters (defaulting to 30):

```
> getVarsSet <- function(cluster,nvars=30,seed=NULL,verb=FALSE) {
+     if (!is.null(seed)) set.seed(seed)

+     cls <- cutree(cluster,nvars)
+     tots <- table(cls)
+     vars <- c()
+     vars <- sapply(1:nvars,function(clID)
+     {
```

```
+            if (!length(tots[clID])) stop('Empty cluster! (',clID,')')
+            x <- sample(1:tots[clID],1)
+            names(cls[cls==clID])[x]
+        })
+    if (verb)  structure(vars,clusMemb=cls,clusTots=tots)
+    else       vars
+ }
> getVarsSet(vc$hclust)

  [1] "X40127_at"  "X745_at"    "X35694_at"   "X187_at"    "X34877_at"
  [6] "X39929_at"  "X32156_at"  "X39738_at"   "X32724_at"  "X38980_at"
 [11] "X38732_at"  "X33772_at"  "X245_at"     "X33283_at"  "X34362_at"
 [16] "X1453_at"   "X34850_at"  "X36412_s_at" "X38748_at"  "X37213_at"
 [21] "X36275_at"  "X36795_at"  "X32824_at"   "X506_s_at"  "X33999_f_at"
 [26] "X40745_at"  "X38158_at"  "X41559_at"   "X1616_at"   "X36550_at"

> getVarsSet(vc$hclust)

  [1] "X40505_at"   "X40409_at"  "X1635_at"    "X37981_at"   "X41498_at"
  [6] "X39837_s_at" "X40323_at"  "X39650_s_at" "X40495_at"   "X32621_at"
 [11] "X39377_at"   "X34335_at"  "X36493_at"   "X32963_s_at" "X174_s_at"
 [16] "X39781_at"   "X539_at"    "X33325_at"   "X35670_at"   "X37304_at"
 [21] "X809_at"     "X40575_at"  "X34785_at"   "X38956_at"   "X41146_at"
 [26] "X40425_at"   "X33429_at"  "X33920_at"   "X33528_at"   "X39135_at"
```

Each time we call this function, we will get a "new" set of 30 variables. Using this function it is easy to generate a set of datasets formed by different predictors and then obtain a model using each of these sets. In Section 7.4 we present a function that obtains ensembles using this strategy.

Further readings on feature selection

Feature selection is a well-studied topic in many disciplines. Good overviews and references of the work in the area of data mining can be obtained in Liu and Motoda (1998), Chizi and Maimon (2005), and Wettschereck et al. (1997). Further information and references can be obtained in Section 3.3.4.2 (page 82).

7.4 Predicting Cytogenetic Abnormalities

This section describes our modeling attempts for the task of predicting the type of cytogenetic abnormalities of the B-cell ALL cases.

7.4.1 Defining the Prediction Task

The data mining problem we are facing is a predictive task. More precisely, it is a classification problem. Predictive classification consists of obtaining models designed with the goal of forecasting the value of a nominal target variable using information on a set of predictors. The models are obtained using a set of labeled observations of the phenomenon under study, that is, observations for which we know both the values of the predictors and of the target variable.

In this case study our target variable is the type of cytogenetic abnormality of a B-cell

ALL sample. In our selected dataset, this variable will take four possible values: `ALL1/AF4`, `BCR/ABL`, `E2A/PBX1`, and `NEG`. Regarding the predictors, they will consist of a set of selected genes for which we have measured an expression value. In our modeling attempts we will experiment with different sets of selected genes, based on the study described in Section 7.3. This means that the number of predictors (features) will vary depending on these trials. Regarding the number of observations, they will consist of 94 cases of B-cell ALL.

7.4.2 The Evaluation Metric

The prediction task is a multi-class classification problem. Predictive classification models are usually evaluated using the error rate or its complement, the accuracy. Nevertheless, there are several alternatives, such as the area under the ROC curve, pairs of measures (e.g., precision and recall), and also measures of the accuracy of class probability estimates (e.g., the Brier score). The package `ROCR` provides a good sample of these measures.

The selection of the evaluation metric for a given problem often depends on the goals of the user. This is a difficult decision that is often impaired by incomplete information such as the absence of information on the costs of misclassifying a class i case with class j (known as the misclassification costs).

In our case study we have no information on the misclassification costs, and thus we assume that it is equally serious to misclassify, for instance, an `E2A/PBX1` mutation as `NEG`, as it is to misclassify `ALL1/AF4` as `BCR/ABL`. Moreover, we have more than two classes, and generalizations of ROC analysis to multi-class problems are not so well established, not to mention recent drawbacks discovered in the use of the area under the ROC curve (Hand, 2009). In this context, we will resort to the use of the standard accuracy that is measured as

$$\overline{acc} = 1 - \frac{1}{N} \sum_{i=1}^{N} L_{0/1}(y_i, \hat{y}_i) \tag{7.1}$$

where N is the size of test sample, and $L_{0/1}()$ is a loss function defined as

$$L_{0/1}(y_i, \hat{y}_i) = \begin{cases} 0 & \text{if } y_i = \hat{y}_i \\ 1 & \text{otherwise} \end{cases} \tag{7.2}$$

7.4.3 The Experimental Procedure

The number of observations of the dataset we will use is rather small: 94 cases. In this context, the more adequate experimental methodology to obtain reliable estimates of the error rate is either the bootstrap or the Leave-One-Out Cross-Validation (LOOCV). LOOCV is a special case of the k-fold cross-validation experimental methodology that we have used before, namely, when k equals the number of observations. Briefly, LOOCV consists of obtaining N models, where N is the dataset size, and each model is obtained using $N - 1$ cases and tested on the observation that was left out. Package **performanceEstimation** also includes this method as one of the estimation methods you may specify in the definition of the estimation task. The bootstrap is another method that is frequently used with small samples as is the case of our problem. It essentially consists of drawing a random sample with replacement of the same size of the original dataset. As the sample is drawn with replacement it means that some cases will appear repeated while others will not be drawn. These latter will form the test set where we will apply the model obtained with the former. This random sampling is typically repeated a large number of times (e.g. 100 or 200). The bootstrap estimate is obtained by the average of the scores obtained in these repetitions. Package **performanceEstimation** provides two implementations of the bootstrap estimation method: ϵ_0 and .632 bootstrap (details on Section 3.5.3, page 179). Below is a small illustration of ϵ_0 bootstrap with the *Iris* dataset:

```
> library(performanceEstimation)
> library(DMwR2)
> data(iris)
> exp <- performanceEstimation(
+     PredTask(Species ~ ., iris),
+     Workflow(learner="rpartXse", predictor.pars=list(type="class")),
+     EstimationTask(metrics="acc",method=Bootstrap(nReps=100)))


> summary(exp)


== Summary of a  Bootstrap Performance Estimation Experiment ==

Task for estimating  acc  using
100  repetitions of  e0  Bootstrap experiment
 Run with seed =  1234


* Predictive Tasks ::  iris.Species
* Workflows  ::  rpartXse

-> Task:  iris.Species
  *Workflow: rpartXse
               acc
avg     0.94488494
std     0.02534310
med     0.94736842
iqr     0.03569024
min     0.87931034
max     1.00000000
invalid 0.00000000
```

7.4.4 The Modeling Techniques

As discussed before, we will use three different datasets that differ in the predictors that are used. One will have all genes selected by an ANOVA test, while the other two will select 30 of these genes. All datasets will contain 94 cases of B-cell ALL. With the exception of the target variable, all information is numeric.

To handle this problem we have selected three different modeling techniques. Two of them have already been used before in this book. They are random forests and support vector machines (SVMs). They are recognized as some of the best off-the-shelf prediction methods. The third algorithm we will try on this problem is new. It is a method based on distances between observations, known as k-nearest neighbors.

The use of random forests is motivated by the fact that these models are particularly adequate to handle problems with a large number of features. This property derives from the algorithm used by these methods that randomly selects subsets of the full set of features of a problem. Regarding the use of k-nearest neighbors, the motivation lies on the assumption that samples with the same mutation should have a similar gene "signature," that is, should have similar expression values on the genes we use to describe them. The validity of this assumption is strongly dependent on the genes selected to describe the samples. Namely, they should have good discrimination properties across the different mutations. As we will see below, k-nearest neighbors methods work by assessing similarities between cases, and thus they seem adequate for this assumption. Finally, the use of SVMs is justified with the goal of trying to explore nonlinear relationships that may eventually exist between gene expression and cytogenetic abnormalities.

Both random forests and support vector machines were described in previous chapters. Detailed information on random forests and other types of ensembles was presented in Section 3.4.5.5 (page 165). SVMs, on the other hand, were described in detail in Section 3.4.5.3 (page 151).

The k-nearest neighbors algorithm belongs to the class of so-called *lazy learners*. This type of techniques do not actually obtain a model from the training data. They simply store this dataset. Their main work happens at prediction time. Given a new test case, its prediction is obtained by searching for similar cases in the training data that was stored. The k most similar training cases are used to obtain the prediction for the given test case. In classification problems, this prediction is usually obtained by voting and thus an odd number for k is desirable. However, more elaborate voting mechanisms that take into account the distance of the test case to each of the k neighbors are also possible. For regression, instead of voting we have an average of the target variable values of the k neighbors.

This type of model is strongly dependent on the notion of similarity between cases. This notion is usually defined with the help of a metric over the input space defined by the predictor variables. This metric is a distance function that can calculate a number representing the "difference" between any two observations. There are many distance functions, but a rather frequent selection is the Euclidean distance function that is defined as

$$d(\mathbf{x}_i, \mathbf{x}_j) = \sqrt{\sum_{k=1}^{p}(X_{i,k} - X_{j,k})^2} \tag{7.3}$$

where p is the number of predictors, and $\mathbf{x}_i$ and $\mathbf{x}_j$ are two observations.

These methods are thus very sensitive to both the selected metric and also to the presence of irrelevant variables that may distort the notion of similarity. Moreover, the scale of the variables should be uniform; otherwise we might underestimate some of the differences in variables with lower average values.

The choice of the number of neighbors (k) is also an important parameter of these methods. Frequent values include the numbers in the set $\{1, 3, 5, 7, 11\}$, but obviously these are just heuristics. However, we can say that larger values of k should be avoided because there is the risk of using cases that are already far away from the test case. Obviously, this depends on the density of the training data. Too sparse datasets incur more on this risk. As with any learning model, the "ideal" parameter settings can be estimated through some experimental methodology.

In R, the package **class** (Venables and Ripley, 2002) includes the function **knn()** that implements this idea. Below is an illustrative example of its use on the *Iris* dataset:

```
> library(class)
> data(iris)
> idx <- sample(1:nrow(iris), as.integer(0.7 * nrow(iris)))
> tr <- iris[idx, ]
> ts <- iris[-idx, ]
> preds <- knn(tr[, -5], ts[, -5], tr[, 5], k = 3)
> table(preds, ts[, 5])
```

```
preds         setosa versicolor virginica
  setosa        13         0         0
  versicolor     0         9         0
  virginica      0         2        21
```

As you see, the function `knn()` uses a nonstandard interface. The first argument is the training set with the exception of the target variable column. The second argument is the test set, again without the target. The third argument includes the target values of the training data. Finally, there are several other parameters controlling the method, among which the parameter **k** determines the number of neighbors. We can create a small function that enables the use of this method in a more standard formula-type interface:

```
> kNN <- function(form, train, test, stand = TRUE, stand.stats = NULL, ...) {
+     require(class, quietly = TRUE)
+     tgtCol <- which(colnames(train) == as.character(form[[2]]))
+     if (stand) {
+         if (is.null(stand.stats))
+             tmp <- scale(train[, -tgtCol], center = TRUE, scale = TRUE)
+         else tmp <- scale(train[, -tgtCol], center = stand.stats[[1]],
+                           scale = stand.stats[[2]])
+         train[, -tgtCol] <- tmp
+         ms <- attr(tmp, "scaled:center")
+         ss <- attr(tmp, "scaled:scale")
+         test[, -tgtCol] <- scale(test[, -tgtCol], center = ms, scale = ss)
+     }
+     knn(train[, -tgtCol], test[, -tgtCol], train[, tgtCol], ...)
+ }
```

```
> preds.stand <- kNN(Species ~ ., tr, ts, k = 3)
> table(preds.stand,ts[, 5])
```

```
preds.stand  setosa versicolor virginica
  setosa         13         0         0
  versicolor      0        10         2
  virginica       0         1        19
```

```
> preds.notStand <- kNN(Species ~ ., tr, ts, stand = FALSE, k = 3)
> table(preds.notStand, ts[, 5])
```

```
preds.notStand setosa versicolor virginica
  setosa           13         0         0
  versicolor        0         9         0
  virginica         0         2        21
```

This function allows the user to indicate if the data should be standardized prior to the call to the `knn()` function. This is done through parameter **stand**. In the example above, you see two examples of its use. A third alternative is to provide the centrality and spread statistics as a list with two components in the argument **stand.stats**. If this is not done, the function will use the means as centrality estimates and the standard deviations as statistics of spread. In our experiments we will use this facility to call the function with medians and IQRs. The function `kNN()` is actually included in our book package so you do not need to type its code.

Further readings on *k*-nearest neighbors

The standard reference on this type of methods is the work by Cover and Hart (1967). Good overviews can be found in the works by Aha et al. (1991) and Aha (1997). Deeper analysis can be found in the PhD theses by Aha (1990) and Wettschereck (1994). A different, but related, perspective of lazy learning is the use of so-called local models (Nadaraya, 1964; Watson, 1964). Good references on this vast area are Atkeson et al. (1997) and Cleveland and Loader (1995).

7.4.5 Comparing the Models

This section describes the process we have used to compare the selected models using a bootstrap estimation procedure.

In Section 7.3, we have seen examples of several feature selection methods. We have used some basic filters to eliminate genes with low variance and also control probes. Next, we applied a method based on the conditioned distribution of the expression levels with respect to the target variable. This method was based on an ANOVA statistical test. Finally, from the results of this test we tried to further reduce the number of genes using random forests and clustering of the variables. With the exception of the first simple filters, all other methods depend somehow on the target variable values. We may question whether these filtering stages should be carried out before the experimental comparisons, or if we should integrate these steps into the processes being compared. If our goal is to obtain an unbiased estimate of the classification accuracy of our methodology on new samples, then we should include these filtering stages as part of the workflows being evaluated and compared. Not doing so would mean that the estimates we obtain are biased by the fact that the genes used to obtain the models were selected using information of the test set. In effect, if we use all the dataset to decide which genes to use, then we are using information on this selection process that should be unknown as it is part of the test data. In this context, we will include part of the filtering stages within the user-defined workflow functions that implement the models we will compare.

The approaches we will compare involve different alternative feature selection procedures and also different classification tools to apply to the resulting filtered datasets. More specifically, we will consider in terms of feature selection: (i) using the genes resulting from the ANOVA filtering; (ii) applying the random forest filtering on top of the ANOVA result; and (iii) applying the filtering based on ensembles of clustered variables after the ANOVA filtering. Each of these three strategies will be combined with different classification tools.

The following function implements the approach involving creating an ensemble of models, each applied to a different set of predictor variables. This function will be called from within the function that implements our workflow (the solution to the prediction task) that we will present later.

```
> varsEnsemble <- function(tgt,train,test,
+                          fs.meth,
+                          baseLearner,blPars,
+                          predictor,predPars,
+                          verb=FALSE)
+ {
+     require(Hmisc,quietly=TRUE)
+     v <- varclus(as.matrix(train[,-which(colnames(train)==tgt)]))
+     varsSets <- lapply(1:fs.meth[[3]],function(x)
+         getVarsSet(v$hclust,nvars=fs.meth[[2]]))
+
+     preds <- matrix(NA,ncol=length(varsSets),nrow=NROW(test))
+     for(v in seq(along=varsSets)) {
```

```
+            if (baseLearner=='knn')
+                preds[,v] <- do.call("kNN",
+                                    c(list(as.formula(paste(tgt,
+                                                    paste(varsSets[[v]],
+                                                        collapse='+'),
+                                                    sep='~')),
+                                        train[,c(tgt,varsSets[[v]])],
+                                        test[,c(tgt,varsSets[[v]])]),
+                                    blPars)
+                                )
+            else {
+                m <- do.call(baseLearner,
+                            c(list(as.formula(paste(tgt,
+                                                paste(varsSets[[v]],
+                                                    collapse='+'),
+                                                sep='~')),
+                                train[,c(tgt,varsSets[[v]])]),
+                                blPars)
+                            )
+                preds[,v] <- do.call(predictor,
+                                    c(list(m,test[,c(tgt,varsSets[[v]])]),
+                                        predPars))
+            }
+        }
+
+    ps <- apply(preds,1,function(x)
+        levels(factor(x))[which.max(table(factor(x)))])
+    factor(ps,
+            levels=1:nlevels(train[,tgt]),
+            labels=levels(train[,tgt]))
+ }
```

The first arguments of this function are the name of the target variable, the training set, and the test set. The next argument (**fs.meth**) is a list containing the sets of variable names (the obtained clusters) from which we should sample a variable to generate the predictors of each member of the ensemble. We then have two arguments (**baseLearner** and **blPars**) that provide the name of the function that implements the learner to be used on each member of the ensemble and respective list of learning parameters. Finally, we have the name of the function to be used to obtain the predictions of the model and its parameters. The result of the function is the set of predictions of the ensemble for the given test set. These predictions are obtained by a voting mechanism among the members of the ensemble. The difference between the members of the ensemble lies only in the predictors that are used, which are determined by the **fs.meth** parameters. These sets result from a variable clustering process, as mentioned in Section 7.3.4.

Given the similarity of the tasks to be carried out by each of the classification algorithms, we have created a single user-defined workflow function that will receive as one of the parameters the learner that is to be used. The function **ALLb.wf()** that we present below implements this idea:

```
> ALLb.wf <- function(form, train, test,
+                    learner, learner.pars=NULL,
+                    predictor="predict",predictor.pars=NULL,
+                    featSel.meth = "s2",
+                    available.fsMethods=list(s1=list("all"),s2=list('rf',30)),
```

```
+                                          s3=list('varclus',30,50)),
+                    .model=FALSE,
+                    ...)
+ {
+     ## The characteristics of the selected feature selection method
+     fs.meth <- available.fsMethods[[featSel.meth]]
+
+     ## The target variable
+     tgt <- as.character(form[[2]])
+     tgtCol <- which(colnames(train)==tgt)
+
+     ## Anova filtering
+     f <- Anova(train[,tgt],p=0.01)
+     ff <- filterfun(f)
+     genes <- genefilter(t(train[,-tgtCol]),ff)
+     genes <- names(genes)[genes]
+     train <- train[,c(tgt,genes)]
+     test <- test[,c(tgt,genes)]
+     tgtCol <- 1
+
+     ## Specific filtering
+     if (fs.meth[[1]]=='varclus') {
+       pred <- varsEnsemble(tgt,train,test,fs.meth,
+                     learner,learner.pars,
+                     predictor,predictor.pars,
+                     list(...))
+
+     } else {
+       if (fs.meth[[1]]=='rf') {
+         require(randomForest,quietly=TRUE)
+         rf <- randomForest(form,train,importance=TRUE)
+         imp <- importance(rf)
+         rf.genes <- rownames(imp)[order(imp[,"MeanDecreaseAccuracy"],
+                           decreasing = TRUE)[1:fs.meth[[2]]]]
+         train <- train[,c(tgt,rf.genes)]
+         test <- test[,c(tgt,rf.genes)]
+       }
+
+       if (learner == 'knn')
+         pred <- kNN(form,train,test,
+                   stand.stats=list(rowMedians(t(as.matrix(train[,-tgtCol]))),
+                       rowIQRs(t(as.matrix(train[,-tgtCol])))),
+                   ...)
+       else {
+         model <- do.call(learner,c(list(form,train),learner.pars))
+         pred <- do.call(predictor,c(list(model,test),predictor.pars))
+       }
+
+     }
+
+     return(list(trues=responseValues(form,test), preds=pred,
+                 model=if (.model && learner!="knn") model else NULL))
+
+ }
```

This user-defined workflow will be called from within the package **performanceEstimation** bootstrap routines for each iteration of the process. The workflow function accepts the formula, train and test sets as the first three arguments, which are mandatory for any workflow function in the context of the infra-structure provided by package **performanceEstimation**. After these we have the parameters specifying the learning and prediction stages. Finally, we have parameters `featSel.meth` and `available.fsMethods` that let the user select one feature selection approach from within a set of alternatives. By default these alternatives are: (i) "s1" that represents using all features obtained after the ANOVA filtering; (ii) "s2" that involves using a random forest to select the top 30 features according to mean decrease in accuracy; and (iii) "s3" for using the variable clustering ensemble approach based on 50 models each build using 30 predictors randomly chosen from 30 clusters of the original features. On top of these three alternatives in terms of feature filtering we will also consider several parameter variants for each of the classification algorithms we will try. The following list holds all variants that are to be considered in our estimation experiments:

```
> vars <- list()
> vars$randomForest <- list(learner.pars=list(ntree=c(500,750,1000),
+                                  mtry=c(5,15)),
+                           preditor.pars=list(type="response"))
> vars$svm <- list(learner.pars=list(cost=c(1,100),
+                           gamma=c(0.01,0.001,0.0001)))
> vars$knn <- list(learner.pars=list(k=c(3,5,7),
+                           stand=c(TRUE,FALSE)))
> vars$featureSel <- list(featSel.meth=c("s1", "s2", "s3"))
```

This means that we will compare 6 (3×2) parameter variants of random forests combined with the 3 alternative feature selection methods (thus a total of 18 variants using random forests as classifiers), plus another 18 variants based on SVMs and 18 variants based on the k-nearest neighbor classifier. Each of these 54 alternatives will have their classification accuracy estimated through 100 repetitions of a bootstrap experiment. This estimation process will take a long time to compute. In this context, we do not recommend that you run the following experiments unless you are aware of this temporal constraint. The objects resulting from this experiment are available at the book Web page so that you are able to proceed with the rest of the analysis without having to run all these experiments. The code to run the full experiments is the following:

```
> library(performanceEstimation)
> library(class)
> library(randomForest)
> library(e1071)
> library(genefilter)
> load('myALL.Rdata')  # loading the previously saved object with the data
>
> es <- exprs(ALLb)
>
> ## simple filtering
> ALLb <- nsFilter(ALLb,
+                 var.func=IQR,var.cutoff=IQR(as.vector(es))/5,
+                 feature.exclude="^AFFX")
> ALLb <- ALLb$eset
>
> ## the source dataset after the basic filtering
```

```
> dt <- data.frame(t(exprs(ALLb)),Mut=ALLb$mol.bio)
>
> set.seed(1234)
> ## The learners to evaluate
> TODO <- c('knn','svm','randomForest')
> for(td in TODO) {
+     assign(td,
+         performanceEstimation(
+             PredTask(Mut ~ .,dt,'ALL'),
+             do.call('workflowVariants',
+                 c(list('ALLb.wf',learner=td,varsRootName=td),
+                   vars[[td]],
+                   vars$featureSel
+                 )
+             ),
+             EstimationTask(metrics="acc",method=Bootstrap(nReps=100)),
+             cluster=TRUE
+         )
+     )
+     save(list=td,file=paste(td,'Rdata',sep='.'))
+ }
```

The code starts by applying the simple filtering that eliminates the control probes and the genes with very small variability. The remaining genes form the dataset that is use to run the bootstrap experiments that estimate the accuracy of the different workflows we are considering for the task of predicting the type of mutation. The main part of the code consists of a loop that goes through the three classification algorithms. This means we run separately the variants of each of these methods. Given the large number of variants and also the fact that we are using 100 repetitions of a bootstrap experiment for each variant, this code takes some time to run. In this context, we have used the **cluster=TRUE** parameter setting in the fourth argument of the function **performanceEstimation()**. This will use all but one of the cores of the computer where the experiments are being executed, with each core running one of the iterations in parallel. Depending on the number of cores of your machine this will lead to a considerable speed-up. At the end of each iteration, the results of the respective classification algorithm are saved in a file. These files are available at the book Web site so that you can avoid running all experiments and yet being able to analyse their results by downloading the files from the site. Assuming they were saved in the current working directory of your R session, you may load the content of the files as follows:

```
> ## load results of the exps
> load("knn.Rdata")
> load("svm.Rdata")
> load("randomForest.Rdata")
```

The results of all variants of a learner are contained in a separate **ComparisonResults** object. For instance, if you want to see which were the best SVM variants, you may issue

```
> rankWorkflows(svm, maxs = TRUE)

$ALL
$ALL$acc
  Workflow  Estimate
1  svm.v8  0.8126319
2  svm.v12 0.8112365
```

```
3   svm.v10 0.8064391
4    svm.v6 0.8046412
5    svm.v7 0.7978988
```

The function `rankWorkflows()` takes an object of class **ComparisonResults** and obtains the best performing variants for each of the statistics that were estimated in the experimental process. By default, the function assumes that "best" means smaller values. In case of statistics that are to be maximized, like accuracy, we can use the parameter `maxs` as we did above.[4]

In order to have an overall perspective of all the workflows tried, we can join the three objects:

```
> all.trials <- mergeEstimationRes(svm, knn, randomForest, by ="workflows")
```

With the resulting **ComparisonResults** object we can check the best overall score of our trials:

```
> rankWorkflows(all.trials, top=10, maxs = TRUE)
```

```
$ALL
$ALL$acc
     Workflow  Estimate
1     svm.v8 0.8126319
2    svm.v12 0.8112365
3     knn.v7 0.8084350
4     knn.v8 0.8084350
5     knn.v9 0.8084350
6    knn.v10 0.8084350
7    knn.v11 0.8084350
8    knn.v12 0.8084350
9    svm.v10 0.8064391
10    svm.v6 0.8046412
```

Surprisingly, no random forest variant appears in the top 10 solutions. The top score is obtained by a variant of the SVM method. Let us check its characteristics:

```
> getWorkflow("svm.v8", all.trials)
```

```
Workflow Object:
Workflow ID       ::   svm.v8
Workflow Function ::   ALLb.wf
    Parameter values:
 learner.pars  ->  cost=100 gamma=0.01
 learner  ->  svm
 featSel.meth  ->  s2
```

This variant uses 30 genes filtered by a random forest (the "s2" strategy), and uses an SVM with parameter settings of 100 for cost and 0.01 for gamma. It is also interesting to observe that among the top 10 scores, only the last one ("svm.v6") does not use the 30 genes filtered with a random forest. How to obtain that information programatically without having to run the above `getWorkflow()` function by hand on all 10 workflows? The following code shows you how to do this:

---

[4]In case we measure several statistics, some that are to be minimized and others maximized, the parameter `maxs` accepts a vector of Boolean values, as many as there are statistics in the estimation task.

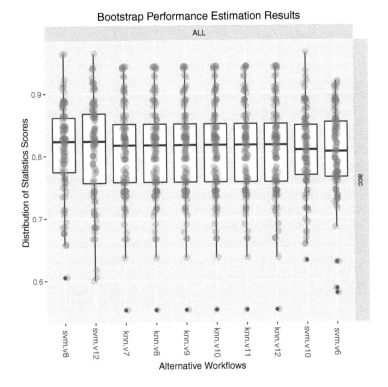

FIGURE 7.5: The accuracy results of the top 10 workflows.

```
> top10WFnames <- rankWorkflows(all.trials, top=10,
+                             maxs = TRUE)[["ALL"]][["acc"]][,"Workflow"]
> sapply(top10WFnames, function(WFid) getWorkflow(WFid,all.trials)@pars$featSel.meth)

 svm.v8 svm.v12  knn.v7  knn.v8  knn.v9 knn.v10 knn.v11 knn.v12 svm.v10
  "s2"    "s2"    "s2"    "s2"    "s2"    "s2"    "s2"    "s2"    "s2"
 svm.v6
  "s1"
```

We first use the output of function `rankWorkflows()` to obtain the names of the top 10 workflows. For each of these names we apply the function `getWorkflow()` to obtain the respective workflow object, from which we extract the slot containing the learner parameters (slot `pars` of these objects), which is a list, where we finally obtain the value of the `featSel.meth` parameter. As you can observe, only the last workflow uses the "s1" feature selection method, i.e. uses all genes resulting from the simple filtering.

Figure 7.5 shows the results of these top 10 workflows on the 100 iterations of the bootstrap estimation procedure. The figure was obtained with,

```
> plot(subset(all.trials,workflows=top10WFnames))
```

We can observe that the results of the different workflows seem very similar. We may obtain a more formal answer to the question of whether the score of the winning workflow is significantly better than the scores of the other workflows in the top 10 as follows,

```
> ps <- pairedComparisons(subset(all.trials,workflows=top10WFnames),baseline="svm.v8")
> ps$acc$WilcoxonSignedRank.test
```

```
, , ALL
```

	MedScore	DiffMedScores	p.value
svm.v8	0.8235294	NA	NA
svm.v12	0.8235294	0.000000000	0.7000463
knn.v7	0.8169856	0.006543766	0.7941389
knn.v8	0.8169856	0.006543766	0.7941389
knn.v9	0.8169856	0.006543766	0.7941389
knn.v10	0.8169856	0.006543766	0.7941389
knn.v11	0.8169856	0.006543766	0.7941389
knn.v12	0.8169856	0.006543766	0.7941389
svm.v10	0.8086312	0.014898200	0.2240278
svm.v6	0.8055556	0.017973856	0.4055620

As you see, there are no statistically significant differences among these 10 workflows. We have used the Wilcoxon signed rank test for this, as this experiment only includes a single prediction task. This test allowed us to make paired comparisons between the different workflows and the top scorer.

Sometimes we are interested in checking the behavior of a certain workflow on one particular iteration of these estimation experiments (maybe because the scores of the workflow at that iteration are unusual). For instance, we could try to obtain the confusion matrix of some workflow on one iteration. To obtain confusion matrices (see page 142) we need to know what the actual predictions of the models are. Our user-defined workflow function (`ALLb.wf`) returns this information. We can inspect the true and predicted class labels for any of the iterations of the bootstrap method and obtain the respective confusion matrix with this information. The following code provides an illustration for a particular iteration:

```
> iteration <- 1  # any number between 1 and 100 in this case
> itInfo <- getIterationsInfo(all.trials,workflow="svm.v8",it=iteration)
> table(itInfo$trues, itInfo$preds)
```

	ALL1/AF4	BCR/ABL	E2A/PBX1	NEG
ALL1/AF4	3	0	0	0
BCR/ABL	0	12	0	3
E2A/PBX1	0	0	0	1
NEG	0	1	1	14

In this example we can observe that the model correctly predicts all cases with the `ALL1/AF4` mutation. Moreover, we can also observe that most of the errors of the model consist of predicting the class `NEG` for a case with some mutation, i.e. false negatives which is not particularly interesting in this application domain. Nevertheless, the reverse also happens with two samples with no mutation, incorrectly predicted as having some abnormality.

We should remark that the `getIterationsInfo()` function can be used to obtain any component of the list returned by one of the workflows involved in the experiment. In particular, for user-defined workflows it is the user who decides the return value of the workflow functions, which means that you can include whatever information you think is useful in the list that results from running the workflow.

7.5 Summary

The primary goal of this chapter was to introduce the reader to an important range of applications of data mining that receives a lot of attention from the R community: bioinformatics. In this context, we explored some of the tools of the project Bioconductor, which provides a large set of R packages specialized for this type of applications. As a concrete example, we addressed a bioinformatics predictive task: to forecast the type of genetic mutation associated with samples of patients with B-cell acute lymphoblastic leukemia. Several classification models were obtained based on information concerning the expression levels on a set of genes resulting from microarray experiments. In terms of data mining concepts, this chapter focused on the following main topics:

- Feature selection methods for problems with a very large number of predictors

- Classification methods

- Random forests

- k-Nearest neighbors

- SVMs

- Ensembles using different subsets of predictors

- Bootstrap experiments

With respect to R, we have learned a few new techniques, namely,

- How to handle microarray data

- Using ANOVA tests to compare means across groups of data

- Clustering the variables of a problem

- Obtaining ensembles with models learned using different predictors

- Obtaining k-nearest neighbors models

- Estimating the accuracy of models using bootstrap.

Bibliography

Acuna, E., members of the CASTLE group at UPR-Mayaguez, and Rico., P. (2009). *dprep: Data preprocessing and visualization functions for classification*. R package version 2.1.

Aggarwal, C. C. (2013). *Outlier Analysis*. Springer.

Aggarwal, C. C. (2015). *Data Mining: The Text Book*. Springer.

Aggarwal, C. C. and Reddy, C. K., editors (2014). *Data Clustering: Algorithms and Applications*. CRC Press.

Agrawal, R. and Srikant, R. (1994). Fast algorithms for mining association rules. In *Proc. 20th Int. Conf. Very Large Data Bases, VLDB*, pages 487–499. Morgan Kaufmann.

Aha, D. (1990). *A study of instance-based learning algorithms for supervised learning tasks: Mathematical, empirical, and psychological evaluations*. PhD thesis, University of California at Irvine, Department of Information and Computer Science.

Aha, D. (1997). Lazy learning. *Artificial Intelligence Review*, 11.

Aha, D., Kibler, D., and Albert, M. (1991). Instance-based learning algorithms. *Machine Learning*, 6(1):37–66.

Aiello, S., Kraljevic, T., Maj, P., and with contributions from the H2O.ai team (2016). *h2o: R Interface for H2O*. R package version 3.8.1.3.

Alfaro, E., Gámez, M., and García, N. (2013). adabag: An R package for classification with boosting and bagging. *Journal of Statistical Software*, 54(2):1–35.

Atkeson, C. G., Moore, A., and Schaal, S. (1997). Locally weighted learning. *Artificial Intelligence Review*, 11:11–73.

Barnett, V. and Lewis, T. (1994). *Outliers in statistical data (3rd edition)*. John Wiley & Sons.

Beck, M. (2015). *NeuralNetTools: Visualization and Analysis Tools for Neural Networks*. R package version 1.4.0.

Bengio, Y. (2009). Learning deep architectures for ai. *Foundations and Trends in Machine Learning*, 2(1):1–127.

Bengio, Y., Courville, A. C., and Vincent, P. (2012). Unsupervised feature learning and deep learning: A review and new perspectives. *CoRR*, abs/1206.5538.

Bergmeir, C. and Benítez, J. M. (2012). Neural networks in R using the Stuttgart neural network simulator: RSNNS. *Journal of Statistical Software*, 46(7):1–26.

Bischl, B., Lang, M., Richter, J., Bossek, J., Judt, L., Kuehn, T., Studerus, E., Kotthoff, L., and Julia, S. (2016). *mlr: Machine Learning in R*. R package version 2.8.

Bontempi, G., Birattari, M., and Bersini, H. (1999). Lazy learners at work: the lazy learning toolbox. In *Proceedings of the 7th European Congress on Intelligent Techniques & Soft Computing (EUFIT'99)*.

Borgelt, C. (2003). Efficient implementations of apriori and eclat. In *FIMI'03: Proceedings of the IEEE ICDM Workshop on Frequent Itemset Mining Implementations*.

Branco, P., Ribeiro, R. P., and Torgo, L. (2016a). UBL: an R package for utility-based learning. *CoRR*, abs/1604.08079.

Branco, P., Torgo, L., and Ribeiro, R. P. (2016b). A survey of predictive modeling on imbalanced domains. *ACM Comput. Surv.*, 49(2):31:1–31:50.

Breiman, L. (1996). Bagging predictors. *Machine Learning*, 24:123–140.

Breiman, L. (1998). Arcing classifiers (with discussion). *Annals of Statistics*, 26:801–849.

Breiman, L. (2001). Random forests. *Machine Learning*, 45(1):5–32.

Breiman, L., Friedman, J., Olshen, R., and Stone, C. (1984). *Classification and Regression Trees*. Statistics/Probability Series. Wadsworth & Brooks/Cole Advanced Books & Software.

Breunig, M., Kriegel, H., Ng, R., and Sander, J. (2000). LOF: identifying density-based local outliers. In *ACM Int. Conf. on Management of Data*, pages 93–104.

Burges, C. (1998). A tutorial on support vector machines for pattern recognition. *Data mining and knowlege discovery*, 2(2):121–167.

Carl, P. and Peterson, B. G. (2014). *PerformanceAnalytics: Econometric tools for performance and risk analysis*. R package version 1.4.3541.

Carlson, M. (2016). *hgu95av2.db: Affymetrix Human Genome U95 Set annotation data (chip hgu95av2)*. R package version 3.2.2.

Chambers, J. (2008). *Software for Data Analysis: programming with R*. Springer.

Chan, R. (1999). Protecting rivers & streams by monitoring chemical concentrations and algae communities. In *Proceedings of the 7th European Congress on Intelligent Tecnhiques & Soft Computing (EUFIT'99)*.

Chandola, V., Banerjee, A., and Kumar, V. (2007). Outlier detection: a survey. Technical Report TR 07-017, Department of Computer Science and Engineering, University of Minnesota.

Chang, W., Cheng, J., Allaire, J., Xie, Y., and McPherson, J. (2016). *shiny: Web Application Framework for R*. R package version 0.13.2.

Chapelle, O., Schölkopf, B., and Zien, A., editors (2006). *Semi-Supervised Learning*. The MIT Press.

Chawla, N., Japkowicz, N., and Kokz, A. (2004). Sigkdd special issue on learning from imbalanced datasets.

Chawla, N., Lazarevic, A., Hall, L., and Bowyer, K. (2003). Smote-boost: Improving prediction of the minority class in boosting. In *Seventh European Conference on Principles and Practice of Knowledge Discovery in Databases*, pages 107–119.

Chawla, N. V., Bowyer, K. W., Hall, L. O., and Kegelmeyer, W. P. (2002). Smote: Synthetic minority over-sampling technique. *Journal of Artificial Intelligence Research*, 16:321—-357.

Chen, C., Hardle, W., and Unwin, A., editors (2008). *Handbook of Data Visualization*. Springer.

Chiaretti, S., Li, X., Gentleman, R., Vitale, A., Vignetti, M., Mandelli, F., Ritz, J., and Foa, R. (2004). Gene expression profile of adult t-cell acute lymphocytic leukemia identifies distinct subsets of patients with different response to therapy and survival. *Blood*, 103(7).

Chizi, B. and Maimon, O. (2005). *The Data Mining and Knowledge Discovery Handbook*, chapter Dimension Reduction and Feature Selection, pages 93–111. Springer.

Cleveland, W. (1993). *Visualizing Data*. Hobart Press.

Cleveland, W. (1995). *The Elements of Graphing Data*. Hobart Press.

Cleveland, W. and Loader, C. (1995). Smoothing by local regression: Principles and methods (with discussion). *Computational Statistics*.

Cortez, P. (2015). *rminer: Data Mining Classification and Regression Methods*. R package version 1.4.1.

Cover, T. M. and Hart, P. E. (1967). Nearest neighbor pattern classification. *IEEE Transactions on Information Theory*, 13(1):21–27.

Cristianini, N. and Shawe-Taylor, J. (2000). *An Introduction to Support Vector Machines*. Cambridge University Press.

Deboeck, G., editor (1994). *Trading on the edge*. John Wiley & Sons.

Demsar, J. (2006). Statistical comparisons of classifiers over multiple data sets. *Journal of Machine Learning Research*, 7:1–30.

Dethlefsen, C. and Højsgaard, S. (2005). A common platform for graphical models in R: The gRbase package. *Journal of Statistical Software*, 14(17):1–12.

Devogelaere, D., Rijckaert, M., and Embrechts, M. J. (1999). 3rd international competition: Protecting rivers and streams by monitoring chemical concentrations and algae communities solved with the use of gadc. In *Proceedings of the 7th European Congress on Intelligent Techniques & Soft Computing (EUFIT'99)*.

Dietterich, T. G. (2000). Ensemble methods in machine learning. *Lecture Notes in Computer Science*, 1857:1–15.

Dimitriadou, E., Hornik, K., Leisch, F., Meyer, D., , and Weingessel, A. (2009). *e1071: Misc Functions of the Department of Statistics (e1071), TU Wien*. R package version 1.5-19.

Domingos, P. (1999). Metacost: A general method for making classifiers cost-sensitive. In *KDD'99: Proceedings of the 5th International Conference on Knowledge Discovery and Data Mining*, pages 155—-164. ACM Press.

Domingos, P. and Pazzani, M. (1997). On the optimality of the simple bayesian classifier under zero-one loss. *Machine Learning*, 29:103–137.

Dougherty, J., Kohavi, R., and Sahami, M. (1995). Supervised and unsupervised discretization of continuous features. In Prieditis, A. and Russell, S., editors, *Machine Learning: Proceedings of the Twelfth International Conference*. Morgan Kaufmann Publishers.

Dowle, M., Srinivasan, A., Short, T., with contributions from R Saporta, S. L., and Antonyan, E. (2015). *data.table: Extension of Data.frame*. R package version 1.9.6.

Drapper, N. and Smith, H. (1981). *Applied Regression Analysis*. John Wiley & Sons, 2nd edition.

Drees, M. (2013). Implementierung und analyse von tiefen architekturen in r. Master's thesis, Fachhochschule Dortmund.

Drummond, C. and Holte, R. (2006). Cost curves: An improved method for visualizing classifier performance. *Machine Learning*, 65(1):95–130.

Elkan, C. (2001). The foundations of cost-sensitive learning. In *IJCAI'01: Proceedings of 17th International Joint Conference of Artificial Intelligence*, pages 973–978. Morgan Kaufmann Publishers Inc.

Ester, M., Kriegel, H.-P., Sander, J., and Xu, X. (1996). A density-based algorithm for discovering clusters in large spatial databases with noise. In *Proceedings of 2nd International Conference on Knowledge Discovery and Data Mining (KDD-96)*.

Feinerer, I. and Hornik, K. (2015). *tm: Text Mining Package*. R package version 0.6-2.

Feng, L., Nowak, G., Welsh, A. H., and O'Neill, T. J. (2014). *imputeR: A General Imputation Framework in R*. R package version 1.0.0.

Flach, P. (2012). *Machine Learning: The Art and Science of Algorithms that Make Sense of Data*. Cambridge University Press.

Fox, J. (2009). *car: Companion to Applied Regression*. R package version 1.2-16.

Freund, Y. (1990). Boosting a weak learning algorithm by majority. In *Proceedings of the Third Annual Workshop on Computational Learning Theory*.

Freund, Y. and Shapire, R. (1996). Experiments with a new boosting algorithm. In *Proceedings of the 13th International Conference on Machine Learning*. Morgan Kaufmann.

Friedman, J. (1991). Multivariate adaptive regression splines. *The Annals of Statistics*, 19(1):1–144.

Friedman, J. (2002). Stochastic gradient boosting. *Comput. Stat. Data Anal.*, 38(4):367–378.

Friedman, J. and Stuetzle, W. (1981). Projection pursuit regression. *Journal of the American Statistical Association*, 76(376):817–823.

Friedman, J. H. (1999). Greedy function approximation: A gradient boosting machine. Technical report, Department of Statistics, Stanford University.

Fritsch, S., Guenther, F., and following earlier work by Marc Suling (2012). *neuralnet: Training of neural networks*. R package version 1.32.

Gagolewski, M. and Tartanus, B. (2015). *R package stringi: Character string processing facilities*.

Gama, J. and Gaber, M., editors (2007). *Learning from data streams*. Springer.

Gama, J., Medas, P., Castillo, G., and Rodrigues, P. (2004). Learning with drift detection. In Bazzan, A. and Labidi, S., editors, *Advances in Artificial Intelligence-SBIA 2004*, volume 3171 of *Lecture Notes in Computer Science*, pages 286–295. Springer.

Gama, J. a., Žliobaitė, I., Bifet, A., Pechenizkiy, M., and Bouchachia, A. (2014). A survey on concept drift adaptation. *ACM Comput. Surv.*, 46(4):44:1–44:37.

Gentleman, R., Carey, V., Huber, W., and Hahne, F. (2010). *genefilter: genefilter: methods for filtering genes from microarray experiments*. R package version 1.28.2.

Gentleman, R. C., Carey, V. J., Bates, D. M., et al. (2004). Bioconductor: Open software development for computational biology and bioinformatics. *Genome Biology*, 5:R80.

Goethals, B. and Zaki, M. (2004). Advances in frequent itemset mining imple mentations: Report on fimi'03. *SIGKDD Explorations*, 6(1):109–117.

Grolemund, G. and Wickham, H. (2011). Dates and times made easy with lubridate. *Journal of Statistical Software*, 40(3):1–25.

Guyon, I. and Elisseeff, A. (2003). An introduction to variable and feature selection. *Journal of Machine Learning Research*, 3:1157–1182.

Hahne, F., Huber, W., Gentleman, R., and Falcon, S. (2008). *Bioconductor Case Studies*. Springer.

Hahsler, M., Buchta, C., Gruen, B., and Hornik, K. (2016). *arules: Mining Association Rules and Frequent Itemsets*. R package version 1.4-1.

Hahsler, M. and Chelluboina, S. (2016). *arulesViz: Visualizing Association Rules and Frequent Itemsets*. R package version 1.1-1.

Han, J., Kamber, M., and Pei, J. (2012). *Data Mining: concepts and techniques (3rd edition)*. Morgan Kaufmann Publishers.

Hand, D. and Yu, K. (2001). Idiot's Bayes - not so stupid after all? *International Statistical Review*, 69(3):385–399.

Hand, D. J. (2009). Measuring classifier performance: a coherent alternative to the area under the roc curve. *Machine Learning*, 77(1):103–123.

Harrell Jr, F. E. (2009). *Hmisc: Harrell Miscellaneous*. R package version 3.7-0. With contributions from many other users.

Harrell Jr., F. E., with contributions from Charles Dupont, and many others. (2015). *Hmisc: Harrell Miscellaneous*. R package version 3.17-0.

Hastie, T. and Tibshirani, R. (1990). *Generalized Additive Models*. Chapman & Hall.

Hastie, T., Tibshirani, R., and Friedman, J. (2001). *The elements of statistical learning: data mining, inference and prediction*. Springer.

Hastie, T., Tibshirani, R., and Friedman, J. (2009). *The elements of statistical learning: data mining, inference and prediction (2nd edition)*. Springer.

Hawkins, D. M. (1980). *Identification of Outliers*. Chapman and Hall.

Hennig, C. (2015). *fpc: Flexible Procedures for Clustering.* R package version 2.1-10.

Hinton, G. E., Osindero, S., and Teh, Y. (2006). A fast learning algorithm for deep belief nets. *Neural Computation,* 18:1527–1554.

Hodge, V. and Austin, J. (2004). A survey of outlier detection methodologies. *Artif. Intell. Rev.,* 22(2):85–126.

Hornik, K., Buchta, C., and Zeileis, A. (2009). Open-source machine learning: R meets Weka. *Computational Statistics,* 24(2):225–232.

Hothorn, T., Hornik, K., and Zeileis, A. (2006). Unbiased recursive partitioning: A conditional inference framework. *Journal of Computational and Graphical Statistics,* 15(3):651–674.

Hu, Y., Murray, W., Shan, Y., and Australia. (2015). *Rlof: R Parallel Implementation of Local Outlier Factor(LOF).* R package version 1.1.1.

Ihaka, R. and Gentleman, R. (1996). R: A language for data analysis and graphics. *Journal of Computational and Graphical Statistics,* 5(3):299–314.

Ishwaran, H. and Kogalur, U. (2016). *Random Forests for Survival, Regression and Classification (RF-SRC).* R package version 2.1.0.

James, G., Witten, D., Hastie, T., and Tibshirani, R. (2013). *An Introduction to Statistical Learning with Applications in R.* Springer.

Japkowicz, N. (2000). The class imbalance problem: Significance and strategies. In *Proceedings of the 2000 International Conference on Artificial Intelligence (IC-A1'2000):Special Track on Inductive Learning.*

Kahle, D. and Wickham, H. (2013). ggmap: Spatial visualization with ggplot2. *The R Journal,* 5(1):144–161.

Karatzoglou, A., Smola, A., Hornik, K., and Zeileis, A. (2004). kernlab – an S4 package for kernel methods in R. *Journal of Statistical Software,* 11(9):1–20.

Kifer, D., Ben-David, S., and Gehrke, J. (2004). Detecting change in data streams. In *VLDB 04: Proceedings of the 30th International Conference on Very Large Data Bases,* pages 180–191. Morgan Kaufmann.

Kira, K. and Rendel, L. (1992). The feature selection problem : Traditional methods and a new algorithm. In *Proc. Tenth National Conference on Artificial Intelligence,* pages 129–134. MIT Press.

Kira, K. and Rendell., L. (1992). A practical approach to feature selection. In Sleeman, D. and Edwards, P., editors, *Proceeedings of International Conference on Machine Learning,* pages 368–377. Morgan Kaufmann.

Klima, G. (2016). *FCNN4R: Fast Compressed Neural Networks for R.* R package version 0.6.2.

Klinkenberg, R. (2004). Learning drifting concepts: example selection vs. example weighting. *Intelligent Data Analysis,* 8(3):281–300.

Knuth, D. E. (1984). Literate programming. *The Computer Journal (British Computer Society),* 27(2):97–111.

Komsta, L. (2011). *outliers: Tests for outliers*. R package version 0.14.

Kononenko, I. (1991). Semi-naive bayesian classifier. In *EWSL-91: Proceedings of the European working session on learning on Machine learning*, pages 206–219. Springer-Verlag New York, Inc.

Kononenko, I. and Kukar, M. (2007). *Machine Learning and Data Mining: introduction to principles and algorithms*. Horwood Publishing.

Kononenko, I., Simec, E., and Robnik-Sikonja, M. (1997). Overcoming the myopia of induction learning algorithms with relieff. *Applied Intelligence*, 17(1):39–55.

Kubat, M. and Matwin, S. (1997). Addressing the curse of imbalanced training sets: one-sided selection. In *Proceedings of the Fourteenth International Conference on Machine Learning*, pages 179–186.

Kuhn, M. (2016). *caret: Classification and Regression Training*. R package version 6.0-68.

Leisch, F. and Dimitriadou, E. (2010). *mlbench: Machine Learning Benchmark Problems*. R package version 2.1-1.

Leisch, F., Hornik, K., and Ripley., B. D. (2009). *mda: Mixture and flexible discriminant analysis, S original by Trevor Hastie and Robert Tibshirani*. R package version 0.3-4.

Li, X. (2009). *ALL: A data package*. R package version 1.4.7.

Liaw, A. and Wiener, M. (2002). Classification and regression by randomforest. *R News*, 2(3):18–22.

Lichman, M. (2013). UCI machine learning repository.

Liu, H. and Motoda, H. (1998). *Feature Selection for Knowledge Discovery and Data Mining*. Kluwer Academic Publishers.

Maechler, M., Rousseeuw, P., Struyf, A., Hubert, M., and Hornik, K. (2015). *cluster: Cluster Analysis Basics and Extensions*. R package version 2.0.3 — For new features, see the 'Changelog' file (in the package source).

McCulloch, W. and Pitts, W. (1943). A logical calculus of the ideas immanent in nervous activity. *Bulletin of Mathematical Biophysics*, 5:115–133.

Milborrow, S. (2009). *earth: Multivariate Adaptive Regression Spline Models, derived from mda:mars by Trevor Hastie and Rob Tibshirani*. R package version 2.4-0.

Milborrow, S. (2015). *rpart.plot: Plot 'rpart' Models: An Enhanced Version of 'plot.rpart'*. R package version 1.5.3.

Minsky, M. and Papert, S. (1969). *Perceptrons: an introduction to computational geometry*. MIT Press.

Murrell, P. (2006). *R Graphics*. Chapman & Hall/CRC.

Myers, R. (1990). *Classical and modern regression with applications*. Duxbury Press, 2nd edition.

Nadaraya, E. (1964). On estimating regression. *Theory of Probability and its Applications*, 9:141–142.

Nieweglowski, L. (2013). *clv: Cluster Validation Techniques.* R package version 0.3-2.1.

Oakland, J. (2007). *Statistical Process Control, 6th edition.* Butterworth-Heinemann.

Oksanen, J., Blanchet, F. G., Kindt, R., Legendre, P., Minchin, P. R., O'Hara, R. B., Simpson, G. L., Solymos, P., Stevens, M. H. H., and Wagner, H. (2016). *vegan: Community Ecology Package.* R package version 2.3-5.

Pebesma, E. (2012). spacetime: Spatio-temporal data in r. *Journal of Statistical Software,* 51(7):1–30.

Pebesma, E. and Bivand, R. (2005). Classes and methods for spatial data in r. *R News,* 5(2).

Peters, A. and Hothorn, T. (2015). *ipred: Improved Predictors.* R package version 0.9-5.

Provost, F. and Fawcett, T. (1997). Analysis and visualization of classifier performance: Comparison under imprecise class and cost distributions. In *KDD'97: Proceedings of the 3rd International Conference on Knowledge Discovery and Data Mining,* pages 43–48. AAAI Press.

Provost, F. and Fawcett, T. (2001). Robust classification for imprecise environments. *Machine Learning,* 42(3).

Provost, F., Fawcett, T., and Kohavi, R. (1998). The case against accuracy estimation for comparing induction algorithms. In *Proc. 15th International Conf. on Machine Learning,* pages 445–453. Morgan Kaufmann, San Francisco, CA.

Pyle, D. (1999). *Data preparation for data mining.* Morgan Kaufmann.

Quinlan, R. (1993). *C4.5: programs for machine learning.* Morgan Kaufmann Publishers.

R Core Team (2015a). *foreign: Read Data Stored by Minitab, S, SAS, SPSS, Stata, Systat, Weka, dBase, ...* R package version 0.8-66.

R Core Team (2015b). *R: A Language and Environment for Statistical Computing.* R Foundation for Statistical Computing, Vienna, Austria.

R Special Interest Group on Databases (2014). *DBI: R Database Interface.* R package version 0.3.1.

Rätsch, G., Onoda, T., and Müller, K. (2001). Soft margins for adaboost. *Machine Learning,* 42(3):287–320.

Ridgeway, G. (2015). *gbm: Generalized Boosted Regression Models.* R package version 2.1.1.

Rijsbergen, C. V. (1979). *Information Retrieval.* Dept. of Computer Science, University of Glasgow, 2nd edition.

Rish, I. (2001). An empirical study of the naive bayes classifier. In *IJCAI 2001 Workshop on Empirical Methods in Artificial Intelligence.*

Robnik-Sikonja, M. and Kononenko, I. (2003). Theoretical and empirical analysis of relieff and rrelieff. *Machine Learning Journal,* 53:23–69.

Robnik-Sikonja, M. and Savicky, P. (2015). *CORElearn: Classification, Regression and Feature Evaluation.* R package version 1.47.1.

Roger S. Bivand, Edzer Pebesma, V. G.-R. (2013). *Applied spatial data analysis with R (2nd ed.)*. Springer.

Rogers, R. and Vemuri, V. (1994). *Artificial neural networks forecasting time series*. IEEE Computer Society Press.

Rojas, R. (1996). *Neural Networks*. Springer-Verlag.

Romanski, P. and Kotthoff, L. (2014). *FSelector: Selecting attributes*. R package version 0.20.

Rong, X. (2014). *deepnet: deep learning toolkit in R*. R package version 0.2.

Ronsenblatt, F. (1958). The perceptron: a probabilistic models for information storage and organization in the brain. *Psychological Review*, 65:386–408.

Rosenberg, C., Hebert, M., and Schneiderman, H. (2005). Semi-supervised self-training of object detection models. In *Proc. of the 7th IEEE Workshop on Applications of Computer Vision*, pages 29–36. IEEE Computer Society.

Rosenblatt, F. (1958). The perceptron: A probabilistic model for information storage and organization in the brain. *Psychological Review*, 65(6):386–408.

Rousseeuw, P. (1987). Silhouettes: A graphical aid to the interpretation and validation of cluster analysis. *J. Comput. Appl. Math.*, 20:53–65.

Rumelhart, D., Hinton, G., and Williams, R. (1986). Learning internal representations by error propagation. In et. al., D. R., editor, *Parallel distributed processing*, volume 1. MIT Press.

Ryan, J. A. (2009). *quantmod: Quantitative Financial Modelling Framework*. R package version 0.3-13.

Ryan, J. A. and Ulrich, J. M. (2014). *xts: eXtensible Time Series*. R package version 0.9-7.

Sarkar, D. (2010). *lattice: Lattice Graphics*. R package version 0.18-3.

Schapire, R. (1990). Strength of weak learnability. *Machine Learning*, 5:197–227.

Schölkopf, B. and Smola, A. (2002). *Learning with Kernels*. MIT Press.

Schloerke, B., Crowley, J., Cook, D., Briatte, F., Marbach, M., Thoen, E., and Elberg, A. (2016). *GGally: Extension to ggplot2*. R package version 1.0.1.

Schmidhuber, J. (2014). Deep learning in neural networks: An overview. *CoRR*, abs/1404.7828.

Seeger, M. (2002). Learning with labeled and unlabeled data. Technical report, Institute for Adaptive and Neural Computation, University of Edinburgh.

Seligman, M. (2016). *Rborist: Extensible, Parallelizable Implementation of the Random Forest Algorithm*. R package version 0.1-1.

Shapire, R. (1990). The strength of weak learnability. *Machine Learning*, 5:197–227.

Sing, T., Sander, O., Beerenwinkel, N., and Lengauer, T. (2009). *ROCR: Visualizing the performance of scoring classifiers*. R package version 1.0-4.

Smola, A. and Schölkopf, B. (2004). A tutorial on support vector regression. *Stat. Comput.*, 14:199–222.

Smola, A. J. and Schölkopf, B. (1998). A tutorial on support vector regression. In *Neuro-COLT Technical Report TR-98-030*.

Steele, J. and Iliinsky, N., editors (2010). *Beautiful Visualization: Looking at Data through the Eyes of Experts (Theory in Practice)*. O'Reilly Media.

Takens, F. (1981). Detecting strange attractors in turbulance. In Rand, D. and Young, L., editors, *Lecture notes in mathematics*, volume 898, pages 366–381. Springer.

Therneau, T. M. and Atkinson, B. (2010). *rpart: Recursive Partitioning*. R port by Brian Ripley. R package version 3.1-46.

Tobler, W. R. (1970). A computer movie simulating urban growth in the detroit region. *Economic Geography*, 46.

Torgo, L. (1999a). *Inductive Learning of Tree-based Regression Models*. PhD thesis, Faculty of Sciences, University of Porto.

Torgo, L. (1999b). Predicting the density of algae communities using local regression trees. In *Proceedings of the 7th European Congress on Intelligent Techniques & Soft Computing (EUFIT'99)*.

Torgo, L. (2007). Resource-bounded fraud detection. In et. al, N., editor, *Proceedings of the 13th Portuguese Conference on Artificial Intelligence (EPIA'07)*, LNAI. Springer.

Torgo, L. (2014a). An infra-structure for performance estimation and experimental comparison of predictive models in r. *CoRR*, abs/1412.0436.

Torgo, L. (2014b). An infra-structure for performance estimation and experimental comparison of predictive models in r. *CoRR*, abs/1412.0436.

Tufte, E. (2001). *The Visual Display of Quantitative Information, 2nd Edition*. Graphics Pr.

Ulrich, J. (2009). *TTR: Technical Trading Rules*. R package version 0.20-1.

Urbanek, S. and Arnold, T. (2015). *iotools: I/O Tools for Streaming*. R package version 0.1-12.

Vapnik, V. (1995). *The Nature of Statistical Learning Theory*. Springer.

Vapnik, V. (1998). *Statistical Learning Theory*. John Wiley and Sons.

Venables, W. N. and Ripley, B. D. (2002). *Modern Applied Statistics with S*. Springer, New York, fourth edition. ISBN 0-387-95457-0.

Watson, G. S. (1964). Smooth regression analysis. *Sankhya: The Indian Journal of Statistics, Series A*, 26:359–372.

Wei, T. (2013). *corrplot: Visualization of a correlation matrix*. R package version 0.73.

Weihs, C., Ligges, U., Luebke, K., and Raabe, N. (2005). klar analyzing german business cycles. In Baier, D., Decker, R., and Schmidt-Thieme, L., editors, *Data Analysis and Decision Support*, pages 335–343, Berlin. Springer-Verlag.

Weiss, G. and F.Provost (2003). Learning when training data are costly: The effect of class distribution on tree induction. *Journal of Artificial Intelligence Research*, 19:315–354.

Weiss, S. and Indurkhya, N. (1999). *Predictive data mining*. Morgan Kaufmann.

Werbos, P. (1974). *Beyond regression - new tools for prediction and analysis in the behavioral sciences*. PhD thesis, Harvard University.

Werbos, P. (1996). *The roots of backpropagation - from observed derivatives to neural networks and political forecasting*. John Wiley & Sons.

Wettschereck, D. (1994). *A study of distance-based machine learning algorithms*. PhD thesis, Oregon State University.

Wettschereck, D., Aha, D., and Mohri, T. (1997). A review and empirical evaluation of feature weighting methods for a class of lazzy learning algorithms. *Artificial Intelligence Review*, 11:11–73.

Whickam, H. (2014). *Advanced R*. The R Series. Chapman & HallCRC.

Wickham, H. (2009). *ggplot2: elegant graphics for data analysis*. Springer New York.

Wickham, H. (2014). Tidy data. *The Journal of Statistical Software*, 59.

Wickham, H. (2015a). *readxl: Read Excel Files*. R package version 0.1.0.

Wickham, H. (2015b). *stringr: Simple, Consistent Wrappers for Common String Operations*. R package version 1.0.0.

Wickham, H. (2015c). *tidyr: Easily Tidy Data with 'spread()' and 'gather()' Functions*. R package version 0.3.1.

Wickham, H. (2016). *forcats: Tools for Working with Categorical Variables (Factors)*. R package version 0.1.0.

Wickham, H. and Francois, R. (2015a). *dplyr: A Grammar of Data Manipulation*. R package version 0.4.3.

Wickham, H. and Francois, R. (2015b). *readr: Read Tabular Data*. R package version 0.2.2.

Wickham, H., Francois, R., and Müller, K. (2016). *tibble: Simple Data Frames*. R package version 1.1.

Wilkinson, L. (2005). *The Grammar of Graphics*. Springer, 2nd edition edition.

Xie, Y. (2015). *Dynamic Documents with R and knitr*. Chapman and Hall/CRC.

Yarowsky, D. (1995). Unsupervised word sense disambiguation rivaling supervised methods. In *Proc. of the 33rd Annual Meeting of the Association for Computational Linguistics (ACL)*, pages 189–196.

Zaki, M., Parthasarathy, S., Ogihara, M., and Li, W. (1997). New algorithms for fast discovery of association rules. Technical Report 651, Computer Science Department, University of Rochester.

Zeileis, A. and Grothendieck, G. (2005). zoo: S3 infrastructure for regular and irregular time series. *Journal of Statistical Software*, 14(6):1–27.

Zhou, Z.-H. (2012). *Ensemble Methods, foundations and algorithms.* CRC Press.

Zhu, J., Zou, H., Rosset, S., and Hastie, T. (2009). Multi-class adaboost. *Statistics and Its Interface*, 2:349–360.

Zhu, X. (2005). *Semi-supervised learning with graphs.* PhD thesis, School of Computer Science, Carnegie Mellon University.

Zhu, X. (2006). Semi-supervised literature survey. Technical Report TR 1530, University of Wisconsin-Madison.

Zirilli, J. (1997). *Financial prediction using neural networks.* Thomson Computer Press.

Subject Index

Index of Data Mining Topics

Index of R Functions

Milton Keynes UK
Ingram Content Group UK Ltd.
UKHW050455071024
449327UK00015B/390

9 780367 573980